# Game Plan
## for Disaster

*Books by Clark R. Mollenhoff*

Game Plan for Disaster: An Ombudsman's Report on the Nixon Years

Strike Force: Organized Crime and the Government

The Pentagon

Despoilers of Democracy

Tentacles of Power

Washington Cover-Up

# Game Plan for Disaster

*An Ombudsman's Report on the Nixon Years*

*by* Clark R. Mollenhoff

W · W · NORTON & COMPANY · INC · *NEW YORK*

*First Edition*

꙰. THE TEXT of this book was typeset in Linotype Times Roman. Composition, printing, and binding were done by the Vail-Ballou Press, Inc.

Library of Congress Cataloging in Publication Data
Mollenhoff, Clark R
    Game plan for disaster.
    Includes index.
        1. United States—Politics and government—1969–1974.
2. Watergate Affair, 1972–   3. Nixon, Richard
Milhous, 1913–      4. Mollenhoff, Clark R.
I. Title.
E855.M64   1976      320.9'73'0924      75–17887

ISBN 0 393 05543 4

1 2 3 4 5 6 7 8 9 0

*To Judge John Sirica and that group of investigative reporters whose devotion to obtaining the full truth exposed the Watergate affair and the use of "executive privilege" to hide massive federal crimes and obstruct justice.*

᷇.   ᷇.   ᷇.   ᷇.   ᷇.

*Associated Press*
Jean Heller
D. Brooks Jackson

*Chicago Tribune*
Harry J. Kelly
James Squires

*Los Angeles Times*
Robert L. Jackson
Jack Nelson
Ronald J. Ostrow

*Minneapolis Tribune*
Frank G. Wright

*New York Daily News*
Joe Volz
James G. Wieghart

*New York Times*
Seymour M. Hersh
James M. Naughton
Anthony Ripley
Walter Rugaber
Wallace Turner

*Newsday*
Robert Greene
Martin J. Schram
Russell Sackett
Anthony Marro

*Newsweek*
Nicholas Horrock

*Scripps-Howard Newspapers*
Dan K. Thomasson

*Time, Inc.*
Hays Gorey
Sandy Smith

*United Press International*
Helen Thomas

*Wall Street Journal*
Jerry Landauer

*Washington Merry-Go-Round*
Jack Anderson
Brit Hume
Leslie H. Whitten

*Washington Post*
Carl Bernstein
Ronald Kessler
Morton Mintz
Spencer Rich
Laurence M. Stern
Barry Sussman
Robert Woodward

*Washington Star-News*
James R. Polk

# Contents

*"America is in trouble today not because her people have failed but because her leaders have failed. And what America needs are leaders to match the greatness of her people."*

Richard M. Nixon, Republican National Convention,
Miami Beach, August 8, 1968

*Introduction*

# THE ROYAL PREROGATIVES
# OF PRESIDENTS

IN THE LAST two hundred years the people of the United States have permitted the office of the president to accumulate royal prerogatives which would have shocked the men who founded this nation. One of those prerogatives, I believe, represents the most serious threat to the functioning of our American democracy and to our freedoms.

"Executive privilege" is explained by its promoters and defenders as a natural evolution of the separation of powers doctrine or as a simple "presidential confidentiality" necessary for any chief executive of the United States to handle his enormous duties. But nowhere does the United States Constitution suggest justification for executive privilege, nor was it even mentioned in the laws passed by Congress or in United States Supreme Court decisions until its use to bar Congress and the courts from information became intolerable. In the Watergate affair, executive privilege was the major tool for criminal obstruction of justice and for arrogant concealment of evidence that serious criminal acts had been committed by White House officials, by Cabinet officers, and by the president himself. Only because of the firm evidence of the White House tapes did the nation learn and understand fully the extent of presidential involvement in crime and the use of executive privilege by the White House in impeding investigators.

Respect for the office of the president is incumbent upon all of us, including the holders of that office. However, events of recent years should have made it clear that the unhealthy deification of our presidents threatens our freedoms and presents a serious danger to the functioning of our democratic system. While various Watergate investigations have exposed the crimes and forced the resignation of a president, there is still too little understanding of the fact that the deep-rooted cause of the Watergate problem is in our adulation of the president, allowing him to claim executive privilege. The danger of another Watergate will not end until we eradicate our belief in the divine right of our chief executives and insist on court and congressional mechanisms to force a president to be accountable under all circumstances for the manner in which the laws are administered and enforced. Richard Nixon did not invent executive privilege. He only used this arbitrary secrecy doctrine to conceal evidence of crime under circumstances which dramatized the falsity of a thesis promoted and defended in several prior administrations.

Looking down the long road of history, Watergate was a disguised blessing in that it exposed executive privilege as a serious threat to a democratic form of government. It not only concealed from the voters information which they needed to make judgments regarding the manner in which the government was being administered, but it proved to be a corruptive influence on the executive itself. The president and his advisers believed that privilege endowed them with a right to bar production of records and testimony and thus bar access to the evidence of their crimes. The precedence cited in various attorneys general's opinions convinced them they could get away with it, even though the claim of executive privilege had no support in the Constitution, in the laws, or in high court opinions.

In *The Twilight of the Presidency,* George Reedy, a White House staff member in the Johnson administration, deals effectively with the problems arising from creating too many privileges for a chief executive and requiring too few checks on his use of the awesome power a president holds. Although it was clear that most of Reedy's examples were drawn from his own experience in the Lyndon B. Johnson White House, he avoided the details of specific cases. The problems flowing from worship of the president were also dealt with by Arthur Schlesinger in *The Imperial Presidency.* Schlesinger explored the history of economic problems and war which rationalized and justified the flow of power and privilege to the office of the president and to the holders of that office. Schlesinger frankly admitted his responsibility and that of other members of the academic community in encouraging presidential adulation and increased presidential power. "It must be said that historians and political scientists, this writer among them, contributed to the rise of the presidential mystique," Schlesinger wrote in his foreword to *The Imperial Presidency.*

Many other fine books explore the unhealthy political condition created by deification of our presidents and the danger posed to our system of government, but I believe my experiences within the Nixon administration and outside present a uniquely specific insight into what went wrong and why all of us—the public, the press, the politicians—should have recognized the danger signs much earlier.

Serving in the capacity of a presidential ombudsman, I came to the conclusion that any honest and dedicated president has the forum to refute malicious falsifications which may be charged against him or top officials of his administration. I also became convinced that honest and fair administration of the government was good, and that a rigid requirement for presidential accountability to Congress would protect rather than harm any holder of that office. There is danger to our system of government in the belief that presidents are entitled to credibility. We should exercise reasonable skepticism in judging all political figures, including the president. Special skepticism should be reserved for presidential words and actions accompanied by arbitrary secrecy. Occasionally it may be necessary to trust a president's word for a brief period, but we should be suspicious of any reluctance to make an accounting to Congress, the courts, or the press.

Richard Nixon's game plan in the spring of 1973 was to use the secrecy of executive privilege to bar the courts and Congress from testimony or documents pertaining to the Watergate cover-up. By this artifice, he could have stalled and "stonewalled" Chief United States District Judge John J. Sirica and Chairman Sam Ervin of the Senate Select Watergate Committee. It was his plan to take advantage of the public's belief in the honesty of presidents to spread false statements denying the involvement of anyone in the White House while heaping scorn on those who would hint at presidential wrongdoing. The defections of Jeb S. Magruder, deputy director of the Committee to Re-elect the President, and White House Counsel John W. Dean III, in April 1973, required a new strategy. It was hoped the sacrifice of Magruder, Dean, and former Attorney General John N. Mitchell would appease the demand for further prosecution and allow Chief of Staff H. R. (Bob) Haldeman, Special Assistant John D. Ehrlichman, and President Nixon himself to escape unscathed. This required withholding testimony and documents which would corroborate John Dean, and engaging in a malicious smear campaign to destroy his credibility as a witness.

President Nixon still relied completely on executive privilege to block the court and Congress from access to White House documents, and his White House taping system continued through May and June, and into July, when its existence was revealed in public testimony by Alexander Butterfield, a former deputy assistant to President Nixon. Confident that he was protected by executive privilege and by the American people's traditional trust in their president, Mr. Nixon, on May 22, 1973, tried to beat John Dean to the punch by revealing some White House efforts to use "national security" and the Central Intelligence Agency (CIA) to hamper an FBI investigation of money found on the Watergate burglars on June 17, 1972. In that speech, filled with misrepresentations and laced with false claims about "national security," President Nixon sought to terminate the Watergate investigation by destroying John Dean as a credible witness. Had it not been for the White House taping system, which eventually corroborated Dean's story of the involvement of Nixon, Haldeman, Ehrlichman, Colson, and Mitchell in the criminal obstruction of justice, the game plan might have succeeded.

With executive privilege in effect and without the White House tapes, Dean's credibility would have remained in doubt, under challenge by the impressive array of Nixon, Ehrlichman, Haldeman, Mitchell, and Colson. Had unlimited executive privilege been established, Special Prosecutor Archibald Cox would have had no solid ground from which to demand the incriminating White House documents and tapes without that demand there would have been no "Saturday night massacre." Without the "Saturday night massacre" and the following "firestorm" of public protest, it is unlikely that Chairman Peter Rodino's House Judiciary Committee would have had the courage to tackle the president with an impeachment investigation. Without firm knowledge of the White House tapes, it is doubtful whether Judge Sirica, then under criticism for his extensive questioning in the original Watergate trial, would have felt confident enough to rule that presidential documents had to be produced for his inspection in his chambers while the president's lawyers clouded the air with claims of national security implications.

Even though the Supreme Court's unanimous 8 to 0 decision in the case of *United States* v. *Nixon* forced the president to produce the tapes for the Special Grand Jury, and then to resign on August 9, 1974, the Supreme Court decision included a dictum on executive privilege which could create serious problems in the future. Judge Sirica and the United States Appeals Court had sharply limited the president to "a presumptive privilege" of confidentiality in his communications that must give way when there is evidence of crime. The lower court opinion indicated that the courts can in all cases insist on the right to examine the documents *in camera* (in chambers) to determine whether presidential confidentiality is being properly invoked. But Chief Justice Warren Burger, through acceptance of a part of the minority opinion of the Appeals Court decision, rooted executive privilege in the Constitution for the first time in history. Burger, a Nixon appointee, wrote that the necessity of "confidentiality" in high-level communications "is too plain to require further discussion." That dictum is an open invitation to future presidents to use executive privilege broadly, with the blessing and backing of the highest court, unless criminal conversations are involved.

The chief justice not only legitimatized executive privilege for the first time, but carelessly distributed dicta of "presumptive privilege" and the indispensability of "confidentiality." Chief Justice Burger even warned the lower courts against insisting upon *in camera* examination of "military, diplomatic, and sensitive national security secrets." On behalf of Chief Justice Burger, whose opinion treated Mr. Nixon's cover-up as a conscientious constitutional claim, it must be conceded that at the time his opinion was written the court was not aware of the full sordid story of the president's crude use of executive privilege as an instrument to obstruct justice. Hopefully, the Supreme Court will take the conspiracy in the Oval Office into account and will require court review of all presidential efforts to use "national security" as a justification of executive privilege.

Raoul Berger, Charles Warren Senior Fellow in American Legal History at Harvard Law School, has commented critically upon Chief Justice Burger's dictum in the White House tapes case: "It cannot often enough be repeated that the Founders did not view the president with awe but with apprehension," Berger commented in his treatise on "The Incarnation of Executive Privilege" in *United States* v. *Nixon*. "Given the sorry role played by executive secrecy in recent years—secret executive agreements, secret bombings of Cambodia, President Nixon's secret obstruction of the Watergate investigation—and given its proven capacity to hamper the legislative process, the nation is entitled to a better explanation of how executive secrecy is protected by the Constitution," Berger wrote. On the Court's exclusion of executive privilege claims involving "national security secrets," Berger quoted former Supreme Court Justice Robert Jackson: "Security is like liberty in that many crimes are committed in its name." In a telling sentence, Berger, as the foremost authority on the dangers of executive privilege, wrote: "Current events, one might suspect, should have persuaded the [United States Supreme] Court that a Judge John J. Sirica or Gerhard Gesell is more to be trusted 'in camera' with such [national security] matters than a John Ehrlichman or his like."

These warnings from Raoul Berger, whose credentials on executive privilege are well recognized, are in line with my own concern that future presidents will grasp at Chief Justice Burger's comments as Richard Nixon did a few hours after the opinion was released. Although the unanimous decision forced him to relinquish the tapes and resign, Mr. Nixon found comfort in Burger's opinion and stated: "I was gratified, therefore, to note that the Court reaffirmed both the validity and the importance of the principle of executive privilege. . . . This [case] will prove to be not the precedent that destroyed the principle but the action that preserved it."

Subsequent to the writing and release of the Supreme Court decision, tapes were released by the White House, by the Judiciary Committee, and in the Watergate cover-up trial that disclosed in full the squalid story of Nixon's willful distortions and his resort to claims of national security and executive privilege to cover up serious federal crime. But until the Supreme Court modifies the dictum in *United States* v. *Nixon* there remains the possibility that present or future presidents may use executive privilege for a cover-up of serious crime under the guise of protecting national security. With the Watergate story a part of our history, we cannot be content to believe that it will not happen again. Richard Nixon, under the pressure of political problems and political expediency, employed vicious dictatorial practices to destroy John Dean and to frustrate and subvert the investigations of Congress and the Special Prosecutor.

I do not believe Richard Nixon wished to be a dictator when he took the oath of office on January 20, 1969. Nor do I believe that White House Chief of Staff H. R. Haldeman or Special Assistant John Ehrlichman expected to engage in the totalitarian tactics and the gross misuse of the power of the presidency that eventually took place. I do believe all were obsessed with a desire to use every power of the presidency to try to win a landslide election victory in 1972 to compensate for Nixon's losses in 1960 and 1962 and his narrow victory over Vice President Hubert Humphrey and Alabama Governor George C. Wallace in 1968. A landslide victory was his goal, and he was willing to invoke all the power of the presidency to achieve it, even a criminal obstruction of justice. Though he knew there was no support for the doctrine of executive privilege in the Constitution, in the law, or in any ruling by the Supreme Court, he believed he could compel acceptance of it. Some future president, caught with the need to cover up crimes or political embarrassment, will probably predicate his plea on an interpretation of Chief Justice Burger's opinion in *United States* v. *Nixon* as having "reaffirmed both the validity and the importance of executive privilege."

Another presidential power grab of Watergate proportions is entirely possible unless the Congress, the press, and the academic community understand the seeds of dictatorship buried in the opinion written by Chief Justice Burger. I am hopeful that the following narrative of executive privilege in action will help demonstrate the evil in terms not quickly forgotten. Otherwise, the tremendous price the nation paid for the Watergate scandals will have been in vain, and we will be easy prey for some future authoritarian president.

# Book 1

*Chapter One*

# RICHARD NIXON—BEST ALTERNATIVE?

T HE NIGHT OF November 5, 1968, I checked out of the Century Plaza Hotel in Los Angeles to catch a night plane to Washington to cast my vote the next day for Richard M. Nixon for president of the United States. Busy covering the political campaign, I had failed to make arrangements for an absentee ballot, and the cross-country night flight was the only way I could vote as well as cover the last days of the Nixon campaign for the *Des Moines Register* and *Tribune.*

After the scandals of the Democratic years, I felt it important that a Republican administration be elected. In 1961 I had had high hopes for the administration of John F. Kennedy, but had watched it destroy its potential with the attempted cover-up of the Billie Sol Estes scandals, the scandal in the award of the TFX warplane contract, the police state tactics of the State Department in the ordeal of Otto F. Otepka, the foreign policy fiascoes of the Bay of Pigs, and the initial troop commitments in the Vietnam War. For years I had been a frustrated journalist trying to persuade a Democratic Congress to make a full investigation of the continuing perjury, falsification of records, and obstruction of justice those scandals typified. The Bobby Baker case, just prior to the November 22, 1963, assassination of President Kennedy, had been a preview of the flagrant favoritism, secrecy, and heavy-handed arrogance of the Lyndon B. Johnson years in the White House.

Hubert H. Humphrey, the Democratic candidate, seemed to me to represent a continuation of the secrecy and partiality of the Johnson administration. As a Washington correspondent for the *Minneapolis Star* and *Tribune* and the *Des Moines Register* and *Tribune,* I had been friendly toward Humphrey, then a United States senator from Minnesota, but a coolness developed in our relationship during his period as vice president. Hubert was bouncy and loquacious on any side of any subject. His bubbling humor, grave frowns, and profound sincerity could be called forth as the occasion demanded. Although basically honest in his motivations, he was careless in his associations and his choice of subordinates. He spouted a good line about the importance of open government and the evils of secret decisions. However, I knew of his early efforts to sweep the Bobby Baker investigation under the rug of party solidarity when Republican Senator John Williams of Delaware was trying to force an investigation into that sordid affair. As vice president and also as a candidate for the presidency, Hubert had been elusive and unavailable when questions arose about some Small Business Administration and foreign aid frauds involving political associates. Efforts to question him on these matters in public press conferences when he was the Democratic candidate for president resulted in frustrating evasions and my personal conclusion that he would be a disaster as President.

My night flight from Los Angeles to Washington, D.C., was to cast my vote for the things Richard Nixon said he stood for—open, honest, efficient operation of the federal government. Candidate Nixon had declared in the campaign that "there are occasions on which a president must take unpopular measures. He is trusted, after all, not to follow the fluctuations of the public-opinion polls, but to bring his own best judgment to bear on the best ideas his administration can muster," Mr. Nixon said. "But, after he has decided, then the people have a right to know why. It's time we once again had an open administration—open to ideas from the people, and open in the com-munication with the people—an administration of open doors, open eyes, and open minds."

More than twenty-five years of investigative reporting had opened my eyes to the corruptive influence of secret government decisions at all levels—from the Des Moines City Hall, the Polk County Courthouse, and the Iowa State House to essentially all of the departments of the federal government in Washington. And the policy with the greatest potential for destruction of American democracy was the claim of "executive privilege" that had emerged in Washington in the early years of the Eisenhower administration. "Executive privilege" had no foundation in federal law and no support in the decisions of the Supreme Court, yet recent presidents had asserted the right to with-hold any documents or testimony from the Congress or the courts in "the national interest." This shield had covered up crimes and mismanagement in the Eisenhower, Kennedy, and Johnson administrations, but Mr. Nixon had assured me that he would put a stop to it. In addition to his speeches on the importance of an open policy to assure fair play in government decisions, I had a private twenty-minute conversation with him on the subject just a few days before the 1968 election. It occurred on the campaign plane one week-end on a flight from Texas to Los Angeles as the quest for votes was drawing to a close. Few members of the press were being permitted access to Mr. Nixon in those final days, but I was regarded as "friendly" and unlikely to break the "background only" rules of the interview either by quoting or misquoting the candidate just before the election. My purpose was simply to catch the mood of the man who at that moment was regarded the favorite and to distill his interpretations of "law and order" and the "open government" assurances he had been giving during the campaign.

Greeting me warmly, Mr. Nixon urged me to take a seat across from him in the small forward compartment of the campaign plane. Although I had known him since 1951 I addressed him formally as Mr. Vice President—his last government position prior to his defeat by John Kennedy in 1960. "Well, it looks like you are going to be the man," I commented, alluding to his favored position in the polls. He replied that although the late slippage in the polls con-cerned some of his people he was still confident he would win by several mil-lion votes. Mr. Nixon was deploring what he and his entourage considered an "unfair" use of "the power of the presidency" by President Johnson to give Vice President Humphrey a boost in the last few days before the election. On October 31, 1968, President Johnson had ordered a halt to all American air, naval, and artillery bombardment of North Vietnam and had announced that the Saigon government and the North Vietnamese would be brought into broadened and intensive peace talks in Paris. Mr. Nixon expressed the same opinion that his friend and political intimate Robert Finch had earlier—that it was "a phony political move" to try to bail out Humphrey. (Mr. Nixon considered it a violation of commitments Johnson had made to him to refrain from active campaigning for Humphrey.)

Our discussions turned almost immediately to what he intended to do about "executive privilege" and the big job of keeping scandals out of the federal government. He offered the view some scandals will inevitably arise in a multi-billion-dollar government, and that the way to avoid damage was to recognize and get on top of problems quickly. He reviewed his own experience with Democratic attempts to cover up the Alger Hiss case and his own success in getting Hiss prosecuted for perjury. His role in the Hiss case had made him a national figure, a hero of the conservative Republicans, and General Eisenhower's choice for a vice presidential running mate. We also talked about the Truman administration's tax scandals. He argued that Mr. Truman had been mistaken to defend his highest aides at the time Senator John J. Williams and others first started raising questions about major corruption in what was then known as the Bureau of Internal Revenue. He also agreed with my view that cooperation with congressional committees in their investigations can be an effective means for a president to keep an administration clean. We both commented on the potential evil in the secrecy of "executive privilege" as used by past Democratic and Republican administrations.

While discussing the problems of eradicating corruption from government, I said I had heard disturbing reports that Jimmy Hoffa, the convicted Teamsters Union boss, had been promised a pardon if the Nixon-Agnew ticket was elected. "I have no deals with Jimmy Hoffa," Mr. Nixon said bluntly and with a touch of irritation. "In fact, I have instructed my people not to accept any Teamsters money for the campaign." He contended that he had specifically cautioned his long-time friend and political supporter, former Congressman Oakley Hunter, to have no contacts with the Teamsters officials. "We got burned on the Teamsters in 1960," he said. "It would be stupid to get burned again on the same thing." Nixon declared with some feeling that the 1960 incident involving Hunter's contact with Hoffa "was innocent" but that "Drew Pearson and the Kennedys tried to make something out of it."

I said that I had been informed by someone in the Kennedy group of a Republican deal to spring Hoffa from prison which involved New Hampshire publisher William Loeb, a Nixon friend and supporter of long standing. "I wanted to find out your explanation of this report," I said. I didn't identify my sources but I did insist that they were well-informed investigators and not inclined to talk loosely, particularly on matters involving Hoffa. However, my personal assessment was that my informants, strongly anti-Nixon as a result of events in the 1960 campaign, might have read a bit more into the situation of the "Hoffa deal" than the evidence merited. Also, I had no material clearly contradicting Mr. Nixon's assurance that he had no arrangement with Hoffa and had cautioned his campaign workers against any pledges. It made sense that Nixon would be wary of Hoffa and the Teamsters union after that earlier criticism, and with apparent sincerity he said he recognized my concern over a possible deal to free Hoffa. He assured me again that he had "no deal and no intention of freeing Hoffa" before he had served his federal prison term.

I turned the conversation back to the dangers of government secrecy by saying I had been impressed with his comments on the importance of open decision-making and hoped he would follow through after he was in the White House. Nixon assured me that he would run an open administration and touched on the importance of his personal experience as a congressional investigator, which he said had taught him the corrupting influence of secret decisions. "Jack Kennedy said the same thing before he became president," I told him, and related conversations I'd had with Kennedy when he was campaigning for the Democratic nomination in 1958, 1959, and 1960, and after he became president. "Kennedy told me he agreed with me on executive privilege, but in a few months he was using it as a cover-up for embarrassments," I said, making reference to the TFX scandal, the Billie Sol Estes case, and the Otto Otepka case. I explained that my conversations with Kennedy had given me the impression he had some historic comprehension of the manner in which arbitrary executive branch secrecy had led to the Truman scandals in the Justice Department, the Bureau of Internal Revenue, and the Reconstruction Finance Corporation.

Mr. Nixon recalled that secrecy and misinformation had led President Eisenhower into embarrassing moments on the Dixon-Yates case and the Sherman Adams–Goldfine affair. That same secrecy was at the bottom of the Eisenhower administration's bungling of the Wolf Ladejinsky security case and of several foreign aid and military scandals, I added.

I expressed the opinion that White House Chief of Staff Sherman Adams' overprotectiveness toward Eisenhower had been a disservice to the president and had been responsible for Mr. Eisenhower's making a number of serious factual mistakes at presidential press conferences. Mr. Nixon said he believed the Eisenhower White House functioned better after Sherman Adams was forced to resign in 1958. "My study of Washington scandals indicates presidents get in trouble because they are misinformed on the facts," I said, reminding him that Presidents Grant, Harding, Truman, Eisenhower, and Kennedy were misled by relying on reports through the chain of command from the very same people involved in the corruption or mismanagement. I omitted President Lyndon Johnson initially, and commented that LBJ was an actively corrupt figure and not likely to have been misled for long by his subordinates.

Nixon agreed about Johnson and accepted my assertion that a president must have a source for his information that is not dependent upon the channels of the bureaucratic government. Such a source would function like the office of ombudsman in Sweden; Nixon characterized it as a "kind of presidential ombudsman." Jack Kennedy had suggested the same general solution in our discussions of the problems of a president in keeping his administration honest while cleaning up the little pockets of corruption and mismanagement inevitably infecting a multi-billion-dollar government.

Nixon asked how Kennedy had visualized such a system working and how big a staff it would take. "Jack thought he could do it by naming Bob as attorney general and having Carmine Bellino as an independent investigator assigned to the White House staff," I said. "It broke down because Bobby was too much involved in the political operations, and Carmine didn't have the political clout or personality to demand direct access to President Kennedy," I said, summarizing a complicated problem of personal and political relationships that permitted the Billie Sol Estes scandal to get out of hand, protected the outrageous multi-billion-dollar blunder of the TFX warplane contract, and resulted in cruel misuse of power in the firing of Otto Otepka from the State Department.

Nixon had known the legendary Carmine Bellino as a staff member of the Senate Permanent Investigating Subcommittee, of which Nixon had been a member, and later as a persistent accountant-investigator inquiring into Nixon's financial links to Howard Hughes and the questionable activities of Nixon's friend and political mentor Murray Chotiner. My reference to Bob Kennedy and Bellino was fleeting because I knew Nixon disliked them intensely. I merely wanted to emphasize two points with regard to a White House ombudsman:

1. An effective presidential ombudsman must have total independence in gathering facts as well as ready access to the president to make certain he understands all implications of those facts.

2. The ombudsman should not have his objectivity jeopardized by partisan political responsibilities or administrative duties in any government agency.

I explained to Mr. Nixon that the ombudsman should not require a large staff because the purpose of the office would not be to duplicate the post audits of the General Accounting Office (GAO) or the standard internal investigatory functions of any of the government agencies. Nor would it take the place of the investigative functions of the congressional oversight committees. "It should be an independent, nonpolitical watchdog for the president to use as a check on the information he was receiving through his own appointees and the executive branch bureaucracy," I said.

Mr. Nixon indicated an interest in being the first president to establish a White House ombudsman as a watchdog on government corruption. Derisively calling the television properties acquired by Mrs. Johnson while her husband was in the House and Senate "a clear conflict of interest," he remarked that no one was fooled by the fact that Mrs. Johnson was holder of the title. "What hell would be raised," he commented, "by some segments of the press if Mrs. Nixon had acquired radio and television interests while I was in the House and Senate." He then volunteered the information that he had taken special precautions to avoid any conflicts of interest if elected president by selling all stocks and investing everything in real estate. "Real estate is the only way to avoid potential conflicts of interest with government contracts," Mr. Nixon said. "I don't want to give anyone any opportunity to criticize my investments."

Somewhat skeptical about Mr. Nixon's rhetoric, I nevertheless believed that his experience in seeing scandals exposed might cause him to conclude that the most expedient politics in the long run was honest and efficient operation of the government. Experience had convinced me that open, honest government could be the best politics, and that the best protection for any president is an open administration policed by the press, the public, the Congress, and the GAO. I harbored no illusions about the purity of Nixon's early record, despite his assurances, because I'd had reason to challenge it personally in connection with a campaign contribution of five thousand dollars he had received from Henry (the Dutchman) Grunewald, a mysterious bipartisan tax fixer whose name was synonymous with the dirtiest aspects of the Truman administration's tax scandals.

My first direct conversation with Richard Nixon, in 1951, concerned that controversial $5,000 contribution to his campaign for the United States Senate seat from California. I do not recall how the subject of the contribution surfaced, but Nixon's membership on the Senate Permanent Investigating Subcommittee, which was then exploring the fringes of the tax scandal, made it important, so I interviewed him in his office in the Old Senate Office Building. Young Senator Nixon's explanation seemed plausible. He had received the $5,000 through Senator Styles Bridges, veteran New Hampshire Republican, who was a friend of Grunewald. At the time, Nixon said, he was not aware of the unsavory nature of Grunewald's background but relied upon the good judgment of the senior Republican senator. Grunewald had received no favors and had asked none, Senator Nixon said, adding that he did not believe he had ever met Grunewald. The senator's manner was candid and forthright, and there was no way and no real reason to try to go behind his explanation. Although the emerging picture of Grunewald's bipartisan corruption of Democrats and Republicans grew more sordid every month, no evidence was ever presented to indicate that Grunewald's money had bought any political favors from Richard Nixon.

In the 1952 campaign, the controversial Nixon political fund of $18,000 emerged, momentarily darkening Nixon's future as Mr. Eisenhower's running mate. The controversial Checkers speech and an overwhelming public response saved his place on the 1952 ticket alongside Eisenhower. As vice president, Nixon moved with a low profile, avoiding entanglements and seeking to be all things to all men in the Republican Party. It was not an unusual stance for a vice president set on succeeding a highly popular president.

The activities of Murray Chotiner, Mr. Nixon's long-time political adviser, resulted in minor political embarrassment in 1956 in connection with question-able contacts at various federal regulatory agencies. For example, Chotiner, who derived his political punch from his relationship with Nixon, successfully halted the deportation of a New Jersey racket figure, Marco Reginelli, who had a record of white slave activities. Robert Kennedy, as chief counsel for the Senate Permanent Investigating Subcommittee, was hot on Chotiner's trail for what he interpreted as improper influence at a federal agency. Kennedy developed evidence that Chotiner had used Nixon's name in setting up some of his appointments and saw the possibility of delivering a karate chop to the vice president in the 1956 presidential campaign. Whatever documentation Robert Kennedy had was not sufficient to convince Chairman John L. Mc-Clellan, Arkansas Democrat, that the investigation should be pushed in the middle of a presidential campaign. Chairman McClellan directed that the probe be dropped, and an irate Bob Kennedy obeyed.

"If there is anything to it, the investigation can be continued after the elec-tion," Chairman McClellan told me. "I'm not going to have this investigating committee used for partisan politics." But, before the investigation was sus-pended, Chotiner and vice president Nixon had some anxious moments even though Chotiner denied that he had used Nixon's name or that there had been anything improper about his activities. The vice president likewise denied knowledge of the deportation case, and said he had never authorized Chotiner to use his name to seek favors at government agencies. With the Senate inves-tigation dead until after the election, there was no way to dispute his state-ments. Vice President Nixon seemed to split sharply with Chotiner to demon-strate deep displeasure with his political adviser over the questionable nature of his representing Reginelli. But in a few months Chotiner was forgiven his careless ethics and the Nixon-Chotiner association resumed its open character. The renewal of old political ties with Chotiner was not a good omen as far as I was concerned, but few active, viable presidential candidates in either party did not have some questionable associates.

Richard Nixon was entitled to be judged by the same standards as Harry Truman, Thomas Dewey, Adlai Stevenson, John Kennedy, and Lyndon John-son. On the basis of his record as of 1968, he appeared to be a reasonably honest presidential candidate. A slim majority of the voters agreed with me that he was the best of three alternatives available to bring some order and decency to the chaotic, corrupt federal establishments. Nixon's victory over Democratic candidate Humphrey and George Wallace, the American Inde-pendent Party candidate, was even narrower than Kennedy's victory over Nixon in 1960. Not until 11:35 A.M. on November 7, did Illinois—the state that had robbed him of the election eight years earlier—put him over the top. That squeaker victory in 1968 meant that Nixon and his political cohorts im-mediately began plotting to assure a landslide victory in 1972.

*Chapter Two*

# FIRST PRESIDENTIAL OMBUDSMAN

A POST in government had never attracted me, even though for years I had mulled over the need for someone to be able to send storm signals to a president when he was being either overprotected or denied information by aides grinding political axes. Even when discussing such a necessity with Kennedy and, later, with Nixon, I never thought of myself as filling such a job.

When Richard Nixon quipped, at a cocktail party celebrating his winning the Republican nomination at Miami in August 1968, that he would name me his secretary of defense, I knew it was a reference to my widely publicized differences with Secretary McNamara over the disastrous TFX contract. Consequently, I was not prepared for a call from Harry Dent in December to inquire whether I would be interested in being director of the U.S. Information Agency. Dent, a former legislative aide to Senator Strom Thurmond of South Carolina, was given major credit for Nixon's crucial victories in southern states and was one of a handful of recruiters as President-elect Nixon prepared to take over the federal government. Harry was a friend of several years' standing, and I told him I was flattered to be considered but wasn't sure I would be interested in leaving the news business for government.

Privately, I gave it some thought, for I had been fascinated by inside knowledge gained as a Kennedy appointee to the five-man United States Advisory Commission on Government Information Policy, which was empowered to monitor the operations of the U.S. Information Agency and write an annual report to Congress. I had shied away from federal jobs offered by Bob and Jack Kennedy, other than the non-paying advisory post, because I relished my freedom as a newspaper reporter and could not see relinquishing my independence. I had been well aware that being on the outside in dealing with Bob on the labor racket investigations was an advantage. It gave me a leverage not enjoyed by his staff as they tried to persuade him certain steps should be taken. I felt that Nixon would be less demanding and more amenable to reasonable argument than the Kennedys, who were accustomed to an awed compliance. I felt that USIA was within my area of experience, but the decision was never forced on me because the post went to Frank Shakespeare, a vice president of CBS, who had been active in the 1968 campaign.

No further thought of government service had occurred to me until Dent, by then a deputy counsel to the president, again called in April and asked me to come to his office in the Executive Office Building. He said that the president wondered whether I would be interested in joining the administration as a kind of trouble-shooter and ombudsman. He said my name had come up several times and that the president had given him the job of sounding me out and finding out how I would visualize the job. I told Harry of my talks with Mr. Nixon about my ideas in the last days of the campaign in 1968, but added that I had not pictured myself in the role of ombudsman. I did say that former Congressman Robert Ellsworth, then a deputy counsel in the White House, seemed to have some corresponding chores for congressional committees but that his other functions placed limitations on the job as I envisioned it. However, I told Dent that if a satisfactory salary and access to the president could be arranged, I would seriously consider the job. I emphasized that the title did not concern me but that jurisdiction would have to be as broad as that of the General Accounting Office or the Senate Permanent Investigating Subcommittee.

For several weeks we explored ideas and searched for a suitable spot. These ranged from assistant director of the Office of the Bureau of the Budget to assistant comptroller general. The latter post held considerable appeal because of the independence it would possess as a result of being outside the White House and not accountable to the White House. Later I found that Haldeman and Ehrlichman disapproved that independent status and wanted me within the White House complex. I quipped that I'd heard about the "Berlin Wall" (Pat Buchanan's phrase for Haldeman and Ehrlichman), but Dent quickly assured me that he had no problem getting to see President Nixon and was sure I'd be ingenious enough to evade their clutches. From Bob Ellsworth, a former Kansas congressman, I'd heard some mild complaints about being hampered by the Haldeman and Ehrlichman combine, which was referred to in tandem. I had known Ellsworth through several congressional investigations in which I'd been interested and thought him highly effective in securing the cooperation of executive agencies with congressional investigating committees. However, I had seen his influence wane and was aware of his frustrations. Dent explained that Ellsworth had taken issue with Haldeman on a few occasions and that Haldeman had retaliated. Dent seemed to feel it was a clash of personalities rather than a factor I needed to consider.

My superiors—Richard Wilson, chief of the Cowles New Bureau, and Kenneth MacDonald, editor of the *Des Moines Register* and *Tribune*—tried to dissuade me from venturing into the government bureaucracy, but I was anxious to try. After spending twenty-five years exposing government corruption and mismanagement, I wanted to test some of my theories on preventive efforts. I requested a year's leave of absence, but MacDonald said I would have to sever my relationship with the paper completely if I joined the Nixon administration.

My wife's response, when I told her of Dent's approach, was to ask whether they hoped to pull my fangs, since I had never been a presidential favorite—of any president. My son's and daughters' instinctive reactions were the same. They asked, "Is he trying to buy you?" and "Do they hope to neutralize you?"

I agreed that some of Nixon's aides undoubtedly expected to neutralize a potential threat but maintained that the president's apparent interest in the need for an ombudsman as an intermediary to promote fair play and honest government gave me an opportunity to test my theory that honest, fair operation of government could be the best politics. As a final clincher I told my children: "It doesn't really make any difference what Mr. Nixon or his associates may think. I'm not for sale. They'll find out quickly enough if they have ideas to the contrary." I knew many of my colleagues in the press would be astonished and would raise questions of a "sell-out," but without the sympathetic concern of my family. I recognized that some of the so-called knee-jerk antagonism toward Richard Nixon would be directed at me, but I was certain that eventually my attempts to stamp out government corruption would be recognized as a sincere non-partisan effort.

Although I had not yet been able to talk with the President or Haldeman, my discussions with Dent and Ehrlichman were completely consistent with my pre-election conversation with Nixon. The problem I encountered initially in getting to see President Nixon should have tipped me off to what would lie ahead. For two months appointments were made and then broken with seemingly plausible explanations about the president's travel schedule or busy calendar. I began to doubt whether Ehrlichman or Haldeman, despite their cordiality, wanted an independent investigator on the loose in the White House.

I talked with only two other people about my prospective change of job. Republican Senator John Williams of Delaware, who had rightly earned the title "the conscience of the senate," said I should insist on hearing directly from Nixon that we were in agreement on my responsibilities, that he would grant me access, and that he would back me. Senator Williams was troubled by the difficulty he had in seeing the president on some tax problems and government salary levels. "It is worse than Sherman Adams," he said. Usually a White House tries to woo senior senators and congressmen, but the Nixon White House was alienating Republican members of Congress and seemed bent on setting its course without consultation. I received the same message and advice from Representative H. R. Gross of Iowa, another old friend whose integrity and courage I admired and whose counsel I sought. "Don't take the job until you get the word straight from Nixon," Gross advised. "There is room enough for misunderstandings if you have it straight from the man and in writing."

Becoming restless, I finally told Dent I was discouraged, and that unless I was permitted to see the president I wished to withdraw, but he assured me that President Nixon was enthusiastic and had asked that I write a job description. When I submitted the job description, Dent said, "The president thinks it is great and even Haldeman and Ehrlichman have okayed it" (actually, their acceptance had been qualified). My written job description called for the title of "special counsel" * reporting directly to President Nixon. By

* I am a graduate of Drake University law school and duly admitted to practice in Iowa, in the District of Columbia, and in federal courts, up to and including the United States Supreme Court.

the time I saw the president, Ehrlichman had reduced my title to "deputy counsel," which placed me under his jurisdiction on the White House organizational chart, though he affably assured me that this would in no way interfere with my direct access "when needed" and that it was "the way the president and Bob want it for housekeeping purposes." Title meant nothing to me as long as the written job description was reviewed with the president and direct reporting guaranteed; Ehrlichman assured me that it was. The president was preparing for a trip around the world, and Ehrlichman explained that this had crowded his schedule and might make it impossible for him to see me until he returned in August. I told Ehrlichman that if I didn't see the president before I left on vacation that they could forget the whole thing. I knew the president was busy, but if this ombudsman job was worth doing it was worth making some adjustment in his schedule to iron out any possibility of misunderstandings ahead of time.

After two or three broken appointments in the last week, I finally saw the president for a half hour on July 17, 1969—a day before I left for a month's vacation. I'd spent forty-five minutes with Ehrlichman before we went to the Oval Office. We went over the job description, and the president spoke approvingly of every aspect of the mechanism for keeping government honest.

It was all very flattering as he suggested some things he was anxious for me to examine and expressed the wish that I could accompany him on "this historic trip" around the world because there were some things he wanted to ask my advice about. He also mentioned that there were some problems of corruption in connection with the Vietnam War that he wanted me to examine. He instructed Ehrlichman to arrange top security clearances for me because some of the problems would involve high "national security" classifications, "because, as you know" the military classifications are often used as a device to cover up corruption. The president also told me he wished to have access to tax returns so that we could avoid any Internal Revenue Service scandals. He reminded me that President Eisenhower had done a good job of cleaning up the IRS but said there had been two intervening terms for corruption and favoritism to creep back into the system. He said that I should "get together with Randy Thrower," the commissioner of Internal Revenue, to work out a satisfactory arrangement for access to returns.

When I left the Oval Office with Ehrlichman, it seemed everything was settled. I was to have whatever staff I needed and unlimited access to all government agencies at all levels to develop the facts needed to provide full information on any problem. The president's enthusiasm was contagious, but some aspects of his interpretation of the job perplexed me. Those I would have to explore in detail sometime later. Did he expect me to take over an inspector general function to the military in Vietnam? Was I to examine all "national security" classifications to be sure nothing was amiss? Perhaps he had in mind some specific instances in which I would review investigations of the inspectors general to assure an adequate follow-through and no cover-ups. In that context, it made sense.

Ehrlichman was all smiles and good wishes as he shook my hand and welcomed me aboard. I was to report for duty in mid-August and to let Lawrence Higby in Haldeman's office know my needs for office space and secretaries. He apologized for the fact that they had only a GS-18 slot open at $33,500 a year (roughly $5,000 a year below what I'd been led to believe I would receive) but said they would try to find something at a higher scale in a few months. "We've all taken salary cuts to perform government service," Ehrlichman consoled me.

I was also due for another setback when the announcement of my appointment was made by the White House Press Office. Press Secretary Ronald Ziegler took pains to explain that as deputy counsel to the president I would report "through" John Ehrlichman and work "under" John Ehrlichman. I hoped it was another case of Ziegler's not knowing what he was saying, but it had all the earmarks of a clever bureaucratic put-down before I was even settled in my job in the White House.

It was too late to turn back even if Haldeman and Ehrlichman didn't want an ombudsman looking over their shoulders.

My concept of the ombudsman job was described in a three-page memorandum submitted to the president in the first week in July 1969 and generally reviewed and approved by Mr. Nixon in my Oval Office conference with him late in the afternoon (5:25 P.M. to 6:00 P.M.) of July 17, 1969. The text follows:

This post should have a title of "special counsel to the president on government operations problems."

To be effective, the man who holds this post must have direct access to the president and must have the authority for direct access to departments and agencies at all levels.

This post should permit a maximum of mobility to provide for direct contacts at the House, the Senate, and various points in the departments and agencies as well as with others outside of government.

This post should be devoid of any authority or responsibility to make policy decisions or general administrative decisions. Any decisions that flow from the recommendations must come from the president.

The purpose of this post is to give the president an independent source of information and evaluation of problem areas and potential problem areas within his administration. In alerting the president to potential problems within the administration at the earliest stage, the special counsel will make it possible to do the planning necessary to correct the malfunctioning of government before a crisis is reached.

The special counsel should also provide for an effective follow-through on problems by someone who is not burdened by the responsibilities of normal housekeeping chores or administrative or political responsibilities.

The mobility of the special counsel should provide a listening post for complaints from Congress, the press, and the public. The investigation and evaluation of these complaints can result in presidential action to communicate the information to proper administrative or political officers.

In addition to alerting the president to possible future problems, the special counsel would provide a follow-through on problems of past administrations to assure effective action and to alert the Nixon administration to the dangers of entanglement with problems of the past. This follow-through could be coordinated with the proper assistant to the president in the fields of politics, legal problems, administrative problems, or communications problems.

The follow-through by the special counsel would include the TFX contract, the Apollo contract award and related problems, the problems related to the operations of the Small Business Administration in Maine, the waste and mismanagement in foreign aid in connection with NAPCO industries of Minnesota, the Universal Fiberglass problem at the GSA and the SBA, and the handling of the Banks extradition matter. This would assure a cooperation and coordination with senators and congressmen with similar views and objectives in examining the details of the problem areas and establishing a responsibility for either corruption or mismanagement.

The problems faced by the Safeguard ABM in the Senate arise in a large part from the delay in understanding and dealing with Pentagon problems in a manner that places the issue in perspective. The issue of the Safeguard ABM has been permitted to become enmeshed in controversy involving corruption, misjudgments, and mismanagement of the McNamara regime at the Pentagon. This could have been avoided, for the potential for this problem was apparent in January. Proper coordination between the White House, Pentagon and Congress can still be helpful in this area.

Much of the problem in the current ABM dispute arises from an avalanche of stories of corruption, mismanagement, and misjudgment flowing from decisions in the Kennedy and Johnson administrations. The problems of the Kennedy and Johnson period have been dealt with in a vague manner that has often left the impression that these problems are the responsibility of the Nixon administration and the Laird Pentagon. (An article in the June 5, 1969, issue of the *New York Review of Books* entitled "The War Machine Under Nixon" is typical of these articles. The article is by I. F. Stone.)

There has been a failure to recognize the danger that the Nixon administration might be blamed for the errors of the past and carry that burden into each major defense controversy. The reasons for the failure are many, and not the least of these is the overwhelming job that any new defense secretary faces in taking charge. Some carry-over of personnel is essential for a continuity in running the Defense Department, but this must be done with total awareness of the danger of too much reliance upon men who were involved in the problems of the Kennedy and Johnson period. Those who were parties to a series of misjudgments of the past have an inevitable desire to hide or minimize those errors and a considerable stake in seeking to saddle the Nixon administration with a defense of those policies and decisions.

Because there has been no clear break with the past there has been a tendency to defend past decisions and operations, and this has blurred the line between the Johnson administration and the Nixon administration. It is essential to place the responsibility for errors on the Johnson and Kennedy administrations where that responsibility belongs. There are dozens of ways that this can be done in such a dramatic manner that the press and the public will not miss the point."

The only change was my title, and Ehrlichman assured me that the change from special counsel to deputy counsel would not interfere with my reporting directly to the president. I did not discuss that change with President Nixon because of Ehrlichman's assurance, and that was a major mistake. Such a discussion at the outset would have permitted a degree of frankness in dealing with the problems of access that was impossible later, thus seriously hampering my effectiveness, creating frustration, and eventually leading to my resignation.

*Chapter Three*

# THE BERLIN WALL

I DO NOT KNOW what the motivations of Bob Haldeman and John Ehrlichman were when they arrived on the Washington scene in January 1969 without prior experience in Washington or, for that matter, in local or state government. Since both were reported to be devout Christian Scientists and teetotalers, we must assume that they had no carefully worked out *Mein Kampf* for the destruction of American institutions. But their priorities from the beginning placed re-election of Nixon ahead of any political accomplishments during the first term, and certainly ahead of the ultimate good of the country.

Haldeman, a vice president of the J. Walter Thompson advertising agency, and Ehrlichman, a zoning lawyer from Seattle, contrived to secure for themselves the two most powerful positions in government within a few months of Mr. Nixon's inauguration as president. Both were superficially bright, but these fledgling government servants were completely lacking in understanding of the bipartisan political accommodations normal in the day-to-day dealings with Congress and government agencies. Almost immediately, their zealous pursuit of power in the president's name, their obsession with secrecy, and their vicious assaults on those they considered enemies created an atmosphere of totalitarianism within the White House and an arrogant disregard for cabinet officers, senators and congressmen. This maladroit team provided a contemporary illustration of Lord Acton's thesis that power tends to corrupt and absolute power corrupts absolutely. Whether they were given authority or just assumed it I can only speculate, but they made it impossible to determine which of the orders they transmitted were from the president and which were their own personal whims. I have often seen how impossible it is for the best-intentioned men to withstand the temptation to misuse unlimited power with the mistaken rationalization that "for this one time" the end justifies the means. Then "one more time" seems warranted, and soon repetition makes it standard conduct.

I joined the White House staff believing that I was assured access to the president. My first experiences gave me reason to be optimistic, but gradually the vise tightened and my efforts to correct situations involving blatant corruption and misuse of power were increasingly frustrated.

Haldeman and Ehrlichman justified their obsessive secrecy as being necessary in dealing with those they characterized as Nixon's "enemies" in the press. There *was* bias against Nixon in the press, and the opposition to the Vietnam War made it easy for the president and his supporters to rationalize their anger at the networks and at certain large metropolitan newspapers in Washington and New York. But erroneous reporting, emotional or ideologically based conclusions, and superficiality are the right of a free press and will remain its right as long as the press is really free.

Haldeman and Ehrlichman did not understand that the greatest strength of American democracy is the right of the free press to be wrong. That is not to say that government officials do not have the right to demand that errors be corrected or to point out evidence of bias, inconsistency, or other weaknesses, but Haldeman and Ehrlichman believed it was necessary to bring discipline to the broadcasting industry and newspapers in order to accomplish their single objective—the re-election of Richard Nixon by as great a majority as possible. This compulsion meant they assigned the highest priority to projects which would boost the president's popularity in the polls, neglecting the time-consuming and difficult task of making the government operate a little more efficiently and fairly.

Neither Ehrlichman nor Haldeman had enough knowledge of government operations to distinguish between good government and bad government, between acceptable ethical standards and political corruption. They assumed it would suffice to paper over corruption and mismanagement with a public relations crusade, a technique they had mastered as advance-men in Mr. Nixon's many campaigns.

Their control of Nixon's time was not apparent during the 1968 campaign, although I learned later that it had caused Richard Whalen, author, speech-writer, and consultant on military matters, to leave in anger shortly after the Miami convention. Some grumblings about the "Berlin Wall" issued from speech-writer Patrick Buchanan and from Robert Ellsworth, who served as deputy counsel to the president for several months in early 1969. But the complaints were muted by a desire to be cooperative and to present a united front to the world outside the Nixon White House. Harry Dent, who was a deputy counsel and a consultant on Southern political strategy, conceded that there was some staff irritation with Haldeman and Ehrlichman but assured me that "progress is being made on working it out" as he discussed with me President Nixon's desire to have me join the White House staff in "an ombudsman role."

I discounted early warnings by Richard Whalen because they were too general and because they were sprinkled with caustic comments about "evil influences of the Berlin Wall and the Germans." I erroneously believed that Whalen's initial comments were unnecessarily bitter or were a humorous exaggeration. By the time I realized Whalen was deadly serious about the menace of the Haldeman-Ehrlichman team it was too late, for I had resigned from the *Des Moines Register* and *Tribune* and was serving as deputy counsel to President Nixon. Two quick triumphs in which I managed to circumvent the influence of Haldeman, Ehrlichman, and Attorney General John Mitchell led me to be overly optimistic in assessing my chances of overcoming the unhealthy totalitarian atmosphere at 1600 Pennsylvania Avenue. For several weeks, I actually believed that by patient persistence I could demonstrate that open and accountable government would be politically advantageous. Gradually, however, evidence piled up that the team of advisers was insulating President Nixon from all influences they could not control.

Subtly they cut the authority of Herbert Klein, Dr. Arthur Burns, and Rose Mary Woods. Herb Klein, an experienced newsman and an old friend of Nixon, was given the impressive title of communications director but denied any effective role on White House information policy or planning. The unflappable Klein was thrust into the public eye on television programs to explain major controversies and to defend the administration line to editors from coast to coast. He had no authority over White House Press Secretary Ronald Ziegler, who took most of his orders from Haldeman and some from Ehrlichman or the president. Haldeman finally seized control of Klein's office by installing his protégé, Jeb S. Magruder, as deputy director in charge of administration. The shift was for the ostensible purpose of freeing Klein from administrative chores so that he could more actively move toward his stated goal of "making the Nixon administration the most open in history." This excuse didn't fool anyone; even the secretaries were gossiping about Haldeman's takeover. Klein was well liked, but Haldeman was feared. This blatant undercutting of one of his earliest supporters was a vivid example of the conniving twosome's influence over Nixon.

While Magruder had many of the same traits as the hard-driving, ambitious Haldeman, he was younger than the curt White House chief of staff and was a pleasant conversationalist. When he moved from the west wing to the Executive Office Building, I dropped by his office for a chat about the advantages of forthright information policies. I wanted to give him a soft sell on open government and, hopefully, a subtle warning about the corrupting influence of covert government and, specifically, executive privilege.

I took a copy of my book *Washington Cover-Up*, intending to lend it to him for historical background on the manner in which executive privilege had been used to hide crimes and mismanagement, proving in the long run to be disastrous to the people who had relied on it to conceal their activities. Jeb Magruder, congenial and receptive, seemed to grasp the general subject so quickly that I decided it would be worth giving him a copy from my dwindling supply. Though he later told me he had read the book, his involvement in the cover-up of the Watergate affair in 1972 indicated that he had either missed the message or forgotten it in his endeavor to please Haldeman and the president.

Ehrlichman and Mitchell were irritated by my constant campaign against executive privilege. It served their purposes to subscribe to the theories fabricated by Secretary of State William P. Rogers when he served in the Eisenhower administration as deputy attorney general and later as attorney general. They found comfort and security in the belief that neither Congress nor the courts could penetrate the shield over the White House, contending that all conversations between White House personnel and all communications within the executive branch were covered by executive privilege. It was pointless to argue that no federal law nor any opinion of the U.S. Supreme Court supported this thesis. Rogers had even admitted this to me, but he argued—with a few truths and many half-truths—that a line of precedents going back to George Washington established a president's constitutional right to authorize withholding of material under the "separation of powers" doctrine. Rogers' only means of supporting this view was a series of attorneys general's opinions that various presidents had had such all-embracing power, which to me was simply accepting the assumption by the king's lawyers that the king could do no wrong.

Rogers' opinion was considered to be without legal foundation by such experts as Senator Sam Ervin, North Carolina Democrat; Senator Thomas Hennings, Missouri Democrat; Representative John Moss, California Democrat; and Professor Raoul Berger, author of the much-praised books *Impeachment* and *Executive Privilege—Constitutional Myth*. My own experience indicated that executive privilege had seldom been used except to conceal mismanagement, corruption, and crime, and that this pernicious doctrine would create problems for any administration because it encouraged officials to believe they could avoid responsibility and accountability for their acts. I believed that acceptance of Rogers' faulty concept could be particularly destructive in the Nixon White House, staffed as it was by so many young, inexperienced, and impressionable men and women operating under the almost complete control of the obsessively secretive Haldeman and Ehrlichman.

In hindsight, it is clear that Dick Whalen's experiences were the most significant indication of the deep problems ahead, but I could not see this then. I had been aware that Whalen's problems with Haldeman had caused him to walk off Nixon's speech-writing team a few weeks after Nixon won the nomination and that his desire for a Republican victory that year had been dampened by the advance-man mentality dominating the Nixon campaign. Although I respected Whalen's ability and integrity, I attributed part of the problem to a personality clash that was possibly not entirely Haldeman's fault. Whalen believed things very deeply, usually knew what he was talking about, and could be very brusque in his comments. Even though he was pleased with the Republican victory, Whalen voiced concern over the iron grip that Haldeman was tightening on control of Nixon's time. Whalen told of an unsuccessful effort Haldeman had made to dislodge Rose Mary Woods, Nixon's long-time secretary, from her White House office next to the Oval Office. The lure had been more spacious quarters in the Executive Office Building, preceded by the sending of a dozen roses. Miss Woods accepted the flowers but declined the larger quarters.

Another incident, involving Dr. Arthur Burns, counselor to the president, was related by Whalen to demonstrate Haldeman's rude disregard for senior White House personnel and for Mr. Nixon's old friends and advisers. It happened prior to April 1969 as Dr. Burns was emerging from an Oval Office conference with the president. Dr. Burns suddenly remembered something the postmaster general had asked him to mention to the president and turned to re-enter the room. Haldeman stood in his path with a curt: "Your appointment is over, Dr. Burns." The president's highest-ranking White House adviser said he wanted only a moment in order to keep his promise to a cabinet officer to deliver a brief message. Haldeman continued to block his path and coldly suggested that he "submit a memorandum" which would be delivered to the president before the end of the day. Frustrated and at a loss for words, Dr. Burns quietly walked away.

When Whalen related the incident in the summer of 1969, I suspected that perhaps he was embellishing it a little because of his dislike for Haldeman. However, it was confirmed for me later in conversation with Dr. Burns and Dr. Martin Anderson, an able and thoroughly trustworthy assistant to Dr. Burns. In my first weeks at the White House, however, I was still skeptical about such criticism and a little overconfident as a result of a few quick victories which seemed to illustrate that "good government is good politics."

I had worked at the White House less than four weeks when the Whalens invited my wife and me to dinner at the Cosmos Club on September 9, 1969. I had been able to obtain the resignation of General Carl Turner as chief United States marshall only a few days earlier (see Chapter Four) and was enthusiastic about several specific projects. I even expressed optimism that eventually Haldeman and Ehrlichman would come to understand both that secrecy in government was corruptive and that it was foolish to believe that there would be no accountability. "I'm sure I will be able to convince them that there are no real secrets in Washington and that it is only practical common sense to operate in the open," I commented.

"You know it and I know it," Whalen replied, "but I still don't believe you know what you are dealing with. Don't be fooled by Haldeman's crewcut Boy Scout look. He's an evil son of a bitch, and don't let him get behind you." Whalen termed Haldeman "a bright angler, almost totally ignorant about issues" and uninterested in them unless they could be used in making Nixon a more salable political product. I explained that I hoped to be able to demonstrate that simple good government was a salable issue if the voters believed a president was sincere. "You are the optimist," Whalen replied. When the evening was over, Whalen wished me "luck—you'll need it," and again warned: "Don't let Haldeman get behind you." The cold reality slowly dawned even while I still believed that eventually the president would see the political wisdom of integrity in government decisions. The inescapable fact was that I had to go through Haldeman or Ehrlichman to see the president, and when I *was* permitted to talk to him it was almost always in the company of one of them. They explained that they weren't trying to bar frank and forthright reports but were simply trying to increase administrative efficiency by freeing the president from the necessity of taking notes and passing instructions to them.

Chilled by the utter futility of trying to get through, over, or around the Berlin Wall, I regretted giving up a thoroughly satisfying job to move into the frustrating White House bureaucracy. I had turned down a similar job feeler from President Kennedy in 1961 because I knew the Kennedys expected to buy your independence as well as your talent, but I had believed Nixon would be less demanding of conformity. I was absolutely right about the insecure Nixon, but I had not taken into account the arrogant possessiveness of Haldeman and Ehrlichman. Ruthlessly wielding the power they derived by controlling access to President Nixon, they resorted to untraceable verbal directives invariably preceded by the phrase, "The president wants you to . . ." or, "It is the president's desire that you . . ."

My requests that "the president's desire" be put in writing always evoked cold hostility and an arrogant reminder that a word from Haldeman or Ehrlichman was to be regarded as a direct command from the president. "Do you doubt my word?" Haldeman asked on a number of occasions. When I responded that I preferred written orders so that there would be no doubt as to the nature of the instructions or the responsibility, Haldeman replied: "The president's time is valuable. This is the system. It is the way the president wants it, and that's the way it's going to be.

On one occasion I reminded Haldeman that my written job description, as approved by President Nixon, called for me to have direct access to the president as I needed it. "There are problem areas where only the president can make a decision as to what should be done," I explained in a conference in Haldeman's office. "Delays on some decisions can only mean major mistakes and irreparable damage." "Even John Mitchell has to come through me," Haldeman gloated as I was protesting my lack of access. "Put it in a memo, and either John or I can decide if it's important enough to take up the president's time," Haldeman snapped.

On still other occasions Haldeman or Ehrlichman suggested that my reports and recommendations be "staffed out" through the very federal agencies in question or through the White Hounse personnel serving a liaison function to the agencies involved. Such a process would have nullified the whole purpose of having an independent ombudsman to warn the president of potential problem areas in his administration.

Irritated with Haldeman's stonewalling, on one occasion I told him that he was "worse than Sherman Adams" and that it could only lead to trouble for the administration, as it had in the Adams case. "I'm not a Sherman Adams," Haldeman retorted, defensively insisting that he took no part in decisions and did not try to guide policy in any government agencies. "I serve the president," Haldeman said, adding that he didn't try to know the substance of problems before the president or to have opinions as to good or bad programs, but merely systematized the president's schedule "so his time will be used in the best way possible." There was no point in further antagonizing him by asking how anyone devoid of opinions and substantive knowledge of matters could determine the best way for the president to use his time.

Though Haldeman and Ehrlichman were both energetic, skillful maneuverers in bureaucratic control, they isolated themselves and their little band of trusted young aides. Haldeman explained the predominance of young men in their twenties and early thirties among his key assistants as being "the best bargain in manpower." He asserted, "You can buy more young brains and energy for less money, and they are not set in their ways." Subservient and pliant sycophants were less inclined to question or challenge a superior who had made them and could break them with no one noting their passing.

Haldeman's bargain-basement manpower consisted of intelligent, handsome, obedient, and inexperienced young men. They included White House Press Secretary Ronald Ziegler, White House Appointments Secretary Dwight Chapin, Jeb S. Magruder, Gordon Strachan, Lawrence Higby, and Hugh Sloan. Ehrlichman's crew included Deputy Counsel Egil (Bud) Krogh, Deputy Counsel Ed Morgan, Todd Hullins, Charles Stewart, John Whittaker, and Kenneth Cole.

The only person who could have taken action against this unhealthy wielding of the power of the presidency was Richard M. Nixon, who seemed placidly unaware and, in fact, pleased to have his privacy assured. This is not to contend that he had relinquished presidential authority to Haldeman or Ehrlichman, but only that he permitted a situation to be created in which it was virtually impossible to determine whether Haldeman and Ehrlichman were speaking for the president or for themselves when they uttered those magic words, "The president would like to have you . . ." The only sure way to test the validity of questionable projects was to state clearly and emphatically: "I will do that when the president tells me to do it," or, "Put that in writing so there won't be any misunderstanding later about what the orders were or where they came from." While effective in avoiding unwanted assignments, such responses put me on the wrong list with both Haldeman and Ehrlichman almost from the start. My recalcitrance led them to seek others who would be anxious to do their bidding without question in return for a kind word or an appreciative pat on the head. Seldom was I able to get them to make a written record of their requests. By contrast, they insisted that the rest of the staff make written reports on everything "for the convenience of the president."

My years as an investigative reporter had made me familiar with that general pattern of operation. The most successful practitioner of this tricky business was President Lyndon B. Johnson, and the most notorious recent example was Robert G. (Bobby) Baker, who, as Johnson's right arm in the Senate, had learned from LBJ himself and from the equally effective political pragmatist Senator Robert Kerr, self-made millionaire from Oklahoma. Johnson, Baker, and Kerr were not amateurs in the Washington political game, but it was difficult to determine whether Haldeman and Ehrlichman were merely precocious students of the cover-up or had an instructor skilled in the art of duplicity.

Although President Nixon was fully responsible for the two men and the conditions they created, I was not sure he completely understood the kind of government that was evolving from their domination of his time and his thinking. Disturbing signs of political favoritism and political corruption were seeping under the edges of the executive privilege blanket they had pulled over the White House staff and were trying to stretch to cover the whole executive branch of government. Unless the president took charge and halted this corrupting arbitrary secrecy, they were headed for disaster.

*Chapter Four*

# GENERAL TURNER—THE FIRST ROTTEN APPLE

THE APPOINTMENT OF retired Major General Carl Turner gave me my first opportunity to test the Nixon administration on a question involving provable dishonesty of one of its appointees. Less than six months before I joined the administration, President Nixon had named General Turner to be the chief United States marshal, on the recommendations of Attorney General John Mitchell and Deputy Attorney General Richard Kleindienst.

The first indication that General Turner was involved in questionable or illegal activity came in a conversation with LaVern J. Duffy, associate counsel for John McClellan's Permanent Senate Investigating Subcommittee, only a week after I went to work at the White House. Duffy, an old friend of mine with an Iowa background, called me at the White House to give me a gruff needle about "the obstructionist tactics" the Army was using to thwart his investigation of the multi-million-dollar Vietnam service club scandals. Duffy wanted my help in breaking through the executive privilege barrier the Army bureaucracy was wrapping around some of the key documents involving an Army cover-up of the club scandals. He explained his problem briefly and described the approximate scope of his investigation of a group of Army sergeants involved in black market activities, kickbacks, and similar corruption. The leader of what he called the "khaki Mafia" was the highest-ranking noncommissioned officer in the Army, Sergeant Major William O. Wooldridge.

Duffy had already concluded that a relatively small group had been able to use Wooldridge's prestige and connections to establish a racket ring in the noncommissioned officers' clubs in Augsburg, Germany, and similar rings in the United States, at Fort Benning, Georgia, and in South Vietnam, where the build-up of troops provided a multi-million-dollar gravy train. Many complaints from military personnel stemmed from the illegal enterprise, which touched every aspect of service club operations—a big skim from the earnings of the club slot machines, kickbacks on liquor and beer sales, shakedowns of entertainers at the service clubs, black market dealings involving the Vietnam money exchanges, and illegal use of club privileges to import everything from refrigeration equipment to Datsun cars from Japan.

Duffy was being facetious when he needled me about being a part of the cover-up, but he was genuinely angry with the Army general counsel's office, which he charged was obstructing the work he and accountant-investigator Carmine Bellino were doing to try to pin down responsibility for lax enforcement of Army regulations and U.S. laws that should have stopped such activity months earlier. The widespread racketeering by the khaki Mafia was so open that it was common talk among the officials of the firms dealing with the service clubs in Vietnam. Some investigations conducted by lower-ranking officials had been whitewashed, Duffy said. The official investigating reports by the lower-ranking officers and enlisted men were needed from the Army for Duffy to prove who had killed earlier investigations.

What he had been able to determine without those reports indicated that at least a major part of the responsibility fell on Brigadier General Earl Cole, who was in charge of the operations of the service clubs in Vietnam and had some administrative control over the Criminal Investigation Division (CID) forces there. General Cole was a close friend of General William C. Westmoreland, who commanded the United States forces in Vietnam and later became Army chief of staff. No evidence indicated Westmoreland was a part of any racketeering, but Duffy had no doubt that the Army secretary's office, the CID, and the Army counsel's office were trying to block a full congressional exposé of General Westmoreland's close friend.

Defense Secretary Melvin A. Laird had agreed several months earlier to give Chairman John L. McClellan's investigators full cooperation, and abandon claims of executive privilege the Army had used to bar access to the Army's internal reports. From long experience with federal government investigations I knew that without these reports it was difficult for investigators for congressional committees or the General Accounting Office to distinguish between simple bureaucratic laxity and criminal obstruction of justice. Duffy's request for assistance in obtaining access to investigative reports was a proper one and in line with Laird's agreement to cooperate with McClellan's investigating subcommittee. This was supposed to correct a precedent set by Defense Secretary Robert S. McNamara when he had arrogantly refused to make information available on the notorious TFX contract.

I agreed to call the Army counsel's office to help Duffy jar loose the crucial internal reports, but I had one last question: "Are there any potential problems for the Nixon administration in your investigation?"

"We aren't completely certain yet," Duffy said. "It could be that there will be a problem involving the new chief United States marshal. We won't be able to tell for sure until we get our hands on some of these documents."

"Give it to me straight," I asked. "What does it look like at this stage?"

"All signs point to General Turner being responsible for the cover-up of the Wooldridge gang," Duffy replied. "Also, there is some indication that General Turner has been collecting guns from police departments, claiming that he is doing it for the Army, and then selling them and pocketing the money." At this stage, said Duffy, the evidence was largely circumstantial, but the case would ultimately depend upon material in the criminal investigation files of the Army. Those files would show what information was available to General Turner at the time he made specific decisions on certain illegal activities in Germany and at Fort Benning.

I had asked Duffy whether he would object to my making inquiries to determine whether the Army challenged his circumstantial evidence or his tentative conclusion on General Turner. Within a few hours I was able to gain release from the Army of the documents Duffy had requested and had assured myself that the Army did not have an adequate answer to the questions he was raising about Turner's handling of the club investigations in Germany, Georgia, and South Vietnam. The Army counsel's office was extremely reluctant to divulge facts which would reveal wrongdoing by either Turner or Cole. A day or two later I was certain that General Turner would be the storm center of a Senate investigation if he were not fired. President Nixon was at the Western White House at San Clemente, so I called directly to the Justice Department.

Before placing the call I knew the revelation that the Nixon administration's chief United States marshal was dishonest was going to be a blow to the pride of Mitchell and Kleindienst. Mitchell had been cool to my appointment as presidential ombudsman, but my personal relationship with Dick Kleindienst, going back over a long period of years, had always been excellent. I had met him briefly in 1964, during Senator Barry Goldwater's campaign for the presidency. Although he was a strongly partisan figure, he had struck me as being genuinely concerned over the ethical standards of Lyndon B. Johnson as demonstrated by the Billie Sol Estes and Bobby Baker cases. And in the 1968 campaign Kleindienst had approached me concerning Hubert Humphrey's role in certain illegal decisions at the Small Business Administration and in the administration of a foreign aid loan to a firm in India. I had written extensively about those scandals and had tried unsuccessfully to question Vice President Humphrey about them in the 1968 campaign. Kleindienst seemed to have a legitimate political interest in researching these matters as campaign issues for Richard Nixon's campaign. I told him what I had written, identified the General Accounting Office investigations, and told him of the unanswered questions raised in the *Congressional Record* by Representative H. R. Gross of Iowa. Although Nixon never effectively explored the issues in the campaign, I had been impressed with Kleindienst's intelligent inquiry and apparent interest in questions of integrity and non-partisan fairness in government decisions. He seemed properly outraged that friends and political associates of Humphrey could drain millions of dollars from the U.S. Treasury on the basis of political favoritism in obtaining government loans.

When Kleindienst became the Number Two man at the Justice Department, his duties included the screening of candidates for appointments as federal judges, United States attorneys, and United States marshals. In the first months of 1969, as a newspaperman, I had several conversations with Kleindienst in connection with various of these appointments. Always he stressed the importance of high-caliber people for the bench and for prosecution positions to keep the government clean and avoid scandals. Kleindienst's comments included disparaging ones about some of the political appointments made by the Kennedy and Johnson administrations, and he reminded me with pride that Will Wilson, a Texas Democrat, was assistant attorney general in charge of the Criminal Division and that Henry Peterson, another Democrat and a career government lawyer, was Wilson's chief deputy. Peterson, an old friend of mine, had been head of the Organized Crime Division under Kennedy and Johnson. I regarded him as a fine public official and I considered it a mark of non-partisan good judgment that he had been retained by the Nixon administration.

Kleindienst was my guest at the annual Gridiron Dinner in March 1969; he came to my home in a black government limousine shortly after five-thirty on the night of the dinner. Dapper in his white tie and tails, enthusiastic about his job, and pleased with the invitation, the former Phoenix lawyer bubbled about a landmark appointment the Nixon administration was going to make. "We are going to take politics out of the U.S. marshal's office," he said proudly. "We are going to name a former Army general—a real career law enforcement man—as our chief United States marshal." A decision had been made to name retired Major General Carl Turner, former provost marshal for the Army, to the post. "He's been the top cop for the Army for years, a real career military policeman," Kleindienst said. He said he didn't even know what political party General Turner belonged to, and added that FBI Director J. Edgar Hoover was "high on Turner." Kleindienst couldn't resist contrasting this "non-political appointment" to those of the "political hacks" appointed by Kennedy and Johnson. He stressed that the Republicans planned to get politics out of what had traditionally been patronage jobs. He also had some comments about the effectiveness of court-authorized wiretapping as a weapon against organized crime, criticizing former Attorney General Ramsey Clark for his adamant refusal to use this effective legal tool to convict the Mafia bosses. My reply to this was that there were indications that Bobby Baker and Lyndon Johnson had had some highly questionable associations with the Las Vegas gambling crowd and that wiretaps could have proved embarrassing.

Although political background was stressed in selecting appointees in the Kennedy and Johnson administrations, I knew of notable exceptions, including Herbert J. Miller, a self-styled Taft Republican named by Bobby Kennedy to be assistant attorney general in charge of the Criminal Division, and John Doar, a registered Republican from Virginia, who headed the Civil Rights Division. James McShane, a former New York City detective and Senate investigator appointed chief United States marshal by the Kennedy administration, was also high on my list. Jim was a Democrat and a Kennedy loyalist, but he was a strong professional law enforcement man with deep and tested integrity. I considered him one of the straightest, most knowledgeable law enforcement officials I had ever observed closely.

With no effort to correct Kleindienst's political oversimplification of the past, I applauded the decision to appoint General Turner as an effort to be nonpartisan in law enforcement. So when I made my first calls to the Justice Department to follow through on Duffy's charges, I knew it was a delicate matter because of Kleindienst's close personal relationship with Turner. I had tried to reach Attorney General Mitchell about the Turner problem but was relieved to find he was not there, making Kleindienst my top man to contact at Justice. (I felt I had a good personal relationship with Kleindienst, but I was unsure about Mitchell. There was nothing frank and forthright about him. Although he presented a quiet impression of pipe-smoking geniality, there was a cold and calculating manner under the mask.)

I expected that Dick Kleindienst would be upset to learn that instead of a dazzling example of integrity General Turner was a rotten apple. I tried to soften the information in our first conversation by stating the evidence more vaguely than I knew it to be, to allow him to adjust slowly to a new opinion of his man. I did not wish to put him on the defensive. He said that the Army had already alerted him to the possibility that Turner might present some problem in connection with questions raised by the Senate committee regarding some of Turner's decisions as provost marshal. It did not seem to be a serious matter, Kleindienst commented, and he didn't believe the Army was too concerned. He himself was satisfied with Turner's explanations. I did not challenge him, wishing only to alert him to the fact that there might be more. I said that my information might be wrong, but that, as presented to me by a Senate investigator, I considered it serious, particularly in the light of the administration's stated pledges to operate honestly and efficiently. I offered to double-check my facts, but Kleindienst's answers to my specific questions indicated that he really hadn't examined the problem in any depth and was only relying on Turner's explanation of a far-understated Army report, affirming my lack of confidence in the Army investigating the Army.

Following another conversation with Duffy and further questioning of an Army source, I called Kleindienst again. This time I could state certain minimum conclusions about General Turner's misconduct and suggest that the deputy attorney general make his own recheck with the Army and raise specific points with General Turner. I urged him to resolve it quickly because the McClellan committee investigation would go into open hearings within two weeks. "Do you think McClellan will call General Turner?" Kleindienst asked.

"I am certain that McClellan will call General Turner as a witness," I replied. "I can't tell you what to do, but I know what I would do if I were making the decision. I just wanted to make certain that you know all the facts involved when you decide whether General Turner should be identified as chief United States marshal when he testifies or whether he will be former

chief United States marshal." I offered to send a written memorandum outlining the case, but Kleindienst said this would not be necessary. There was no
question about his concern as he assured me he would take care of the matter.

A day or so later, he called to tell me that General Turner had "resigned"
and that there would be a follow-through investigation by the Justice Department. He did not thank me for my assistance to the Justice Department and
the administration in warning them and thus helping them avoid a serious embarrassment. In fact, Kleindienst's air of resentment carried the implication
that I had created the Turner problem. He was probably reflecting the annoyance I found in Attorney General Mitchell because I had pressed them to
come to grips with the problem of Turner's misdeeds.

Both Mitchell and Kleindienst regarded it as a reflection on their judgment that they had selected him in the first place. Too many public figures
make the error of insisting that the record show them to be completely accurate in their judgments of men and in forecasting events. It is unrealistic to
expect anyone to be right all the time in matters contingent upon so many un-
controllable conditions. The most public officials should expect is to arrive at
reasonably consistent decisions on the basis of the best facts available, set up
machinery for catching errors early, and quickly admit and correct the inevitable mistakes.

While Mitchell and Kleindienst did not fully appreciate my efforts on the
Turner case, President Nixon was pleased and commented: "We can't avoid
errors, but we can catch them at the earliest point and correct them. That's
what you're here for." I was happy, and used the Turner incident to demonstrate to various academic, government, political, and press groups that "good
government can be good politics" and that it can avoid the long-range, self-
defeating entanglements of trying to conceal evidence of mismanagement and
corruption.

Generals Turner and Cole later were convicted of fraud, sentenced to federal prison terms, and stripped of their Distinguished Service medals. Reports
of the McClellan committee charged them with responsibility for obstructing
justice and a wide range of military corruption that took place under their
commands. It blamed the Army's laxity in investigating its general officers and
the secrecy that barred Congress from access to information files for maintain-
ing a climate in which such corruption could flourish.

The same major problems were to show up in connection with the My Lai
massacres in Vietnam, which even more vividly dramatized the insidious evil
of a military cover-up.

*Chapter Five*

# THE HOFFA-NIXON PROBLEM

WALTER SHERIDAN telephoned with a startling message just a few weeks after I joined the White House staff. "It's all set for the Nixon administration to spring Jimmy Hoffa," Sheridan said. His information from "Teamsters sources and some people at Justice" indicated that former Teamsters Union president James R. Hoffa was to be freed within a few weeks from the federal prison at Lewisburg as part of "a Chotiner deal" made during the 1968 presidential election campaign. "I'm told Murray Chotiner is handling it with the Las Vegas mob," Sheridan said. "John Mitchell and John Ehrlichman have something to do with it, and I'm told it has been cleared with Nixon."

I explained that I was sure Nixon had had no such pre-election deal because he had told me so in a conversation on the campaign plane a few days before the election. I had asked direct questions about any deals with Hoffa. In relaying Nixon's assurances to Sheridan, I added for additional emphasis that Mr. Nixon had personally told me he agreed with my assessment of Hoffa as a menace to the labor movement and politics. Although Nixon was suspicious of the Kennedys' motivations in pursuing Hoffa, he said he was moved by the arguments of his friend Senator John L. McClellan, the Arkansas Democrat who had chaired the Teamsters investigations.

Sheridan persisted in treating the reports of clemency for Hoffa as a "Nixon-Chotiner deal," but I tried to reject the notion of duplicity by Nixon. I even told Sheridan I was leaving my mind open to the possibility that Attorney General Mitchell and White House Counsel Ehrlichman had naïvely bought the Teamsters lawyers' claim that Bob Kennedy had misused the Justice Department's power to investigate and prosecute in order to frame Jimmy Hoffa. I reminded Sheridan that the International Brotherhood of Teamsters had many able, articulate, and frequently deceptive lawyers who had put together what might appear to the casual observer a convincing case that Bob Kennedy had used false testimony to send Hoffa to prison. Sheridan knew that I was convinced the prosecutions of Hoffa were sound and fair, for we both knew intimately the decade of court proceedings involving Jimmy Hoffa and his racketeering associates. He also knew I had differed with Bob and Jack Kennedy on many policies during the short and tragic Kennedy administration but that I admired the persistence of their pursuit of Hoffa and other labor racketeers. The Kennedy brothers, with a big bipartisan assist from Senator McClellan and from Senator Irving Ives of New York, had been a major force in passage of the Landrum-Griffin labor reform act.

Sheridan and I had been soul mates with Bob Kennedy on the investigations and prosecutions of labor racketeering that eventually led to Hoffa's conviction for attempts to tamper with a federal jury in Chattanooga, Tennessee, and for fraud in connection with Teamsters union pension funds in Chicago. I had attended both trials, had followed Hoffa's countless unsuccessful appeals to the United States Supreme Court, and had written a book (*Tentacles of Power*, 1965) on the menace of Hoffa's ties with the Mafia and politics. Although Sheridan and I had widely differing views on the potential of Richard Nixon as a president, he respected my opinions and my hopes that I could keep the Nixon administration free from the illegal or unethical actions which had plagued all other administrations, including Kennedy's. Likewise, I respected his judgment as well as his right to have a skeptical opinion of the motivations of President Nixon. For even though Sheridan had been a loyal political supporter of the Kennedys throughout some of their scandals, he acknowledged later that I had been right in my criticism of the handling of the TFX contract and the Billie Sol Estes case.

Several telephone and face-to-face conversations with Justice Department and White House sources over a period of weeks verified Sheridan's claim that there was indeed some movement to win Hoffa's release through a pardon or a presidential grant of executive clemency. In spite of this I told Sheridan that I still did not believe President Nixon was involved in any Hoffa deal, but that I would make every effort to convince the president that the prosecution of Hoffa had not been unjustified persecution, and that only by determined persistence could the wily Hoffa and his associates have been convicted.

Sheridan reminded me that William Loeb, publisher of the largest daily newspaper in New Hampshire, was one of those attempting to obtain freedom for Hoffa. Loeb's newspaper, the *New Hampshire Union-Leader,* had received a loan of more than $2 million from the Teamsters Union pension fund, and the bulk of that loan was still outstanding. Loeb's support for Richard Nixon in the early New Hampshire primary in 1968 had been an important factor in his top-heavy 79 percent of the Republican vote. An outspoken supporter of Hoffa and critic of the Kennedys, Loeb was a welcome guest at the Nixon White House.

My first inquiries established that Loeb had been lobbying for Hoffa's release at the White House and at the Justice Department. Assistant Attorney General Will Wilson, a Texas Democrat, told me Loeb had contacted him on the Hoffa matter and had talked to Deputy Attorney General Kleindienst. Wilson said he had been pleasant to Loeb as a long-time Nixon supporter but had made no commitment and was not moved to sympathy for Hoffa. Attorney General Mitchell had also apparently had some discussions with Loeb on this matter, but Wilson did not have details.

Wilson, head of the Criminal Division of the Justice Department, had been attorney general in Texas in the early 1960s and had played a major role in forcing the exposure of the Billie Sol Estes scandals during the Kennedy administration. Although he was a Democrat, his warnings on the Estes matter were disregarded, and a bitterness developed that resulted in his supporting

Nixon for president in 1968. I had dealt sympathetically with Wilson in news stories in the *Des Moines Register* and in my 1965 book *Despoilers of Democracy,* in the chapter detailing Estes' crimes, and had a generally good rapport with him. Aware of my experience in the investigations and prosecution of Hoffa, he agreed that it would be "damned foolishness" for the Nixon administration to spring Hoffa. Wilson told me he would make his views on Hoffa known if consulted but said he knew little about "what was going on upstairs" with Mitchell and Kleindienst. Since they were obviously irritated by what they considered my "meddling" to force the firing of Chief Marshal Turner, I decided to avoid a direct approach to either of them on the Hoffa matter. Moreover, it was obvious that Mitchell regarded me with suspicion because President Nixon had not consulted him before appointing me as White House ombudsman. To Mitchell, the appointment of a White House lawyer to police the government for the president was a reflection on his own abilities as attorney general and as the highest-ranking law official in the administration. I discovered later that Mitchell had assumed my installation in the White House was a Haldeman-Ehrlichman maneuver to second-guess him and cut into the final authority he could have exercised on law enforcement matters. On the surface, Mitchell, Haldeman, and Ehrlichman were congenial to one another, but the veneer covered a bitter rivalry for political influence and control of the president.

I chose to direct my inquiry to Ehrlichman, then counsel to the president and my line of communication with Mr. Nixon. Although my original agreement with the president was for direct reporting, Haldeman and Ehrlichman had already usurped complete control over my contacts with the president. This vigilant pair, dominating access to Mr. Nixon, made it impossible for me to remind him of our conversation on Hoffa and to warn him of the possibility of justifiably severe criticism if Hoffa was released from prison. A low-key inquiry to Ehrlichman was the only way to determine what was going on, so I relayed to him my concern over reports of a plan to release Hoffa, stressing my belief that such a move would not be to the political advantage of the Nixon administration.

Ehrlichman avoided putting a reply in writing but sent his young assistant, Todd Hullins, to tell me: "Mr. Ehrlichman says you should not concern yourself with the Hoffa matter. He is handling it himself with John Mitchell." This confirmed Sheridan's report that something was working for Hoffa and that it involved Mitchell and Ehrlichman. Now I was genuinely worried that they would get the administration into avoidable troubles by moving quickly to spring Hoffa as part of a highly questionable political deal or because they were too damned stupid to understand what a treacherous character he could be. I was permitted only one short telephone conversation with John Ehrlichman to try to summarize my concern over the Hoffa matter. He did not allow me to go into detail because he was "in a hurry," as usual, but said pointedly: "The president does not want you in this. It is highly sensitive. John Mitchell and I have it under control."

Up to this point my relations with Ehrlichman had been exceedingly cordial. I had not known him well, but I had seen him several times in the 1968 campaign, had visited with him on a few occasions, and had had a couple of long conferences with him on Defense Department matters while I was a Washington correspondent for the *Des Moines Register* in early 1969, before I joined the White House staff. In almost any other organization except the White House there is some possibility of catching the top man under conditions where the chain of command can be circumvented, but because of the tight security required by a president of the United States that possibility is absent. In September 1969 I was still new to the White House and still confident that right could prevail in this regime if it were diligently pursued and the facts presented persuasively enough to demonstrate that questionable or dishonest decisions would lead only to political disaster.

First, it was necessary to persuade Ehrlichman that Jimmy Hoffa had been prosecuted and convicted in a fair manner and that he did in fact have a long record of links with the underworld and with political corruption. I sent him *Tentacles of Power,* documenting Hoffa's crimes and his links with Johnny Dioguardi, Tony (Ducks) Corallo, and Joey Glimco. Second, it was necessary to demonstrate that both Ehrlichman and the president could be badly burned by careless involvement with Loeb, Hoffa, or any of the Teamsters lawyers who were constantly buzzing around with hints of big campaign contributions.

I recalled that Cartha D. (Deke) DeLoach, veteran assistant FBI director, had been greatly embarrassed as a result of a meeting on the Hoffa matter with William Loeb in 1966. DeLoach, one of J. Edgar Hoover's long-time press assistants, had discussed with Loeb the possibility that Attorney General Robert Kennedy had used an illegal wiretap on the Hoffa case. Hoffa and his lawyers had been searching for evidence of an illegal wiretap for years because it would mean almost automatic reversal of Jimmy's convictions if it could be linked to any of the evidence against him. Loeb swore in an affidavit that DeLoach had told him that three of Bobby Kennedy's associates—Sheridan, Carmine Bellino, and Eddie Jones—had placed an illegal tap on Hoffa. Hoffa used that affidavit in seeking to upset his criminal convictions, and an embarrassed DeLoach had to admit to conversations with Loeb on the possibility of such a wiretap. However, DeLoach denied having stated that he knew Hoffa's wire had been tapped or having confirmed to Loeb in any manner that Sheridan, Bellino, or Jones had done any wiretapping. It seemed to me that the Loeb-DeLoach incident would illustrate to Ehrlichman that if one of the most skillful and able operators in Washington (DeLoach) had been singed in dealing with Loeb, he, as a novice, could also be burned.

I wrote a memorandum covering the Loeb-DeLoach affair which I hand delivered to Ehrlichman and briefly explained. I then related one of my experiences with Hoffa in 1955 which pretty well dramatized his cynical attitude that every man has his price. Jimmy had interrupted a breakfast conversation at the Mayflower Hotel in Washington to make a direct and crass effort to bribe me. I repeated the conversation to Ehrlichman: "Now, look here,

Clark," Hoffa had said. "They don't pay newspaper reporters enough for you to be giving me the bad time that you've been giving me. Everyone has his price. What's yours?"

I intended the story as an illustration to Ehrlichman of the total cynicism of Hoffa and the danger of dealing with him, but his response showed that he had missed the point. He smugly retorted: "We know your price—a White House title and $33,500 a year." I held my tongue with difficulty. Whether his remark stemmed from ignorance or callousness, I had to work with him, so I let it pass by declaring that the press critics of the Nixon administration "would want nothing better than to catch Nixon granting favors to Jimmy Hoffa."

In the next few weeks I became so deeply involved in the Haynsworth matter (see Chapter 6) that I made no further inquiry on the Hoffa matter; I was prepared for a decision to release him. It was a pleasant surprise when I received a call from the Justice Department informing me Mitchell and Ehrlichman had dropped their efforts to obtain executive clemency for Hoffa before Christmas. Privately, I rejoiced: at least temporarily, and perhaps permanently, the possibility of a Hoffa pardon scandal had been disposed of. I knew Hoffa never gave up, but it was pleasant to believe that a careful compilation of facts and a persistent effort for a proper goal made it possible to win a few important victories. I hoped the president had recognized that the bitter medicine of reneging on a political deal was better than being exposed as selling out for money or political support.

Basking in my little victory, I wondered what would happen if I ever needed to protect Mr. Nixon from misconduct conceived by those three advisers. If Mitchell were implicated, the other two would probably take some devious satisfaction in getting the facts to the president. But could I penetrate "the Berlin Wall" if either or both of them was the culprit or interested in a political cover-up?

## Chapter Six

# THE ORDEAL OF CLEMENT HAYNSWORTH

I WAS SUBMERGED in the defense of the record of United States Circuit Judge Clement F. Haynsworth, Jr., for six weeks in October and November 1969. His ordeal ended on November 21, 1969, when the Senate refused to confirm his nomination to the United States Supreme Court by a vote of 55 to 45, but I carried scars for many months. Many of my friends considered my active defense of Judge Haynsworth an error, and there were moments when I regretted being so deeply involved in the heated judicial confirmation fight. But, looking back on that losing battle, I have only a few regrets, involving errors of judgment that might have made some small difference in the defense of a basically decent man.

When emotions cooled, it was agreed that Judge Haynsworth had none of the conflicts of interest as charged and was indeed a fine scholar who would have been a credit to the United States Supreme Court. But during September, October, and November the AFL-CIO lobbyists were doing a hatchet job on him, with a willing assist from many of the nation's newspapers and magazines. However, reporters and editors were not to blame for the Nixon administration's blundering that plunged the Haynsworth nomination into trouble in the first place. When the first charges of conflicts of interest were raised in August, they could and should have been answered fully and clearly to demonstrate the factual inaccuracies and distorted legal thinking behind charges stimulated by AFL-CIO lobbyists and their allies in the press. But the Nixon administration chose to remain aloof from the allegations, and Attorney General John N. Mitchell instructed Haynsworth not to discuss them.

White House Press Secretary Ronald Ziegler, under the direction of President Nixon and White House Chief of Staff Haldeman, refused to respond to the specific assertions leveled against Haynsworth and only stated there was "no substance" to the charges and that President Nixon continued "to have faith" in Judge Haynsworth. Attorney General Mitchell, still basking in the success of his silent maneuvers resulting in the resignation of Associate Supreme Court Justice Abe Fortas, wrongly assumed that a cloistered approach would always be effective. He did not recognize that refusal to discuss the details of serious charges against a sitting Supreme Court justice could be the proper stance to force his resignation, but that refusing to explain serious charges involving your own nominee for the Supreme Court would raise suspicions that the claims were true and could not be answered.

The disappointing defeat of the Haynsworth nomination taught me much about the Nixon administration, about politics in general, and about the press that I could not have learned in one thousand victories. It was exhilarating to be a major spokesman for the president on a highly controversial, emotional political issue, but in a sudden panic I realized that some members of the Nixon team were "leaking" false information about my role to the press to set me up as the fall guy.

Some people in the administration who were supposed to be convincing their contacts in the press that no conflict of interest existed were, in fact, completely uninformed on the merits of the case and were faltering in the political crossfire. I learned of the abysmal shallowness of White House Press Secretary Ziegler, who did not understand the charges against Haynsworth and was incapable of understanding the facts, the law, or the ethical problems. Haldeman or Ehrlichman would tell him what to say and he would repeat it. Usually, he would say only that President Nixon had discussed the issue in his last press conference and that he, Ziegler, would not expand upon it. On most issues this sufficed, but when a Nixon administration nominee for associate justice of the Supreme Court was being charged with specific improprieties, a "no comment" from the White House press office was equivalent to Frank Costello pleading the Fifth before the Kefauver crime committee.

My first hint that Judge Haynsworth would be nominated for the Supreme Court vacancy created by Abe Fortas' resignation came in early July in a visit with Senator James O. Eastland, the Mississippi Democrat who was chairman of the Senate Judiciary Committee. Clement Haynsworth was simply a circuit court judge from South Carolina who might be nominated to the Supreme Court to please the South. I had no knowledge of his background or record, and no opinion on his fitness. The nomination was announced in mid-August, while I was on vacation, and within a few days news stories were mentioning a possible conflict of interest by Haynsworth in casting the deciding vote in a 3-to-2 decision in favor of Deering Milliken, a textile firm which was in a dispute with the Textile Workers' Union of America.

The Fourth Circuit Court of Appeals, on which Haynsworth was serving, had infuriated the powerful AFL-CIO with its reversal of a National Labor Relations Board finding that Deering Milliken had been guilty of an unfair labor practice in closing a plant to avoid bargaining with the union. The union had charged that Haynsworth was first vice president of and owned considerable stock in Vend-a-Matic, which had contracts to supply vending services to Deering Milliken. The Textile Workers' Union contended that the textile firm had increased its business with Vend-a-Matic in the period immediately following the Fourth Circuit Court decision for Deering Milliken.

I read the news stories casually, but with the view that the conflicts of interest charge was certainly something that deserved careful investigation. Judge Haynsworth was quoted as saying that he had resigned his corporate position with Carolina Vend-a-Matic when the case was in litigation and that Deering Milliken, subsequent to the Fourth Circuit opinion, had awarded a contract, bid on by Vend-a-Matic, to a competitor. But when Haynsworth was asked whether he had owned shares in Carolina Vend-a-Matic at the time of the decision, he declined to answer, on the advice of the Justice Department. The Justice Department also declined comment, and White House Press Secretary Ziegler said only that there was "no substance" to the charges.

It was not my problem. However, when I reported for duty at the White House on August 18, I received a call from Harry Dent. "The Haynsworth nomination is coming in for some criticism, and I wonder if you could get in touch with Senator John J. Williams [R., Del.] and Senator Jack Miller [R., Iowa] and have them say something in support of Haynsworth," Dent said. I told him I didn't know what to think of the nomination myself yet, but that I would ask Senators Williams and Miller whether they had any objection to making a statement for Haynsworth. Since I had not made any personal inquiry on the merits of the charges against Judge Haynsworth, I solicited questions from Senators Williams and Miller on the ethics and qualifications of Judge Haynsworth.

I had covered Senator Miller closely from the time he was elected to the Senate in 1960. Senator Williams I had known since 1950, when I was assigned to the Washington bureau by the *Des Moines Register,* and it had been a particularly warm and mutually beneficial relationship, since we were both deeply interested in investigations of corruption and mismanagement in government and had cooperated on more than a dozen major investigative projects. I knew both Miller and Williams would be interested in details of the allegations against Haynsworth, and I was sure they would have been apprised of the administration's side of the controversy by the Justice Department or the White House liaison people. It surprised me to find that neither had been briefed, and of course both had serious questions they wanted answered before they would consider a statement of support for Haynsworth. I believed their questions were valid, and I offered to get answers for them and for myself.

Neither Mitchell nor Deputy Attorney General Richard Kleindienst was available, but Jack Landau, Mitchell's press officer, returned my call. I told him I wanted to get some information on the Haynsworth nomination and that I had wanted to talk to the attorney general personally. Landau said that the Justice Department wasn't saying anything about the Haynsworth matter except what had been said, and that Mitchell had said all inquiries were being handled through the White House Press Office. I explained that I was calling as deputy counsel to the president, not as a newspaperman, and that I needed answers for some senators who might be important to the administration if the controversy became more heated.

"The attorney general and Ehrlichman have this under control and will do any explaining that needs to be done," Landau said.

"Tell the attorney general that Harry Dent has asked me to request support for Haynsworth from two of my friends in the Senate and that I promised them I would get them answers," I snapped. "If I don't, I am not going to ask them to do anything, because I am not sure this nomination can be supported," I declared in exasperation.

"That's the way the attorney general wants it," Landau said. I had no way to contact Mitchell to find out whether that was true.

I immediately called Harry Dent back, related the experience at Justice, and told him I would not ask any senator to support the nomination until I had satisfied myself that Haynsworth was an ethical person. Dent moaned that "the liberals are beating Haynsworth's brains out and we can't even get the Justice Department to answer questions for Republican senators."

I replied: "Ehrlichman and Mitchell are the keys to getting answers. I'm not turning another wheel on it until I get a reasonable response."

I called Senators Williams and Miller, told them to forget that I had even suggested that they make a statement in support of Haynsworth, but recommended that they try directly through Justice Department channels. Later I learned that the Justice Department policy under Attorney General Mitchell was to answer only Chairman James Eastland, as the representative of the majority, and Senator Roman Hruska, the Nebraska conservative, as the representative of the Senate Republicans. It was hardly a system to court any middle-of-the-road or liberal support for a controversial nominee.

The Haynsworth nomination was not my responsibility and I concentrated my efforts in other directions, finding plenty to concern myself with. There were irregularities in the State Department involving allegations of perjury, falsification of documents, and favoritism; a problem involving frauds and favoritism in the loan programs of the Economic Development administration (EDA), in the Department of Commerce; and irregularities and favoritism in connection with a federally financed $15,000,000 geriatric center in Texas. So for a month I paid scant attention to the foundering Haynsworth nomination. It was in worse trouble with each passing week, for the Justice Department had muzzled Judge Haynsworth except for his appearance before the Senate Judiciary Committee, and the unyielding silence at the White House contributed nothing to Judge Haynsworth's defense. While reading the newspapers I was glad it was John Ehrlichman's or John Mitchell's baby.

Reporters sympathetic to the Nixon administration called to say I should warn the president the nomination was in serious trouble and that even such a staunch administration supporter as Senator Robert Dole (R., Kans.) was considering voting against confirmation because no explanations were forthcoming from the Justice Department. I knew that Senator Robert Griffin (R., Michigan) was irritated because he couldn't talk to Mitchell and because the "no comment" position of the White House left him without a defense against the AFL-CIO broadsides. Without opposition, the AFL-CIO and civil rights groups joined in an all-out effort to give the Nixon administration its first major defeat.

I was pulled into the Haynsworth case briefly on September 19, when Senator James Eastland called: "Could you come up to my office right away?" he drawled. "It's about the Haynsworth nomination." He gave no explanation, but a call from the chairman of the Judiciary Committee on a pending nomination was top priority. I left the Executive Office Building for the New Senate Office Building, where the Haynsworth hearing was in progress across the hall from Eastland's second-floor office. I walked past a line of reporters in the hall who wanted to know "What's up?" Eastland's secretary motioned me through the door into the large corner office I had visited so many times as a newspaperman.

"This Haynsworth nomination is in deep trouble," Eastland began. "A new problem has come up, and I'd like to have you listen to the facts and give me your best judgment as to its seriousness." Eastland offered the opinion that "the folks they have working on this at the Justice Department don't know what they're doing. There is no real reason for the Haynsworth nomination to be in trouble, but they aren't explaining things and it is being bungled at every stage."

I said that I had not delved enough into it to have made any judgments but that "Mitchell and Ehrlichman have been calling the shots."

"Well, I have been following it and I can say they don't know what they are doing," Eastland said. His assessment was that he could hold the conservative Democrats, but only if the Republicans didn't desert the ship.

The new problem was another conflict-of-interest allegation involving "the Brunswick case"; Eastland offered to have Assistant Attorney General William Rehnquist brief me on it. When Rehnquist and Judge Haynsworth entered the room, I recall having a spontaneous feeling of pity for this sad little man who was caught in the political-judicial badminton game. He shook my hand warmly, with the air of a drowning man reaching for a life raft. I had talked with Rehnquist on the telephone several times and had met him on at least one prior occasion, when he was a young lawyer fresh from Phoenix, Arizona. He now headed the Office of Legal Counsel in the Justice Department.

Obviously, Rehnquist was doing most of Mitchell's legal work and leg work on the Haynsworth nomination but was frustrated by the restrictions placed on him by the White House and by Mitchell and Kleindienst in the Justice Department. I felt sorry for Bill because he was bewildered by the failure of the press to examine the facts in the public record and distressed at the lack of perspective in comments by Senator Birch Bayh, a liberal Democrat from Indiana. Senator Bayh had listed *Brunswick Corporation* v. *Long* as one of five cases in which Judge Haynsworth held a financial interest "substantial enough" to require disqualification under the law. Bayh contended that Judge Haynsworth's failure to disqualify himself "constitutes impropriety" under the canons of judicial ethics. Most of Bayh's charges were ludicrous and clearly political obfuscation, but as I listened to Rehnquist's recital of the facts of the Brunswick case I could see it was troublesome. I was to be the devil's advocate raising all possible ethical questions.

Judge Haynsworth's stockbroker had purchased one thousand shares of Brunswick Corporation stock in December 1967. Judge Haynsworth served on an appeal court panel that dealt with a case involving Brunswick in November 1967, with a ruling made public on February 2, 1968.* Two questions appeared likely to be raised:

1. Was it a conflict of interest for Judge Haynsworth to take part in the Brunswick decision, which was announced on February 2, 1968, when he held stock in the company? The facts, as related by Senator Eastland and Judge Haynsworth, were these: Judge Haynsworth had no stock interest in the Brunswick Corporation on November 10, 1967, the date the panel made the decision affirming the decision of the lower court which favored Brunswick. This was a unanimous decision, and Judge Haynsworth did not write the opin-

---

* The Brunswick Corporation had supplied equipment to a bowling alley in South Carolina under a conditional sales contract. When the bowling alley went out of business, a dispute arose as to whether Brunswick's claim to the equipment had precedence over the claim of owner of the building, who said that the rent was overdue. The court held that Brunswick's contract had precedence. The United States Supreme Court denied certiorari (review) on June 3, 1968.

ion; it was assigned to Judge Winter. Under these circumstances, there would be no legal conflict of interest because he held no stock at the time the decision was made. Bill Rehnquist of Justice concurred in this belief.

2. Another question was raised by the purchase of one thousand shares of Brunswick stock at approximately $16 per share on December 26, 1967. This was more than six weeks after the decision, but prior to Judge Winter's distribution of the opinion and publication of it on February 2, 1968. The question could be raised as to whether Judge Haynsworth, in purchasing Brunswick stock, relied in some manner upon inside information about the decision prior to the time it was made public.

I was informed by the Justice Department and Judge Haynsworth that the suit itself involved no more than $40,000 to $50,000 and that the outcome of the case would be insignificant in its impact on the assets of the corporation, which they estimated to be in the neighborhood of $1 billion. Brunswick had 18,479,969 shares of outstanding stock, and the value of the entire thousand shares owned by Haynsworth would have been affected less than $5.00 by the decision. If there had been a substantial fluctuation in this stock at the time the decision was rendered, it might present a potential problem, but Judge Haynsworth and Justice Department officials stated that there had been no significant fluctuation in the stock in the crucial period between November 10, 1967, and the period immediately after the February 2, 1968, announcement of the decision.

Also important in analyzing this aspect of the case is the fact that Judge Haynsworth purchased the stock through his regular broker, who was authorized to make purchases for him. It was not clear in Judge Haynsworth's mind whether this specific purchase was made by the broker on his own volition and later approved, or whether Judge Haynsworth approved prior to the time of purchase. This point would seem to be immaterial because of other circumstances. Judge Haynsworth's broker made purchases of the stock for forty-seven other people during the time in question, and it is logical to believe that he rather than Judge Haynsworth would have initiated the purchase of Brunswick stock. It was ludicrous to think that Judge Haynsworth's decision might have been influenced in any manner by the stock he did not acquire until more than a month after he and his fellow judges unanimously agreed on a disposition of the case on all issues.

I told the judge and Rehnquist that if they had been accurate about the dates of the opinion, the stock purchase, and the amounts, I did not believe there was any impropriety. I said I thought the only possible mistake Judge Haynsworth had made was in permitting his broker to go ahead with any purchase, regardless of how inconsequential. The more the public knew about the Brunswick case the more they would understand that there was no possible way that Judge Haynsworth could have enriched himself unjustly through the stock purchase. I advised that the Justice Department and some of Haynsworth's supporters in the Senate engage in a lengthy discussion of the Brunswick case to counter the distortions being used by Senator Bayh and other opponents of the nomination. I also suggested that the Justice Department prepare clear, accurate fact sheets on all of the controversial cases and distribute them widely rather than continue the lofty silence that had put the nomination in jeopardy. "If you have good explanations on these controversial points, make them public," I advised.

I returned to the office and a short time later called my friend Senator Williams. Following an explanation of the facts, Senator Williams said he saw no real problem in the Brunswick case but that the accumulation of more than a dozen charges of conflicts of interest confused the public as well as many of the senators who did not do their homework and were unduly moved by public opinion. I told him of my talk with Eastland, Haynsworth, and Rehnquist and of my advice to "get the facts out in the open, if you've got a good case." I assured him that Judge Haynsworth felt confident that all of the various charges could be answered, but that he had been muzzled by Mitchell and that no one was taking the initiative to explain.

Senator Williams commented that President Nixon was in danger of losing many Republicans, including Assistant Minority Leader Griffin, who had been an outspoken leader of the critics of Justice Abe Fortas in the period just prior to his forced resignation. The Delaware Republican, who was symbolic of aggressive, non-partisan integrity in the Congress, complained that he and others had trouble getting factual explanations from the Justice Department or even an opportunity to talk with John Mitchell. On the rare occasions when it was possible to speak to Mitchell, Senator Williams said, he was disturbed at the lack of emphasis on issues of integrity, the stress placed on party loyalty, and hints that lack of loyalty would not be forgotten. Senator Williams was as much concerned by the stories he had heard from other Republican Senators about White House tactics as he was about anything he had heard regarding Judge Haynsworth. I was glad the Haynsworth nomination was not my responsibility, even though I felt sorry for the jurist President Nixon had thrown into a major political brawl to make Brownie points in the South.

The administration's handling of the Haynsworth case up to that point demonstrated to me that Nixon's White House team captains were rank amateurs in the operation of government. Through arrogance, superficiality, ignorance, and ethical insensitivity they could destroy the very people they hoped to use to their political advantage. These irresponsible, superficially bright children were playing with the awesome power of the presidency, unmindful of the inherent danger to themselves and the nation in the misuse of that power. Their obsession with secrecy, and fear of sharing that power, presented additional difficulties for those who sought to persuade them that corrective action was needed.

*Chapter Seven*

# THE HAZARDS OF HELPING HAYNSWORTH

LATE IN THE AFTERNOON OF October 2, 1969, John Ehrlichman called from Air Force One to say President Nixon was worried about Senator Birch Bayh's opposition to the Haynsworth nomination. The president wanted me to try to ascertain the substance of the charges. President Nixon was concerned about a real estate transaction in South Carolina allegedly linking Judge Haynsworth and Bobby Baker, Ehrlichman said. Senator John J. Williams had raised the question in a conference with the president. It was important to keep Williams favorably inclined toward Haynsworth because of his impact on those still undecided. When I told Ehrlichman that I had not had very good luck in getting information from the Justice Department on the Haynsworth matter, he suggested that I let Attorney General Mitchell know that Ehrlichman and the president had asked me to call.

In an hour Mitchell returned my call, commenting caustically that Senator Bayh's sixty thousand dollar campaign contribution from organized labor had undoubtedly prompted his opposition to Haynsworth. He then turned to the president's concern over the questions Senators Williams and Griffin had raised.

Mitchell said that although President Nixon had "been firm" behind Haynsworth at a leadership meeting, Senator Griffin had gone to Senator Eastland's office at 3:00 P.M. that afternoon suggesting that it might be wise to withdraw Haynsworth's name. Mitchell related that Senator Williams had been "totally noncommittal" in talking with him on Wednesday afternoon and during a conversation with President Nixon Thursday. Mitchell said that the president and he felt that Senator Williams had "a kind of hang-up" on some aspects of the case dealing with business enterprises involving Bobby Baker. The transactions were "all legal and ethical," the attorney general said, and he asked what to do about Senators Williams, Griffin, and several others whose support appeared wobbly.

I wanted to remind him that he and Ehrlichman had made a mess of it and that they should damned well figure it out for themselves. But I remembered that pleasant little man in Senator Eastland's office whose reputation was being brutally assaulted because they had not defended him. I pointedly remarked that I had avoided the Haynsworth case except for the Brunswick stock matter, which I had reviewed briefly with Senator Eastland, Bill Rehnquist, and Judge Haynsworth. I was convinced there was nothing illegal or unethical about that particular case and had been able to explain it to the satisfaction of Senator Williams and others.

It was decided that I would get into the Bobby Baker case to determine whether Judge Haynsworth's role in the transaction had been questionable in any respect. Mitchell became balky at the suggestion that I might conclude that there had been any impropriety and questioned whether I should be permitted to talk to Haynsworth. He suggested I relay questions through Bill Rehnquist, but I said that that would be totally unsatisfactory and that unless I had complete freedom to question Judge Haynsworth I would not touch the investigation, and he (Mitchell) could explain to the president why I was not doing anything on it.

At 9:50 A.M. on October 3, the attorney general called and again made a half-hearted effort to get me to accept an arrangement for relaying questions to Haynsworth. I again explained the necessity of having full access to all Justice Department information and the right to question Judge Haynsworth. If I found this to be a solid case, I told him, I would be putting my own name on the line, and I did not intend to do so unless I had a clear understanding that I had all information. "It is necessary to protect myself as well as the administration," I declared. Mitchell then asked if I could interrogate Judge Haynsworth at Rehnquist's Justice Department office so that there might be some coordination of our efforts. I said it was my intention to question him with Rehnquist present so that we could have a complete understanding on every aspect of each of the controversial cases.

For the moment, my job was to clear up the questions Senator Williams had on the reports of a Bobby Baker investment link with Judge Haynsworth.

It was easy to understand why Republicans were frightened by headlines stating: "Haynsworth Linked to Bobby Baker Land Deal." By Saturday, October 4, I was able to send a letter to Senator Williams totally demolishing the allegation of a questionable business relationship between Judge Haynsworth and Bobby Baker. I also sent copies to Senator Carl Curtis (R., Nebr.), Senator Griffin, and Senator Margaret Chase Smith (R., Maine), who had exhibited some concern over the Bobby Baker connection. "Judge Haynsworth says he has had three casual conversations with Robert G. Baker, and that the last of these was in September of 1958. He states they have never had a conversation involving any business transaction." To the letter I attached a detailed memorandum on the Greenville Memorial Gardens cemetery in South Carolina, in which both Judge Haynsworth and Baker were among the investors. Haynsworth said he was unaware of Baker's interest when he invested and, had he noted Baker's name, would not have been troubled by it in 1958 because that was five years before the Bobby Baker scandals broke in Washington. The letter to Senator Williams fully answered his questions and was released for Sunday morning newspapers. The exhaustive four-page memorandum and letter ended Judge Haynsworth's problem with the alleged Baker involvement, as it should have.

A few days later Ehrlichman called me, saying the president was pleased with the manner in which the Bobby Baker matter had been disposed of and that he wanted me to probe all aspects of the Haynsworth case to try to answer the questions still being asked by senators. I agreed but said that if I ran into any improprieties I would not, and could not, ask any senators to support the nomination and would probably suggest that it be withdrawn. He assured me that "that is the way the president would want it."

As a starting point, I took Senator Birch Bayh's eight-page bill of particulars on the alleged conflicts of interest of Judge Haynsworth. Then, with Judge Haynsworth and Bill Rehnquist, I went over them one by one, prying into all possibilities for hidden interests or improper motivation. Having satisfied myself that there was nothing illegal or unethical, I asked Senator Williams and Senator Griffin to tell me what troubled them most or to pick holes in my arguments. Neither one of them raised any argument about improprieties in any specific case, but both were gravely concerned with the overall impression that had been permitted to develop. Senator Griffin argued that the Justice Department's failure to meet each allegation as it arose had resulted in charge being piled upon charge, thus many conscientious reporters and editors in Michigan had become committed to opposing the nomination. Nothing in Haynsworth's record troubled Senator Williams as much as the tactics being used by the White House in its efforts to force a united Republican front on the appointment. The White House didn't do it directly but operated through influential businessmen and professional men in various states.

Senator Leonard Jordan (R., Idaho) was furious because he was asked to vote for Judge Haynsworth in the same breath as an official from the Department of Agriculture mentioned an agriculture project the senator had been seeking for months. The impression was left by the spokesman for the executive branch that if the senator voted for Haynsworth he would have his project approved but that otherwise he could not expect much help from the Nixon administration. Jordan, outspoken critic of Bobby Baker and Lyndon Johnson's "bribery and blackmail" adaptation of carrot and stick strategy, said, "I thought we got rid of LBJ and Bobby Baker and the things they stand for." Every White House flexed its muscles from time to time to clear a pet project, but Williams and Jordan had little patience for such tactics in any administration. Although the strategy irritated me, I found the falsifications and distortions used against Clement Haynsworth more despicable.

By October 2, 1969, the major problem in defending Haynsworth was the sheer number of charges that had not been explained and the intricacy of some of the cases.

To those attacking Judge Haynsworth, the best strategy was to keep the picture confused so that the public and press would believe there must be something to the charges. My job was to analyze each allegation in clear enough terminology so that even Ron Ziegler could understand the accusations and explain them to the reporters who were rightly infuriated with the non-answers and stonewalling at the White House and the Justice Department. In the process of explaining the cases to Ziegler, I was amazed to discover that he knew absolutely nothing about the merits of any of the charges and that his "no comments" covered a vast ignorance of facts and total insensitivity on ethical issues. He was Haldeman's puppet and not really interested in knowing whether the administration was right or wrong on an issue. It was easy and safe to be an unthinking conduit.

Starting with Birch Bayh's allegations and proceeding through Bill Rehnquist's legal explanations, I sorted the whole thing down to five categories. Then I put together a relatively short, pithy explanation of each case, adding in every instance a lengthy detailed explanation. It was a grueling chore going over the legal details with Rehnquist and asking innumerable questions of Haynsworth to be certain every detail of my clarification was accurate. When finished, I had pulled together a complete defense of Haynsworth in one place for the first time.

Communications Director Herb Klein understood the value of my analysis immediately and used it to try to turn the tide running strongly against the nomination. He duplicated the Haynsworth package and mailed it out to editors and Republican political leaders in all parts of the country. Herb said it was the first time he had been able to get fully satisfactory answers to questions raised by even staunch Republicans who wanted to believe the nomination was a good one but were beginning to have doubts. Against that background I assembled a twenty-five page detailed analysis of all of the charges leveled against the South Carolina judge in the seven weeks since his name had been announced as Mr. Nixon's choice to fill the Fortas vacancy on the United States Supreme Court.

In addition to my own critique, I leaned heavily on the fact that on October 10, 1969, the six other judges of the Fourth Circuit, with full knowledge of the charges by Senator Bayh and the AFL-CIO, had stated their "unshaken confidence" in the ability, the honesty and integrity of Judge Haynsworth. They were Simon E. Sobeloff, Herbert S. Boreman, Albert V. Bryan, Harrison L. Winter, J. Braxton Craven, Jr., and John D. Butzer. Also in my corner on the ethical issues were the American Bar Association and a number of leading authorities on conflicts of interest and the standards by which a judge was required to disqualify himself from sitting on cases in his jurisdiction.

John Ehrlichman, on October 10 or 11, told me the president wanted me to be prepared to brief the Republican leaders on the Haynsworth case in the Cabinet Room on the morning of October 14. He suggested that I mention the firing of General Turner as indicative of President Nixon's desire to get rid of bad appointees and recommended that I specify that I had been asked not to defend Judge Haynsworth but to investigate the charges and make an objective report on the legal and ethical questions raised by Haynsworth's critics.

I was in the office by 6:00 a.m. on October 14 to put the last-minute touches on my speech to make sure I had it firmly enough in mind to freely edit or expand it as I went along. It was 8:28 when I entered the Cabinet

Room for what I considered an opportunity to use the Haynsworth case to do a little missionary work on my favorite theme that "good government is the best politics." There would undoubtedly be some cynics in the crowd, but I knew a few, such as Senator Bob Griffin, Senator Margaret Chase Smith, and Representative John Rhodes, would share my views.

I explained that all of Senator Bayh's charges were inaccurate with regard to Judge Haynsworth's investments in corporations or ludicrous because of the small amounts of money involved. The case of *Merck* v. *Olin Mathieson Chemical Corporation* was one in which Senator Bayh had suggested it was illegal and unethical for Judge Haynsworth to participate because of a "substantial interest" in one of the litigants. "The truth is that Judge Haynsworth never owned any Merck stock and never owned any Olin Mathieson stock," I said. "Bayh now says his staff researcher misread a business transaction" and that this charge against Judge Haynsworth was "in error."

I told the Republican leaders that Senator Bayh had also alleged improprieties by Judge Haynsworth in sitting on a case involving the Greenville Community Hotel Corporation because he held stock in that firm. "It was contended that this was illegal and unethical, and superficial reporting made it appear that it might be questionable," I said. "The facts demonstrated that Judge Haynsworth sat on a case involving the Greenville Community Hotel Corporation in 1962—nearly five years after he disposed of his stock. The only stock interest he ever held in that company was one share worth twenty-one dollars. He drew only a fifteen cent dividend on that stock in 1957" (which, incidentally, he reported in his income tax).

And then I went into the most ludicrous charge of all, in connection with Judge Haynsworth's gift of his home to Furman University. Some columnists hinted at "impropriety" and a "tax dodge." "Far from being a reprehensible act," I said, "it was in fact a commendable act by a public-spirited citizen who conducted himself within the rules and regulations of the Internal Revenue Service. In fact, Judge Haynsworth had not taken full advantage of the transaction." I explained that in 1963, when Judge and Mrs. Haynsworth made the gift to Furman University, they held clear title to the home, for which they had paid $115,000 and upon which they had expended more than $10,000 in improvements. Although the appraised value at the time was $153,000, the replacement value was $184,000. Judge and Mrs. Haynsworth claimed only a $115,000 tax deduction—the precise amount of money they had paid for the property.

Judge and Mrs. Haynsworth could have retained the home for their estate, or they could have sold it for something in the neighborhood of $153,000, I explained to the Republican leaders. They could have made a gift of the home to any other university and properly claimed a tax deduction of at least $125,000 (the cost plus improvements), and perhaps as much as $153,000, as a base for deductions on federal tax returns. Instead, Judge Clement Furman Haynsworth chose to give the home to the university from which he had graduated and which was named after one of his ancestors. This generous gesture became the focal point for a series of critical stories, although my comprehensive fact sheets on the gift and my willingness to answer any and all questions relative to the transaction did quiet some of the press uproar. In the atmosphere of October and November, 1969, some columnists and commentators who were ideologically opposed to Haynsworth continued to criticize the gift of the house to Furman University and other alleged improprieties down to the final vote.

On the day after my briefing of Republican congressional leaders in the Cabinet Room, I spoke before a packed meeting of House and Senate Republicans and key staff members. It was to be the start of a series of speeches, television, and radio appearances to air the facts on the Haynsworth case and clear up misconceptions. Dick Whalen called to warn: "Watch yourself; they are pushing you out in front to make you the fall guy for a nomination that is already dead." I assured him I was moving cautiously and was being careful to keep track of every letter I wrote and every conversation. He reminded me that Haldeman and Mitchell were deceptive and would put a knife in my back without a second thought.

Starved for factual explanations from an administration spokesman, newspapermen and broadcast newsmen swamped me with requests for interviews. The majority were excellent to deal with and did a balanced job of trying to straighten the distorted record. However, a few notable exceptions to impartiality prevailed. And it was unfortunate that their prejudice, stemming in part from an unreasoned bias against President Nixon, was carried in some prime-time spots by popular commentators and in influential newspapers.

Although I was allowed time to explain the lack of substance to the charges against Haynsworth in most forums, a few were rigged against me. For example, I was invited to appear on an evening news show at a Washington television station and was given the impression that I would have at least fifteen minutes of the one-hour show to answer questions on the allegations against Haynsworth. I arrived at the studio and sat through forty-five minutes of news and commentary loaded with distortions against Judge Haynsworth. But I was confident that I could straighten the record with fifteen minutes to respond, even to hostile questions. But fifty minutes passed, and I became restless. I was told that some segments had run a little longer than anticipated but that I would be on "in a moment." As it finally turned out, I had just over three minutes on the end of the program to get in a fast pitch for Haynsworth. It wasn't enough time to adequately cover more than one of the complicated issues. When the first question was finally asked, I replied I was "flattered" they believed I could adequately correct weeks and months of complicated distortions and falsehoods against Haynsworth in three minutes. Even my efforts to explain a couple of the alleged "conflicts of interest" were interrupted by the introduction of additional confusing charges. I doubt seriously that I won many converts.

Still later, almost on the eve of the Senate vote on Haynsworth, I appeared as a member of a six-man panel on the Haynsworth controversy. I knew it would be an unsatisfactory forum, for the moderators' anti-Haynsworth bias had been apparent for weeks and two of the panelists had criticized Judge Haynsworth's gift of his home to Furman University as an impropriety. In the course of a confusing discussion in which my explanations were constantly interrupted, I suddenly blazed with the angry charge that one of the panel members had perpetrated a "fraud" on the public with his "false" stories on Judge Haynsworth. The ensuing exchanges added heat, but little light, to the Haynsworth debate. Although the whole bitter exchange took less than a minute, sixty seconds can be a long time on television. I was the loser by briefly losing my temper, even though my accusation was accurate and well-worded even in hindsight. The columnist and commentator had little to lose in provoking "a lively show," but I had not helped the cause by letting anything other than cool reason project to the millions who had tuned in to the special broadcast. Haynsworth's partisans called with hearty, well-meant congratulations for "really telling them off." But that had not been my goal, and it did not serve Haynsworth's best interest at that critical juncture.

Before that television show, Senator Williams had told me he was going to vote against confirmation of Haynsworth. He found no specific impropriety or "conflict" but stressed a "lack of sensitivity" that he could not accept. It was one of the few questions of ethics upon which I ever disagreed with Senator Williams. It was my feeling at the time that he was being unfair to the judge by leaning over backwards to avoid any possible blemish on his own record if something derogatory to Haynsworth should surface later. I made a last-minute plea as a friend to John Williams in a personal letter that my secretary, Ernestine Hersey, delivered a few hours before the vote on the nomination. Probably a half dozen votes could have been influenced by honest John Williams, but he was unmoved. The 55 to 45 vote by which the Senate rejected the nomination was within a couple of votes of what I had expected it to be if John Williams voted in opposition to confirmation.

Months later, Senator Williams said his decision had resulted from a conversation with Attorney General Mitchell and another Republican political figure and was not based on Haynsworth's record. Mitchell had argued to Williams that Judge Haynsworth was a conservative and could be counted upon to vote for his political friends on the Supreme Court. It was the wrong argument to use with Senator Williams, who wanted only the assurance that the appointee was an able man who would vote his conscience. A prominent Republican lawyer also called on Senator Williams following the meeting with Mitchell to assure Williams that he knew from experience "that Judge Haynsworth would stick by his friends" if confirmed to the Supreme Court. Again it was the wrong approach to use to woo Senator Williams, and he drew an admission from the Delaware lawyer that he had been asked to approach him by John Mitchell. Whether the representation about Judge Haynsworth's political loyalty was true or not, Senator Williams resented the tactics.

Even before the final vote was taken, I was aware that "anonymous White House sources" were leaking stories designed to blame me for the defeat that was now expected. And a few irresponsible reporters were willing to use the planted stories on the failure of my "arm-twisting tactics" without trying to identify any senator whose arm I was alleged to have twisted. When I made inquiry of their sources, they said they were "confidential," as I had expected they would. But none of them could name even one senator I was alleged to have dealt with "in bare knuckle" fashion. I named those senators to whom I had written personal letters—Len Jordan, Margaret Chase Smith, Mark Hatfield, Jack Miller, George Aiken, and John Williams—and made my letter file available to anyone who was interested, in an effort to combat the continued "leaks" from the White House and the sly comments of Attorney General Mitchell hinting that he, too, was blaming me but didn't wish to say so outright.

Unfortunately, my brief display of anger on the television show, when I hurled the word "fraud" at one of the columnists, gave some weight to the impression that I might have resorted to tough tactics on senators and that they backfired. It was true that a large number of senators were bitter toward the Nixon administration for the "blackmail and bribe" methods some spokesmen were using to try to push the nomination through. But that bitterness had been created weeks before my involvement, and my major problem had been soothing the ruffled legislators who could not get in to see President Nixon to express their irritation.

Some reporters availed themselves of my offer and examined some or all of my correspondence with the various senators; they saw that the thrust of my appeal was that they should continue to demand the highest standards of ethics in the men they supported. I said that I respected their independence, admired their quest for men of integrity, and hoped to retain their friendship. I conceded that in hindsight Judge Haynsworth could have refrained from investing in Brunswick so soon after a decision was rendered, even though he had not profited. All of us can improve our images in hindsight. To Senator Williams I added: "Judge Haynsworth is honest and ethical. He has not used his office to try to enrich himself. Defeat of Judge Haynsworth will be a triumph for George Meany and the AFL-CIO and the money power reported by Jerry Landauer in today's *Wall Street Journal*. It will be a triumph for those cynical men who defended Fortas and now conspire to ruin an honest man. I know you, and I have full confidence in your motivation and that of a number of others. Yet, I know that your vote is being used as a crutch by men who have had little concern for ethics. They use your name to justify their submission to the power of the AFL-CIO."

Months after the Haynsworth battle was over, occasional reports still blamed me for his defeat because I was the visible defender. Although I had complete documentation to establish that I had used no improper tactics in dealing with senators, or even one senator, the fact that I was on the White House staff prohibited me from speaking out to place the blame where it should have been—on Mitchell, Ehrlichman, Haldeman. I also believed that President Nixon had to take major responsibility for not making himself available for discussions with various Republican senators during late September and October. Not only should they not have been denied access, he should have taken the initiative in discussing the question with them, explaining it fully, and possibly salvaging a significant number of Republican votes.

When it was over, the president invited Clement Haynsworth to the White House to make a personal request that he continue as chief judge of the Fourth Circuit Court of Appeals. "I must say that after the brutal, vicious, and, in my opinion, unfair attacks on his integrity, I would well understand why the judge would retire to private life," Mr. Nixon said.

I also wrote to urge him to remain on the federal bench and again expressed my belief in him as an able and honest man:

> The months of digging by an aggressive and well-financed opposition failed to surface any evidence to the contrary. It was noteworthy that in the final days the most vociferous opponents conceded that you were an honest man. The news stories and columns since the vote have made the same point over and over as they have pointed up the real forces that defeated the nomination. It is obvious now that many writers and others are ashamed of what they did to you, and the shame will be more evident as the months go by.
>
> I hope you will continue on the Fourth Circuit bench for those who believed in you and put forth so much effort on behalf of your nomination.

Also worth mentioning is the support Judge Haynsworth received from a well-intentioned cabinet wife whose backing was more impassioned, if less conventional. It was not until December 6, 1969, that the *Washington Daily News* revealed in a front-page story that Martha Mitchell had personally lobbied for the votes of Senator Albert Gore, a Tennessee Democrat, and Senator J. William Fulbright, from Mrs. Mitchell's home state of Arkansas. The wife of the attorney general had been emerging as an unusually outspoken cabinet wife, with a gift for frank and unrestrained comment on governmental affairs. In this, her first association with political action, *Time* magazine labeled her the "warbler of the Watergate," in those days when Watergate was known only as a plush apartment complex with a magnificent view of the Potomac River.

*Chapter Eight*

# THE FITZGERALD FIASCO

THE CASE OF A. Ernest Fitzgerald gave President Nixon his finest opportunity to demonstrate an active and effective interest in fighting waste in Pentagon spending. It was a chance to do the right thing for the right reason:

protect a courageous public servant who had defied the bureaucracy to testify truthfully, praise him for exposing huge overruns on a contract awarded during Robert McNamara's tenure, and legitimately make political hay by revealing incompetence in the previous Democratic administration.

Because of Mr. Nixon's personal experience in congressional investigations, and because of past conversations with him, I believed he would be particularly understanding of the importance of assuring government employees they would be protected if they were frank and forthright in testifying before Congress. Instead, he hesitated, floundered, and bungled the case so badly that it became a symbol of abuse of power.

In November 1968, weeks before President Nixon was inaugurated, A. Ernest Fitzgerald, deputy for management systems in the Air Force, testified before the Proxmire Joint Economic Subcommittee that overruns on the C-5A Galaxy jet transport would be between $1 and $2 billion.

Shortly after the contract had been awarded in 1967 it was reported the Pentagon had given it to the Lockheed Corporation, which had a huge plant in Marietta, Georgia, to keep peace with Senator Richard Russell, veteran Georgia Democrat, who then chaired the Senate Armed Services Committee. Lockheed at that time was the Number One defense contractor. The highly touted aim of McNamara's "Total Package Procurement Contract" (TPPC) was to control costs and assure economy in a major weapons system. Like so many of Bob McNamara's ballyhooed ideas, this now had to be discarded as another misjudgment. The Air Force, displeased by Fitzgerald's frankness, initially denied the accuracy of his figures. Then they conceded that the contract arrangement had not lived up to its much publicized origins and reluctantly admitted that new agreements were underway which would guarantee Lockheed substantial profits. Questions in this area had arisen before Melvin Laird's confirmation as secretary of defense, and he had testified that he was prepared to take "corrective action."

I had not followed the issue closely but was aware of material being developed by Proxmire's committee. I discussed it with Defense Secretary Laird and William Baroody, and we agreed on the three main points: 1. the C-5A was a problem of the McNamara era; 2. Fitzgerald testified against the wishes of his Air Force superiors; 3. the testimony was prior to Nixon's inauguration.

It seemed clear to me there could be no excuse, morally or politically, for a cover-up of any aspect of the case. This seemed a tailor-made opportunity for the Nixon administration to engage in a no-holds-barred investigation. I so stated to Laird and Baroody, and in our brief conversation I thought we were in agreement.

Years of covering Defense Department scandals had demonstrated to me the capacity of the military system for vicious retaliation against those it characterized as not being "team players." Now the Air Force bureaucracy was determined to use the Nixon administration to shield itself from exposure of decisions that were the responsibility of the Johnson administration. This was precisely the type of situation I thought should be guarded against when

I wrote months before in the job description I submitted. "In addition to alerting the president to possible future problems, the special counsel would provide a follow-through on problems of past administrations to assure effective action, and to alert the Nixon administration to the dangers of entanglement with problems of the past." "There has been a failure to recognize the danger that the Nixon administration might be blamed for errors of the past and carry that burden into each major defense controversy." I had written this in July 1969, with the bungled TFX contract award, Vietnam War decisions, and the anti-ballistic missile program in mind.

Other considerations I mentioned at the time I joined the White House staff applied equally well to the C-5A procedure. I warned that while carry-over personnel are essential for continuity, every new secretary of defense must be on guard against relying too much on the men involved in previous administrations: "Those who were parties to a series of misjudgments of the past have an inevitable desire to hide or minimize those errors and a considerable stake in seeking a defense of those policies and decisions."

In the first week of November 1969, Washington newspapers carried the story that Air Force cost analyst A. Ernest Fitzgerald was being fired. I was surprised because I had thought Laird's office shared my view that if there were any doubts about the merits of the charges against Fitzgerald, he would be retained or even promoted if the facts weighed heavily enough in his favor. I thought a courtesy call prior to the action should have apprised me of the situation we had been mutually concerned about. I was a little miffed when I called Baroody after reading the papers. "What happened?" I asked. He knew my inquiry referred to the Fitzgerald case.

"We were just as surprised as you were," Baroody replied. "The Air Force just did it and then notified us."

I asked whether Laird planned to reverse the decision, but Baroody explained that since it had been announced publicly, Secretary of Defense Laird would have to persuade or direct Air Force Secretary Robert C. Seamans, Jr., to rehire Fitzgerald. This could cause a serious breach in Laird's relationship with Seamans in other areas, Baroody said, and he thought Laird hoped to work out something. I offered the opinion that if this was the kind of cooperation Laird was receiving on other Air Force projects it hardly seemed worth the effort to retain Seamans.

By firing Fitzgerald, the Air Force had forced a showdown with the Nixon Administration. It had to defend either its secretary of the Air Force or Fitzgerald. "The firing of Fitzgerald was probably a mistake, but Bob Seamans isn't a bad guy to work with," Baroody said. "We could do worse." Baroody commented that it is seldom that one gets perfect solutions for problems in government and that, in this case, it was a matter of balancing off the value of Dr. Seamans against Fitzgerald. Seamans was no more than a nodding acquaintance of mine at that time, and, not recalling, off the top of my head, any glaring examples of his involvement in either mismanagement or fraud, I didn't question the reluctance to challenge the decision. I had never met

Fitzgerald, but newspaper accounts of his work were highly favorable. However, those stories were written by reporters who had strong views against what President Eisenhower had called the "military-industrial complex," and they might tend to overlook serious flaws in Fitzgerald's record to score a point against any major defense contractor.

About this time I received calls from newsmen who expressed the view that Fitzgerald was being fired for telling the truth. The initial calls were from reporters not unfriendly to President Nixon but concerned about what they considered an injustice and anxious to call it to my attention. With no preconception as to whether he was right or wrong, I read some reports of the hearings and called the Air Force, which immediately denied Fitzgerald was being fired in retaliation for his testimony on the C-5A. To counter my persistent questioning, Assistant Secretary Spencer Schedler hinted that there were "some important aspects of the C-5A matter" that he did not want to discuss on the telephone but would like to explain to me at my office.

On the afternoon of November 13, 1969, Schedler came to my office on the first floor of the Executive Office Building accompanied by Colonel James Dudley Pewitt, whom he introduced as having full background on the C-5A and the Fitzgerald problem.

It was quickly established that Schedler and Pewitt had no quarrel with the accuracy of Fitzgerald's testimony on the C-5A. In a conspiratorial tone they assured me that they could understand my concern over the sharply critical editorial reaction, but they were sure "other things" in the case justified the termination of Fitzgerald's employment and the abolition of his job. I agreed that there were frequently unexplained factors in such cases, but while some of those factors could be handled on a confidential basis, the only defensible case is the one that can be made publicly.

Schedler said he was confident I would agree abolishing the job had been the most satisfactory way for all concerned when I knew all the facts, and mentioned a "security problem" and "conflict of interest" which might have proven embarrassing to Fitzgerald if the Air Force had chosen to fire him for cause. He hinted that it might be awkward for the White House or Congress to make an issue of the case and said they were pretty sure the Armed Service Committees of the House and Senate were on their side.

I called attention to the fact that news stories were already describing the abolition of Fitzgerald's job as "the firing of a man for giving honest testimony." When I pressed for details on Fitzgerald's "conflict of interest" and "security problem," they charitably claimed they did not want to go into detail but said I could rest assured the case was there. Nevertheless, I pressed them, and Schedler said Fitzgerald had leaked C-5A information to Proxmire's committee. I snapped that it was hardly a case of "security violation," even if they could prove Fitzgerald had given highly classified documents to a properly authorized committee of Congress. Nothing in Fitzgerald's public testimony was alleged to have violated security. I asked Schedler whether he realized that if the Air Force was firing Fitzgerald because he had "leaked" information to Senator Proxmire, it was in fact engaging in the very retaliation Proxmire charged. I advised them to consider their arguments very carefully before using them with anyone else.

Then I moved to the alleged "conflict of interest" and asked for details. Between them, they came up with a vague answer that boiled down to the charge that Fitzgerald was the owner of a corporation and that the corporation had received defense contracts. "Has Fitzgerald retained his interest in the corporation?" I wanted to know. Schedler said Fitzgerald claimed to have sold his interest. Did they have evidence to contradict him? After fumbling around, they offered to look at the files. "Has Fitzgerald used his Air Force position to favor his former firm?" Again, they would have to look at the files.

They still insisted that there was a security problem and something that constituted a conflict, but neither could remember precisely what it was, and said they needed to refresh their minds on all points of fact. I commended them for their desire to be accurate and suggested they get a fair and accurate report to me by the end of the next day, a Friday. I suggested these alternatives:

1. If the case against Fitzgerald was serious and could be proved in a public forum, I suggested that they should fire him on those grounds or confront him with the charges and ask for his resignation.

2. If only a technical case of a conflict of interest or a security violation could be made, it should be documented and made a part of the record with the decision to abolish his job; if it was a minor conflict, he should be moved to a position where that particular conflict would not be a factor.

3. If they were unable to substantiate a case against Fitzgerald, he should be retainied or promoted, depending upon the balanced weighing of all factors.

Because of their hesitation and groping, I again stressed that, under the circumstances, if there were any doubts they should be resolved on Fitzgerald's side.

No memorandum was delivered on Friday, Saturday, or even Monday. By this time I was convinced they had no case. After all, the Air Force counsel's office should have compiled charges before they proceeded with the firing, and it would have been simple to draft a memo had such an analysis existed.

I called Bryce Harlow, counselor to the president. I went over the case briefly, emphasized the lack of response from the Air Force, and said I felt the president should be informed immediately, before he stumbled into a problem without receiving adequate warning. Harlow had an appointment with the president shortly and offered to take a memorandum to him for the quickest action. I was sure this would be much better than my channel through Haldeman's office, where it might be delivered that day, held until the next, or perhaps just forgotten. Bryce cautioned me not to say anything because Haldeman might be irritated with both of us for going around him. We agreed, however, that, should the point be raised, we would state precisely what had taken place.

In that November 17, 1969, memorandum to the president I pointed out the "dangers involved in the Air Force decision to abolish the job of Mr. A. Ernest Fitzgerald." I avoided an opinion as to Fitzgerald's honesty or lack of it.

> The abolition of the job held by Mr. Fitzgerald has been pictured in the press as "the firing" of this man for giving honest testimony on the cost over-runs on the C-5A program.
> Unless there are clear and overwhelming reasons why Mr. Fitzgerald should be fired, this decision should be modified in some manner to avoid most serious embarrassment to Secretary Laird and the White House. In my judgment, this decision is likely to plague the administration for years to come.
> I do not believe this matter was well handled by the Air Force in the first instance, for it should have recognized that this case represents particularly sensitive problems.

I understated my conviction that some smug Air Force officers had suckered Nixon administration appointees into a totally untenable position.

Bryce Harlow assured me that he had given the memo to the president and discussed it with him, but I heard of no plans for corrective action. I sent two other memos stressing the possible hazards to the administration, and, with a press conference scheduled for December 8, I contacted Patrick Buchanan, whose responsibility it was to anticipate questions that would be put to the president and suggest suitable responses.

Pat quickly grasped the danger in defending the Air Force and agreed to prepare a response to avoid trouble. He suggested this answer: "It is true that Mr. Fitzgerald's job is being abolished, but it is not because of his performance in it; he has, to my knowledge, been a dedicated and effective public servant. After looking into it, I have decided to direct the defense secretary to find Mr. Fitzgerald another position, of equal pay and stature—not a make-work job—where his talents can continue to be used by this administration." The feedback from the Oval Office indicated that the president was pleased with the answer as a solution to a problem which by now was creating a minor tempest among Republicans in Congress, as well as Democrats.

The Fitzgerald firing came up as predicted in that December 8, 1969, press conference, but the question was phrased in such a rambling, complicated way that President Nixon answered with a quip which brought belly laughs from the assembled journalists and convinced John Ehrlichman and Bob Haldeman that the case was laid to rest with a joke. In the next few days, Ehrlichman commented sarcastically that the Fitzgerald case was less serious than I had indicated, and Egil Krogh sent me a curt note saying that the Fitzgerald problem appeared to have been without substance. Others also belittled my concern. I tried to point out that repartee avoiding the issue did not deal with the basic wrong and that they were deceiving themselves if they felt one brush-off could dispose of the well-documented complaints about Fitzgerald's firing.

Wanting to be on record in the matter, I sent the following memo to Ehrlichman on the second of January:

I hope the decision [not to retain Fitzgerald] was made with a full understanding of the facts as well as the potential for serious political damage. I say this because many of the initial decisions in this matter were made without a full understanding of what was involved.

Unless Fitzgerald can be clearly implicated in some serious mismanagement or conflict of interest, this can well be a possible political hazard for months, for it is obvious that Senator Proxmire does not intend to drop this matter.

The question asked by Sarah McClendon at the press conference and the lack of concern by the press in the days after this incident should not lull us into any false sense of security. "Senator Proxmire and his investigators will be more difficult to deal with, particularly since they have allies in the liberal press and a few allies in the conservative press who regard Fitzgerald as a symbol of what was wrong with the C-5A.

I do not like to harp on this subject, but there were too many errors in the initial handling of this matter for me to have any confidence that all the facts are getting through.

Within a period of a few weeks, critical comment appeared in newspapers in all parts of the country, including such diverse editorial pages as the *Washington Post* and the *Chicago Tribune,* the *Wall Street Journal* and the *Des Moines Register,* the *Washington Star* and the *Washington News.*

Senator Proxmire demanded that the Justice Department investigate to determine whether the Air Force had violated federal laws prohibiting intimidation or retaliation against government employees who tell the truth to Congress.

The *Washington Star,* on January 12, 1970, commented that Fitzgerald "was eased out under the palpably absurd guise of saving the government money by eliminating his $31,000-a-year position." "But the matter must not be permitted to rest there," the *Star* said, and commented on the importance of a Justice Department probe to "determine if any federal laws were broken. This inquiry should, by all means, be carried forward on a priority basis. . . . Needless to say, the results of the Justice Department probe into possible Air Force misbehavior will be awaited with considerable interest by the hard-pressed American taxpayer."

Willard Edwards, in his column in the *Chicago Tribune,* wrote:

The Nixon administration now has its own Otepka case, and the president has been warned by one of his top advisors that it may plague him for years. As a symbol of government harassment and intimidation for telling the truth to Congress, A. Ernest Fitzgerald has replaced Otto Otepka, a State Department security chief, whose persecution lasted from 1963 to 1969.

Fitzgerald is, like Otepka, a calm and determined man, well-equipped to wage a long battle for vindication. He has put his case in the hands of attorneys, who may appeal his dismissal to the Civil Service Commission or sue in federal courts for restoration of his job.

Edwards quoted Fitzgerald as saying: "I won't give up on this. I plan to give them hell."

Fitzgerald, a solidly built man in his mid-forties, had a good-humored toughness in his demeanor that made Proxmire's staff call him the "happy warrior." The highly skilled cost analyst retained just a touch of his Alabama drawl. He had graduated in 1951 from the University of Alabama with a bachelor's degree in industrial engineering. Neither a doctrinaire liberal nor a doctrinaire conservative, he had the rare ability to view his own situation with an objective eye. It was his good-humored objectivity and his meticulous care in dealing with the facts in his case that won him the support of virtually all the writers who met him over the years, with a resulting avalanche of columns and editorials critical of the Air Force for firing him.

My efforts to use these critical columns to prod Ehrlichman and Haldeman into recognizing the need for corrective action was an exercise in futility. Adamantly refusing to take action, they tossed verbal barbs in my direction because of my concern for Fitzgerald, who was now characterized by them as "Proxmire's man."

When I left the White House in July 1970 to become Washington Bureau Chief for the *Des Moines Register,* a major disappointment was my inability to convince the president and his inner circle of the wisdom of straightening out the Fitzgerald matter. In more than seven months, I still had not received the written report on Fitzgerald from the Air Force and had long since concluded they had no case against him. Not until more than three years later did I learn that an Air Force investigation in the summer of 1969 had cleared Fitzgerald of conflict of interest and security violation charges. It was highly significant that the clearing of Fitzgerald took place at least four months before Schedler and Colonel Pewitt had called on me at the Executive Office Building to explain the case "in perspective".

I also did not know that Haldeman had discussed the Fitzgerald case with Alexander P. Butterfield, a former Air Force colonel who served as a chief deputy assistant to Haldeman in the White House. Through his Air Force contacts Butterfield had picked up information about the Air Force's interest in getting rid of Fitzgerald. A January 20, 1970, memorandum from Butterfield to Haldeman referred to an earlier conversation on Fitzgerald at San Clemente in which he apparently had expressed the same views:

Fitzgerald is no doubt a top-notch cost expert, but he *must* be given very low marks in loyalty; and after all, loyalty is the name of the game.

Only a basic no-goodnik would take his official business grievances so far from normal channels.

We should let him bleed for a while at least. Any rush to pick him up and put him back on the federal payroll would be tantamount to an admission of earlier wrongdoing on our part.

We owe "first choice on Fitzgerald" to Proxmire and others who tried so hard to make him a hero.

Following this advice, the Nixon White House "let him bleed for a while." No one outside the Haldeman-Butterfield group was aware of Butterfield's role until his memorandum surfaced in the summer of 1973 in the Senate Watergate investigation.

*Chapter Nine*

# THE MY LAI COVER-UP— THE EVIL OF SECRECY

IN THE summer and fall of 1969 two widely publicized cases arising out of the Vietnam War pointed up more clearly than any others up to that time the evil inherent in secret actions by government officials. Both made the point of the conflict of interest involved in permitting investigations to be under the direction of individuals who might have a stake in the outcome.

In September 1969, Army Secretary Stanley Resor announced the Army had dropped murder charges against six U.S. Special Forces men suspected of killing Thai Khac Chuyen, alleged to be a South Vietnamese double agent. This was known as the Green Beret case. In making the announcement, Resor declared that the scheduled courts-martial of the Green Beret personnel had had to be abandoned because the Central Intelligence Agency (CIA), "though not directly involved in the alleged incident, has determined that in the interest of national security it will not make available any of its personnel in connection with the pending trials. Under these circumstances the defendants cannot receive a fair trial," the Army secretary said, trying to explain the unexplainable situation by which one arm of the government says its operations are so secret and so important it cannot make its information available even when the question of responsibility for a murder is involved. Secretary Resor emphasized that "the acts which were charged [against the men of the Green Beret unit], but not proved represent a fundamental violation of Army regulations, orders, and principles," and that "the army will not and cannot condone unlawful acts of the kind alleged."

The merits of any case in a war zone are difficult to weigh, but efforts have been made to establish international standards of conduct even in war. However, because unexplained operations of the CIA put vital evidence out of the reach of the Army courts-martial proceedings, the Army and the CIA made arbitrary secret decisions in the Green Beret incident on the question of whether men would be punished, or even tried, for murder.

The CIA was reported to have ordered Chuyen's death as a double agent and then rescinded that order a few days after the Green Beret unit had carried out the execution on June 20, 1969. Because of the arbitrary secrecy necessary for an effective international intelligence-gathering operation, the public will probably never have another opportunity to weigh the merits of the arguments in this case, but it should have been obvious to everyone that our much-cherished "due process of law" and standards of justice cannot survive in secret proceedings.

At about the same time as the Green Beret case broke, the press forced public hearings on the even more tragic My Lai massacre, in which officers and men of a U.S. infantry unit had slaughtered a large number of unarmed men, women, and children. First Lieutenant William L. Calley, Jr., a twenty-six-year-old infantry officer, was eventually tried and convicted of "unlawfully" killing men, women, and children "without justification or excuse." Lieutenant Calley's defense was that he was following orders from superiors and that his actions took place during a war and in a war zone. He was guilty of a senseless slaughter and was punished in an action that will be a subject of heated controversy as long as wars are fought. But the most significant point on the whole My Lai matter involved the question of responsibility for the Army's failure to investigate the incident and its successful cover-up of the affair until forced by the press and the Congress to conduct a full investigation.

The massacre took place in March 1968, and not until November 24, 1969, did Army Secretary Resor and General William Westmoreland, then the Army chief of staff, announce the appointment of Lieutenant General William R. Peers "to explore the nature and scope of the original Army investigation" of the My Lai massacre. That investigation was initiated months after Representative L. Mendel Rivers, South Carolina Democrat, who headed the House Armed Services Committee, had forwarded to the Army a letter from Ron Ridenhour of Phoenix, Arizona, stating that a large number of civilian inhabitants of My Lai had been killed by troops from C Company, First Battalion, Twenty-ninth Infantry, on March 16, 1968. The letter from Ridenhour, who had been assigned to the Eleventh Infantry Brigade in Vietnam, contained specific details, including map coordinates of the village, names of individuals involved, and names of witnesses. The usual Army reliance upon chain-of-command reports stalled the matter until the press focused on the massacre in the fall of 1969, thus forcing Resor and Westmoreland to appoint an investigator who had no direct stake in the outcome.

The Army, conducting its own investigation under General Peers, adopted a thoroughly uncooperative attitude toward the independent investigations of the House Armed Services Subcommittee, headed by Representative F. Edward Hébert, Louisiana Democrat. Instead of releasing all information on the incident to the subcommittee, Resor procrastinated on the request to supply "all reports, affidavits, photographs, the names and addresses of all American persons at My Lai 4 at the time, and all other pertinent documents and materials which might have any probative value in the inquiry." He said he wanted to review the individual requests for information and documents with "our general counsel, in the light of Mr. Laird's position that he has taken with respect to furnishing files in the case of open matters." Again the problem of "executive privilege" was arising, relative to the right of the Congress to files that would show precisely what the Army had done and had not done at various stages of the case.

Deputy General Counsel R. Kenly Webster dragged his feet in the same bureaucratic manner displayed earlier in connection with the McClellan subcommittee's requests for documents and reports in the Vietnam service club scandal inquiry. On December 19, 1969, weeks after requests by subcommittee Chairman Hébert, Resor was still denying the requests because, "in accordance with long-standing policy recently reaffirmed, it would be inappropriate to release this information at this time." On December 23, 1969, Hébert demanded that Resor supply the documents and witnesses requested or give him a categorical answer to each of the requests by the close of business on that day. Again, Resor's response was not a direct answer. He suggested a meeting with the chariman. Hébert replied that he would be happy to meet with Resor on the entire matter but that he wanted answers in writing. Weeks went by before Hébert, the second-highest-ranking member of the House Armed Services Committee, could force Resor to produce the documents and the witnesses, a classic example of the "cover-up and stall" technique that all government departments have used in varying degrees to avoid and evade public accountability.

It was not until July 15, 1970, that Hebert's subcommittee was able to write a report criticizing the Army's lack of cooperation and documenting the massive Army cover-up. "It can reasonably be concluded that the My Lai matter was 'covered up' within the American Division and by the district and province advisory teams," the Subcommittee stated after reviewing the My Lai massacre and the inadequate investigation by the Army of its own activities.

On the afternoon of March 16, 1968, an order was given by radio to the Commander of C Company of Task Force Barker to return to My Lai 4 that day to determine the sex, age, and cause of death of those civilians killed. That order was immediately countermanded by the commander of the American Division, who was monitoring the frequency on which the order was transmitted. He testified he did so for tactical reasons. However, there is no evidence that American troops ever returned to My Lai 4 for the above purpose, although the situation reports for March 17, 1968, indicate that elements of both A and C companies were in the immediate vicinity . . . on that date and apparently could have easily made such an investigation. . . . To keep the My Lai matter bottled up within the American Division and the District and Province Advisory Teams required the concerted action or inaction on the part of so many individuals that it would be unreasonable to conclude that this dereliction of duty was without plan or direction.

The subcommittee noted that a number of witnesses testified under oath with respect to the existence of investigative reports, statements, affidavits, correspondence, and other documents relating to the My Lai incident.

If they ever existed, virtually all such records have now disappeared. Only one copy of the so-called "Henderson Report" has been found. It had not been kept in the files, but was hidden in the desk drawer of the Brigade Intelligence Sergeant on instructions of his immediate superior.

There is evidence that officers and enlisted men of the Americal Division . . . were informed, directly or indirectly, that the My Lai operation was being investigated and, therefore, were instructed that they should not speculate on or discuss the matter pending completion of that investigation.

While normally this might be considered proper procedure, this warning, coupled with the failure of the division or brigade to conduct any meaningful investigation, tends to substantiate the charge of "cover-up."

The subcommittee called attention to the fact that "the intelligence community at all times during 1968–69 had numerous individuals, both civilian and military, stationed in close proximity to My Lai 4." Yet the intelligence community denied having learned anything about the massacre for more than eighteen months that would have suggested an investigation was in order.

Documentary evidence, however, established that one organization attached to an intelligence agency had a report as early as March 18 (1968) alleging the killing of civilians.

Our intelligence personnel, who one might reasonably expect to be able to detect or verify an incident of such magnitude, apparently saw fit to dismiss all allegations concerning it as communist propaganda, although most of these allegations, which came to them through the South Vietnamese officials, were specific as to time, place and units involved. Failure to investigate and report those allegations to higher authority raises a serious question as to the reliability and usefulness of our intelligence activities in this area.

The subcommittee also found it noteworthy that there was "a surprising and almost unbelievable lack of recollection" on the part of many of the Defense Department witnesses who had responsibility to investigate.

The Army's shocking conduct in the My Lai massacre investigation and the Green Beret affair demonstrated the need for a fully independent government ombudsman with authority to use subpoena power if necessary to obtain records of investigations from the various departments of government. Seldom had the evil of "controlled investigations" been more apparent, particularly when national security classifications could be used to justify hiding the facts from the press and the public.

Minor involvement in inquiries on the fringes of these cases caused me such concern that I wrote a memorandum to President Nixon on January 5, 1970. "There is a need for a White House overview of all of the investigations, prosecutions, and general press coverage of the My Lai matter," I wrote noting that the press often was far ahead of official bodies in alerting the White House to potential cover-ups.

Most of my comments focused on the My Lai case, but they were relevant to the overall problem of permitting government agencies to investigate themselves.

The Defense Department has the primary responsibility in this matter, but I have little faith in the Pentagon bureaucracy doing the type of comprehensive study of all aspects of this matter that is essential to protect the president from mistakes of fact or misjudgments that can be highly embarrassing.

The investigation of this matter will be conducted in a number of forums within the Pentagon itself, and there are certain to be many investigations by the Congress and the press that will raise questions about this matter that will not be resolved by any specific official body. The only manner in which there can be any reasonable assurance that White House statements are based upon the full facts developed in all forums is to assign one man to the job of monitoring all of the various investigations and prosecutions.

It may be that all of these investigations and prosecutions will be carried through in an effective and fully coordinated manner. However, if this is accomplished, it will be for the first time.

Someone within the White House should be authorized to have access to all records and to raise questions relative to any and all facts developed within the Executive Branch of the government.

In a later conversation with Haldeman, I emphasized the importance to the White House on making certain that the Army cooperated with the Hébert Committee and did not engage in a cover-up. Haldeman said he saw no need to give such a project "the priority" which I felt it deserved but said that I should keep myself posted on it and let President Nixon know if there were any developments that might cause political embarrassment. The need for responsible government operations and for assuring that there was no Army cover-up obviously was unimportant to Haldeman. He was unconcerned about evidence indicating mismanagement or corruption in government unless it threatened to embarrass the president or the administration. The My Lai massacre and related problems, as far as he was concerned, were only efforts by the press to discredit our involvement in the Vietnam War during a crucial period for the administration. The need for public accountability was most difficult to explain to this obsessively secretive man.

*Chapter Ten*

# TEXAS DEAL FOR LBJ— THE AUSTIN GERIATRIC CENTER

EXPOSURE OF fraud and mismanagement at the Federal Housing Administration had been a staple in the repertoire of Senator John J. Williams for the nearly twenty years I had known him. I had been intimately aware of his quiet role in pushing the Eisenhower administration to fire more than twenty FHA officials for various types of political favoritism during the last years of the Truman administration. The Delaware Republican consistently followed through against political influence and favoritism in the approval of federal housing loans in the Eisenhower, Kennedy, and Johnson administrations.

So I was not unprepared for a conversation with my old friend, shortly after I moved into the Executive Office Building, in which he related that he was "on to something big" pertaining to housing loans and a geriatric center in Austin, Texas. "Lyndon pulled it off in the last few weeks he was in office," Senator Williams said. "It involved manipulation of decisions in four government agencies, transfer of a piece of choice real estate the government owned in Austin, and several million dollars in grants and loans from FHA." Senator Williams had a good informant and, I assumed, also some help from Senator John Tower, the conservative Texas Republican who Senator Williams said was furious about LBJ's last-minute land grab. Senator Tower would have some political difficulty opposing a project for Texas, even if it involved major irregularities by the Johnson Democrats.

Senator Williams expressed confidence in his information source but said he might need some help getting full answers from the agencies involved and wanted to alert me to his interest in the undertaking.

A week later, on September 2, he had developed more specific information on Lyndon's land grab. The twenty-six acres of choice riverfront land a short distance from downtown Austin had been used by the Interior Department as a fish hatchery, but had been transferred as "surplus" to the Department of Health, Education, and Welfare and then given to a newly created nonprofit corporation known as the Austin Geriatric Center, Inc. The federal treasury would fully finance the corporation through a series of medical contracts and loans handled in a speedy and "irregular manner," Senator Williams said. Final papers were rushed to Texas to be signed on January 20, 1969, the last day Lyndon Johnson was president. The bold feat had been coordinated from the White House by top Johnson appointees in the various agencies rather than through normal bureaucratic channels, which could have taken a year or more to resolve the highly controversial decisions.

Senator Williams was considering a trip to Austin to examine the site in order to have all aspects of the situation clear in his mind before opening fire. Part of the fun in his role as a crusader against government corruption was to appear in the federal offices, ask for routine records, identify himself, and watch the bureaucrats scramble.

A few days later, I called George Romney, secretary of Housing and Urban Development, to discuss the case with the forthright and able former governor of Michigan. Romney was not in, and Under Secretary Richard C. Van Dusen, whom I had known through Romney's unsuccessful campaign for the Republican presidential nomination, took my call. Van Dusen said that he knew of the Austin Geriatric Center project but that G. Richard Dunnells, one of his special assistants, was thoroughly familiar with the details of an investigation HUD was conducting of the circumstances surrounding the FHA grants and loan guarantees. In a telephone conversation, the young HUD lawyer briefed me on the outlines of the program, verifying the general accuracy of the information I had received from Senator Williams. Later, on September 9, Dunnells came to my office and gave me a copy of the August 25, 1969, report he had made to Van Dusen. It was a careful, factual report, but also expressed his personal indignation at the gross manipulation of government decisions.

According to the report, the land, appraised at more than $2 million, had been transferred by HEW at a value of $642,000: "The twenty-six acres is within the city limits, adjoins a public park, school site, and interstate highway. It overlooks the river and lies directly across from a luxury motel and high-income residential areas on the other bank. In short, it is a prime piece of land for development." Dunnells called my attention to the fact that the deed had a "reverter clause stipulating land use for health and health research purposes for the first thirty years." He explained that HEW and HUD had signed a "consent agreement" on January 10, 1969, to make the clause inoperative for title to revert to the federal government as long as FHA had a commitment to insure the mortgages.

It seemed to Dunnells that the arrangement opened the way for the Austin Geriatric Center, Inc., to acquire clear title to this valuable land at the end of thirty years regardless of the use which would then be made of it. "The principals in the nonprofit corporation are prominent Austin residents and close associates of LBJ," he wrote. "At present it would appear that they were directed by LBJ to front this project which would be another monument to the ex-president. . . . I found no evidence of direct or unusual financial gain which has flowed or would flow to the principals," Dunnells said. "However, I am exploring what happens under Texas law when a nonprofit corporation is dissolved and its assets are liquidated." He noted that the contractor and architects involved in the project are "very close to LBJ and have got the lion's share of federal construction work (of which there has been a hell of a lot) in the area," and that "the entire project has been kept extremely quiet in Austin. Even most of the local realtors know nothing about the deal."

Dunnells reported that officials in the Fort Worth FHA office "had serious problems with the project from the outset, i.e., qualification of sponsors, costs, market, tax exemption," and that "their stated earlier concern is borne out by the files." Dunnells' interviews had "borne out what the files indicate—FHA was directed to ram this thing through using as much play in the joints as our regulations would permit." Dunnells said he had directed the Fort Worth FHA office "to open the entire project up for an in-depth technical review emphasizing objectivity and the need for technical substantiation on either a go or no-go disposition."

The geriatric center had asked for "an extension of time" with regard to some technical problems, and Dunnells assured me HUD would take no action on this request until such time as the review had been completed. I told him that Senator Tower's Office had made inquiries of the housing department and that he could expect some from Senator Williams because of his long-standing interest in irregularities at FHA. "As far as I can see, you have acted properly in your review of this, and there is no reason why you should fear making all information available to any senators or congressmen," I advised Tower. I sensed his uneasiness about becoming involved in a congressional investigation but assured him that he had nothing to fear if he were truthful and there were no attempts to cover up the irregularities in the FHA. Dunnells said that HUD would not have approved the project had it come up at that time and said he and others were looking for a proper way to reverse the decision. They were in contact with officials of the Department of Health, Education, and Welfare in an attempt to clarify the circumstances surrounding an HEW grant of $642,000, made on December 10, 1968, which was to provide most of the seed capital for the Austin Geriatric Center.

When Dunnells left, I dictated a memorandum for the files on the manner in which Lyndon Johnson, between October 29, 1968—a few days before the election—and January 20, 1969, had "organized a series of unusual actions by the highest-level personnel in three agencies—HUD, HEW, and GSA."

"I am informed that the file shows that the president wanted a large geriatric center in Austin with a minimum of five hundred units with full financing by the federal government," I wrote, explaining that the land was "donated on the transfer from GSA to HEW under an agreement that required that it be used for 'health purposes' for thirty years. There is considerable doubt as to whether this land would then revert to the federal government or would be subject to disposal by the officers of the nonprofit corporation."

I noted that HEW grants were to provide most, if not all, of the capital and that "FHA provided a total of $8,600,000 in mortgage grants, $80,000 in rent supplement, $300,000 in Section 236 money, and $30,000 in rent subsidies to the sponsor. Normally there is a requirement for 10 percent under Section 236 loans. However, in this case, the nonprofit corporation officers were able to use the land which they received free. I was concerned because he had maneuvered President Nixon into supporting his conduct of the Vietnam War. In return, Johnson's friends were aiding Nixon in the Senate and House in handling the Vietnam War and on the big ABM fight. The president had made several speeches under circumstances which called for laudatory remarks about his predecessor, but I felt he went overboard in praising a man whom, he had told me only a few months earlier, he regarded as "a crooked" political figure. I blamed Mr. Nixon's praise of Johnson on his tendency to overstate in order to make political points needed at the moment, and at this moment the tight fight on the ABM in Congress certainly indicated that President Nixon needed all the support he could get. I hoped no new crisis would arise in which he believed he needed Johnson before the decision on the Austin Geriatric Center was reversed.

Although I had great faith in the rectitude of George Romney at HUD, I had equal reservations about the strength and purpose of Robert Finch, secretary of health, education, and welfare. Though I had been told HEW was reviewing the circumstances surrounding their medical grants and gift of land in Austin, I called HEW to reassure myself because of the reputation Finch had acquired as a weak and vacillating cabinet officer. When I sought information on the status of the geriatric center grants and particularly the transfer of land, Robert Mardian, HEW counsel, assured me that the HEW staff members were aware of the problem and believed that there were irregularities that would justify cancellation and withdrawal; he personally considered it a questionable project.

I pointed out that the firms involved in construction contracts and architectural contracts "are firms closely associated with the Johnson administration."

Although the usual architectural fee is recorded to be 5.3 percent on FHA construction, the Department of HUD approved a 7 percent architectural fee in this case, despite the fact that the plans were lifted almost wholly from the plans of a national medical association in Washington, following some prodding from the White House.

There is an entire pattern of activity in connection with this matter that represents bad government at its worst. The decisions, the high-level personnel involved, and the time involved were all highly unusual and even irregular. The Department of HUD would not have approved this matter if it had come before the department today.

On September 10, Senator Williams came to my office, and I told him that HUD had confirmed his information. We reviewed the general problems and I gave him a copy of my memorandum for his guidance in asking the agencies for files and reports. Although there was a real chance to reverse this multi-million-dollar scheme through the normal operations of honest government officials, we knew from experience that heavy political pressures can frequently break the best-motivated men.

We were both aware that Lyndon Johnson was a tough and able adversary inside government, and we feared he would be difficult from the outside unless he was forced to deal on top of the table. Mardian said that he and George Baffa, an HEW lawyer, had reviewed the record but that while HEW found "many irregularities" in the processing, it is "still a little sticky about whether they can take some action to recover the land."

I suggested that he deal frankly with Senator Williams when he made inquiries, for to do otherwise was borrowing trouble. Williams later told me that he was pleased with the excellent cooperation of HEW and HUD. Their data, coupled with the additional information he had obtained from Senator Tower and other sources, made him decide it was time to lay the facts on the line. On October 30, 1969, he made the Austin Geriatric Center one of the first pieces of Senate business and distributed dozens of copies of his well-documented chronology of Lyndon's $2 million "land grab" during his last days in office. He praised HUD and HEW and built a public case to guard against underground pressures that Lyndon Johnson was almost certain to use to save the multi-million-dollar project in Austin. Spelling out the details, he told the Senate: "I question not only the propriety but the legality of this multi-million-dollar giveaway transaction wherein all rules governing the disposition of government property were ignored. Grants and loans were made and loans approved for this group in a manner which underscores bureaucratic contempt for the American taxpayers."

"This transaction cannot remain unchallenged," Senator Williams said. He asked for a Justice Department investigation and "all proper steps that can be taken to reclaim the land." Senator Williams said that government files "indicate that these liberal transactions were arranged upon orders from the White House and that official approval was given by the secretary of health, education, and welfare, who overrode the strenuous objections of subordinates who recognized this deal as a land grab in which the interests of the government were not properly protected." Williams traced the origin of the project to a special meeting at the White House on October 29, 1968, for the purpose of developing "a definitive program in response to the president's request for a new and innovative nursing home for Austin, Texas, as soon as possible."

Williams reviewed the swift decisions at the Interior Department and GSA to declare the twenty-six acres "surplus" to government needs without their being "screened for use by other federal agencies, as is required by law." He enumerated the serious objections raised by career employees in every department and described the summary overruling by Cabinet officers and others of high rank, with the end result that "the government, in cash grants and free land, furnished collateral for their own loans."

"An examination of this transaction clearly shows that the free gift of this land and the approval of these cash grants and these 8.5 million dollars in loans were obviously a political decision, and as a result of this last-minute scramble to get just one more grab from the federal Treasury, the taxpayers stand to lose millions," Senator Williams said.

Lyndon Johnson was furious, and so was Representative Jake Pickle, the Democratic congressman from Austin, a special friend of the former president. The next day, Representative Pickle rose on the House floor to deplore "a new low blow against a very worthy and humanitarian project." Said Pickle: "The project is a plan to build a home for the elderly poor folks. A public nonprofit organization intends to build and operate it. . . . The home will be built on land given free by the people of Austin to the federal government at the request of then Congressman Lyndon B. Johnson, a number of years ago, for the construction of a fish hatchery. After thirty years of operation, the Department of the Interior recommended that the fish hatchery be abandoned, and the land was returned to the people of Austin as the site of a model home for old people."

Representative Pickle ignored President Johnson's role in pushing the project through in record time, contrary to the advice of career employees who objected because it did not meet agency standards, but he bled for the poor and elderly: "It is difficult for me to understand how people who raise no objection to this land being used as a hatchery for fish object to its being used as a home for our senior citizens in the twilight of their lives. I say shame on those who cast aspersions by innuendo." Alluding to President Nixon's 1968 pledge, the Texas congressman said, "This is a very poor way to bring us together."

On November 7, Representative Pickle wrote to Presidential Counselor Bryce Harlow complaining of "Senator John J. Williams' blast about the proposed geriatric center in Austin and his innuendos that the transaction was illegal and the grant was improper." Wrote Pickle, "I want you and President Nixon to examine the facts," and he called attention to his own House floor statement (completely devoid of facts) attempting to challenge the irregularities Senator Williams had spelled out in a six-page, single-spaced Senate speech. Without explaining or trying to refute Williams, Pickle assured Harlow that the transfer was "absolutely in order" and was the same type of surplus property transfer that "has taken place hundreds of times. Yet, the inference by Senator Williams, notably echoed by the press, has been that 'three chums' have been party to a personal deal with the president." Pickle was particularly distressed that "a representative of HEW is quoted as saying that that agency will demand the return of this property. I cannot believe this. I do know that an application was made for conveyance to the geriatric center. I trust this application will be approved."

Later he called Harlow to make certain that President Nixon knew how seriously he felt about the Austin Geriatric Center and to affirm that President Johnson felt the same way. Harlow was unfamiliar with the details of the Austin Geriatric Center project or what the agencies of government were doing about it, but promised Pickle that I would discuss it with him. In his telephone call to me on November 11, Harlow said that Pickle had been in to see him on Saturday and that on Monday, November 10, "Lyndon called to the president to lean on him on this Austin Geriatric Center. Lyndon wanted to know what the White House 'is trying to do to some of my friends down in Austin.'" "He reminded the Boss [Nixon] that his friends in Congress have been supporting us on the Vietnam War." Harlow mimicked Lyndon's Texas drawl down to his familiar "Veet Nam."

Later his assistant sent me a memorandum: "Bryce Harlow would like for you to have a visit as soon as you conveniently can with Ol' Jake Pickle of Texas. Pickle came in to see Bryce on Saturday about all the attached [a *Congressional Record* transcript of Jake's speech and a *Time* article on my cooperation with Senator Williams on the Austin Geriatric Center]. Purpose of your visit would be to somewhat soothe him, and thereby perhaps soothe Lyndon Johnson. Thanks. LaMar Alexander."

I welcomed an opportunity to talk with "Ol' Jake Pickle" and called HUD for an updating from George Baffa, an assistant to Mardian, who informed me that HEW was "in the process of seeking return of the twenty-six acres in Austin." The action was based on a specified failure of the Austin Geriatric Center to obtain tax-exempt status under the proper section of the Internal Revenue Code. "Although the department . . . feels there were many unusual aspects of this case that they regarded as irregular, the specific action to obtain reconveyance is on a specific technical ground involving the tax-exempt status," Baffa told me. In a hurry to get the plan through, the Geriatric Center had filed for tax exemption under the wrong section. Baffa confirmed that "on Monday, Lyndon Johnson called the president. He was upset over the Austin Geriatric Center." John Ehrlichman had later called HEW "to see if there were any possibility of resurrecting this thing," Baffa said. "Bob Mardian instructed him that there was little or no possibility of resurrecting it because it does not comply with the law."

I also got in touch with Dick Van Dusen at HUD, who informed me that the FHA office in San Antonio was in the process of taking action formally to end the FHA commitment on the Austin project.

Thus fortified, at 1:00 P.M. on November 12 I met with Representative Jake Pickle. After shaking my hand in a most cordial fashion, he said that he "wanted to see what is necessary to get some White House help in getting the Geriatric Center back on the track," and immediately followed this with the statement that "Lyndon Johnson, Jake Pickle, and our friends up here" had given President Nixon great, crucial support with regard to the Vietnam War."

I stopped him short: "Just a minute, Jake. I thought you were supporting the president on Vietnam because you agreed with his policies and you were doing what you thought was right?"

"That's right," he responded.

"And it is your intention to continue to vote your conscience and to do what is right on votes dealing with national defense?"

When he again said, "That's right," I asked, "And that goes regardless of whether the White House assures the approval of the Austin Geriatric Center?"

When he grunted out a reluctant, "I guess so," I suggested that we "start the conversation over, because if someone was listening to this conversation he might get the impression you were trying to bargain for some *quid pro quo* on Vietnam War support."

The Texas congressman squirmed uneasily and said he certainly didn't want to leave that impression but simply wanted to emphasize that he had "been friendly with the White House" and "wanted some White House help in getting this project back on the track," and in "stopping the criticism from Senator Williams."

I stated that no one in the administration knew what Senator Williams was going to say and that no one had suggested what he should say about the geriatric center or any person connected with it. "It would be futile to even try to influence Senator Williams' course of conduct in such matters, and any effort on our part to discuss his comments would probably only make matters more difficult," I said. "The departments of government simply answered Senator Williams' inquiries in the same manner that they should answer proper questions from any senator or representative in connection with the normal business of government unless national security is involved. Anything that is done on this is going to have to be able to pass the scrutiny of Senator Williams, any other interested member of the House or Senate, or other interested party."

Representative Pickle then tried to shift to me or someone else in the White House the responsibility for devising a satisfactory plan for reviving the Austin Geriatric Center by asking for my "advice and recommendation on a modified plan."

I responded that if the Austin Geriatric Center were to be revived under more suitable arrangements, "the initiative for specific new plans should come from officials of the Austin Geriatric Center." In advance of seeing such a proposal, I said, I could not give an opinion as to whether it would be "good or bad" and had "no notion as to White House attitudes." I stated that any new proposal should meet these standards:

1. The plan should be developed by the Austin Geriatric Center, with no prior commitment by the administration to approve or disapprove. In the light of the questionable nature of the earlier program, this plan must be developed so that every step can be made public and examined critically.

2. There should be proper application of FHA laws and regulations by officials of HUD, with no pressure from the White House to approve or disapprove the program.

3. There should be proper application of the laws and regulations of the Department of HEW with regard to grants and land conveyances to nonprofit corporations, again with no White House pressure to approve or disapprove.

When Pickle expressed "a hope for White House help," I explained that "it was the Johnson White House pressure that caused the problem in the first place," and that "I am going to have no part in seeking favoritism from any government agency." I stressed that I could not suggest anything other than the agencies handle each decision "on the merits," and he replied that he "wanted no favoritism" but did not know enough about the details to discuss it on the merits.

"I have confidence in the character of the men involved in the Austin Geriatric Center but do not want to become involved in anything if there was questionable or illegal activity by anyone," he said. He was concerned about a Justice Department investigation.

I told him that at the moment I knew of no action aimed at anything more than the nullification of the HUD and HEW decisions. For my part, I said, I could only assume that those involved in the Austin Geriatric Center were motivated by a desire for a worthwhile project and had acted in a hasty and irregular manner because of their zeal.

Pickle thanked me for coming by and said that a Washington lawyer, Joseph Califano, would get in touch with me for suggestions as to what could be done to "put it back on the track."

I filled Harlow in on my discussion with Pickle and sent him a memorandum on the substance of the conversations. He said that he hoped the conversation with Pickle had "turned it off" but that he really expected that Lyndon would "try to twist the president's arm."

On November 14, Bob Mardian told me that a number of newspapermen were making inquiries about reports that President Nixon was interested in trying to reactivate the giveaway. Mardian said HEW Secretary Finch had told him that former President Johnson, in a conversation with President Nixon, had deplored the actions at HEW and HUD and had said the Austin Geriatric Center was a project "very close to his heart, and had been close to his heart for years." Finch wanted a "review of the record to be certain that the whole matter is being handled in a proper way and that nothing is being done that is biased against former President Johnson and his associates."

I let Senator Williams know of my conversations with Jake Pickle and Bryce Harlow, and conveyed to him the assumption of Mardian at HEW and Dunnells at HUD that rejection of loan arrangements by HUD would terminate any efforts to solidify the land titles and related actions.

HUD Under Secretary Van Dusen wrote to Representative Pickle on December 11 reporting adverse findings after a "full technical review of the processing and feasibility of the project." Wrote Van Dusen: "These findings showed that the project was not feasible on the basis of cost estimates, market absorption, and insufficient operating funds and that the FHA mortgage commitments should not have been initially issued. It is my understanding that the sponsor's representatives attending this meeting did not take exception to these findings." This seemed to indicate that the project had been finally and fully terminated, and I was pleased that Lyndon Johnson's efforts to twist President Nixon's arm had not diverted Nixon from the right course.

Months later, Senator Williams heard rumblings "about some new movement" on the Austin Geriatric Center. But I was leaving my post in a few weeks, and it was obvious that since John Ehrlichman, as special assistant in domestic affairs, was making inquiries himself, I was being dealt out intentionally.

On July 6, 1970, the day before I left the White House, the December decision was reversed, on direct orders from President Nixon.

LaMar Alexander came by my office at about 10:00 A.M. to talk with me because of Bryce Harlow's great concern that he would be left in the middle of this rip-off. Johnson, obdurate, had again approached President Nixon in December or January to clear the approval of the Austin Geriatric Center, and, said Alexander, "the president made a commitment to see that such an approval was started."

The decision was referred to Harlow to implement, and in the light of my memorandums he was concerned over the position Senator Williams might take on its revival. Senator Tower, said Alexander, "is opposed to the project but has apparently agreed not to make a fuss about it." That the president was so spineless against Johnson's coercion as to give a "casual commitment to approve this project" before the sponsors had filed application was extremely disappointing to me. LaMar said Harlow felt "compelled to carry out the presidential directive." The decisions had been made "by the book," Alexander said, except that "in line with presidential wishes, Bryce has asked that the Austin Geriatric Center be expedited and be given preferential treatment with regard to funding."

I agreed to make inquiry of Senator Williams, but was startled and shocked at the news and believed that his reaction would be the same. I asked Alexander to convey to Harlow my conviction that "White House involvement in 1970 in a commitment to approve the same project was the same as the initial involvement, and a decision to 'go back and do it by the book' was no different from adjusting the record to reach a preconceived conclusion."

The memorandum of my conversation with LaMar Alexander was one of my last acts as special counsel to the president of the United States. I was thoroughly disgusted with this pliable president, so malleable by wheeler-dealers and public relations men but unavailable for serious discussion of ways to make government agencies perform efficiently and fairly.

No official announcement was made on the government decision to move forward on the Austin Geriatric Center, but Dan Thomasson, an investigative reporter from the Scripps-Howard Washington Bureau, broke a story on the reversal in late August. Thomasson quoted congressional sources as saying "an angry Mr. Johnson" had prodded President Nixon into the revival after having "pointedly reminded" Mr. Nixon he had supported the president's Vietnam policy.

*Chapter Eleven*

# JOHN MITCHELL AND EXECUTIVE PRIVILEGE

THE APPREHENSIVE expression on Ernestine Hersey's face and her worried demeanor forecast the tenor of the memorandum she placed on my desk. As a career White House secretary, she was extremely sensitive to criticism by superiors and ever alert to little indications that I might be in trouble with the ruling inner circle in the Nixon White House, which was frequently the case. "The attorney general is upset about your giving those files to Congressman Moss," she said cautiously, testing my mood while attempting to cushion the blow she expected me to feel at criticism from Mitchell. "I am not at all surprised. I had expected it," I responded.

Known as "Big John" around the White House because of his well-recognized political clout with President Nixon, Mitchell was a tough adversary regardless of the merits of a particular case. A few months earlier, I would have been concerned over any direct confrontation with him, but now, in March 1970, I welcomed a confrontation on the issue of excessive secrecy because I had already decided to resign in a few weeks.

I had known Mitchell as Mr. Nixon's 1968 campaign manager and as attorney general—not well, but we had chatted on a number of occasions. In June 1969, I had hitched a ride back to Washington on his chartered plane from Knoxville, Tennessee, where we both had been speakers before the Tennessee Bar Association. That conversation was the longest I had had with him. Our talk ranged over the law enforcement field from the recent forced resignation of Abe Fortas from the United States Supreme Court to the war on organized crime. I approved of his quiet, restrained handling of the Fortas matter, which had been taken care of effectively through private communication with Chief Justice Earl Warren.

The resignation of Fortas under the pressure of public criticism was the first such resignation in the 178-year history of the Supreme Court. It came on May 14, 1969, ten days after *Life* reporter William Lambert exposed a questionable financial transaction. Lambert's story was so solid that resignation was inevitable. It was revealed that Fortas had accepted and then returned eleven months later a twenty-thousand-dollar retainer from the family foundation of Louis E. Wolfson, who was then serving a one-year prison term for selling unregistered securities.

Although Fortas issued a statement denying any wrongdoing, demands from Congress for his resignation, coupled with stories that Attorney General Mitchell had met secretly with Chief Justice Warren to warn of "far more serious" information, left little alternative action. Rather than face a congressional inquiry led by Senator John J. Williams, crusading Delaware Republican, Fortas resigned. Judge Warren Burger of the United States Court of Appeals was appointed to replace retiring Chief Justice Earl Warren. Justice Burger was an old friend and a man I admired, so it was easy for me to praise the steps the administration was taking in the war against crime during those first months President Nixon was in office.

However, two of Mitchell's comments disturbed me. One was a criticism of former Attorney General Robert Kennedy's prosecution of Teamsters boss James R. Hoffa. The other was praise for Chief United States Marshal Carl Turner, coupled with a snide comparison to the former chief marshal, James McShane. I resented hearing my friend Jim McShane called a "corrupt political hack" but let it pass in the interests of harmony. The attorney general's apparent sympathy for Hoffa concerned me, but I decided I could discuss with him the corruption, brutality, and Mafia connections of the Teamsters leadership at a later time.

My next encounter with Mitchell was at a party in Washington in September 1969. Our hostess wasn't sure we had met, so she made a light reference to our both being members of the Nixon team. "Are you?" Mitchell responded coldly. None of the genial good humor of our last meeting was evident. Since this was our first meeting since the announcement of my appointment, I had expected at least a routine "Welcome aboard." His manner made it clear where he considered I belonged in the pecking order of the Nixon administration.

I was puzzled. I thought perhaps he had not been consulted and therefore resented my appointment. For two years prior to the 1968 campaign Mitchell had been the Nixon's law partner, and he had served as his campaign manager. He was considered to be the cabinet member closest to the president and the one with the most influence on policies and appointments. I wracked my brain, trying to recall what I might have written since the June plane ride that might have caused this sharp change in Mitchell's attitude. Suddenly I remembered: he must have known that I had been involved in the reports that led to the firing of Carl Turner as chief U.S. marshal. That probably accounted for the grim freeze he was giving me.

Now, in March 1970, I decided to give Representative John Moss, a liberal California Democrat, the Agency for International Development (AID) files on Vietnam fraud investigations, after several telephone calls from Republican members of the House and White House legislative liaison men.

Congressman Moss, chairman of the House Government Operations Subcommittee on Government Information and Foreign Operations, already had about 90 percent of the picture on the Vietnam frauds but was being barred from the other 10 percent by an AID decision to claim "executive privilege" on its investigative files. The Justice Department had approved AID's use of "executive privilege," but a final decision would come from the White House. It was immediately apparent to me that Moss already had most of the picture and would eventually be able to piece it together from other sources to reveal a massive fraud on U.S. tax dollars. He was operating within his proper sphere and no one could quarrel with his objectives or his conduct. In fact, I believed Moss was doing the Nixon administration a favor by doing his job.

When Bud Krogh, John Ehrlichman's alter ego on such politically sensitive problems, presented the case, I laid out my reasons for believing there was no justification for withholding the files from the Moss subcommittee.

In the first place, President Nixon had said he wished to cooperate fully with Congress in its investigations unless there was an overriding reason for withholding records or testimony. Neither the Justice Department nor the State Department had presented any justification for withholding files from Moss other than "executive privilege."

No law passed by Congress, and no court decision, supported the withholding of testimony or documents from properly authorized committees of Congress, I explained to Krogh. The only justification that had ever been claimed for the concept of executive privilege was an historically inaccurate list of precedents and a self-serving argument by various attorneys general that the president had a constitutional right to arbitrarily pull down a blanket of secrecy. (It was like the king's lawyer arguing that the king was right because the king had always been right even when he engaged in acts that would have been crimes if done by anyone else.)

Further, the case before us was not one in which a sensitive negotiation momentarily necessitated holding up the release of documents or the giving of testimony.

I spelled the situation out to Krogh in one, two, three fashion. The request by Moss was a valid one. There was no legal justification for withholding the documents that Moss sought. From a practical viewpoint, the records he was requesting were only the last 10 percent of a case of fraud and mismanagement he was seeking to expose, and he was already in a position to sustain a charge that withholding the documents was "a cover-up of crime." It appeared that the infractions Moss was seeking to expose were not partisan but rather the usual type of government bureaucratic bungling that had occurred in connection with the administration of foreign aid under every president since the creation of the programs after World War II.

I advised Krogh that the wise policy would be to give Moss the documents he wanted and to do it quickly in order to avoid giving the impression that the Nixon administration would cover up evidence of mismanagement or crime. Krogh then overruled the Justice Department and State Department legal offices and gave the documents to the Moss subcommittee.

On March 23, 1970, I received a telephone call from Bud Krogh. Big John Mitchell was angry with us for giving Moss the foreign aid files and wanted an explanation. Krogh had told the Justice Department that he had acted on my advice, and now he wanted me to explain my reasoning in a memorandum which could be forwarded to the Justice Department. As John Ehrlichman's protégé, he was upset because the action had displeased both Mitchell and Ehrlichman. The nervous young lawyer said he would send Mitchell's memorandum to me for comment because he did not recall the details of my reasoning for giving Moss the files.

The memorandum Mrs. Hersey placed on my desk was from Krogh, and attached to it was Mitchell's memorandum of complaint to John Ehrlichman. Without question, John Mitchell knew that I was the offending party, but the dour and aloof attorney general had not challenged me directly. Despite his title and standing with the president, he had no confidence in a direct confrontation based on the issues. Mitchell talked only to President Nixon and to those in the top power structure at the White House. In turn, they would contact me or send their errand boys with their complaints. In our few direct confrontations they had found me not properly subservient and eager to please.

I did not automatically accept their instructions but tried to apply some common sense in carrying out the assignments they suggested. I did not fly into action automatically when they used the magic words, "The president wants you to do this." On occasion I questioned whether the president would want me to involve myself in some of the petty, silly assignments they suggested. When Ehrlichman and Haldeman pressed the argument that my only reason for being there was to do what the president wanted done, I usually ended the discussion with the comment: "I'll do it when the president tells me personally that he wants it done, after hearing the arguments on the other side." Equally effective in turning off requests for strictly political chores was the comment: "When you give me that instruction in writing, I might do it."

Both Ehrlichman and Haldeman followed the Lyndon Johnson tradition of avoiding a written record of their role, and they were thoroughly unappreciative of my long written explanations as to why matters should not be handled in the manner they suggested. I had determined from the first to make such a record so that my actions and intent would always be apparent. The complaint from John Mitchell through Ehrlichman gave me one of those rare opportunities to respond with an explicit memorandum which would be instructive and would, I hoped, correct their course of action.

The memorandum from Bud Krogh on the "release of investigative files to Congressman Moss" was brief and to the point:

The attached memorandum from the Attorney General indicates his deep displeasure at our decision to release that file.

As I remember our conversation that afternoon, you indicated there was basic legal and policy justification for releasing that file.

I would appreciate your reviewing the attached memorandum and supplying whatever comments you feel are appropriate. It will be necessary for me to explain the grounds for the decision to release the file.

Attached was Mitchell's three-page memorandum to Ehrlichman dealing with "executive privilege regarding executive files." It also went directly to the point: "I was deeply disturbed to learn within the past few days that a decision had apparently been made to release material in the files of the Department of Justice to the chairman of a congressional committee, contrary to the recommendations of this department." Then he launched into the usual bunk about "a previously unbroken line of authority" and the duty of the Justice Department being to avoid "impairment of the executive's constitutional duty to take care that the laws are faithfully executed." It was what I expected from a politically motivated campaign manager with an arrogant disdain for the right of Congress to have access to evidence as to how the laws are administered and enforced.

"The principle of confidentiality of investigative files is one which simply does not admit to any exceptions," the memorandum stated, a broad, all-embracing statement that would wipe out any accountability of the Justice Department as to why it had prosecuted or failed to prosecute any cases it handled. The acceptance of Mitchell's thesis would mean that an attorney general would not have to answer to anyone for the cases he settled or did not settle. "To try to justify the furnishing of such files in isolated cases because of the power of the particular committee requesting it . . . can only lead to a complete breakdown in the principle," Mitchell argued. "Congressional committees have proved in the past that they are willing to accept this claim of executive privilege when it has been applied across the board; but it will become increasingly difficult to obtain such acceptance in the future if examples of cases in which such files have been furnished become known on the Hill."

Clearly, John Mitchell did not wish to be accountable to Congress for his administration of the Justice Department, but wanted flexibility to tell the public and the Congress what he wanted them to know without fear of being contradicted by the documents in the files of the department or by the testimony of subordinates.

The memo concluded with the statement that he would regard it as "the most serious sort of mistake to retreat in the slightest from the long-established principle that material in the investigative files of the Department of Justice shall not be furnished upon the demand of a committee of Congress."

The arbitrary, all-embracing secrecy doctrine Mitchell laid out was directly contrary to the tone and intent of President Nixon's letter to Representative Moss in April 1969, in which he said, "Under this administration executive privilege will not be asserted without specific presidential approval. . . . I want open government to be a reality in every way possible."

It was a pleasure to send Ehrlichman my answer to Mitchell's complaint. In four single-spaced pages I dealt with his arguments with the full assurance that the writings of Harvard Law professor Raoul Berger would back every assertion I made, and that every committee of Congress that had studied the executive privilege claims in any depth had rejected them as myths. It was not unusual for attorneys general to make claims of completely encompassing power for presidents. I felt fully confident of my subject. My book *Washington Cover-Up*, written in 1962, was a case-by-case documentation of the manner in which claims of executive privilege had been used to cover up frauds, perjury, destruction of records, and general mismanagement and obstruction of justice by high government officials.

I had concluded that executive privilege was a thoroughly evil doctrine because denying access to evidence permitted subordinate officials to engage in crimes believing they could hide the proof from Congress, the press, the public, and even the president. I knew from personal experience that this had happened in the administrations of Presidents Truman, Eisenhower, Kennedy, and Johnson. The notorious scandals of the Grant and Harding administrations had thrived in the secrecy imposed by imperious aides who concealed their actions from even the president. My 1962 book on executive privilege was supported completely by Raoul Berger's definitive study, published in 1965 in two issues of the *University of California Law Review*.

First, I challenged Mitchell's arguments that the release of files to Moss might in any manner "prejudice law enforcement" or result in an "injustice to innocent individuals." I agreed that care must be taken to avoid any action that might "prejudice law enforcement" or harm "innocent individuals," and then noted: "The president's use of executive privilege has been accepted by the Congress on many occasions, but a close examination of those cases will demonstrate that the executive branch was usually on sound political ground that made it possible for the president to put his personal political approval on the decision to withhold information from the Congress."

"Certainly there have been hundreds and thousands of incidents where the executive branch gave investigating committees access to the investigative files," I wrote, flatly contradicting Mitchell's superficial and erroneous conclusion that such files had never been made available to committees of Congress. I reviewed the disastrous history of executive branch efforts to withhold information from Congress that had actually been harmful to the Truman and Eisenhower administrations.

The Truman administration . . . after being criticized for months for alleged efforts to cover up evidence of [tax] scandals," made most of the information available to Congress.

In almost all of these cases the Truman administration suffered as much from the allegations that it was hiding evidence of scandal as it did from the scandals themselves. The Eisenhower administration made a number of unsuccessful attempts to withhold investigative files from Congress and in almost every instance suffered severe political damage and in the end produced essentially all the information from the files.

There are no federal statutes and there are no court cases that support the right of the executive branch to withhold information from the properly authorized committees of Congress when they are operating within their jurisdiction and in a responsible manner. Any right to withhold records flows from the personal right of the president to instruct officials of the executive branch to deliver the records to him to withhold the specific documents in the national interest.

Then I dealt with the specific problem of the records which Chairman Moss had requested:

1. Chairman Moss had developed a substantial amount of evidence of frauds involving the operations of the AID program under the Johnson administration.

2. Through his own investigations and through outside sources, he was already privy to at least 90 percent of the information that was available in the investigative file in Saigon.

3. Congressman Moss was prepared to make an issue over a Nixon administration decision to withhold the files.

This situation created the possibility that the Nixon Administration could be blamed for trying to hide scandals of the prior administration. There was no political percentage in putting the president's name on the line to hide evidence of the kind of scandals we are trying to eliminate. Even if we had wanted to hide the record there was little possibility of doing it because Moss and his investigators were already in possession of most of the information and had the leverage to obtain the rest of it if they wished to do this.

In giving the files to Congressman Moss we have simply avoided a battle that we could not win, have saved the president from possible political embarrassment, and have set no precedent that will interfere in any measure with later decisions to properly withhold investigative files.

I am sure the president understands this issue from his own extensive experience in connection with congressional investigations. In commenting on President Truman's efforts to withhold files from Congress, the then Representative Richard M. Nixon stated, on April 22, 1948: "I say that this proposition cannot stand from a constitutional standpoint or on the basis of merit for this very good reason: They would mean the president could have arbitrarily issued an Executive Order in the [Bennett] Meyers case, the Teapot Dome case, or any other case, denying the Congress of the United States information it needed to conduct an investigation of the executive department, and the Congress would have no right to question the decision."

There are many ways that the president can properly withhold information from Congress in the national interest, but in each case he must be prepared to weigh all of the political advantages and disadvantages flowing from the decision.

I heard nothing further from either Ehrlichman or Mitchell on that issue and hoped that my arguments had been persuasive. Had they heeded the warning, Mitchell, Ehrlichman, and Nixon would not have had many of the problems they later encountered. It was already apparent to me that they felt too secure behind the power they wielded in the name of the president to heed my advice with regard to the inevitable result of their treating Congress as an errand boy for the White House. My frequent requests to talk with President Nixon about this and other problems were rejected or stalled by the iron control that Haldeman had on information flow to the president.

"Can't you put it in a memorandum?" Haldeman would snap. "I'll see that he gets it."

"I was to have direct access to the president," I frequently reminded him, to which he usually responded:

"The president's time is valuable. Don't you trust me to give him your memorandums?"

I didn't trust Haldeman to deliver anything except a Haldeman version on any subject that dealt with the obsessive secrecy he had imposed upon the whole White House. Everyone grumbled about it but few complained because the spy system inevitably delivered the message back to Haldeman. A dissenter in the ranks could not be tolerated unless he could be programmed to serve a useful political purpose.

For nine months I had been dodging their efforts to use me on improper or illegal political projects. I was wary of the constant problem posed by their ignorance of government and the ethical insensitivity apparent whenever I had to deal with them. But I still believed that President Nixon had too much experience and too strong an instinct for political survival to approve some of the abuses of power suggested in his name.

*Chapter Twelve*

# PETER FLANIGAN AND THE *SANSINENA* AFFAIR

EVEN AT quick glance Peter M. Flanigan posed the greatest threat of a "conflict of interest" in the Nixon White House. His personal fortune was largely in the stock of Anheuser-Busch, Inc., inherited from his mother, but his investments and connections were spread across the whole spectrum of the financial community, with particular emphasis on oil and tankers owned by the Barracuda Tanker Corporation.

As special assistant to the president for commercial and economic matters,

Flanigan was Mr. Nixon's ambassador to the business community and the business community's representative on the White House staff. The New York investment banker had been one of the leading fund-raisers in the 1968 campaign, when he served as deputy campaign manager, working with Attorney General John Mitchell and Commerce Secretary Maurice Stans. Before Flanigan officially joined the White House staff in April 1969, he had been "an unpaid consultant to the administration, advising with regard to personnel for high-level government positions," according to the press release announcing his appointment.

Flanigan had not sought the $42,500-a-year job of special assistant that placed him on the same salary level as Haldeman and John Ehrlichman and, initially, on a par with them from the standpoint of influence with President Nixon. He had reluctantly accepted the position at the urging of the president so that he could be more active in the staffing of government agencies with Nixon men, particularly the "big six" regulatory agencies: the Federal Communications Commission (FCC), the Civil Aeronautics Board (CAB), the Interstate Commerce Commission (ICC), the Federal Power Commission (FPC), the Federal Trade Commission (FTC), and the Securities and Exchange Commission (SEC).

I questioned the president's judgment in placing a major fund-raiser in a position where he could influence personnel selection at the regulatory agencies which had been plagued with scandals in every administration for as long as I could remember. It seemed to me that a heavy layer of insulation was needed between the big business contributors, who will nearly always expect and seek favored treatment before federal agencies if they have problems, and the personnel selection process, which is really better off in the hands of people whose only interest is fair and efficient government.

But in the absence of specific complaints of illegalities or improprieties at the regulatory agencies or in department decisions, I had no reason to make inquiry into Flanigan's holdings or the specific appointments he was recommending at various agencies. The press, caught up in criticizing the handling of the Vietnam War, was paying too little attention to the staffing of high-level posts and irregularities in government decisions, which were at least equally significant.

Flanigan had been with Dillon, Read & Company since 1947, and had served as vice president since 1954. His father, Horace C. Flanigan, had been a director and chairman of the board of Manufacturers Hanover Trust Company and a director of the Union Oil Company. A brother, John Flanigan, was a vice president and member of the board of directors of Anheuser-Busch, Inc., in charge of its West Coast operations.

Senator William Proxmire (D., Wis.) raised some questions about the possibility that the oil industry was using Flanigan as a means of approaching "the back door of the White House" to influence the Task Force on Oil Import Control, but his remarks did not specify Flanigan's and Nixon's links to the big oil contributors or the fact that Dillon, Read & Company had served as an investment firm for Union Oil Company, or that Flanigan's tanker firm, Barracuda Tanker Corporation, had long-term contracts with Union Oil. I was not surprised when, in the first week of March, I received a call from a White House liaison man at the Capitol saying that Senate and House committees were investigating Treasury Department decisions which would give the Barracuda Tanker Corporation millions of dollars in windfall profits. My caller feared a scandal which would be damaging to the president, yet he was eager to avoid identification with any complaint involving Flanigan. Although Haldeman and Ehrlichman wielded more direct power, it was recognized that Peter Flanigan had more influence with President Nixon for a number of reasons. The primary one was that Flanigan had some real expertise in the New York financial world, in international economics, and in the real world of Washington politics, where Haldeman and Ehrlichman were simply inexperienced meddlers pulling power levers. The congressional liaison man wanted to be assured of anonymity in connection with the investigation of possible favoritism toward the Barracuda Tanker Corporation.

The potential conflict was summed up in the following facts:

1. On March 2, 1970, the Treasury Department had granted the *S.S. Sansinena,* a sixty-thousand-ton tanker registered in Monrovia, Liberia, a waiver of the Jones Act, which limits coastal trade to ships of American registry. This waiver was worth several million dollars in "windfall profits" because it permitted the tanker to operate between United States ports and Alaska.

2. This, the first such waiver by the Treasury Department, had been granted on "national security" grounds but without support from the Defense Department.

3. The *Sansinena* was owned by Barracuda Tanker Corporation, a Bermuda firm organized by Peter Flanigan, who served as president and managing director until 1969 when he became assistant to the president.

4. Although Flanigan had resigned those positions, he had retained his stock in the Barracuda corporation until February 25, 1970—a few days before the Treasury Department granted the valuable waiver from the Jones Act.

These facts indicated serious trouble ahead even if Flanigan had had no role in the Treasury Department decision. Even if he and his family derived no financial gain, who would believe it?

In the process of checking the basic facts with Republican staff members, I learned that Maryland Democratic Congressman Edward A. Garmatz, chairman of the House Committee on Merchant Marine and Fisheries, had protested the waiver of the Jones Act as an unwarranted dilution of the barriers created to protect the U.S. shipbuilding industry. Senator Joseph Tydings, another Maryland Democrat, was investigating the Treasury Department action through a subcommittee of the Senate Commerce Committee and was planning hearings within a few days unless the waiver was cancelled.

On March 5, 1970, the *Weekly Bulletin* of the Shipbuilders' Council of America carried an article making it obvious why there was no time to be lost in getting Treasury to cancel the waiver: The same day Assistant Treasury

Secretary Eugene T. Rossides signed the waiver on the Sansinena, Maritime Administrator Andrew E. Gibson testified before a Senate commerce sub-committee that he "strongly" supported the Jones Act as a tool for strengthening the U.S. shipbuilding industry. The *Bulletin* declared that on this subject the Nixon administration "apparently speaks with split personality." Noting Rossides' action on the Liberian-registered *Sansinena,* the *Bulletin* estimated that "upwards of sixty tankers, in comparable category" could qualify for similar waivers by virtue of being U.S. built but of foreign registry. Such waivers would result in a diminution of market opportunities for new tanker construction in American yards over the next five years.

The Shipbuilders' publication noted that the *Sansinena,* built in 1958, was under a time charter to the Union Oil Company of Los Angeles. Since 1967, Union Oil had been seeking a waiver of the Jones Act to permit opera-tions in U.S. domestic waters—principally between Alaskan and West Coast ports. The waiver applications, made under "national defense" exceptions in the Jones Act, had been rejected as lacking justification. Three years later, with virtually no change in circumstances, a renewed application by Union Oil Company had been approved by the Treasury Department—not the Defense Department—on national defense grounds. There was, said the *Bulletin,* "no explanation, no reason, no rationale, and no justification."

A few hours after the first warning from the White House liaison man, in early March, I called White House Counselor Bryce Harlow to alert him to the potential problem. I also told Rossides, at the Treasury Department, that the granting of the waiver appeared to have been a serious mistake. He assured me that he had had no contact with Flanigan but had handled the *Sansinena* waiver "on its merits"; he gave me a complicated explanation.

I requested a complete chronological breakdown explaining the *Sansinena* decision from General Counsel of the Treasury Paul Eggers. It was important to have it quickly because it seemed likely administration witnesses would be called to appear before a House committee to explain under oath. On Friday, March 6, I received a three-page memorandum from Roy T. Englert, acting general counsel for the Treasury Department.

The Treasury Department's best foot forward on the *Sansinena* was none too good. Their memorandum verified all of the basic facts I already had but argued that Secretary of the Treasury David Kennedy had the power to waive authority "either upon his own initiative or upon written recommendations of the head of any other department or agency . . . in the interest of national defense." Englert stated that Assistant Secretary Rossides decided on Sep-tember 23, 1969, "that he could not recommend that the waiver be granted" but that he had called attention to this power.

A memorandum from the general counsel to Kennedy on February 18, 1970, stated that "the case was not an easy one" but that it was being approved because of the possibility of a "cutoff of Middle East imports." Attached to the memorandum was a letter to the Union Oil Company informing them the *Sansinena* would have to be purchased by a United States–domiciled corporation owned by United States citizens, be manned by American-licensed and unlicensed crews, and be used primarily for the transportation of Alaskan crude oil to West Coast refineries if the waiver was to remain in force.

Englert commented that I "should be aware" that "as of December 31, 1969, P. M. Flanigan [was listed] as owner of 308 shares, or 3.95 percent," of Barracuda Tanker Corporation stock. "Subsequently," Englert wrote, "we were advised that this list was in error and we were furnished a new list which did not include P. M. Flanigan, but which did include Horace C. Flanigan as trustee, as owner of 308 shares. A memorandum in our files indicates that at one time Mr. Peter Flanigan was president of Barracuda Tanker Corporation."

A new corporation would buy the *Sansinena* from Barracuda, Englert said, to fulfill the terms of the waiver. "A proposed list of stockholders of the new corporation, stated to be a partial list of persons who are presently expected to be stockholders in the new corporation, does not include the name Flanigan."

"The Flanigan interest in the Barracuda Tanker Corporation was not involved in the decision, nor was any aspect of this matter ever discussed by Treasury with Mr. Peter Flanigan," Englert said, hoping to absolve the assistant to the president, who had jurisdiction over Treasury, Commerce, and Maritime Commission, and oil policy, from having had any role in the unusual decision.

I talked with Flanigan, who denied any role in the matter, and with Haldeman and Ehrlichman, who exhibited no great concern. Their only interest was in how to stop the investigation proposed by Senator Tydings, not to correct improper action. They proposed to have Senator Norris Cotton of New Hampshire, senior Republican on the Senate Commerce Committee, "make an arrangement with" Senator Warren Magnuson, Democrat from Washington, chairman of the Commerce Committee.

Prodded by my warnings, Flanigan prepared a memorandum of his association with Barracuda for Secretary of the Treasury Kennedy, who was slated to go before the House Merchant Marine and Fisheries Committee on Tuesday, March 10. I received a copy of the letter and the memorandum, which verified everything I had been told but included admissions making the picture even worse.

For example, Flanigan related that "for many years [Dillon, Read & Co.] . . . have been investment bankers for Union Oil Company of California. From time to time over the years, officers of Dillon, Read have organized corporations for the purpose of acquiring and leasing ships and other assets to Union." Since its organization in 1956, Flanigan said, Barracuda's "sole activity has been the ownership of tankers and their charter to Union on long-term charter contracts."

He stated that since he had joined the White House staff his father had had "complete discretion in the management" of his securities.

I am informed that on February 25, 1970, the president of Barracuda telephoned my father and said that to avoid my being placed in a position where there was any possibility of an appearance of conflict, he would buy the trust's shares for $20,000, and my father as trustee agreed to the sale at this price without any consultation with me.

He [Horace Flanigan] was informed that this price was determined solely with reference to Barracuda's liquid assets, the rentals under the existing charters, and estimated salvage values, following a method employed in determining price when certain shares were bought by Barracuda in 1966.

Flanigan concluded by denying financial gain or any discussions with any government employees on the waivers for *Sansinena* by him: "Neither I nor the trust has obtained or can obtain any benefit from the Treasury's action on Union's application. I did not discuss the application to the Treasury Department for waiver of the coastwise trading restrictions on the *Sansinena* with any government official or employee."

On the basis of Flanigan's statement I recommended to Harlow and Haldeman immediate cancellation of the waiver, on the grounds that the administration's explanation still left the appearance of a conflict of interest that would be hard to dispel. I told them I had received allegations that sharply disagreed with Flanigan's position and that Secretary Kennedy should not be required to testify before a congressional committee until all doubts about Flanigan's position had been resolved. In my conversations with John Ehrlichman, speech-writer Pat Buchanan, and Bob Haldeman, I stressed that there was potential for great harm to the credibility of several high officials of the administration." "The choice is between a long-drawn-out series of confrontations or a quick decision (to upset the waiver) that will eliminate most of the possibilities for conflict," I told Haldeman.

Haldeman and Harlow sided with Flanigan in his assertion that he could not be required to appear before a congressional committee because "executive privilege" covered all the actions taken by assistants to the president. Without getting into the basic inaccuracy of the "executive privilege" idea, I explained that if Flanigan or Secretary Kennedy refused to testify, the president might suffer serious political injury. "If the hearings proceed and there is no cancellation of the waiver, there will be increasing demands for testimony from Kennedy, as well as Flanigan," I said. "At that point, the president would be placed in the position of deciding whether he should direct Kennedy and Flanigan to testify or to refuse to testify. That would not be a pleasant political predicament for the chief executive."

On March 9, Senator Joseph Tydings gave a speech in which he characterized the Treasury Department action on *Sansinena* as a decision to give the tanker owners an immediate "windfall" of "at least five million dollars; "the cost to U.S. shipyards and steelworkers . . . may well be hundreds of millions of dollars." The Maryland Democrat found it very strange that the Treasury Department could justify such a waiver as being in the interests of national defense without consulting the Defense Department. Tydings declared: "The opposition to granting a waiver by the Defense Department evidently again was stated in November when Chairman Garmatz of the House Merchant Marine and Fisheries Committee wrote Mr. Andrew Pettis, president of the International Union of Marine and Shipbuilding Workers of America, AFL-CIO, and stated that he had been advised by the office of the under secretary of the Navy that the policy opposing the *Sansinena's* waiver had not changed."

Quoting from a March 7 letter in which Assistant Secretary of Defense Barry J. Shillito assured Senator Tydings that the Defense Department had "no direct or indirect interest" in Union Oil Company's application for waiver, Tydings asked: "How can the secretary of the Treasury issue a waiver on the basis of national defense when the Defense Department 'has no direct or indirect interest' in the matter?"

"Positions of power within the judicial, legislative and executive branches are a public trust," Tydings said. "A breach of this trust is an abuse of power. It will destroy the respect and confidence upon which free government rests. Ultimately and inevitably, it will destroy free government itself."

Tydings declared that "impropriety or even the appearance of impropriety has no place in the government of the United States of America" and called attention to the fact that Flanigan, an assistant to the president, had been president and managing director of the Barracuda Corporation and had held stock in that firm until five days before Secretary Kennedy issued the waiver.

Tydings also called attention to Flanigan's key role in White House financial affairs and his reputation as a "White House pipeline to financiers and corporation executives." Tydings also noted that Fred L. Hartley, the president and chief executive officer of Union Oil, "is a frequent financial supporter of the Republican party." "What is the exact relationship of Mr. Hartley, Union Oil Company, Barracuda Tanker Corporation, and Mr. Flanigan?" Tydings asked. "Who benefits from the increased value of the *Sansinena?* . . . What expertise does the secretary of the Treasury possess . . . on national defense? Why did he step in and, by the stroke of a pen, create a million-dollar windfall?"

After reading a copy of Tydings' speech, I talked with Flanigan briefly and met with Haldeman and Harlow to again stress the importance of an early decision to cancel the waiver. At 7 P.M. Flanigan called from Bryce Harlow's office and asked me to join them in a discussion of the *Sansinena* matter. It was a full room, with Gene Rossides and Paul Eggers from Treasury, Harlow, Ehrlichman, Krogh, and a third man from Treasury whose name I missed.

The discussion, led by Ehrlichman, was centering on ways to stop the Senate investigation by using Republican Senator Cotton, by "doing something for Magnuson," and by finding some way "to take care of" Tydings. I listened for a few minutes, then asked if they had read Tydings' speech. Flanigan was the only one who had, so I carefully laid out the situation as I understood it:

Tydings already had all the facts he needed for an investigation that would embarrass the administration unless there were much better explanations than the ones I had gotten from Flanigan or from anyone at Treasury. Although Senator Cotton was an able advocate of Republican positions, he

had fumbled and floundered trying to save Boston industrialist Bernard Goldfine and White House Chief of Staff Sherman Adams from an investigating
committee.

Ehrlichman suggested that the White House could stonewall with "executive privilege." I reiterated that it was not a proper legal defense, that it
wouldn't work, and that if it did President Nixon would still be embarrassed
by having his name associated with a questionable decision. I asked what
answers Flanigan and Kennedy would give to Tydings' questions and then
suggested some of my own. At that point Bryce Harlow agreed that I "had it
summed up just about right" and that "there is no need to bring the Boss
[Nixon] into this if it can be settled otherwise." Flanigan then reversed the
position he had taken with me only a few hours earlier and announced that he
had "thought from the first" that it had not been a good idea to grant the
waiver "because it did not look good," but that he had wanted to "remain
completely out of it."

Within a few minutes a decision had been made to cancel the waiver and
to issue a brief press release from the Treasury Department stating that it had
been cancelled for re-review. The announcement would be attached to a
Treasury comment denying involvement by Flanigan or the White House in the
decision. Flanigan's statement on his financial interests would be attached.

Although the cancellation of the waiver on the *Sansinena* ended the possibility of an early hearing, neither Flanigan nor Haldeman appreciated my interference in rescuing the administration from a series of confrontations. Brief
stories of the Monday-night meeting appeared in the newspapers, revealing the
reversal of the *Sansinena* decision, and I know Haldeman blamed me for leaking it to the press, though I had not. Before the end of the next day I received
a "confidential" memorandum from Haldeman: "In order to make sure that
there is absolutely no misunderstanding, let me emphasize that no member of
the White House staff—and this very specifically includes you—is to have any
communication with or make any statement or provide any information to
any member of the press without prior consultation with Ron Ziegler. It is
absolutely imperative that this rule be followed at all times and under all
circumstances—with no exceptions." It was signed with a big *H*. A copy had
gone to Ziegler.

The demand for "consultation with Ron Ziegler" would have been reason
for my leaving had my plans to return to the *Des Moines Register* not already
been made. Now it only solidified my judgment that Haldeman had the kind
of mentality that could not comprehend the strength of and necessity for open
government policies.

Although there were still hazards for the Nixon White House in Flanigan's
duties, I knew the "big three" would welcome a confrontation to justify my
being fired for insubordination and to refuse me the opportunity to explain
the controversy to President Nixon, who I still believed was too experienced
in politics to endorse the corruptive secrecy dominating his White House.

To cope with questions I had raised about Flanigan's father controlling his son's "blind trust," Haldeman asked me to prepare a memorandum on the "blind trust" that former Defense Secretary Robert S. McNamara had proposed for his Ford stock in his initial discussions with the Senate Armed Services Committee. McNamara had suggested giving up all control under an arrangement by which he would receive no information on the purchases and sales from his stock portfolio or even the details of his stock income for income tax purposes. "Even this tight arrangement to bar McNamara from knowledge or control of the stock portfolio did not satisfy the Senate Armed Services Committee," I wrote Haldeman. "The members of the committee demanded that McNamara sell all of his stock in the Ford company, and he swept the counter clean by disposing of all of his stock prior to taking office as defense secretary."

In explaining the standard Peter Flanigan should try to meet, I called attention to the fact that "the Senate Armed Services Committee insisted that McNamara not invest the proceeds of the Ford stock and other stock in any firm that did more than $10,000 a year in business with the Defense Department. The Defense Department initially ran off a list of more than eighteen thousand firms that did at least $10,000 a year in business with the government. This meant that McNamara's investment counselor was limited to purchases of stock that was not of a particularly lucrative nature." I stressed: "The control of the blind trust must be in the hands of someone or some organization where there would be a public acceptance of the concept of no knowledge and no control." This was hardly the case if Flanigan's father was in charge of his investments.

That memorandum was written on March 12, the same day that the Senate Commerce Committee voted to launch an investigation of Barracuda Tanker Corporation and any role that Flanigan might have had in it. Senator Vance Hartke (D., Ind.) was chairman of the Commerce Subcommittee, and Senator Tydings was a member. Although Senator Cotton was not a member of that particular subcommittee, as ranking Republican of the full committee he could sit in on subcommittee meetings. "Senator Cotton would probably be the strongest and most effective defender of the Administration if there is a good defense that can be made," I said in my memorandum. I also recommended that Flanigan "assume the best possible posture prior to the time" the hearings started. I suggested that someone review and adjust his investment portfolio and also make a careful study of the many important conflicts between Flanigan's statements and Tydings' speech of May 9.

For several weeks my prodding was gentle, but I became a little sharper in my demands that Flanigan sell his stock or change his White House responsibilities to spare the administration embarrassment. In a communication to Haldeman, I suggested that it would be difficult to convince anyone that Peter Flanigan and his father would not communicate about financial decisions on the stock when such decisions would involve the welfare and future of Peter Flanigan's children. "It would appear to me that it is virtually impossible for Peter Flanigan to isolate himself from his stock interests without a full divesture," I wrote. "Since Flanigan considers the sale of the stock to be out of the question, the only manner in which possible conflicts can be avoided is through some clearly worked out restriction on his duties as assistant to the president where his responsibilities might require direct involvement."

In early May, a memorandum to Peter Flanigan from Maritime Administrator Andrew E. Gibson surfaced. It indicated that Flanigan had asked questions of Gibson in connection with the *Sansinena* matter. This didn't tally with Flanigan's earlier denial of any contact whatsoever with any government officials regarding the waiver of the Jones Act.

With less than two weeks left before my resignation would be announced, I tackled Flanigan's problems with a memorandum for the president. On May 18, 1970, I wrote:

> I have the most serious doubt about whether it will be possible to make a successful political defense of the *Sansinena* decision and the role of Peter Flanigan. . . .
>
> The correspondence between Flanigan and the Commerce Department officials [Gibson and Fanseen] cannot be hidden from the Tydings investigators. It is apparent that it deals to some degree with Union Oil Company, the Barracuda Corporation and the *Sansinena* matter. Senator Tydings, the press, and the cartoonists can be expected to put the worst possible interpretations on these transactions involving Dillon, Read & Company and Union Oil. The chronology of events and the letters create some serious credibility problems.
>
> To overcome the problems it will take a strong, aggressive, continuing defense of Flanigan from the president and from those in the Congress who will be willing to take the political risk. . . . The first step should be an effort to determine if there are six or more members of the Senate or House who will be willing to defend this case. These must be men who project a firm and honest image on their own. All of the facts must be disclosed to those who indicate they are willing to undertake the defense.

I warned of the hazards of the president involving himself in a losing fight, defending questionable ethical standards and alleged favoritism. "The whole pattern of Peter Flanigan's contacts with the Commerce Department in the late summer and fall of 1969 makes this a dangerous political situation," I wrote.

I pointed out that "the general laziness and superficiality of some segments of the press might be helpful if the members of the press were sympathetic to the administration."

> However, it would be the greatest disservice for me to try to minimize the potential dangers in the Tydings hearings. These points stand out.
>
> 1. The decision by the Treasury Department was without precedent.
> 2. The decision that national security was involved was diametrically opposed to the view of the Defense Department.
> 3. The decision would result in large profits flowing to a number of business entities with which Flanigan has been associated—Dillon, Read & Company, and the Barracuda Corporation."

I closed my last memorandum on *Sansinena* by saying: "I will not presume to suggest a solution. The decision can only be made by those with the major stakes—the president and Peter Flanigan."

Senator Tydings rose on the Senate floor at the end of May to reveal that he had discovered a document casting doubt on Peter Flanigan's statements to the Treasury Department and Congress that he "did not discuss the application to the Treasury Department for waiver of the coastwise trading restrictions on the *Sansinena* with any government official or employee."

"I have acquired a document proving that Mr. Flanigan did make a direct inquiry from the White House to the primary agency within the government on the merchant marine about the *Sansinena*," Tydings told the Senate. The document in question was a memorandum sent by Andrew E. Gibson, the maritime administrator, to Peter Flanigan at the White House on October 9, 1969. The subject was given as "S.S. *Sansinena*," and the first paragraph said: "In response to your inquiry last week regarding the use of subject vessel in domestic trades, you should be aware that such use is specifically prohibited by Section 27, Shipping Act, 1920 (the Jones Act)." After citing the provisions of the law, Gibson concluded: "Union Oil has previously requested the Department of Commerce to support its request for a waiver on the coastwise restrictions on the *Sansinena*. By letter of December 3, 1968, that request was denied. Earlier this year I had a similar request which had to be answered in the same vein. I am informed that there is no way these restrictions can be removed short of a change in the existing law."

To Senator Tydings it was clear that, contrary to Flanigan's disclaimer, there had indeed been discussions with Maritime Commissioner Gibson and with James F. Fanseen, acting chairman of the Maritime Commission.

A defense of Flanigan was placed in the *Congressional Record* by Senator Cotton, who accused Tydings of using the Senate floor to make a questionable charge which should have been taken up in an executive session of the Commerce Subcommittee. "The opportunity of indirectly taking a stab in the back of the president of the United States was apparently too attractive to let pass," Senator Cotton lectured the young Maryland Democrat.

Senator Cotton introduced into the record a new statement from Flanigan in which he changed his broad contention that he had never had any conversations with government officials about the *Sansinena* to the narrower: "I took no part in any way, directly or indirectly, in anything relating to the Treasury's granting of a waiver from the prohibitions of the Jones Act to permit the tanker *Sansinena* to engage in U. S. coastal trade. Nothing in the memorandum of October 9, 1969, from Maritime Administrator Andrew Gibson to me, to which Senator Tydings refers, or in the circumstances leading up to it, in any way contradicts that."

Senator Cotton said that Flanigan had assured him that he would respond to any request to appear in a closed session of the Commerce Committee and had said he would not claim "executive privilege" relative to documents or testimony. As Senator Tydings tried to pin this down as a promise that Flanigan would appear to answer questions on the *Sansinena* matter at a later date, Senator Cotton slipped away from an unqualified commitment. "The senator from New Hampshire has not conferred with the president of the United States on this matter," Senator Cotton said. "The senator from New Hampshire does not have the authority to indicate when executive privilege will be invoked and when it will not be invoked."

With the *Sansinena* waivers cancelled there was not sufficient incentive to comb the record for contradictions, and Republican maneuvering in the Commerce Committee allowed Flanigan and others to avoid making their explanations under oath.

While President Nixon and others in the White House gave lip service to concern over the potential conflict of interest between Flanigan's investments and his White House responsibilities, they quietly encouraged Special Counsel Charles W. Colson to counter Tydings' threatened expose of Flanigan. Colson initiated a retaliatory investigation of Tydings for alleged use of his Senate office to advance his own financial interests. No one revealed this action to me. However, in my last hours at the White House I inadvertently learned of the "Tydings project" through a conversation with *Life* magazine writer William Lambert, who assumed that I knew of the "White House cooperation" on his story. The details of the "Tydings project" were completely unfamiliar to me and I had no way to assess the merit of Lambert's story. However, I had a high regard for him as a reporter.

Although I held no brief for Senator Tydings, I was sorry to hear that the Maryland Democrat had potential conflict-of-interest problems of his own. I had hoped the threat of Tydings' investigation would exert continuing pressure on President Nixon to narrow Flanigan's authority in the area of business and finance to avoid the appearance of conflicts of interest.

*Chapter Thirteen*

# POLICING TAX TAMPERERS

FAMILIARITY WITH John Marshall's statement that "the power to tax involves the power to destroy" influenced my perspective on the special sensitivity of federal income tax matters. The corollary of that famous quotation from the *McCulloch* v. *Maryland* decision in 1819 is that in our era of heavy income taxes the power to tax is the power to bestow great wealth.

I know of no way in which access to tax returns can be used to harass an honest man, but an unscrupulous taxing agency can grant favored treatment in many different ways to political favorites when protected by the secrecy encompassing the Internal Revenue Service.

Tax favoritism generated the Internal Revenue Service scandals of the Truman administration during my first years in Washington. The sordid pattern exposed by Senator John Williams involved bribery and favored treatment resulting from failure to investigate aggressively or to prosecute major tax cheaters. Senator Estes Kefauver's Crime Committee exposed the connivance of federal tax agents with mobsters and sheriffs in Florida, Louisiana, Missouri, and Illinois who were not reporting payoff money. Senator Williams and a House Ways and Means Subcommittee chaired by Representative Cecil King, a relatively obscure California Democrat, and a House Judiciary Subcommittee chaired by Representative Frank Chelf of Kentucky, exposed major corruption permeating the old Bureau of Internal Revenue from top to bottom.

In 1952, 174 Internal Revenue Service officials were fired, fifty-three for taking bribes, twenty-four for embezzlement, and twenty-one for failing to pay their own taxes. Six of sixty-four district directors were ousted, three were convicted, and a former commissioner of internal revenue, Joseph D. Nunan, Jr., was indicted and convicted. The Number Two man in the tax-collecting agency, Assistant Commissioner Daniel L. Bolich, was indicted on charges of personal tax fraud for unreported income and was also indicted and convicted as a key man in the nationwide tax-fix ring that centered around Henry (the Dutchman) Grunewald and his influence in the Washington, D.C., office. Although the Bolich conviction was overturned because of an erroneous instruction to the jury, the facts as established by the congressional investigation were never seriously questioned.

Fraudulent tax shenanigans reached right into the White House when President Truman's appointments secretary, Matthew Connelly, was convicted with T. Lamar Caudle on charges of defrauding the government by accepting oil royalties to help a St. Louis shoe manufacturer escape criminal prosecution for tax frauds. Strong suspicion of involvement also fell on top officials in Treasury Secretary John Snyder's office.

Although the Eisenhower administration introduced major reforms in the Internal Revenue Service in the aftermath of these massive tax scandals, certain rogues were able to avoid exposure because of their political ties.

I was aware that Mike Acree, the assistant commissioner in charge of internal inspection, had been dissatisfied with the lack of tenacity which had allowed abuses to persist in the New York and New Jersey areas. I considered it one of the first orders of business to give Acree, a career government investigator, the kind of White House support he needed to clean up these pockets of corruption. Aggressive action to eradicate favoritism at the Internal Revenue Service and to prosecute violators would show the public, Congress, and Republican appointees that the Nixon administration would not tolerate cheating or fixing of tax cases.

In July 1969, before my appointment had been announced, I conferred with Acree on a problem he had mentioned months earlier. After I officially joined the White House staff I again talked with him. On August 29, I had lunch at the White House with Acree and Internal Revenue Commissioner Randolph Thrower. We discussed the problem of obtaining adequate skilled personnel to probe the tax affairs of the major underworld bosses, the problems of political corruption in the past, the difficulty of policing tax agents in racket-ridden cities, and also an acceptable system to permit me to examine returns from time to time consistent with the president's request. I told them that I was aware of great abuses through earlier loose handling of access to tax returns, but I wanted authorization under a system that would protect us both. I was familiar with the laws restricting availability of tax returns and the fact that a government official who permitted unauthorized access to federal tax returns was in violation of the law.

On September 18, 1969, Commissioner Thrower sent me a memorandum pertaining to my "inspection of tax returns and related files."

"I have been thinking about ways that we can meet those situations in which you may want to inspect tax returns or other Internal Revenue Service files when at the same time carrying out our responsibilities under the disclosure statutes," Thrower wrote, calling attention to the rules governing disclosure and the penalty provisions of the law. He suggested a written memorandum stating which returns for which years were required, and added: "Naturally, we will infer in every case that the request is either at the direction of, or in the interest of, the president." He attached a suggested form for me to file with each request.

I made no requests for tax returns in 1969 and had only two occasions to request tax information. One of these requests involved United States Circuit Judge Clement Haynsworth's handling of tax deductions on the home he had given to Furman University. Although I went over the details with Judge Haynsworth, I also made inquiries at the Internal Revenue Service to ascertain whether the information Judge Haynsworth had given me was correct as to fact and to law. In replying to requests of reporters for full explanations of the facts and the law, I talked with Commissioner Thrower, Assistant Commissioner Don Bacon, and General Counsel Martin Worthy, as well as others. And, just to check against the possibility that I was getting a bureaucratic line from the top officials at the IRS, I called an old friend, Maurice Stark, an able tax lawyer in Fort Dodge, Iowa, who I knew would be objective and thoroughly honest in his assessment of such matters. Only after this many-sided examination was I willing to inform the press that there was no error of fact and no questionable interpretation of the law involved in the transfer of Haynsworth's house or the tax deductions he had taken in making the gift to Furman University.

As a result of the controversy over Judge Haynsworth's outside business interests while on the federal bench, I received a flood of mail complaining of corruption and payoffs to federal judges and charging conflicts of interest in the manner in which they assigned bankruptcy cases to law firms in which relatives were partners. I also received a great number of complaints about the financial irregularities of many congressmen and senators who were critical of Haynsworth's outside business interests and voted against him. Most of them, anonymous telephone calls or anonymous letters, were not worth pursuing.

Requesting the tax returns of a senator or congressman would be asking for trouble unless I had incontrovertible evidence that he was taking graft and failing to report the income, and that the IRS was not following through in a proper manner. Such a laydown hand would be almost impossible, so I chose to err on the side of not asking for federal tax returns of any elected officials. However, it did seem that a complaint by a sitting federal judge that two other federal judges were taking payoffs in connection with their duties on the federal court was substantial enough to follow through. And when the protesting judge claimed that "favoritism" toward the judiciary by IRS officials was the only reason the judges had been getting by with infractions of the law for so long, I felt a personal look at their tax returns was justified.

Specific complaints also charged that two judges were involved in improper real estate transactions with lawyers who appeared in their courts, that three judges were running bankruptcy rackets out of their courts, that a Southern political operator was operating as a bag man, and that payoffs were being channeled through a minor city official in northern Ohio whose name came to me in a newspaper clipping with some rather specific allegations. One of the judges had paid no federal or state taxes in the eight-year period just prior to his appointment to the federal bench, and he was reported to be operating a tax-fix ring out of his federal court.

These were the nine cases for which I had obtained federal tax returns. All of my investigations were the result of letters, visits, or telephone calls from persons outside of the White House political structure. No one in the White House except my two secretaries was aware that I had requested the returns. They did not see them. I examined them personally, kept them in a locked safe in my office, and took care never to have them on my desk when visitors were in the room. I returned them to the IRS without showing them to another individual. No information was leaked from the returns, nor were there any leaks revealing that I had the returns. There were news stories on only two tax matters that involved information I received from the Internal Revenue Service at the request of others in the White House.*

Because of newspaper reports that West Virginia Governor Arch Moore had some unspecified tax problem, Harry Flemming, special assistant to the president for personnel matters, asked me to check with the IRS to determine whether it would be wise for the president to appoint Moore to a federal advisory commission post. I received a memorandum, not Moore's tax return, from the IRS on March 25 and told Harry Flemming I did not believe that

---

* The president, as head of the federal government, can lawfully designate a subordinate to have access to tax returns. It is improper to use this authority for political purposes or for blackmail. It would be a violation of the law for anyone to disclose this tax information to persons outside of government or to persons in government who have no official reason for having such access.

the appointment should be made until the tax matter was cleared up. The memorandum I wrote to the president on the status of the case included this note: "The Tax Division examination of this matter indicates that it is serious. It is being assigned to a senior tax lawyer with instructions to handle it in a normal manner." Before and after I sent the memorandum to President Nixon through Haldeman and discussed it with Harry Flemming, there were numerous leaks on the Arch Moore tax matter. However, I discussed the matter with no one but Flemming, who, as a White House personnel official, had to find out whether a potential appointee had tax problems. Afterwards I acknowledged to reporters only that I had made an inquiry on published reports in connection with a possible appointment to an advisory commission.

The other problem was more serious, for it was a substantive leak concerning the tax affairs of a brother of Alabama Governor George Wallace, and whoever was responsible was guilty of a law violation. Bob Haldeman called me in late February or early March to request that I obtain information on Gerald Wallace's tax problem for the president. I requested Gerald Wallace's returns for a period of three years, but the IRS informed me that they were being worked on in the field and asked whether a memorandum on the status of the investigation would be sufficient. On March 21, I received a brief one-page status report on the general allegation with no proof and no assessment of its seriousness.

Murray Chotiner, also a special counsel, called me requesting a copy of the Gerald Wallace tax information, stating that Haldeman had authorized him to "pick up a copy." I advised him that handling tax information was touchy business and refused to make it available to him except on written instructions from the president. He took this with good humor, but a little later I received a call from Haldeman suggesting that I should consider his (Haldeman's) call an authorization from the president for Chotiner to have the Gerald Wallace tax information. I explained to Haldeman the extreme sensitivity of information from tax returns and refused to turn over the information to Chotiner unless I received the authority in writing. Haldeman said I was being "stuffy" and "difficult to deal with," and hung up, with instructions to send a copy to him. I personally took the information to the Xerox machine, made a single copy, and sent it through Bob Haldeman to the president with a premonition that Chotiner would probably receive a copy.

In late March, a conversation with Senator Williams revealed what appeared to be unfair tactics in connection with the federal income tax liabilities of Bobby Baker and Don B. Reynolds, a Maryland insurance man who had been a key witness and informant in the initial exposure of Baker's illegal activities. At about the same time I had discussions with several newsmen and with Reynolds about allegations that IRS had displayed vindictiveness toward Reynolds while treating Baker lightly. One of the reports was that the IRS was about to settle Baker's tax liabilities for approximately seven cents on the dollar. At the same time, the squeeze was being put on Reynolds for $190,000 in delinquent taxes.

In an "eyes only" memorandum to the general counsel of the Internal Revenue Service I requested an investigation of these reports of "harassment" of Reynolds and "favoritism" toward Baker.

The $190,000 figure represents an IRS decision to make Reynolds responsible for payment of tax on large sums of money that went through his bank account but which he contends were in fact payments for Baker and other political figures.

The evidence demonstrates conclusively that in some cases Reynolds was a conduit for money to Baker and to some other political figures.

The testimony of Reynolds and also the documents establish that he was not in a position to command large payoffs in cash but was probably serving as a conduit for someone with political punch. If the money traced to and through the Reynolds bank account was in fact to be paid to Baker or others, it would seem that it would be unfair to claim tax deficiencies from Reynolds while permitting Baker to settle on some limited figure.

I am not familiar with the governing details on these transactions, but I am familiar with an attitude that prevailed in the IRS under the Johnson administration. This attitude amounted to an all-out effort to heap the biggest possible tax burden upon Reynolds, who had testified in a manner that linked Baker to Lyndon Johnson. At the same time, there was a concerted effort to kill Senate investigations of Baker and to stifle the prosecutors who were working on the Baker investigation in the Justice Department.

I only want to be sure that those handling this matter now are not following along on the same pattern and that there is some effort to measure the Reynolds case and the Baker case by the same standards."

I have no doubt that Mr. Reynolds has considerable income tax deficiency, but the decisions of the present should not be simply a continuation of certain harassment that followed his cooperation in exposing Baker.

At about this time, Murray Chotiner dropped by the office with a list of people who he said had been making political contributions to the Democrats and were believed to be illegally dipping into business expenses to reimburse themselves, in addition to miscellaneous other kinds of skullduggery. "Haldeman said he would like to have them investigated by Internal Revenue and that you were the man to do the job," Chotiner said. Wary of Chotiner's political sophistry and of Haldeman's devious *modus operandi* (designed to hide his involvement if anything went wrong) I said that it was dangerous but that if Haldeman wanted it done Haldeman knew how to get in touch with me. Chotiner, a likable scoundrel, pushed no further and said he would have Haldeman call, which he did a short time later. Uneasy about the Gerald Wallace information and the "leak" of information on Governor Arch Moore, I asked Haldeman whether the investigation of Democratic contributions was something the president wanted. I do not remember whether his reply was a direct answer or one of his haughty quips that when he called it was always for the president.

On March 31, 1970, I forwarded that list to the commissioner of internal revenue with a note: "I'm attaching a list of individuals who I am informed have been involved in a number of financial transactions that raise some serious questions about the manner in which they have been reporting their income."

"There is a great interest here in seeing that at least a preliminary study is made of their returns in recent years to determine if they have been filing and reporting properly," I wrote, making the most limited request I could. If there was some obvious deficiency in the manner the returns had been filed, or if no returns had been filed, the Internal Revenue Service could make its own judgments. I intended my note as little more than the request any taxpayer is entitled to make to determine whether another taxpayer has filed returns or whether Internal Revenue agents have found any deficiency in the returns. I had used this avenue often during my years as a newspaper reporter in seeking to learn whether a taxpayer had filed or was delinquent in his filing. Senator Williams had piloted that provision into the law in the wake of the Truman tax scandals to rip open the curtain of secrecy used to protect tax fixers and cheaters.

On April 2, I went to breakfast with a group of Washington reporters. In the course of answering their questions, I was asked if in my investigations of government corruption I had access to federal tax returns. I acknowledged that I did, and that although I had used it infrequently I considered it an essential tool if I was to perform effectively as the president's ombudsman.

There were only two or three questions on the subject, and I answered them frankly. Had I looked at any newsmen's returns? I said I hadn't for, being a former newsman, I knew they didn't make enough money to cheat on taxes.

Whose returns had I examined? I said I was barred by law from discussing names or contents of any returns.

Could I get anybody's return? I pondered that for a moment and said that I supposed I could get any return if I had a proper reason for it.

Most of the reporters I knew in Washington would have understood that any law enforcement or tax official in state, county, and federal government may obtain access to federal tax returns upon a proper written request. It should have been no surprise that a special counsel to the president, with ombudsman functions, would need access to tax returns and tax information from time to time to check on appointees or on allegations of governmental corruption. But a couple of reporters in the group were naïvely amazed or simply seeking a reason to criticize. I saw only two stories on my access to returns immediately following the breakfast, but one of these was a cry of alarm that a political appointee had access to sacrosanct tax returns. I was viewed with alarm as a White House "political operator" and "a political hatchetman for Nixon." I was surprised and furious at the misinterpretation of my motives and the misstatements of fact indicating that I was rampaging through the tax files of senators, congressmen and governors in search of political blackmail. (It was amusing in a way because Ehrlichman and Haldeman, too, regarded me as a "hatchetman," but they raged because I endangered goals they had outlined for the Nixon administration.) I felt a factual public statement would calm the storm if it was explained that I'd had access to only nine returns and that there were no senators, congressmen or governors—in fact, no elected officials—involved.

Both Ehrlichman and Haldeman criticised me for creating the problem "by telling the newsmen that you had access to tax returns." "You shouldn't even have had breakfast with them," Haldeman said. He reminded me of his earlier directive that I was not to talk to the press. I had protested the lack of reality in that directive because of my long association with the press and the fact that some of my best tips on potential problems in government came from investigative reporters.

Our conversation on the subject had ended in a stalemate, and since I had protested and he had not repeated his order I considered that it was not in effect until it had been discussed further. For several days afterward I had tried vainly to reach him for another confrontation on the benefits of open government versus the closed White House he was running.

When the heat was on about the tax return issue, I tried daily to get the opportunity to explain publicly. I asked Haldeman. I asked Ehrlichman. Neither returned my calls, so I asked White House Press Secretary Ron Ziegler. Ziegler, of course, had to take it up with Haldeman, and when he came back he said Haldeman had told him the president did not want me to make a public statement and that "it would all blow over in a few days." It was impossible to determine whether or not it was indeed the president's wish that I not explain what was clearly explainable.

Although boxed in by Ehlichman, Haldeman, Ziegler, and my lack of access to the president, I was patient because I would soon be free of shackles of the White House.

Taking advantage of the fact that White House spokesmen were silent, Democratic Chairman Lawrence F. O'Brien made the absurd charge that the president did not have the legal power to authorize a lawyer on the White House staff to have access to federal income tax returns. I knew it was a political shot, and Larry O'Brien knew it, because I was aware of what the situation had been during the Kennedy administration, when he was a member of the Cabinet. But with a straight face, Democratic Chairman O'Brien did his political duty and cited the legal opinions of three Democratic "experts." His stable of experts were Mortimer Caplan, commissioner of internal revenue in the Kennedy administration; Sheldon Cohen, commissioner of internal revenue in the Johnson administration; and Mitchell Rogovin, chief counsel for the Internal Revenue Service and assistant attorney general in charge of the Tax Division in the Johnson administration. All were experts in the tax field and expert Democratic political lawyers, and all knew of the sloppy and undisciplined handling of federal tax returns under both the Kennedy and Johnson administrations. Moreover, all had at least some inkling of my knowledge of such practices and of their own vulnerability.

I was in Iowa on the day Larry O'Brien's blast hit the newspapers, and within a short time I received a telephone call from Murray Chotiner. He said he was calling at the request of President Nixon to determine how I had been given my authority to examine tax returns. "Was it oral, or was there something in writing?" Chotiner asked in an even, soothing tone which I immediately recognized as portending an effort to toss me overboard if they found me defenseless. I paused a moment to word a careful response, and then answered:

"The president should remember it very clearly, for we went over it in our July meeting and touched on it in several other meetings. It came up indirectly in one meeting in the Oval Office when Senator John Williams and Peter Flanigan were present."

"Do you have anything in writing?" Chotiner persisted. "What do you have?"

"I'm not completely sure that it is in any one document," I replied. "But there is sufficient proof in a dozen places in the files to fully corroborate the fact that I wasn't off on my own." I suggested that if President Nixon, Ehrlichman, and Haldeman had any problems recollecting the circumstances under which I was given the authority, they should let me know. "I'm sure I can scrounge around and find a few things to jog their memories," I said. Chotiner thanked me for my cooperation and said he hoped I didn't think he or anyone else questioned the fact that I had been given the authority. "I was just asked by the president to find out what the facts are," he said. "You have them to the best of my ability at this time," I replied. "If there is any problem, I'm sure I can be of more help when I am able to get to my files in the office." Before I hung up, I asked Chotiner to try to use his influence with President Nixon to make a public explanation or let me make one. "I've handled this tax information in a completely proper manner, and I can explain it publicly with no fear of any problems," I said.

That was April 11, and Chotiner had already "leaked" to columnist Jack Anderson a memorandum on Gerald Wallace's tax problems that was to stir new storms when it appeared in the newspapers on April 13, 1970. When I saw Anderson's column that morning I knew that someone in the highest levels of the White House had leaked a copy of the memorandum I had sent to President Nixon through Haldeman. From comments made by Haldeman several months earlier, I knew that Chotiner had some kind of arrangement to make inside information available to Anderson. And I recalled that Haldeman had first asked me to give a copy of the Wallace tax memorandum to Chotiner, which I had refused to do. Unless there was a leak at the Treasury Department or the Internal Revenue Service, there was only one place Jack Anderson could have obtained the information. One copy had gone to the president through Haldeman, and in some manner Chotiner had obtained a copy.

When my secretary told me Commissioner Randolph Thrower was on the line, I knew why he was calling. I assured him that I had not broken faith with him, that I was aware that it was a serious violation of the law for a government official to disclose such confidential information from tax returns outside of proper channels, and that I was in no way responsible for Anderson's having the material. When he asked me if I had any idea how it could have occurred, I said that since I hadn't showed the information to anyone or discussed it with anyone but Haldeman, the leak had to be "at the highest levels of the White House" or through the Internal Revenue Service.

I told him about the one copy I sent through Haldeman to the president and said I believed there was a strong chance it had dribbled away from either Haldeman or Ehrlichman. I explained why I suspected Chotiner was the actual conduit. (K. Martin Worthy, the general counsel for the IRS, talked to me that day, or within a few days, and we reviewed the details of how I had handled the Gerald Wallace tax information.)

For a public official to reveal such information to a newsman was a serious violation of the law for the public official, but not for the newsman or for the newspaper which printed the information. I had long been aware of this, and I thought that any public official who engaged in such unlawful conduct was a damned fool.

Thrower indicated that either he or Worthy was going to talk to Haldeman and Ehrlichman later in the day about the seriousness of such leaks. Late in the afternoon, I received a call informing me that "Mr. Ehrlichman would like to have you come to his office in the West Wing." I welcomed the opportunity to confront Ehrlichman face to face on this problem and several others, for I had been trying unsuccessfully to reach him or Haldeman for more than a week. They simply did not return my calls because they knew I wanted to raise issues in a half-dozen areas where I was prodding them to take corrective action on festering problems. I expected to meet Ehrlichman alone. I was confident I could defend my actions in any matter he might wish to discuss, and at the same time I rejoiced that within a few weeks I would be free from his benighted domination. But when I walked into Ehrlichman's large second-floor office and saw the icy smile of Bob Haldeman and the sickly, uncomfortable grin of Ron Ziegler, I knew this was a special kind of party, rigged three to one against me, and probably being recorded.

They managed awkward amenities about not seeing me for some time, and I retorted that it was not my fault, because I had been trying to reach them with little success. After routine comments about how busy they had been, Ehrlichman attacked:

"Why did you give Jack Anderson that Gerald Wallace tax information?" "Don't you know that's a law violation?"

I responded that because I *did* know it was a law violation I had been damned certain *not* to give it to Jack Anderson or anyone else except one who was properly authorized to receive such information.

He changed to a bland tone in an effort to coax an admission from me. "You know how it was leaked, don't you?"

I replied that I believed I knew how it had been leaked and who had leaked it, and I tossed Murray Chotiner's name up as my Number One suspect. Although Ehrlichman obviously was trying to set me up as a fall guy, he was obtusely unaware of where his questions were leading me.

Then he snapped, "Why did you give that information to Chotiner? He's not supposed to have it."

"I didn't give it to Chotiner," I said, "but I have a pretty good idea of who did, and I think Bob might have the answer to that one. I made one copy and it was sent to the president through Haldeman's office."

When Haldeman denied that he had given a copy to Chotiner, and joined in a rapid-fire assault, I flared up. I accused them of attempting a frame-up, told them that I hadn't been born yesterday and could recognize when I was being set up as a fall guy, and asked if they had bugged the room as part of their dirty scheme. They responded angrily that I had caused the whole tax problem for the president by meeting with the two groups of Washington reporters two weeks earlier "in violation of a direct order" from Haldeman. I thundered that I had simply told the truth about my access to tax returns and that a full explanation would have cleared up the problem at the outset if they hadn't muzzled me. The argument was so furious and noisy, with Haldeman snarling and Ehrlichman injecting other issues, that it disintegrated into sheer bedlam. Ziegler, who took no part after a few feeble early efforts, fidgeted uneasily and then literally darted from the room.

After I had thoroughly destroyed their little ambush and any hidden recordings that might have been part of their plan, we settled down to a reasonably low-keyed but cool conversation about why I had not been permitted to see the president as much as I needed to keep this kind of problem from arising. I suggested they tell the president that I could give a full public explanation of the whole tax controversy, and added that if they couldn't convey the message I would be happy to. In the event that the president did not authorize me to make a public statement, I suggested that some Republican senator or congressman could still the complaints with a speech on the floor. Unless they did it within a few days, I warned, I would take the initiative myself. I would ask Senator Williams to explain why my access to tax returns was legal and proper and to make it clear that I had not abused my authority.

Early next morning I dictated a memorandum to H. R. Haldeman: "I think it is important that I see the president as soon as possible with regard to details of the problem on the tax returns. A brief meeting now so all lines are clear can save untold problems for everyone later."

The next day, on April 15, I addressed a memorandum directly to the president on "the urgent need for a continued access to federal tax returns."

It is vital that there be a public presidential statement, verbal or written, reaffirming the right of access to tax information by the White House for the following reasons:

1. To examine the qualifications of potential appointees as well as of persons holding office.

2. To make inquiries into allegations of corruption and mismanagement by government officials and others where there is a federal jurisdiction.

3. To make inquiries to assure the integrity and fairness of the federal tax collecting system itself."

Past access to federal tax returns has been under proper authority, on a sharply limited number of tax matters, and the information has been kept confidential as required by law.

In brief, there has been no abuse by me of the authority to obtain tax information. Each request has been in writing on a form approved by Commissioner Thrower and under a system he established and he approved. Each request has been for the purpose of obtaining information on the integrity of an administration appointee, or for the purpose of following up allegations of corruption or mismanagement in government. Up to the present time there has been no request for the tax returns of United States senators or United States representatives. This has represented the ultimate in restraint, for there are a number of cases in which inquiry was probably merited but was delayed because of the sensitivity of making requests for such tax information.

I explained the "fine line between this restraint and negligence in not taking proper steps to obtain information." I also said: "I have been concerned that my lack of inquiry in some instances might be interpreted as negligence in not following through on evidence of financial irregularities." I went into detail on specific cases.

Since the memorandum had to go through Haldeman's office, I had no assurance that President Nixon would ever see it. There was no response to it, and I talked to Senator Williams that day to explain my frustration.

Commissioner Thrower issued a public statement defending the legality of my right to examine returns. He also said: "I have seen no suggestion that any tax return information supplied Mr. Mollenhoff was not within the course of his official duties or has been abused. Tax return information has been supplied in response to seven requests involving nine individuals. None of these is an elected public official."

On April 16, Senator Williams rose on the Senate floor to explain that my authority to examine tax returns was certainly more restrictive than in earlier administrations, and he mentioned specific White House aides in the Kennedy and Johnson administrations who had had access to tax returns without the formality of asking for them in writing. He defended the legality of my right to returns, pointing out that I had had access to only nine returns in ten months, and challenged any senator to step forward with evidence of impropriety. None came forward, and Senator Williams cited the case in which I had asked for the tax returns of a federal judge who had not paid state or federal taxes for eight years prior to the time he was appointed to the federal bench. "Just before being confirmed, apparently thinking he was going to get the appointment, he filed belated returns for all those years; and in a matter of months he was nominated and confirmed, and he is serving today," Senator Williams said. "The only way the president can now get rid of him would be to ask him for his resignation unless we in the Senate say that we will back him in removing this particular judge. Why should he [Mollenhoff] not investigate such a charge?"

The lengthy and detailed speech by Senator Williams ended the political sniping about my access to tax returns, but unfortunately the newsmen most eager to harpoon me when they believed I might be acting improperly did not even bother to write a few paragraphs on Senator Williams' speech. However, in time I came to regard even the unfair criticism I received as valuable. In preparing myself to meet inaccurate and unjust assaults, I became even more restrained in exercising my authority in the tax matter and thus less vulnerable to pressures that always exist when one has to define the thin line between legal and proper actions or illegality and impropriety.

*Chapter Fourteen*

# SPACE CONTRACT FAVORITISM

MY GREATEST disillusionment at the White House began when an irregular award of a fifty-million-dollar space contract was made to General Electric Company under conditions suggesting favoritism and when the reactions by top White House personnel to my prodding led me to suspect a political deal. Had I not already decided to resign as special counsel, my frustration with the lack of probity in that contract award for the Application Technology Satellite (ATS), an orbiting space laboratory, would have convinced me to get out.

Representative Clark MacGregor, Minnesota Republican, called on April 8, 1970, to say that Senator Hugh Scott of Pennsylvania had just announced on the floor of the Senate that NASA had awarded the ATS contract to General Electric. MacGregor wanted to warn the president that this award had many of the earmarks of the TFX scandal, which had been a nasty blot on the Kennedy and Johnson administrations. Later, Representative Rogers Morton, Maryland Republican, calling on behalf of his constituent Fairchild-Hiller (which had been competing with GE for the contract), also mentioned the similarity to Defense Secretary McNamara's TFX fiasco.

Representative MacGregor had been friendly to the White House, and there was no doubt in my mind that he was genuinely concerned about the possible scandal arising from the ATS award as well as about equitable treatment for a constituent—the Honeywell Company of Minneapolis, a subcontractor on the Fairchild-Hiller proposal. Likewise, Representative Morton was upset about Fairchild-Hiller's being treated unfairly. However, as Republican national chairman, he was equally concerned about the damage such a scandal could do to the Nixon administration. Neither MacGregor nor Morton asked special treatment for Fairchild-Hiller. They simply wanted the president to get the facts. That they called me was indicative of an intolerable communications problem, when even favored Republicans could not get through the Berlin Wall. Both MacGregor and Morton stressed that they were relying on Fairchild-

Hiller representatives for the chronology of events leading to the award of the contract to General Electric. Of greatest concern to them was the fact that Hugh Scott, minority leader of the Senate, had made that announcement shortly before he voted to support the president's controversial Supreme Court nominee G. Harold Carswell.

The irregularity of the award was clear from my first inquiries at the National Aeronautics and Space Administration (NASA). Dr. Thomas Paine, administrator of NASA and an employee of General Electric for nineteen years before joining NASA, had made the decision, according to NASA Counsel Spencer Beresford. Reports indicated Paine planned to return to General Electric, and he later did. Dr. Paine's previous connection with General Electric constituted a potential conflict of interest comparable to that of former Deputy Secretary of Defense Roswell Gilpatric in the TFX fighter contract.

In initial proposals, in December 1969, Fairchild-Hiller had the best design and the best price. Subsequently, General Electric designs took on Fairchild-Hiller features, suggesting a possible "technological transfusion." General Electric had been given a full week longer than Fairchild-Hiller to submit its final bid and proposal.

Within a few hours, NASA sources confirmed the basic facts to me, giving no rational explanation for the decision to favor General Electric. I concluded that MacGregor and Morton had not overstated the problem, and in the late afternoon I sent a memorandum to President Nixon setting out what appeared to be the ingredients of a major scandal. I expected to receive a call from Bob Haldeman later that evening or early next morning suggesting a meeting with the president, since top Republicans had initiated the complaint. Whether Haldeman gave my memorandum, or merely a Haldeman version, to the president I have no way of knowing, but it was three days before the first response came from Haldeman's office. The matter had been turned over to Peter Flanigan, who had been involved at an earlier stage. Larry Higby, assistant to Haldeman, told me: "Murray Chotiner and Pete Flanigan have the details on this. Please be in touch with them directly." This was hardly reassuring, since Flanigan had been involved in problems of his own regarding the *Sansinena* tanker affair only a few weeks earlier and had demonstrated a remarkable lack of sensitivity on questions of conflicts of interest. I made several unsuccessful attempts to get in touch with him, his special province being big business, the regulatory agencies, and big-money policy matters at the Treasury Department.

Initially, I had felt that the interest of Republican Chairman Morton and Republican Congressman MacGregor might balance any political interest of Senator Scott and provide an incentive to probe the conditions of the award to General Electric. However, it became apparent that Flanigan, Haldeman, and Ehrlichman were not interested in learning that the facts showed irregularities in the handling of the contract, but were only intent on defending the selection of General Electric. Throughout the inquiry they justified the award with distorted information and illogical arguments to me, to representatives of Fairchild-Hiller, and in correspondence with the congressmen. I had no way of checking Haldeman's assurances that the president was informed of the facts and knew of the great concern of Representatives Morton and MacGregor. Haldeman rejected my requests to explain the matter personally to President Nixon, although this was precisely the type of situation in which it had been agreed I should have direct access. Keenly aware that I had made life uncomfortable for a number of the president's advisers on several projects, I was determined to give exceptional care to drafting memorandums from the outset. Pointing out potential illegalities, improprieties, and examples of political favoritism was treacherous in the top ranks of a White House where political pragmatism was so highly valued. I knew that I must be precise and accurate.

Hugh Scott's announcement from the Senate floor made it impossible to delay the official announcement by NASA until certain charges could be examined. Dr. Paine could not be reached. However, Spencer Beresford verified the basic facts I had received from Congressman MacGregor. He admitted that in the initial proposals Fairchild-Hiller had the best design as well as the best price. He was apologetic about the decision being made in favor of General Electric but said that the fifty-million-dollar contract had been awarded by Dr. Paine. He pointed out that Dr. Paine had left General Electric more than two years earlier, assured me that Dr. Paine did not intend to return to General Electric, and said that it probably was not "a true conflict of interest." The NASA general counsel also verified that, in a series of proposals submitted by the two contractors, General Electric's design took on many of the characteristics of the original Fairchild-Hiller proposal. As a result of Fairchild-Hiller complaints, NASA technicians had challenged General Electric. General Electric's explanation that they got their ideas from aviation and space journals and had not engaged in "industrial piracy" was ridiculed by Fairchild-Hiller officials.

Beresford explained that in February 1970 both firms had submitted final bids. By this time the designs were rated as essentially equal, but the Fairchild-Hiller proposal was approximately one million dollars less—about 2 percent lower. At this point, Dr. Paine decided on a "stretch-out" of the program because of NASA budget changes. This resulted in a resubmission of bids in late February. General Electric was able to offer a program about $500,000 lower than its competitor. On that basis, Beresford said, Dr. Paine had made the final decision to award the communications satellite contract to GE. However, Fairchild-Hiller had charged that this was an unrealistic figure because it was based on the possibility of GE building a new plant in a low-labor-cost area. I asked Beresford about the charge that the lower figures were a result of this unusual cost manipulation. He conceded that Fairchild-Hiller had "every reason to feel hurt" but said he would assure them the decision had been made in good faith and that they would be considered most seriously for later NASA contracts. Though expressed in good bureaucratese, this was a thinly veiled threat that those who challenged decisions would not be considered in future contract awards.

In my detailed memorandum to President Nixon, I suggested that NASA should be particularly careful in preparing papers to justify this contract. I stressed that it had been an error-filled memorandum of justification on the seven-billion-dollar TFX contract that made it impossible for Defense Secretary McNamara to defend that monumental bungle. I warned that should the General Accounting Office investigate the award to General Electric it would be difficult to justify. "I suggest that Dr. Paine should be forced to defend it and that it be kept far removed from the White House," I wrote to President Nixon.

William Timmons, special assistant to the president for congressional liaison, called to say that the two Maryland congressmen, Rogers Morton and Glenn Beall, had complained to him about the NASA decision and had warned him the circumstances were questionable. I urged him to have them contact me with any information they felt might be helpful.

I also received a call from Stanley Blair, administrative aide to Vice President Spiro Agnew, requesting that I make an effort to see William Emerson, a public relations man for Fairchild-Hiller. Next day I met for more than an hour with Emerson and with several other Fairchild-Hiller officials. John F. Dealy, vice president and general counsel, and Bill Emerson carried the major part of the discussion. Dr. Coleman Raphael, then vice president of Fairchild-Hiller and general manager of its space and electronics systems division in Germantown, Maryland, accompanied them, and Irving Singer, program director for the ATS, dealt with technical aspects.

They spelled out in detail the irregular manner in which General Electric had been granted an extension of the deadline in the last go-round of the bidding. On February 2, Dr. Paine had ordered both contractors to submit revised proposals reflecting the cost impact of an extended program by February 27. No technical revisions were to be made at this time and there was to be no new technical evaluation. As the deadline approached, Fairchild-Hiller asked for an extension and the request was rejected. NASA officials explained that General Electric had made a similar inquiry and that no extensions were to be allowed. Working around the clock, Fairchild-Hiller officials met that late February deadline. Only after making their own submission did Fairchild-Hiller officials discover that General Electric had not submitted its proposal in time and would in fact be late by a week. Fairchild-Hiller officials immediately protested this special treatment for GE and at the same time requested that the Fairchild-Hiller cost figures be kept confidential until General Electric had submitted its bid. Previous experience indicated that a "leak of significant cost information to General Electric" was possible. Irvin Singer provided a detailed memorandum on the "technical transfusion" that had occurred early in the competition with General Electric. An additional memorandum provided me with more insight into attitudes at NASA that had resulted in a predisposition to award the contract to General Electric and a general assumption in the space industry that the contract would go to General Electric regardless of the merits of GE's proposal.

"In the face of this climate, Fairchild-Hiller decided that the only way to win the competition was to be clearly superior technically and lower in cost," John Dealy said. "Fairchild-Hiller believes that it has accomplished both of these objectives, but that the conduct of the evaluation has eroded the evidence of Fairchild's technical superiority and created a spurious and unfair representation of the program costs." The arguments and documentation convinced me that Fairchild-Hiller had a good case. In addition, Beresford and Paine had made admissions substantially supporting Fairchild-Hiller. I was convinced it would be an injustice if the contract were permitted to go to General Electric.

I was informed that throughout the procurement Senator Scott of Pennsylvania had worked aggressively in GE's behalf, even attempting to get the White House to intervene in GE's favor. This was particularly pertinent, since Senator Scott's office had been advised of GE's selection before NASA made an official announcement. In fact, Scott's office had publicly disclosed the award to GE even before the White House had been informed of it, a Fairchild-Hiller source revealed. "Moreover, Senator Scott publicly took credit for intervening personally with NASA to get the award for GE," Fairchild-Hiller officials said in a memorandum filed with me on April 16. "It is suggested that this type of congressional influence in behalf of industrial giants effectively destroys the best advantages of the competitive procurement process."

In discussing the political circumstances surrounding the ATS award to General Electric with Representatives Rogers Morton and Glenn Beall, I suggested that if Senator Scott had obtained information ahead of time it was not so much the fault of Senator Scott as it was the fault of the agency for giving it to him. I pointed out that Senator Scott could be expected to take certain steps on behalf of a constituent but that the responsibility for a fair decision was still on the shoulders of Dr. Paine.

Representative Morton declared that the facts he had accumulated indicated that Paine had been unfair to Fairchild-Hiller and said he intended to notify him that he felt the firm had been abused. Morton felt that if he, as Republican National Chairman, made a public demand for Paine's resignation, it might be interpreted as a major break with the White House; Morton wanted "a solution, not a bigger political problem."

I shared their concern over the contract award and had explored the points raised by Fairchild-Hiller officials deeply enough to know that they were not frivolous. I suggested that it would be proper to request an investigation by the General Accounting Office (GAO). I thought Morton and Beall should keep their major focus on NASA and Dr. Paine, and I told them to alert me if they found any indications of a White House impediment to a solution.

The GAO investigation was launched in mid-April as a result of joint requests from Fairchild-Hiller and Congressmen Morton and MacGregor. It moved forward slowly and quietly through May and June, simultaneously with a Senate investigation by Chairman John McClellan's Permanent Investigations Subcommittee. I learned from friends on the Senate committee staff that they regarded the ATS award to General Electric as completely irregular. "A little TFX contract," one Senate staff member quipped caustically.

On April 17, Representative Morton wired me at the White House that Dr. Paine had created a critical situation by cutting off funds for Fairchild-Hiller as of the previous day. Funds to General Electric were being continued through July 31. The least the White House could do was to direct NASA to accord the same treatment to Fairchild-Hiller and continue funding until the GAO report was completed. I told Peter Flanigan that I regarded the cutoff as a gross injustice and said that there was no way the White House could justify permitting Dr. Paine to have any role at all in the contract now. The administration could expect to be sharply criticized if Paine were permitted to go ahead with it. Flanigan said that he believed "Dr. Paine is an honest man" and that he had been informed that Dr. Paine was only one member of a committee making the decision. I suggested he should recheck his facts. Although I was aware that Flanigan had had some role in the affair prior to the awarding of the contract and was probably a conduit of information to Senator Scott, I assumed it was a proper role and that Dr. Paine was the man with the responsibility for any impropriety or illegality.

On April 20, Dr. Paine had told Edward Uhl, president of Fairchild-Hiller, that he could not discuss the contract because it was under GAO investigation. It was an obvious stall, but Flanigan would not force action even though Dealy and other Fairchild officials were outraged that contract records were not available to them. They demanded access to the records under the Freedom of Information Act. Representative Gilbert Gude, of Maryland's eighth district, protested to the White House the unfairness of NASA's refusal to make documents available to Fairchild-Hiller or to the GAO. Gude wrote President Nixon:

> I cannot understand the denial of documents requested of NASA by the Fairchild-Hiller Corporation that bear on the latter's protest of the award of the ATS (F&G) to the General Electric Corporation.
> If there is to be public confidence that the tax dollars are wisely spent by federal agencies, every effort must be made to insure against any irregularities in procurement. I personally believe Fairchild-Hiller is entitled to the information requested under the Freedom of Information Act. If there has been no wrongdoing no harm can come from making the information available. If there has been wrongdoing there is an opportunity to set the matter straight before performance on the contract commences. It would appear that NASA's refusal of the requested documentation is an effort to frustrate a full airing of the situation.

On Thursday, April 23, I again tried to warn the president that this wrong decision could result in serious problems for the administration, hoping he would needle Flanigan into action. "As it stands now, the responsibility for this decision is on Dr. Thomas O. Paine," I wrote, spelling out four points of concern and adding that some NASA officials agreed there was reason for Fairchild-Hiller to be critical of the whole procedure. I called attention to congressional complaints and warned that others would certainly join in the criticism if the situation was not corrected quickly. McClellan's investigators and the GAO were already looking into the contract. I recommended "immediate cancellation of the contract award and a direction to Dr. Paine to stand aside and permit some subordinate to make the award." The plea was ignored.

On April 21, 1970, Dealy wrote to GAO requesting access to certain NASA documentation required to support Fairchild's contentions. This letter was forwarded to NASA on April 22. On May 1, Dealy wrote to Dr. Paine again demanding the pertinent documents: "The requested documents are the proper subject of disclosures under the circumstances of this request as well as the pertinent provisions of the Freedom of Information Act and the implementing of NASA regulations." He asked for General Electric's cost proposals and the Source Evaluation Board reports, information on the briefing of February 4, and the final Source Evaluation Board report prepared for the April 7, 1970, briefing of Dr. Paine, just prior to the decision. Dealy's letter said that it was urgent that he receive either the information or a reply indicating that he could not have it. He included his office telephone number for an immediate call. There was no reply and no acknowledgement of this letter by Dr. Paine.

On May 12, Dealy wrote a second letter to Dr. Paine stating that he was "deeply disturbed, both as a lawyer and as a businessman, that our requests for documentation have gone unanswered through today's date—a period of approximately twenty days." "I cannot understand the reluctance of your organization to even reply to our request," he wrote. He noted that prior to the contract decision, "Fairchild executives sought a meeting with you in order to discuss the serious irregularities and inadequate source selection procedures we believe have occurred in the program." The young lawyer said it was "inconceivable" that NASA would not release the appropriate documents for review. He pointed out that the information had been paid for with U.S. government funds and that there could be no justifiable claim that any information was "proprietary." But, Dealy said, he was willing to let NASA hold out any pages they felt might be confidential. He also said Fairchild-Hiller was willing to pay any "reasonable fee" for the documents. He argued the law, and then added that "fundamental fairness" required that the information be made available.

A day later, Dealy received a telephone call from NASA informing him that the documents he requested would not be made available. The next day, May 14, Representative Beall rose on the House floor to denounce NASA's action "I think it is a shocking thing when a public agency throws a cloak of secrecy over its own record, which, under a pre-existing law, not only a protestor but any member of the public is guaranteed the right to examine," Beall said. "In order to maintain the integrity of the appeal procedure in the award of federal contracts, I would hope that NASA would see fit to make information available and cooperate in any way to assure a fair hearing on a matter involving commitment of $50 million of taxpayer's money." He told the House that only full disclosure of records and a full investigation would protect Dr. Paine from a charge of "favoritism" as a former long-time employee of General Electric. Senator Margaret Chase Smith (R., Maine) and Senator Clinton Anderson (D., N. Mex.) expressed their concern in letters to NASA.

On May 19, I sent a memorandum to President Nixon warning of developments that "make it necessary to direct some swift action" on the ATS award: "Within the next twenty-four hours a top official of Fairchild-Hiller will conduct a press conference before more than one hundred space writers in Las Vegas dealing with the ATS. He will probably outline the general pattern of 'irregularities' in the negotiation but will stress NASA's refusal to make records available to Fairchild-Hiller." I suggested that all records be made available:

If he [Dr. Paine] cannot defend this with the full record on the table, then he should not have entered into the contract to start with. If it is his mistake, it is not something that should be permitted to fester until it becomes a blot on the record of the Nixon administration.

My investigation indicates to me that NASA officials were careless, if not irresponsible, in connection with some aspects of this award. It would appear to me that some NASA officials are trying to make up a record after the fact to justify the contract. This is precarious at best and can destroy the credibility of those officials involved, as well as setting the stage for the same kind of prolonged dispute that involved the TFX.

Efforts to see the president were useless, with Haldeman telling me that it should be put in a memorandum or should be taken up with Peter Flanigan. I had no faith in Peter Flanigan's ability to get to the bottom of such matters, and little in his attitude showed any real interest in anything other than a cover-up.

On May 25, 1970, I fired off another memorandum to President Nixon:

This refusal to produce records for Fairchild-Hiller carries with it the possibility of serious political embarrassment for the administration. In the first place, it gives the impression that Dr. Paine, a former official of General Electric, has done something questionable in connection with the award of the ATS contract and is now continuing to cover it up.

It is fine for Dr. Paine to try to place emphasis on the fact that he requested the GAO investigation, but it will be apparent to anyone who takes two looks at this case that Fairchild-Hiller officials were going to demand it if he did not and did, in fact, take their complaints to Senator John McClellan, Congressman Clark MacGregor, Congressman Rogers Morton, and Congressman Glenn Beall.

While conceding that Dr. Paine had probably done nothing against the law, I noted:

His problem is compounded by a simple chronology that indicates that nearly every decision NASA made gave some slight favored position to General Electric. If this contract award to General Electric is a good one, it should be able to stand scrutiny by the public in all details. If there is any uneasiness about the wisdom of this contract, then it should probably be cancelled.

It appears to me that this hiding of the record would not be justifiable under any circumstances. In this case it is seen as a cover-up by such supporters of the administration as Rogers Morton, Clark MacGregor, and Glenn Beall.

I met with Peter Flanigan and put a series of questions to him. Anxious to back Dr. Paine, he declared that my basic thesis was wrong. He again denied that Dr. Paine had made the decision to give the contract to General Electric and seemed to believe that that was the only issue. He obviously had accepted Dr. Paine's statement that he had not been involved in the award.

"My information is that Dr. Paine was involved in the decision," I said. "Can you give me his statement in writing that he was not?"

Flanigan then hedged away from his position and said that Dr. Paine was "only one of three making the decision and he voted last."

"You had better recheck your facts," I snapped. "My information simply does not square with yours, and I'm not going to tell you where it doesn't square. I'm going back and recheck my facts, and I suggest you do the same." I warned that a GAO investigation was in progress, that a Senate or House investigation was likely, and that there would be a demand for accountability.

I then sent a memorandum to John Ehrlichman telling him that a memorandum I had received from Peter Flanigan "raises a lot more questions than it answers."

This is now a problem at the NASA level, and as far as I know there is no White House responsibility for this highly questionable award procedure. The White House could be criticized if it does anything that seems to approve a procedure under which Dr. Paine is permitted to sit as investigator, advocate, judge, and jury in a controversy involving a decision in which he took part.

There are many critics in Congress who would be willing to try to make this case a political issue. Almost all of the facts are in the public domain, and I know that Fairchild-Hiller plans to make an issue of this if it is not resolved.

I sent a copy of this memo to the president through Haldeman.

Unbeknownst to me, that same day Ehrlichman sent a letter to Representative Morton and to others in essence repeating Paine's inaccurate version of the ATS dispute, which apparently had been forwarded to him through Flanigan. The letter demonstrated Ehrlichman's ignorance of the basic controversy:

A charge has been made that in awarding the disputed NASA contract to GE, GE was granted an extension of time while Fairchild-Hiller was denied extension. The facts are as follows: When submissions were called for, a cutoff date by which submission had to be in was stipulated. It was further stipulated that if an extension beyond this date was requested, such request would have to be in several weeks prior to the submission date. GE made such a request in advance of that earlier date and a delay of a week was granted.

After the earlier date by which requests for extension had to be made had passed, Fairchild-Hiller telephoned to the contract officer at NASA and asked for a delay of several days. The contract officer denied this request.

From the above, it is clear that NASA followed the book with regard to this aspect of the contract.

A charge has been made that Dr. Paine was not totally objective in his selection of GE in that he had previously been employed by this firm. This award was made by a three-man board of which Dr. Paine was a member. The vote was unanimous and Dr. Paine voted last. Recognizing the considerable conflict surrounding this award, Dr. Paine warned everyone that the award should be conducted in a way that would stand vigorous investigation. Immediately after the contract was awarded, Dr. Paine asked GAO to conduct an investigation, which is currently underway.

In spite of my memorandum to him, Ehrlichman was either ignoring the facts in his possession or deliberately trying to mislead Morton. When Morton sent the letter to Dealy, the young lawyer was outraged by the misstatements about the award procedures and Dr. Paine's role. NASA's own submissions to GAO contradicted Ehrlichman. He was also contradicted by the statement Beresford, NASA's counsel, gave to Edward Uhl, president of Fairchild-Hiller, and Beresford's explanation to me. Whether sloppy or deliberately deceptive, Ehrlichman's explanation to Representative Morton was as incompetent a blunder as any made in connection with the ATS contract.

Through May and June, Haldeman and Ehrlichman rejected my requests to see President Nixon. My appeals to reason and fair play were disregarded. I had made my decision to leave the White House in March, but even after my resignation was announced in May, I continued to seek an objective review of the contract. At the White House, officials seemed uninterested in establishing the truth and unconcerned about the McClellan investigation and the GAO review.

I stopped just short of a sharp confrontation because I knew Haldeman and Ehrlichman would like nothing better than an excuse for "leaking" a story that I had been fired. When I was unhampered by their interference I would be able to follow through on the irregularities in the ATS contract. Then there would be a fighting chance at success.

## Chapter Fifteen

# OMBUDSMAN WITH PERSPECTIVE

LEAVING THE Nixon White House in July 1970 presented many more problems than had joining it a year earlier. Although frustrated in a number of efforts to get swift corrective action, I was not thoroughly disillusioned with President Nixon or with the idea that an effective White House ombudsman could keep an administration out of trouble.

My extreme irritation with President Nixon's two top aides—Haldeman and Ehrlichman—was tempered by my belief that they were not intentionally bad men, but were ignorant about government operations and about the proper use of the power they held. Because they were admirers of former President Lyndon Johnson and former Texas Governor John Connally, they refused to recognize that ruthless wheeling-dealing politics were in the long run self-defeating. Because Haldeman had so successfully barred my access to the president, my talks with Mr. Nixon had been limited to five conversations in the first eight months, and on each occasion Haldeman, Ehrlichman or Peter Flanigan had been present for all but a few minutes.

Who could determine whether President Nixon had granted them the immense power they wielded or whether they had only assumed it and were brandishing it with an utter disregard for legality, propriety, and common sense? I felt an obligation to state bluntly that the obsessive secrecy and the attempt to exercise absolute control over the thoughts and actions of everyone on the White House staff were not only wrong but doomed to failure even while they were being imposed. But, because Ehrlichman or Haldeman were always present, I expressed this view in an uncharacteristically subtle manner. It was impossible to tell the president that Haldeman and Ehrlichman were the major problem in his relationship with Congress, with Cabinet officers, with the Republican National Committee, and with the White House staff as well. It was particularly difficult to speak with him when I did not know whether he had originated or specifically endorsed their actions in a number of controversial areas.

For example, I did not know whether President Nixon had initiated the efforts to free Jimmy Hoffa or whether he was aware of my efforts to thwart the many moves to grant Hoffa executive clemency as a political deal. Although I had documented the irregularities and improprieties in the Austin Geriatric Center matter, I had no way of determining how many of the details had penetrated the Oval Office before the president directed Bryce Harlow to "put it back on the track." Nor did I know whether Mr. Nixon was directly and personally involved in the Chotiner-managed political deal on the ATS contract awarded to General Electric by NASA. And I could get no straight answer from Haldeman on the leak of the federal tax investigation information about Gerald Wallace. These were typical of the unresolved questions I faced in dozens of minor instances where the rights or wrongs were relatively easy to establish and document but the problems were permitted to fester because Haldeman and Ehrlichman did not recognize the need for action.

When the Gerald Wallace tax information was leaked I tried unsuccessfully to see the president several times. I supplemented verbal and written requests through Haldeman by a direct call to Presidential Appointments Secretary Dwight Chapin in an effort to go around Haldeman. As had previously happened, Chapin called Haldeman to relay my request and Haldeman sent his errand boy, Lawrence Higby, to inquire why I wanted to see the president. Obviously Haldeman wished to prevent my asking the president directly how Chotiner obtained the copy of the tax information which was leaked to columnist Jack Anderson in violation of the federal income tax laws. I was boxed in, and knew it. Commissioner of Internal Revenue Randolph Thrower and General Counsel Martin Worthy knew of my strong suspicions that the memorandum to the president had been given to Chotiner.

With my specific responsibility on that matter in the hands of the proper authorities, I gave my attention to seeking a graceful exit from my frustrating experience as White House ombudsman. Although many of my experiences were disillusioning, 8o percent of the problems I had to deal with were effectively corrected. For example, the mere fact that questions had been raised in a systematic and informed manner had forced cancellation of a decision which would have given the S.S. *Sansinena* five million dollars in "windfall profits" and the Nixon Administration had avoided a disastrous congressional inquiry. By contrast, the refusal to reinstate A. Ernest Fitzgerald as a cost analyst for the Air Force was certain to be a continuing problem for the Defense Department and the White House. Despite persistent prodding and prying, I had been unable to determine why the Oval Office attitude had suddenly changed after Haldeman had told me that Fitzgerald would be rehired by the Bureau of the Budget.

Although I had occasionally been tempted to resign and lash out at Haldeman and Ehrlichman, I knew my criticism must be balanced with the understanding that some aspects of these problems existed in every White House. Never having been on the inside before, I did not feel I could speak or write in comparative terms. The scandals of prior administrations tempered my attitude, and I was not yet ready to conclude that this was "the worst administration in history" or even the most arrogant or most secretive.

As I was preparing to leave I blamed myself in part for my inability to persuade Haldeman and Ehrlichman as well as President Nixon of the advantages of good government and open government. Perhaps I had been too adamant in my view that Hoffa should not be released from prison. Perhaps I could have been more sympathetic to the personal and political problem Attorney General John Mitchell and Deputy Attorney General Richard Kleindienst had in firing their friend, General Carl Turner, from his post as chief United States marshal. Perhaps I had encroached on too many areas in too many departments and had tried to impose an unreasonably high political standard in too brief a time. Quite possibly I could have been more successful with Mr. Nixon and his top aides if I had used unrestrained flattery, as Dr. Kissinger and Dr. Moynihan had done.

Haldeman and Ehrlichman, insecure because of their lack of knowledge, sought to impose a complete gag on all White House personnel and demanded the agreement of cabinet officers and agency heads to extend this control across the whole government. Their faith in the doctrine of "executive privilege" to protect White House personnel from any accountability to Congress remained intact. Though no law and no court decision backed the doctrine of absolute confidentiality, Ehrlichman was confident the president could stall by refusing to comply with subpoenas and using executive branch programs to reward or punish members of congressional committees. Ehrlichman espoused the belief that essentially any committee of the Senate or House could be controlled through enforcement of Republican unanimity combined with a divide-and-conquer manipulation of Democratic members who wanted something from the White House. Although a belief in the pliable venality of a large number of the senators and congressmen probably had some basis, a constant danger in such tactics was the risk of congressional resentment of this ruthless interference with House and Senate independence. Approaching a fiercely honest and independent senator or congressman could quickly undo months of alliances plotted on a dishonest basis.

Periodic warnings about these dangers and even the unsuccessful experience of trying to manipulate the Senate in the Haynsworth and Carswell nominations had not taught Ehrlichman and Haldeman the needed lesson, because they personally had escaped unscathed. In assessing the losing fight of Judge Carswell to the United States Supreme Court, they believed Judge Carswell had become such a symbol of Mr. Nixon's dedication to the South that he would be a sure winner in the general election and President Nixon had personally encouraged him to resign from the Appeals Court to become a candidate for the Republican nomination to the U.S. Senate from Florida.

On May 1, I had put the final touches to my agreement with Kenneth MacDonald, executive editor of the *Des Moines Register,* to become Washington Bureau chief. My decision was irrevocable and was made without consultation with President Nixon or anyone in the White House, but I wanted my resignation accomplished on an amicable basis. Without offering an explanation to Haldeman, I spent a full month seeking a conference with the president in order to tell him that I was resigning as special counsel. I finally had to tell Haldeman the reason for my request, and an appointment was made for the afternoon of May 25.

Meeting with Haldeman at noon, shortly before I met with the president, I had made it clear that my decision to resign was irrevocable. I did not expect him to request that I remain, and he did not. He displayed certain qualms about what I might say or write when I was out of government and implied that I should not divulge information obtained as a result of my government service. He voiced Ehrlichman's reminder that, as a lawyer for the president, I was bound by the lawyer-client relationship against disclosing information I had received while on the White House staff, as well as by "executive privilege." Haldeman and Ehrlichman smugly believed that I was effectively muzzled by their restrictions against revealing my actions and conversations as a member of the White House staff. In fact, I could not think of one single fact I had received that was covered by the lawyer-client relationship, and I knew that no one, President Nixon, Haldeman, or Ehrlichman, could impose "executive privilege" on me if I wished to testify. Certainly there were many things I would not discuss or write about which involved national security or specific requirements of confidentiality under the law. But I did not bother to correct Haldeman's general contention that I was barred from commenting or writing about my time in the White House. Nor did I take the trouble to inform him that I would disregard executive confidentiality on any matters involving crime or impropriety. Haldeman's relief that I was leaving the White House staff was apparent. My prying and prodding had been a constant challenge to his dictatorial control, which was accepted by the young, inexperienced staff members without complaint.

At 3:00 P.M. I met with President Nixon in his office in the Executive Office Building to discuss the contents of an exchange of letters to mark my resignation. At that point there was no purpose in airing my grievances, and I was anxious to be free of White House ties so that I could view the experience from an outsider's perspective. I felt that the president had enough problems at that time in bringing the Vietnam War to a close against a background of criticism of partisan critics who had supported involvement in the war when President Kennedy had sent in the first advisers and when President Johnson and Defense Secretary McNamara had made the decision to put more than 500,000 Americans in Southeast Asia. I had a good deal of sympathy for Mr. Nixon in what I believed was a conscientious effort to extricate the nation from a war which was the responsibility of the Kennedy and Johnson administrations. I believed the carping criticism from some important segments of the press was unreasonable, that it was simply a result of bias against Mr. Nixon because he was a Republican and a conservative. Compromises he made to get programs adopted by the Congress were pictured as dishonest and seamy political manipulation, when similar actions by President Kennedy or President Johnson would have been applauded as "political pragmatism" or "the politics of the possible."

At that time, the press and television had little interest in the details of the political manipulation of NASA, the irregularities of the Austin Geriatric Center, or dozens of cases of perjury, subornation of perjury, and destruction of records permeating many government decisions. That would have required detailed examination of government records and an intelligent analysis of government operations. It was much easier to report the sensational rantings of critics of the Vietnam War.

It was easy to be sympathetic to President Nixon because of the unreasonableness of some of his critics. It was easy to forgive him for some of his blundering, bad decisions. There was no real proof that President Nixon had direct responsibility for the political deals and irregularities in government decisions. There were no indications that Haldeman and Ehrlichman acted out of a desire for personal gain. They were only power-seeking novices, jealously guarding the Oval Office from the truth about their authoritarian practices.

Prior to my meeting with President Nixon, I had tried to analyze the strength and weaknesses of my charter as special ombudsman and to draw up a detailed blueprint outlining the functions of a future ombudsman. Since Haldeman was present, I was barred from telling the president bluntly that Haldeman's iron control of his time represented a sharp restriction on his information and facts. This was a time not for blunt talk but for constructive conversation.

During our conversation, the president said he was "sorry" to have me leave the White House staff, apologized because he had been so busy with foreign relations problems that he had been unable to see me more often, and commented that he believed my work had been effective in alerting the administration to potential scandals. I discussed the need to continue the post of White House ombudsman and suggested that it could be more effective if the office were specified by law to provide independence and access to the president. With Haldeman present, it was difficult to do more than hint at the extent to which my lack of access to the president and lack of clear independent statutory authority to investigate and to make public reports had reduced my effectiveness. I suggested that Senator John J. Williams, Delaware Republican, who was retiring at the end of 1970, would make an excellent ombudsman. The president expressed his high regard for Senator Williams, with whom he had served in the Senate, and professed interest in my opinions on a permanent presidential ombudsman.

I made notes on his suggestions on the letters to be exchanged upon the announcement of my resignation, and said I was eager to have it made quickly before a possible leak could cause speculation that might reflect unfavorably on me or the president. I later suggested letters to be edited by Haldeman, the president, and Special Assistant James Keogh, the president's chief speechwriter.

At 6:10 P.M. on May 26, in Haldeman's office, I gave final approval of the texts of my letter of resignation and of Mr. Nixon's response. From this vantage point, four years later, my letter to President Nixon, while accurate, appears a little naïve and rather amusing. Lacking proof of Mr. Nixon's complicity in the corruption and mismanagement I had observed, I accepted at face value his assurances to the contrary.

THE WHITE HOUSE
Washington
May 28, 1970

Dear Mr. President:

It is with some regret that I submit my resignation at this time, effective in mid-July. I had hoped that it might be possible to continue for many months more before making a decision relative to my own long-time future plans. However, the retirement of Richard L. Wilson as bureau chief for the *Des Moines Register* and *Tribune* makes it necessary for me to take the step now. This last chance to return to the *Des Moines Register* and *Tribune* as chief of the Washington Bureau is too good an opportunity to let slip by despite the great experience it has been to work as "presidential ombudsman" in your administration.

Your instructions were to investigate any indications of wrongdoing or questionable ethical conduct, and to call them the way that I saw them without regard for partisan politics or ideology. You have never changed those instructions. As your special counsel, it has been my responsibility to keep informed on problems dealing with mismanagement or corruption in government, to report to you and other administration officials on the facts where it appeared that illegality, impropriety, or just plain careless practices might be interfering with the honest efficient operations of government. Your personal responses to my reports on these problems in government operations have always been in the highest tradition.

My decision to resign is in no manner an opposition to your policies, and it is certainly not an indication of any dissatisfaction with our personal relationship. There have been no restraints placed upon my work except to be accurate, fair, and firm as I had been in the past in dealing with Democratic and Republican administrations.

It has not been possible to spotlight or to solve all of the problems of government operations, but I believe that much has been accomplished in avoiding the factual errors and the delays in problem solving that have plagued so many of our past administrations. I hope that a good government tone has been set, and that we have made some headway in proving that aggressive good government can be good politics. I also hope that we have been able to right a few wrongs, and to help a few average citizens fight their way through the bureaucratic jungle that our big government has become. I have become more appreciative of the problems of making big government operate effectively, and sympathetic with the problems our presidents face in making the federal government move. The experience has dramatized how important it is that the president have the "right to know" what is taking place at all levels of government, and the right to expect that his will is carried out.

Sincerely,<br>Clark R. Mollenhoff<br>Special Council to the President

The President
The White House
Washington, D.C.

THE WHITE HOUSE
Washington
May 29, 1970

Dear Clark:

It is with regret that I accept your resignation as Special Counsel effective as of mid-July. The work you have done has alerted us to many potential problem areas and has been important in demonstrating that good government can be good politics for any administration.

I hope that seeing this administration from the inside has given you some greater perspective on the problems of government and the difficulties we face in trying to solve them. I am sure that this experience has demonstrated to you that we are trying to come to grips with the great issues of our times in an honest and forthright manner.

As you return to the press corps, I am sure that you will call them as you see them with regard to the Nixon administration. And while I recognize that our relationship cannot be the same as it was when you were in the government, I know that it will always be one of friendship and respect.

With warm personal regards,

Sincerely,<br>[Signed RN]

Honorable Clark Mollenhoff
The White House
Washington, D.C.

White House Press Secretary Ronald Ziegler announced my resignation from the Western White House at San Clemente on May 30, 1970. The letters were quoted liberally in the newspaper on Sunday, June 1, 1970, along with some unattributed quotations about my frustrations in the White House job.

On June 2, Senator Williams went on the floor of the Senate to express his "regret at news of [my] resignation" as one "who has had a great respect both for Mr. Mollenhoff and the job he has been doing at the White House."

"I hope whoever takes his place will exercise the same hard rules of fairness and the same discretion in the administration of this office as have been laid down by Mr. Mollenhoff," Senator Williams said. "I have particular reference to his insistence that anyone holding this position who examines tax returns must file a written request stating why those tax returns are requested. By placing all requests for tax returns in writing, as has been done under Mr. Mollenhoff's administration of this office, it would be a matter of record, and if in later years it were shown that there had been abuse of this power, both the public and the Congress could ascertain the extent and who was responsible for such abuse."

Senator Carl Curtis (R., Nebr.) joined with Senator Williams in characterizing my service as displaying "honor, integrity, and great ability." Senator Williams noted that there were some who "would be glad Mr. Mollenhoff was leaving this position because they feared him."

"I have known Clark Mollenhoff for a number of years," Senator Williams said. "I will state that no man in America need have any fear of Mr. Mollenhoff unless—I emphasize, unless—he had heretofore done—or had contemplated doing—something that was unethical as far as government is concerned. In that instance Clark Mollenhoff would be a most dangerous man to have in public office because he would expose such activities, regardless of who or what political party was involved. Yes, Clark Mollenhoff would not be feared by those who are honest and trying to do a good job in government, but he would be feared by those who had done or who planned to do wrong." John Williams was my friend, and we had been through many trials together since 1950, in Democratic and Republican administrations. Although I knew he was prejudiced in my favor, I appreciated his comments in the *Congressional Record,* particularly in view of our different viewpoints on the nomination of Judge Clement Haynsworth to the Supreme Court.

On June 3, the *Washington Star* carried an unattributed story that "some top officials in the Nixon administration are waiting with a mixture of amusement and apprehension for Clark R. Mollenhoff to drop the first shoe. The suspicion in some high quarters is that Mollenhoff will move quickly to establish his credentials as an unbiased observer by dropping some kind of bomb on the administration he served for eleven months."

Despite my irritation with Haldeman and Ehrlichman and my general disappointment with President Nixon's actions in many areas, I was convinced that I should be restrained and should allow time to temper my opinions and my criticisms of my former colleagues. A scorching series of exclusive articles on the "Berlin Wall" was very tempting, but I was determined not to use information I had received at the White House unless I could justify it as a constructive use of material to supplement issues largely in the public domain.

I spelled out my ideas on the ombudsman role in a memorandum to President Nixon, and also, in essentially the same language, in a series of speeches starting in early June and continuing until July 7—the last day I was special counsel. Expressing my ideas publicly, I hoped, would help assure that Haldeman and Ehrlichman would not bottle up my suggestions because they did not want an effective ombudsman.

In my memorandum to the president I noted that an ombudsman post could be created by the president within the White House or could be established by law independent of the White House. Essential to the proper functioning of this office were the following:

1. Cabinet rank, to assure the ombudsman's authority to obtain records, reports, and testimony.

2. A man of great experience, stature, and impeccable integrity.

3. Job tenure, to guarantee the ombudsman's complete independence.

4. Direct access to the president at all times.

5. Initially, a small staff of lawyers and accountants with years of experience on investigations of government operations.

6. Public reports made to the president and to the Senate and House on an annual or semi-annual basis, with provisions for special reports.

7. The job should be devoid of any partisan political authority or responsibility.

I advised the president that the key to the successful operation of any ombudsman structure was the man named to head the office. "This man must be a man of great experience in the investigation of government who is recognized by the public for his great stature and his impeccable integrity." I suggested in speeches and in another memorandum to the president that Senator John J. Williams "is the only man who comes to mind immediately as having the full credentials necessary to do this job."

His conduct as a member of the United States Senate over a period of twenty-four years is recognized by Democrats and Republicans, liberals and conservatives as having been in the highest tradition of public service.

I believe that the establishment of an ombudsman office headed by Senator John Williams would do more than any other single act to restore faith in the federal government. . . . John Williams and a small staff could break up the old bureaucratic patterns and restore integrity and fair play in many areas where it has been missing for years.

A few weeks after I left the White House staff, Special Assistant Patrick Buchanan confided that "the powers have decided" that the Nixon White House didn't need an ombudsman to keep them alert to potential scandals. "The powers [Haldeman and Ehrlichman] say John Williams would be worse than Clark Mollenhoff," Harry Dent advised me a few days later. Later I learned that Haldeman and Ehrlichman had turned most of the ombudsman duties, as they saw them, over to John W. Dean III, a young lawyer from the Justice Department who had been a protégé of Attorney General Mitchell. Haldeman had allocated a few of the ombudsman functions to Special Counsel Charles W. Colson. I did not believe that John Dean and Charles Colson represented the strength, the independence, or the integrity that Senator Williams would have brought to the job. Dean and Colson were intelligent enough, but both struck me as too smooth, too willing to make compromises, and much too eager to please Haldeman, who did not know (or want to know) the difference between right and wrong, legality and illegality.

# Book 2

## Chapter Sixteen

# AN UNEASY TRANSITION

WHEN I WALKED OUT of my job as special counsel to the president in July 1970, I recognized my earlier naïveté in assessing the influence one man could have in persuading a president and his top political advisers of the long-range political advantages of open and honest government. I had expected that my access to the president and influence on him would be contingent only upon the merits of each case, the accuracy of the facts presented, and the logic and responsibility of the presentation. I had pledged to myself that I would be meticulous in my research on facts, responsible and nonpartisan in my legal conclusions, and so restrained in my recommendations that they could be argued publicly at any point without fear of being branded partisan or ideological in motivation. I was determined to leave political compromises to professional politicians. I believed that an experienced politician such as I believed Richard Nixon to be would immediately see the wisdom of avoiding scandals before they reached epidemic proportions.

However, the mechanics of going through the presidential captors, Haldeman and Ehrlichman, for appointments meant that I had met with Mr. Nixon only five times in a ten-month period, and one of those meetings was an unscheduled request to see me from President Nixon because Senator John J. Williams of Delaware was in his office. In addition, my daily memorandums to the president were at the mercy of Haldeman and Ehrlichman. Though I was assured that they were delivered to the president, and instructions came back through Haldeman and Ehrlichman, rarely was there anything in writing to indicate that Mr. Nixon had received my reports and recommendations. In my infrequent meetings with the president, he occasionally made comments indicating that he had read my memorandums, but his questions suggested either that he had not read them or that he had failed to understand their significance. Short of a direct challenge to the President's credibility, there was no certain way to determine whether Mr. Nixon had in fact read the material I sent him or had merely been briefed by Haldeman or Ehrlichman.

From my standpoint, this was a most unsatisfactory way of handling the vital job of keeping the president informed of possible scandals. But Haldeman and Ehrlichman did not seem to understand that the secrecy they imposed was corruptive, or that political favoritism in contract awards, prosecution decisions, or personnel decisions was undesirable from the standpoint of propriety, of legality, and of practical politics as well. Anything the Kennedy or Johnson administrations "got by with" was justified in the Nixon Administration, as far as Haldeman or Ehrlichman were concerned. Because of their lack of experience in national politics they did not realize that corruption in a Democratic administration is likely to be overlooked by a Democratic-controlled Congress. They were heedless of the furor that Democratic committee chairmen and some segments of the press might raise if the same patterns of favoritism developed in a Nixon administration.

Haldeman and Ehrlichman regarded the Congress as a body of venal, vulnerable politicians willing, in most cases, to barter away their corrupt souls for a project in their state, a social invitation to the White House, a few words of praise from the president, or, in a few instances, to avoid investigation by the Internal Revenue Service or the Justice Department. "Most of them can be bought cheap," Ehrlichman commented as he developed plans to shut off a Senate Commerce Committee investigation of the *Sansinena* affair. One senior Democrat on the committee, he said, "owes us something" because of Justice Department leniency in an investigation of favoritism on a government contract. In that instance, it was wisely decided that cancellation of the Treasury Department concessions to the tanker firm was the best way to avoid a confrontation with Congress, but Ehrlichman contended that a senior Republican had a key Democrat "in his pocket" and could have blocked a subpoena for Special Assistant Peter Flanigan.

While there was some measure of truth in the Haldeman-Ehrlichman assessment of Congress, it did not follow that a majority of the members of the House or Senate were corrupt or corruptible. A great many were tainted to some degree from the years of fund-raising required to get elected, but it could also be said that some of the most dishonorable were the most independent and proud. The most corrupt tended to be the most dangerous to try to coerce with threats or hints of investigation or prosecution. These elected veterans of many congressional wars resented overbearing attempts by appointed White House subordinates to dictate actions they might well have taken if persuasive approaches had been used. In the end, corrupt members of the House and Senate could wield their power only in closed sessions or behind-the-scenes maneuvers. Time after time, I had seen a few senators or congressmen with a good cause triumph over the money and power of corrupters. To risk public debate against a few honest, able men was to risk political destruction. Rather than letting themselves be easily shoved around or bought, as Haldeman and Ehrlichman assumed they would, corrupt legislators often displayed their cunning by agreeing to suggestions while arranging for a colleague to create problems for a would-be oppressor. Also, it was not unusual for the most venal to move to the forefront in popular investigations of corruption in the executive branch, creating for themselves the image of active foes of dishonesty and frauds. Frequently, the biggest knaves in Congress would be among the sponsors of so-called reform legislation.

Haldeman and Ehrlichman made similar misjudgments about the ease with which reporters could be controlled or forced into line. While many would temporarily succumb in exchange for a few early tips on news stories or for White House invitations, resentment festered if they believed they were being used. Haldeman attempted to monitor press contacts with White House personnel by means of the same tight control he exerted over White House Press Secretary Ronald Ziegler's statements. His control was not complete, but it was probably more stringently exercised than in any prior administration.

Since White House reporters are in a highly competitive business, most of them found it necessary to keep peace with the press office in order to avoid being cut off completely from all but routine news releases. And even when some wrote critical stories about President Nixon, the Vietnam War, or general government problems, there seemed to me a studied effort on the part of the White House press corps regulars to avoid criticism of Haldeman, Ehrlichman, or Ziegler. I assumed that some reporters were unaware of the clever restraints Haldeman exerted, but in other cases I had to assume that there was full understanding of his control. A sharp word or memorandum from the despotic Haldeman was often sufficient warning to any White House official that a certain reporter was an "enemy" and therefore not to be given the courtesy of a call back.

During my months on the White House staff I developed many friendly contacts in the administration. The vast majority of the people I met feared and detested Haldeman and Ehrlichman and resented the tyrannical and unforgiving domination of their public and private lives. Many would return my calls after I left the White House, but I knew that others could not if word went out from Haldeman that I was now to be regarded as an "enemy." Although I had had many private conflicts with Haldeman and Ehrlichman during my months in the White House, I had tried to avoid letting my disagreements with them deteriorate into open hostility. In that case I would have been the loser, for they had President Nixon's ear and could have had me summarily fired without an official explanation. White House silence would have given credence to "leaked" smears which could have been distributed through unsuspecting columnists or political figures.

Some of my newspaper colleagues envied my situation, believing that I had the best of both worlds—inside knowledge of White House secrets and a string of high-level sources. It was hardly that simple. While I recognized certain advantages in having background knowledge of specific controversies and personal contacts with numerous high officials, I saw real problems in moving to the outside. Haldeman and Ehrlichman cautioned me against using information I had received as a government official to criticize the administration, claiming that any information I had received was subject to "executive privilege" and was in fact the property of President Nixon. Ehrlichman tossed in a warning that it would be a breach of legal ethics to disclose information I had received as a "White House lawyer." Although I mentally discounted their warnings, I reiterated our differences in interpreting "executive privilege." I expected them to favor me with a few "exclusive" crumbs, as a way of testing whether they could use me, but I knew how vindictively my news sources would be cut if anything I wrote was regarded as "disloyal" or threatening to their power in the White House.

The three blocks from the Executive Office Building to the *Des Moines*

*Register* and *Tribune* office in the National Press Building was a simple physical transition, but now it would be necessary to re-establish my credibility as an objective newsman while avoiding an overly critical posture. This would require time and patience, because I wanted to keep matters in perspective. This was complicated by a certain hostility from a few members of the Washington press corps who were so bitterly anti-Nixon they did not believe a person with honest motivation would go to work for him. Some reporters and editors even believed I was a part of the oppressive secrecy and vindictive policies of the Nixon White House. Had they bothered to read my speeches, it should have been clear to any knowledgeable reporter that I opposed those policies. To a small group of reporters and editors, nothing less than a journalistic bombshell proving their thesis that Richard Nixon was a war criminal would have convinced them of my independence of the White House.

I had to establish that I was neither too close to Nixon, as some of my poorly informed colleagues believed, nor as treacherous as Haldeman and Ehrlichman suspected when I proved I was not a team player by opposing their political deals on government contracts, pardons, and paroles. I knew that unless Haldeman changed the White House's information policies I would become a critic of the administration, but I wanted to avoid either making a complete break or assuming the role of political lapdog.

Some journalists, through the clever duplicity of playing to the presidential power structure, are consistently able to have access to every administration, be it Democratic or Republican. They do not seek out or expose corruption in any administration, but withdraw to the heights to ponder and evaluate political fights, feeling no personal responsibility to spotlight or eradicate wrongdoing. They treat as "exclusive" unattributable information from "reliable sources" as to what the president "is thinking" or what White House strategists "are planning." They are safe conduits of White House propaganda and, through a dignified and properly authoritative style, add to their own prestige as well as the mystique of the presidential decision-making process with relatively little effort. Some become little more than conveyor belts for the White House line. When others expose corruption and mismanagement, they minimize its importance or excuse it as no worse than what other administrations have done. By refusing to examine the facts about bribery, perjury, frauds, favoritism, or abuse of power, they are able to say with good conscience, "It is not as bad as the good-government zealots say it is."

When I left the White House in July 1970, I could have posed as a sympathetic defender of the Nixon administration's position and could have established a degree of credibility as one who had a real inside track on the president's thinking. It would have been a fraud.

I had discovered, as had others, that information circulated around the White House was only the Haldeman-Ehrlichman version of presidential planning which they wanted distributed in a manner that permitted flat denials if they were faced with bad political repercussions. The only exception was Dr. Henry Kissinger, who was a power to himself in the field of foreign affairs, plying President Nixon with a combination of flattery, control of information on the alternatives available to the president, and a baffling, seemingly erudite, spellbinding rhetoric. But even the temperamental Dr. Kissinger saw the expediency of reserving some of his flattery for Haldeman.

I had no desire to be another peddler of the Haldeman-Ehrlichman line or, for that matter, of the Kissinger-Nixon foreign policy line. Neither did I wish to use the freedom of the press to lash out with unrestrained and constant criticism of the president in a manner detrimental to his chances of running a successful administration. Although I was disappointed, I still believed that Richard Nixon might be a good president if he could re-establish good relations with the Senate and the House, with his own cabinet officers, and with those on the White House staff who had the kind of experience, judgment, and independence that might have been useful. Although it was recognized that Herb Klein was "communications director" in name only, I hoped President Nixon might consult his long-time friend and heed his advice.

I rejected the idea of launching my syndicated column with a sensationalized series based on information about government problems I had received as special counsel. In time I would be writing on some of the subjects I had dealt with in the White House, but for the present I decided on this simple rule: Subjects I had dealt with as special counsel would be off limits for my column until such time as they emerged through the normal channels of congressional investigation, investigations by the General Accounting Office, official reports, criminal prosecutions or civil litigation in the courts, or through the news stories of other reporters. With the exception of income tax information and some national defense matters, the information I had obtained was not confidential by law. But to avoid any appearance of a questionable disclosure, I preferred to be able to point to public records as the source of my information, at least until proper governmental authorities had been given a reasonable length of time in which to take corrective action. Application of these guidelines would enable me to deal with a wide range of administration actions involving evidence of mismanagement, possible conflicts of interest, or other misuse of governmental power within a six-month period.

The General Accounting Office and the Senate Permanent Investigating Subcommittee were investigating irregularities in the award of the ATS contract to General Electric, and I could comment on that controversy as soon as the reports were issued. Senator William Proxmire of Wisconsin was following through on an investigation of the firing of Air Force cost analyst A. Ernest Fitzgerald, who was contemplating a challenge before the Civil Service Commission. The Senate Permanent Investigating Subcommittee was keeping presure on the Army and the Justice Department to prosecute two former generals in connection with the Vietnam service club scandals.

In addition, President Nixon's much-heralded Family Assistance Plan (FAP) was in trouble in the Senate Finance Committee, where Senator John J. Williams revealed major flaws in the welfare plan, devised by White House Counselor Daniel Patrick Moynihan. Senator Williams and Senator Carl

Curtis, both conservative Republicans, declared it was excessively costly and would create an incentive for poor people to give up low-paying jobs to go on the welfare rolls—precisely the opposite of President Nixon's and Moynihan's claims. I had not dealt with Moynihan's plan while in the White House, but through my contacts with Dr. Arthur Burns and his assistant, Dr. Martin Anderson, I knew that well-informed people who had worked on its development believed it was false and deceptive. Dr. Moynihan had sold his welfare concept to President Nixon and House Ways and Means Committee Chairman Wilbur Mills (D., Ark.) on the basis of highly questionable statistics from an incomplete study in New Jersey. Reports in the White House criticized the highly articulate Dr. Moynihan for using political flim-flam and flattery to sell Mr. Nixon something he didn't fully understand.

The multi-billion-dollar financial problems of the Penn Central Railroad began to surface when its officials sought to use the influence of President Nixon's former law firm to assist them in obtaining a $200 million loan guarantee under the Defense Production Act. Three congressional committees and the Interstate Commerce Commission were interested in the fact that the law firm of Mudge, Rose, Guthrie, and Alexander, in which Attorney General John N. Mitchell and President Nixon had been partners, had been secretly hired in April 1970 by officials of Penn Central in a frantic effort to win administration approval for the loan guarantee. This was only one of many instances in which Nixon's former law firm had been hired by businesses endeavoring to obtain favored treatment from the White House, the Justice Department, or some other federal agency.

The rescue operation for Penn Central was put together in a May 28, 1970, White House meeting attended by Stuart T. Saunders, who at the time was chairman of the board of Penn Central; Treasury Secretary David Kennedy; Defense Secretary Melvin Laird; Attorney General John Mitchell; and Peter Flanigan, special assistant to President Nixon for financial and commercial matters. Wright Patman (D., Tex.), chairman of the House Banking and Currency Committee, and others in Congress called attention to the fact that of those who attended the meeting only Defense Secretary Laird could state he had no financial or personal interest in Penn Central's future. The others had the following interests:

Treasury Secretary Kennedy was a former chairman of the Continental Illinois National Bank and Trust Company of Chicago, a major Penn Central creditor and one of seventy-four banking institutions subject to a House Banking Committee subpoena.

Horace Flanigan, father of presidential aide Peter Flanigan, was a former director of Manufacturers Hanover Trust Company of New York. This firm was also a major Penn Central creditor and was listed as the holder of a major block of voting stock in the Penn Central holding company.

Attorney General Mitchell and President Nixon had been partners in Mudge, Rose, Guthrie, and Alexander, the firm that represented Penn Central in its financial negotiations.

Under criticism from Congress, the Nixon Administration withdrew its support for the loan guarantee after it became apparent that Penn Central did not intend to pledge all of its assets as collateral for the loan. I did not know whether President Nixon knew of the potential conflicts of interest in his former law firm's representation of Penn Central, but it was typical of the lack of sensitivity on the part of many high officials in his administration. There was trouble ahead, and I was glad I was on the outside as a member of the free and independent press again.

Free of the oppressive spirit of the Nixon White House, I had no desire to return to the misery of the Executive Office Building with its gold-carpeted splendor, its ornate fireplaces, and its ulcer-producing frustrations. I was sorry for the many able and decent people who felt compelled to remain there because of an unrealistic personal loyalty to President Nixon, a loyalty to the Republican Party, or political aspirations that seemed contingent upon living within the Haldeman-Ehrlichman system. They included men of political experience who had finally reached the White House pinnacle and did not want to abandon it as long as there was any hope that they could be of service. They also included a great many energetic and able young men in their twenties and early thirties who had vaulted to the top and would probably fade into obscurity if they displeased Haldeman or Ehrlichman.

*Chapter Seventeen*

# THE FINAL ACT OF
# THE GE-FAIRCHILD AFFAIR

ON JULY 28, 1970—only three weeks after I left the White House staff—Dr. Thomas O. Paine announced that he was resigning as head of the National Aeronautics and Space Administration to return to his long-time employer, the General Electric Company. By this time, the General Accounting Office had issued a scathing report on the irregularities in the ATS contract award, Senator John McClellan's Permanent Investigating Subcommittee had issued an equally stinging criticism of Paine's decision, and an official of Fairchild-Hiller had provided me with all of the information about their highly unsatisfactory dealings with Paine and White House aide Peter Flanigan. Virtually all the facts about the controversy were now in the public domain, and I felt free to deal with it in news stories and in my weekly "Watch on Washington" column.

In resigning, Dr. Paine said that the controversy over the communications satellite contract had absolutely nothing to do with his decision to leave government, though John Dealy had told me six weeks earlier that Dr. Paine had declared in the presence of several others that he had no intention of returning to General Electric. Despite the adverse GAO report, Dr. Paine reiterated that he could see nothing irregular in the manner in which the $50 million contract had been awarded. All of my memoranda pertaining to Dr. Paine's conflict of interest and the many irregularities of the award to GE were ignored as President Nixon expressed his "deep regret" at the resignation and said Paine had "earned a unique and permanent place of honor in the history of man's exploration" through his work in helping to put a man on the moon a year earlier.

By the time Dr. Paine resigned, the General Accounting Office had supported Fairchild-Hiller's complaint by finding that GE was permitted to submit its bid a week after the deadline. NASA had voided the contract in line with a GAO recommendation and was in the process of reassessing both proposals. Part of the reason for the sudden activity to correct the award, as I had advised nearly four months earlier, was discovery by Fairchild-Hiller's lawyers of John Ehrlichman's erroneous explanations of the role Dr. Paine had played.

On June 12, Representative Glenn Beall (R., Md.) had accompanied Dealy to a White House conference to personally determine the validity of the explanations he and Representative Rogers Morton had received in a letter from Ehrlichman. When Flanigan started to repeat Ehrlichman's explanation to Morton, Dealy pulled from his briefcase the NASA report to GAO which established the error in the explanation. Dealy also related conversations that disagreed with Dr. Paine's denial that he had taken part in the award as an individual. Still determined to justify the award to General Electric, Flanigan blandly explained that Dr. Paine had disclosed a GAO rule that permitted an exchange of information when two firms were close in competition. Dealy challenged this and enumerated other reasons for believing Dr. Paine or someone else had made an improper decision. Dealy and Beall felt the futility of any discussion with Flanigan. Was he accepting Dr. Paine's explanation to establish an excuse for his own actions, rather than making a serious attempt to explore the facts of the controversy?

After two months of pressure, Dr. Paine finally agreed to a meeting at NASA on June 19. In that one-hour presentation, stress was placed on the partiality shown General Electric, and Dr. Paine made little protest. Dealy then commented on Dr. Paine's prior relationship with GE, and said the unfairness of the procedures suggested a possible conflict of interest. It was at that time, that Dr. Paine insisted he had severed all ties with GE when he joined NASA in 1968 and had no intention of returning.

Following the early-afternoon meeting with Dr. Paine, the Fairchild-Hiller delegation then went to the General Accounting Office, where they met with Comptroller General Elmer Staats, Assistant Comptroller General Robert Keller, and other GAO officials. These discussions convinced them that GAO would carefully explore all aspects of the conflict and would base its decision on the facts.

Despite Senator Scott's announcement in April, the GAO investigation had blocked formal award of the contract by NASA. Nevertheless, on July 2, 1970, NASA informed the *Commerce Business Daily* that the ATS contract would go to General Electric. Ironically, that same day Comptroller General Staats made his report criticizing "irregularities and deficiencies" in the NASA contract procedures. GAO rejected Dr. Paine's defense of the General Electric award and disputed Dr. Paine's claim that a GAO ruling justified the use of different deadlines for the competing firms. "Our office has never approved any procedure whereby information which would give an unfair competitive advantage to any proposer would be disclosed during the negotiation process," Staats stated. "We do not read this regulation as authorizing such a procedure." The GAO directed "reconsideration" of the award, but to the embarrassment of Dr. Paine and NASA the *Commerce Business Daily* carried the following item a few days later: "For Phase D of the ATSF&G spacecraft. NASA/GSFA procurement office will contract with General Electric Co., Valley Forge." That blooper, a week after the GAO report, was corrected in the July 16 issue of the publication.

On July 9, Senator John McClellan in a Senate speech scored NASA for its unfair procedures. The Arkansas Democrat declared that in February NASA had secretly made a substantial adjustment to the Fairchild-Hiller proposal to reflect what it estimated would be a cost overrun. While NASA officials were arbitrarily boosting the cost figures of Fairchild-Hiller, they were secretly permitting General Electric to use a questionable device to cut costs, McClellan charged. "I believe that the proceedings of such source selection boards should be made fully available to all competitors after the contract decision has been made," he declared, critical of the months of record hiding by Dr. Paine. "There should be no secret decisions which are followed by inadequate and unsatisfactory explanations."

The game had suddenly become too hot for Dr. Paine to continue direct participation and he agreed to establish a blue ribbon seven-member committee to re-evaluate both submissions. He said it would be composed of men with no role in the initial evaluation. However, all were his subordinates, and Fairchild-Hiller officials observed that the actual selection was to be made by a three-man group of Dr. Paine's closest associates. At least one of them, Bernard Moritz, had been a defender of the initial award to General Electric.

Daniel J. Fink, vice president and general manager of General Electric, objected to the GAO report as being unfair to GE and NASA, and said it could "create an imbalance in favor of Fairchild-Hiller" on price and development information. Fink also objected to the airing of allegations that NASA had engaged in a "coaching" procedure to bring GE into a winning position. "The discussion is in the vein of suggesting that such a practice was indulged in, when in fact this was not done, and there is no evidence to sustain that allegation." Fink also declared that "the sole basis for your recommending reconsideration in this case was the procedural problem involving an extension of bid time resulting from the somewhat ambiguous instruction given to both parties by NASA and interpreted differently by the two bidders. Your other observations concerning a 'possible leak' and improper technical transfusion only serve to give an impression different from what your investigation actually established."

In his reply, GAO Comptroller-General Staats quoted from the report that dealt with the complaint of "impropriety" and "leaks" of information:

We agree that there is no evidence of a leak. On the other hand it cannot be conclusively stated that there was no leak. A situation was created where a leak which might have affected the results of competition was possible. And the danger of such a leak existed not only during the two- or three-day period referred to, but during the entire week that intervened between submission of the two proposals. . . . It must be recognized, however, that there is always a danger of premature disclosure of information during the course of a negotiated competitive procurement, and for this reason the concept of cutoff dates and the lateness were introduced into the negotiation process. In this case Goddard [Space Center] failed to follow proper procedures and thereby created a situation where premature disclosure of information in the Fairchild proposal was possible. The comments in our decision were directed at the agency [NASA] action. We did not then and do not now imply there were any improprieties on the part of GE.

Fairchild-Hiller officials knew it would be an uphill struggle to get a reversal from a three-man selection panel named by Dr. Paine, but they were encouraged by their initial contact with the man selected as chairman of the blue ribbon review committee—Bruce Lundin, director of NASA's Lewis Research Laboratory in Cleveland. "It was the first show from a NASA official of any real desire to get all the facts, and the assurance that this would be a fair evaluation," Dealy said later. "We were wary, but we were encouraged."

On July 27, 1970, General Electric made its presentation to the Lundin committee; the following day Dr. Raphael, Irvin Singer, and Dealy submitted Fairchild-Hiller's arguments in a ten-and-a-half-hour presentation. The irregularities apparent to GAO were obvious again, but now Dealy was dealing with Paine's subordinates. Even with confidence in Lundin, Dealy stressed the courage it would take for the board to overrule Paine. Lundin and others assured Dealy that the decision would be based on the facts, and at a break in the proceedings that day Fairchild-Hiller received an unexpected assist. It was announced that Dr. Paine was resigning from NASA, as of September 15, 1970, and would return to General Electric.

At a press conference on July 29, Dr. Paine told reporters that when he came to NASA he had severed all relations with General Electric and had no intention of returning, but that in recent weeks he had changed his mind. He said that he would not be involved in space activities for GE, that while at NASA he had never "cast a vote in favor or against GE," and that he had "rigorously excluded" himself from the ATS competition between General Electric and Fairchild-Hiller. This was certainly a rigorous distortion of the facts.

In his final statement to the Lundin committee, Dealy challenged Dr. Paine's contention that he had never made a decision for or against General Electric:

In press stories concerning Dr. Paine's recent news conference, he was quoted as saying that he had never been in a position during his tenure as administrator [of NASA] to cast a deciding vote for or against General Electric. On the contrary, Fairchild-Hiller was informed by high NASA officials within a week of the ATS selection that the ATS decision was made by Dr. Paine and in fact was made by him on price and general confidence in GE criteria.

In addition, the same NASA officials advised us that Dr. Paine had sometime previously reversed a [Goddard Space] Center's recommendation in awarding another contract to General Electric.

In substantiation of these points, Dealy submitted two memorandums written by Edward Uhl, president of Fairchild-Hiller, on April 8 and April 17, concerning these conversations with NASA officials.

On August 26, 1970, the Lundin committee filed a unanimous (and, at that time, secret) report recommending the award of the $50 million ATS contract to Fairchild-Hiller. The committee found "that Fairchild was superior in nearly all aspects of project organization and overall management. On the technical side, the PRC [Project Review Committee] considered Fairchild superior in the important areas of systems engineering and in several features of the subsystem design," the report said. Although there had been unjustified juggling of costs, the committee said it was impossible to determine whether the $1.3 million savings Fairchild claimed could have been realized. "A very real probability remains that some cost reduction could have been realized by Fairchild had more time been available."

While under serious challenge on this award and one to TRW, Inc., Dr. Paine on September 3 ordered a review of the NASA procurement system. Unwilling to admit his own errors, he suddenly decided there might be something gravely wrong with the system. In that atmosphere it would have been difficult for any NASA selection group to reject the unanimous decision of the Lundin review group. On September 5, 1970, at 6:00 P.M., the committee unanimously voted to reverse Dr. Paine and award the contract to Fairchild-Hiller. Dr. Paine's press release announcing the decision did little to change the fact that it was a direct reversal of a decision he had made in April and had stubbornly clung to, reinforced by Ehrlichman and Flanigan at the White House through May, June, July, and August.

Even at this stage, General Electric did not give up easily. Working with Senator Scott and his staff, they threatened to challenge the decision, thus blocking Fairchild-Hiller from moving ahead on the contract. If Republican complaints couldn't get action to resolve this matter, then I knew the man who could and would hurdle White House blockades if necessary—Senator William Proxmire. Proxmire had done a good job of pointing out big cost overruns on the C-5A military transport plane and had created a furor against the military-industrial complex. I did not agree with all of his attacks on the military-industrial complex, but I had no sympathy with manipulated bidding on government contracts. Copies of my newspaper stories on the ATS contract award interested Senator Proxmire, and he assigned an investigator to examine Dr. Paine's role.

Proxmire's tough questions, read into the *Congressional Record* on September 22, 1970, must have caused Dr. Paine to shudder. "To what extent do the giant aerospace contractors unduly influence the award of government contracts? Is there a conflict of interest when a high government official awards a contract to a firm where he was formerly employed or where he will be employed when his term of public service is over? Are middle-sized and small businesses discriminated against in government procurement matters?" Proxmire pointed out that such questions are raised year after year but that "nowhere have they been raised so sharply as in the $50 million communications satellite contract first awarded to General Electric and later rescinded and awarded to Fairchild-Hiller."

"An investigation by the General Accounting Office into the original award to GE revealed major irregularities—among them preferential treatment for GE at the expense of its rival bidder, Fairchild-Hiller," Proxmire said. "Perhaps the most disturbing fact in the case, however, was that the head of NASA, the agency which made the award, subsequently resigned from the big government position and went to work for GE as a vice president."

Rogers Morton, as national chairman for the Republican Party, though outraged, did not have the political punch to force the issue. Both GE officials and the White House were confident Morton would not embarrass the Nixon administration or anyone in the White House. However, they fully recognized that Senator Proxmire would quite happily embarrass the Nixon White House or Dr. Paine, even though the Nixon administration had inherited Paine from the Johnson administration. Proxmire pointed out that "in 1969, General Electric was NASA's fifth largest contractor, with over $150 million in awards —GE was also the Pentagon's second largest military contractor, with over $1.6 billion in awards." He noted that, by contrast, Fairchild-Hiller was NASA's fortieth-ranked contractor, with $6.9 million in awards, and ranked forty-third as a military contractor.

There were many inconsistencies in the record on the ATS contract, and the times were not such that there was much public sympathy for the industrial giants. This was particularly true of General Electric, for many of its highest officers had been convicted of criminal charges in connection with rigged bidding on government contracts.

Only a few days after the Proxmire investigation started, General Electric decided not to engage in any further challenge, and NASA formally made the award to Fairchild-Hiller. This success represented a giant step forward in challenging space and defense contracts, and the name of Fairchild-Hiller will go down as a giant killer. Upsetting such an award was unprecedented. (The unwritten rules for competing firms in government contracts are: (1) If you protest an award you won't get the contract, but will simply see the agency give it to a third party. (2) Bureaucrats at the agencies should involve top White House figures to gain political clout in support of wrong decisions or challenged procedures. It is difficult for politicians to reverse a case without seeming to reverse themselves.)

The episode was hardly a high mark for the Nixon administration, for their fumbling and ineptitude permitted Dr. Paine to ensnare a number of White House officials into acceptance of his dereliction. The warnings Clark MacGregor and Rogers Morton had given on April 8 fell on deaf ears in the small circle of government servants who were supposed to hear the warnings, understand them, and act on them.

The proof of the wisdom of awarding this government contract to the best-qualified low bidder, however, came four years later, when the Fairchild-constructed ATS communications satellite was launched into perfect orbit with a minimum use of fuel. Shortly after the May 30, 1974, launching of the ATS from Cape Canaveral, Florida, the nation's press reported on its spectacular technical performance and NASA had projected adequate station-keeping fuel on the satellite for seven years of useful operation—more than three times the two-year life called for in the contract.* In this instance, good government procedures were good for the advancement of science and also good for the taxpayers. It wasn't often that it turned out that way in the days when high cost overruns and low performance ratings seemed to be the norm.

But the public was generally unaware of the manner in which the Nixon administration had botched the initial award with conflicts of interest and irregularities, for there were only a few reporters who wrote about the McClellan committee investigation and the GAO report that had forced NASA to correct the errors and give the contract to Fairchild. It was the superficial treatment of such well-documented scandals by the press that led the Nixon White House to believe it would not be held accountable for either venality or blundering, even when it was caught red-handed.


*Chapter Eighteen*

# THEY NEVER LEARN


PRESIDENT NIXON and his top aides learned nothing from the major mistakes of their first eighteen months in office, mistakes caused by their own

---

* The success of Fairchild's ATS project was spotlighted in the National Space Club awards at the annual Goddard Memorial Dinner on April 11, 1975. Two awards were given on the ATS-6, which was characterized as "the world's most powerful communications satellite." One award, for the NASA-Fairchild team effort, was for "significant advance in space communications." The other related to the "excellent management [of the program] and subsequent excellent performance of the ATS-6."

It was noted that the ATS-6 signal could be received by ground station equipment costing less than $4,000, compared with the more than $400,000 minimum required for construction of elaborate antennas to receive from earlier communications satellites. In isolated and sparsely settled regions of the world it made posible high-quality educational and medical services and television for the price of a simple, low-cost ground station.

inexperience and ethical insensitivity. But they were able to make their game plan work because of the equally serious mistakes by Nixon's critics in the press, the Democratic Party, and his own party.

The blundering and venality of the Austin Geriatric Center grants, the ATS communications satellite contract, the *Sansinena* affair, and the firing of A. Ernest Fitzgerald received only minor notice in the press, although essentially all the significant facts were available in public records or could be obtained by interviewing willing witnesses. A few energetic and knowledgeable reporters wrote briefly of these matters, but the stories were buried in the back pages of most newspapers because the editors and television networks were obsessed with coverage of the Vietnam War and the easy job of producing colorful copy out of the unrest and irresponsibility flowing from that unwise involvement. This concentration on the Vietnam War permitted the Nixon White House to emphasize foreign affairs and the winding down of the Vietnam War while superficially going through the motions of running the government.

I do not intend to minimize the importance of the tragedy of our involvement in a war on the other side of the world that was doomed from the start by deceptive political policies and unrealistic goals. But in blaming Mr. Nixon for that war, his critics overlooked these hard facts:

1. Mr. Nixon did not start the war. In fact, many of his major critics supported it when it was launched by President Kennedy and escalated disastrously by President Johnson to the point that 500,000 American men were in Vietnam before Mr. Nixon was inaugurated in January 1969.

2. Whatever faulty policies Mr. Nixon pursued in his conduct of the war, he was winding it down and had no political or financial advantage in sustaining it any longer than was necessary to withdraw the U.S. forces.

It was to the decided political advantage of the Nixon administration to keep the attention of the press focused on problems of foreign affairs and war, an area in which the issues were often complex, a certain amount of secrecy could be justified in the name of "national security" whether merited or not, and the public tended to give all American presidents the benefit of the doubt. By contrast, the public is quick and bitter in its criticism of government officials in any administration for the blundering mismanagement and political favoritism that characterized so many of the Nixon administration's decisions involving domestic programs.

It was not that Nixon, Haldeman, and Ehrlichman intended to run a corrupt government. It was simply that they had moved too quickly to grasp all the power levers of government, and the responsibilities they appropriated to themselves went beyond their experience. The result was a superficial understanding of programs and no comprehension of the patience and tedious work required to make a government work honestly and efficiently. Haldeman and Ehrlichman weighed every decision in terms of the impact it might have on the 1972 election. Fascination with that goal and a passion for efficiency distorted their whole outlook on the American democracy. They were in far over their heads, and the appearance of a smoothly operating White House was a facade born of advertising techniques. The compensating superficiality of the White House press corps helped hide the facts from the public.

Richard Nixon, whose record justified a fear of losing in 1972, wanted very much to end the war, establish peace, and rise to first place in the hearts of his countrymen. He had not really won a political race on his own since his election to the Senate in 1950 in a highly controversial campaign. Winning with Dwight Eisenhower heading the ticket in 1952 and 1956 was not a significant sign of political prowess, particularly when it was followed by the loss of the presidency to John F. Kennedy in 1960 and of the California governorship to Edmund G. (Pat) Brown in 1962. The narrow victory over Vice President Hubert H. Humphrey in November 1968 demonstrated Nixon's tendency to lose support as a campaign progressed and explained why Nixon, Haldeman, and Ehrlichman were obsessed with using all of the power and paraphernalia of the office of the presidency to build a large margin of popularity prior to the campaign of 1972. Getting re-elected is the first order of business with most politicians, and Nixon's lack of easy popularity and his insecurity made him envy the hero status of General Eisenhower while he resented the contrast so often drawn. While Mr. Nixon recognized that the easy Kennedy charm and grace was beyond his reach, the tough-talking and aggressive confidence of Lyndon B. Johnson and John B. Connally was something he could emulate. The pathetic effort to find kinship with LBJ and Connally, win their admiration, emulate their life style, and adopt their political tactics was a major force in shaping the tragic course of the Nixon administration.

After winning in 1968 on the basis of a nonexistent "secret plan" for ending the Vietnam War, Nixon permitted the Democratic liberals to make it the "Nixon war" through his endorsement of Johnson's policies in return for a questionable alliance on the war issue with Johnson's "friends" in the Congress. The compromise barred criticism of Johnson for escalating the war and created the atmosphere in which President Johnson could suggest the Nixon administration reinstate the controversial Austin Geriatric Center land grab over the objections of Senator John J. Williams and some of Nixon's own cabinet officers.

The Nixon-Johnson alliance was of particular concern to me because as a candidate Nixon had told me he believed Lyndon Johnson was one of the most corrupt political figures in Washington, that the Bobby Baker investigations had only scraped the surface, and that the multi-million-dollar Johnson television fortune was constructed on an open and notorious conflict of interest. While I appreciated the complicated problems President Nixon faced in getting the United States out of Vietnam, it seemed to me that an expedient alliance with a former president he believed to be corrupt and deceptive would be self-defeating. It barred a frank criticism of the most questionable decisions in the Johnson years, and the much-publicized meetings and consultations with the discredited former president were certainly not helpful to Nixon's image among the Republicans who had been in the forefront in criticizing Johnson's highly vulnerable record.

I felt the same concern over the first insinuation of former Texas Governor John B. Connally into White House affairs as a consultant. The handsome and articulate Texas lawyer had been Johnson's campaign manager in the highly controversial Democratic primary election in 1948 that first sent Lyndon Johnson to the United States Senate. That tainted eighty-seven-vote victory won Johnson the nickname of "Landslide Lyndon" and demonstrated in some areas that how a man wins is not as important as seizing the power of a political base. Disturbed by the emergence of a Johnson-Connally influence in the White House, and accepting its inevitability, I only hoped it might create another force to counter the control exercised by Haldeman and Ehrlichman. That hope, of course, was futile; Connally flattered and charmed the president, Haldeman, and Ehrlichman by telling them what great men they were and by privately and publicly praising Administration programs and policies.

The three-time Texas governor was appointed to a five-member Advisory Panel on Executive Organization by President Nixon in April 1969 to produce a reorganization plan for the executive branch. Roy L. Ash, president of Litton Industries, Inc., of Beverly Hills, California, who had aided in the transition between the Johnson and Nixon administrations, headed the panel. It was in connection with the development of this reorganization plan that the suave and confident Connally was able to work his way into the inner circles of the White House. Though Ash was chairman, the forceful Texan prevailed in panel meetings and dominated the special seminar on reorganization for all senior White House personnel, which President Nixon attended. His deft flattery of Nixon and key members of the White House staff demonstrated to me that Connally could have just about anything he wanted from the insecure chief executive, who yearned so much for the easy confidence that the handsome Connally exuded.

Nixon's admiration for Johnson, Connally, and other self-made men of wealth partially explained his decision to invest essentially all of his available money in private homes in Key Biscayne, Florida, and San Clemente, California. One home suitable for retirement purposes made sense, but two lavish retreats seemed hardly feasible economically for a president whose net worth was only about $500,000 and who had the White House and Camp David at his disposal.

It was no great surprise to me when Dan Thomasson, a Washington writer for the Scripps-Howard newspapers, wrote in late August 1970 that the Austin Geriatric Center had been quietly revived by the Nixon administration under the personal prodding of former President Johnson. Although I knew that Presidential Counselor Bryce Harlow had been directed to try to reinstate the project, it was a further disappointment to me when it actually happened. I had made no specific inquiry on the project since leaving the White House and had made a decision to deal with it only after it was the object of some government action or congressional complaint.

Thomasson noted that the project had been characterized by Senator John Williams as a "multi-million-dollar giveaway" and reported: "Top congressional sources said today [August 28, 1970] an angry Mr. Johnson urged Mr. Nixon to resurrect the project which involves more than $7 million in Federal Housing Administration grants and loans and transfer of 26.5 acres of federal land to a group of Mr. Johnson's personal friends and business associates." Thomasson recalled that the project had initially been "rushed through in the last days of the Johnson administration" but had been killed by the Nixon administration after its legality was questioned by Senator Williams and by lawyers in several government departments. I assumed that one of Thomasson's congressional sources was Senator Williams, but he quoted the Department of Health, Education, and Welfare as confirming that it had ceased to contest the land transfer to the Austin Geriatric Center, Inc. He also quoted officials of the Department of Housing and Urban Development as confirming reports that "it has worked out a new 100 percent federal financing deal with the Austin organization." "The congressional sources said Mr. Johnson, infuriated by the Nixon administration's rejection of the project, pointedly reminded Mr. Nixon that he [Johnson] was supporting the president's policy on Vietnam and Southeast Asia," Thomasson wrote.

When Senator Williams placed Thomasson's news story in the *Congressional Record* and expressed his extreme displeasure at the turn of events, I felt free to write about those aspects of the controversy that were already in the public domain. From my own experience with the project, as special counsel, I knew that Thomasson's report was essentially accurate. I was also aware of the great disappointment it must have been for the lawyers at HEW and HUD to be required to reverse themselves after they had managed to get the project cancelled less than a year earlier. I was particularly sorry for HUD Secretary George Romney, an honest and straightforward man, who had been pleased to be able to take swift action in response to the complaints from Senator Williams and cancel the housing loan commitments and interest subsidies of $7.3 million. Romney had hoped that his action would demonstrate that aggressive, honest government decisions could prevail against all of the pressures for political accommodation that operated in Washington. Although he undoubtedly insisted that the new HUD loan arrangements were technically proper in the way they were processed, he must have known that they were part of the same old Johnson wheeling and dealing that Republicans had criticized in earlier years.

Senator John Williams asked for a General Accounting Office investigation of the decision to reinstate the Austin Geriatric Center. But even as the Delaware Republican told me of his request, he said he expected that on paper the record of the agencies involved would be proper and correct and would show no evidence of a directive from President Nixon. In this case, we both knew Mr. Nixon had direct responsibility. It was a final demonstration of the power LBJ wielded with Richard Nixon in the White House even in the face of opposition from a Republican Senator who was a symbol of aggressive, nonpartisan opposition to favoritism in government decisions.

*Chapter Nineteen*

# KISSINGER'S *MODUS OPERANDI*

DURING THE first months that I was on the White House staff, I concurred with the prevailing opinion that President Nixon and Dr. Henry A. Kissinger were conducting U.S. foreign policy in a highly competent and professional manner. While Mr. Nixon had not carried out his campaign pledge to "clean out the State Department," there seemed less need for tidying up that contaminated bureaucracy because of the power exercised by Dr. Kissinger as head of the National Security Council (NSC) operating out of the White House and the Executive Office Building. My own duties fell largely within the range of departments and agencies dealing with domestic programs, and only rarely was I called upon to deal with the State Department or the National Security Council. But by the time I left in the summer of 1970, I had had sufficient experience with Dr. Kissinger's direction of NSC to have developed some very definite impressions that it was not the highly effective and efficient performance it appeared to be from outside the government. In the first place, foreign affairs were handled with the same bureaucratic control that H. R. Haldeman and John Ehrlichman exerted on politics and domestic programs and policies. While there is a legitimate need for considerable secrecy in foreign affairs and military procedures, it was not essential that Dr. Kissinger control all information flowing to President Nixon to the exclusion of Secretary of State William P. Rogers and Defense Secretary Melvin Laird.

For several months in early 1970 I tried unsuccessfully to arrange for President Nixon to meet briefly with Admiral Hyman G. Rickover, Laird, and Rogers in connection with a controversial nuclear exchange program involving submarine technology. It was a highly classified issue, and hundreds of people at Defense and State were tied up with a useless jockeying for position. One of Laird's key aides and a technical expert from Admiral Rickover's office told me the whole futile exercise could have been settled in a fifteen-minute conference, with President Nixon as the decision-maker. But Dr. Kissinger was determined to control the information reaching Mr. Nixon on that nuclear exchange issue and did not want Admiral Rickover or Secretary Laird to personally argue the Defense Department position. He skillfully parried all of my efforts to arrange the meeting Laird had requested with the highly knowledgeable Admiral Rickover at his side. Kissinger may have had some highly complicated reason for wanting to keep Defense and State occupied with busywork while he performed marvels. But Defense Department officials concluded that someone in the National Security Council was in collusion with the State Department group that was pushing the nuclear exchange that Admiral Rickover believed unwise.

That episode reminded me of an incident that occurred during the first three months of the Nixon administration, while I was still a newspaper reporter. I had asked Appointments Secretary Dwight Chapin to arrange for me to see President Nixon with regard to a Defense Department controversy held over from the prior administration. Since the discussion was to be in the general area of national security, I was advised that I should meet with Dr. Kissinger, who would accompany me to see the president. I arrived at the West Wing of the White House on time and patiently waited at Dr. Kissinger's basement office for an hour beyond the 5:30 P.M. appointment time. When I was finally ushered into Kissinger's office, he apologized effusively for keeping me waiting, adding in his bedside manner: "The president has asked me to tell you that he is so sorry he won't be able to see you because of some last-minute developments of a very important nature. The president asked that I give you his very warmest regards and assure you that you should talk with me just as if you were talking to him." He went on to comment on "the very high regard the president has for you" and characterized me as "one of his warmest friends in the press." I wondered how often the special assistant to the president for national security affairs similarly soothed the feelings of others who had expected to meet with the president. I had to admit his personal touch made it easy to believe President Nixon had paused to express his heartfelt regret and insist that his Number One foreign policy aide do the stroking in warm and confidential terms.

Since I was unsure of whether I really wished to discuss some of the problems with Dr. Kissinger, I decided to use the opportunity to probe his attitudes on defense procurement matters, which had occupied a great deal of my time. I was also interested in testing his attitudes toward and knowledge of the manner in which the Defense Department had functioned under Robert S. McNamara, for I had found over the years that there are many highly articulate people in high government positions whose retentive memories and facility for quick study allow them to give an impression of brilliance far beyond their real understanding of the problems. Elements of this had emerged in McNamara's highly praised "cost effectiveness" studies and overreliance on "management systems." The weaknesses in McNamara's operation were exposed in a number of congressional investigations. I wondered whether Dr. Kissinger might be very much like McNamara in both his strengths and weaknesses. Certainly his greeting resembled the excessive flattery McNamara had used in our first meeting to discuss his disastrous award of the multi-billion-dollar F-111 war plane contract to General Dynamics.

In the course of our half-hour conversation it became clear that although House and Senate committees had exposed the superficiality of the public relations claims made by McNamara during his tenure at the Pentagon, Dr. Kissinger still accepted McNamara's public image as promoted by the Pentagon press office. I gained an immediate impression that Dr. Kissinger was interested only in "the big picture" of international politics and not at all in the details or economics of Defense Department or State Department programs. He was an uncritical admirer of McNamara, and in the course of the discussion I understood why. Henry Kissinger and Bob McNamara shared many of the same traits. Both were highly intelligent, articulate, and systematic, but were inclined to arrive at fixed conclusions that suited their purposes with too little information. Both were clever manipulators of governmental power levers and the information they controlled. Both were keenly aware of the advantage of personally arguing the case they favored while barring the proponents of alternative viewpoints. While both scorned the government bureaucracy, they were expert at controlling, using, or ignoring that bureaucracy to achieve their goals. Because they were operating in the area of "national security," secrecy aided their deceptive maneuvers to control policy while they insisted they were presenting "all of the alternatives."

After I joined the White House staff my contacts with Dr. Kissinger, the then Colonel Alexander M. Haig, Jr., Kissinger's administrative aide, and other NSC staff members corroborated my initial impression that Kissinger would be a strong force in foreign policy, but that he would be ruthless and cunning in the means he employed to gain the ends he decided were the realistic goals of American foreign policy. He, however, modestly disclaimed any interest in establishing "a Kissinger foreign policy" and asserted that his only ambition was to organize information and decision-making to best implement the president's policies.

But there were widespread complaints about the difficulty of getting information through Dr. Kissinger to the president. Complaints came even from the office of Dr. Arthur Burns, Mr. Nixon's top economic adviser, who, as counselor to the president, was the highest-ranking member of the White House staff. Other complaints issued from the office of the assistant secretary of defense for international security affairs, headed by Dr. G. Warren Nutter; from Assistant Secretary of Commerce Kenneth Davis, an energetic former chief financial officer and treasurer of IBM who had been recruited as a foreign trade specialist; and from Republicans in Congress.

Davis, a moderate Republican, came to my office in desperation after weeks of futile attempts to alert President Nixon to what he believed was Dr. Kissinger's disregard of the impact on American business created by making trade recommendations to accommodate his foreign policy goals. Davis related his repeated unsuccessful efforts to get a telephone call back from Dr. Kissinger and his conviction that Kissinger was uninterested in economic arguments if they interfered with his foreign policy planning. Davis believed strongly that foreign policy should not be made without serious thought to its impact on all segments of the U.S. financial structure and that Kissinger and his staff were failing to place adequate emphasis on economic factors. All would be lost if international political bargaining destroyed substantial sections of our domestic economy. International political triumphs would be hollow if U.S. citizens and industry were left with serious shortages of food or fuel.

Davis resigned in the early summer of 1970 in frustration at his inability to reach either President Nixon or Dr. Kissinger. The NSC explanation to me was that an interdepartmental committee was studying the trade matters Davis was concerned about and that Davis should make his views known there. Davis' assessment was that the rambling discussions of the sub-Cabinet inter-departmental committee wasted the time of many officials and, in the end, would have no influence on the trade accommodations he feared were already part of Dr. Kissinger's planning. I hoped Davis' resignation would awaken President Nixon and Dr. Kissinger to the need for greater attention to the economic factors which many believed were being ignored. But the resignation passed with no significant press reaction, and it is possible that Mr. Nixon was not even aware of Davis' departure from government.

Only the columnists Roland Evans and Robert Novak discerned the story behind the story and the significance of Davis' resignation and his final confrontation with John Ehrlichman in mid-June 1970. The quotations attributed to Davis by Evans and Novak were thoroughly consistent with the version Davis had told me. They reported that Davis told Ehrlichman: "I have no hard feelings, John. . . . I wish you luck. You're going to need it. You're in trouble, John—worse trouble than you know—and I'm worried about the country more than I was before I came down here." Davis had zeroed in on what the Evans and Novak column referred to as the Nixon administration's "chaotic decision-making process" as it involved domestic and foreign affairs. From the inside, I had concluded that Nixon and his top advisers didn't know much about running a government, but they had been able to present a façade of operational efficiency somewhat like that of the Wizard of Oz.

I was pleased that Evans and Novak had perceived that the real weakness of the Nixon White House lay beyond ideology or partisan politics. But too few reporters had either the freedom, the forum, or the courage to deal with the major inadequacies in the face of the outpouring of self-serving kudos flowing out of the White House Press Office, the various departments, the Republican National Committee and Mr. Nixon's press conferences. Usually the counter-arguments by leading Democrats or by Democrat-aligned pressure groups were so partisan they had little credibility. Sound Republican criticism from Senator John J. Williams of Delaware, or from Representative H. R. Gross of Iowa, was usually ignored though they carefully documented their evaluations of the questionable programs and policies of the Nixon administration.

One incident demonstrated to me that Dr. Kissinger was not sufficiently concerned about laxity in personnel selection at the National Security Council. In December 1969 a former foreign service officer called to my attention the fact that one of Dr. Kissinger's key aides at NSC had been accused of giving "top secret" information to "intelligence agents of a foreign power." The problem had never been satisfactorily resolved. The man named was Helmut Sonnenfeldt, a Soviet-American affairs specialist, who, it was claimed, made the disclosure of top-secret information to intelligence agents of the Israeli Embassy in Washington in the late 1950s. Another foreign service officer told me that he had witnessed what he described as "a serious security violation" in connection with arrangements the U.S. had with one of Israel's Arab neighbors. He said that former State Department Security Evaluator Otto F. Otepka had some knowledge of the scope of the initial investigation and of the reasons it was dropped.

Obviously, this was not something I could resolve, but I had an obligation to pass the information on to the proper authorities. I arranged to see Dr. Kissinger to tell him of the charge, the evidence which should be available in State Department files or at the FBI as a result of the original investigation, the questions pending, and witnesses who were willing to testify. Dr. Kissinger expressed "grave concern," assured me I had "done the right thing" in bringing the information to him, cautioned me against telling anyone else about it, and said he would handle it. I offered to arrange for the witnesses to talk to him, but he wanted nothing said to them until he and Al Haig decided how to follow through on the matter. A couple of weeks later, when I called to check on the progress of the case, Dr. Kissinger said that he had "been busy" and had turned it over to Al Haig. I forgot about it for several weeks, until I received a telephone call from an informant at the State Department who said he had learned that Sonnenfeldt was to be promoted to FSO-1 despite a technical lack of qualification because he had spent too little time at foreign posts. That was the least of the problems, as far as I was concerned.

This time I went to see Haig. He declared that he was "concerned" over the charges but did not want to move precipitously and felt it would not be proper to tell me what action was being taken. I made several other calls to Haig to try to determine whether the allegations about Sonnenfeldt had been generally supported or had washed out in the investigation. In each case I was brushed aside with the same assurance that the matter was being properly pursued. Shortly after I left the White House, I learned that Sonnenfeldt had been promoted from FSO-2 to FSO-1 in the career foreign service, on the recommendation of Dr. Kissinger. The men whose names I had supplied to Kissinger and Haig told me they had never been questioned about the Sonnenfeldt matter, and I wondered how it could have been resolved without that elementary investigative step. By this time I had learned that Sonnenfeldt and Kissinger had been friends since their youth in New York, and that Sonnenfeldt was the first man Dr. Kissinger had asked to join him on the NSC after Mr. Nixon hired him for that job in November 1968. Perhaps Dr. Kissinger himself had simply questioned Sonnenfeldt and had been satisfied with his denial of the charges. It was no surprise to learn later that Dr. Kissinger leaned heavily on Sonnenfeldt in making decisions pertaining to the 1972 trips to Peking and Moscow and had, in fact, given Sonnenfeldt responsibility for the 1972 Strategic Arms Limitation (SALT) talks in Moscow and the sale of American wheat to the Soviet Union.

Although participation in such historic agreements is usually prized by foreign service officers, Sonnenfeldt's responsibility in the massive wheat sales to the Soviet Union in 1972 became an albatross around his neck when he was nominated by President Nixon in 1973 to be under secretary of the treasury in charge of all East-West trade agreements. Sonnenfeldt denied that he had given highly classified information to a foreign power in testimony contrary to that of two other witnesses, but the Senate Finance Committee never resolved that conflict. Under questioning by Senator Harry Byrd of Virginia, Sonnenfeldt admitted that he had had a key supervisory role in the wheat transaction and conceded that in hindsight it was a mistake for the U.S. not to have limited the sales. He admitted that there had been no necessity for the $140 million wheat subsidy in connection with the sales to the Soviet Union but said that he had not tried to assess its impact on the national economy because he had no expertise on grain prices, grain supplies, or economics. He said he left those tasks to others.

Controversy over Sonnenfeldt caused his nomination to be stalled in the Senate Finance Committee for more than six months before Chairman Russell Long permitted it to be reported to the Senate floor for action. But before the nomination could be acted upon, it was withdrawn, and Sonnenfeldt was nominated as counselor of the State Department. That nomination, as one of Secretary of State Kissinger's top aides, was confirmed without debate on December 19, 1973.

As early as 1970 an incident occurred that provided evidence of the lack of effective communication at the White House on foreign policy matters. On November 23, 1970, Simas Kudirka, a thirty-two-year-old Lithuanian seaman, tried to defect from a Soviet fishing vessel by jumping to the U.S. Coast Guard cutter *Vigilant*. Kudirka was the radio operator aboard the *Sovietkaya Litva,* a mother ship for trawlers working the Atlantic seacoast. The *Sovietkaya* and *Vigilant* were tied together off Gay Head, at the tip of Martha's Vineyard, for a discussion of fishing rights. Kudirka, whose mother had been born in Brooklyn, had informed a Coast Guard officer that he intended to defect several hours before he leaped to the deck of the United States Coast Guard cutter, and the first Coast Guard request for advice reached the State Department at 2:30 P.M. About 5:00 P.M., Coast Guard Commander Ralph W. Eustis, the skipper of the *Vigilant,* asked First Coast Guard District headquarters in Boston how he should respond to Soviet demands that Kudirka be forced to return. Again Coast Guard headquarters contacted the State Department, which relayed back the message that the Coast Guard should avoid a "provocation" of the Soviets by suggesting that Kudirka return to the Soviet ship of his own volition; the Coast Guard crew could force Kudirka to return or could permit the Russian crew to come aboard the Coast Guard cutter to use force to return him to the *Sovietkaya.*

Kudirka, who spoke English, French, and Spanish, in addition to Russian, visited for more than an hour with Commander Eustis while awaiting orders from Coast Guard headquarters, and the two developed some measure of rapport. When the captain asked Kudirka if he would return to the Soviet ship voluntarily, the response was a flat no. Commander Eustis refused to direct

U.S. Coast Guard personnel to force Kudirka to return to the Soviet ship, but with tears in his eyes he gave the Soviet crew the authority to come aboard the U.S. ship and take the defecting radio operator by force. Eyewitnesses later told a House Foreign Affairs Subcommittee of the brutal agony of watching the Russians aboard the U.S. ship beat Kudirka into submission in an ordeal that lasted several hours. Under orders from his superiors and the State Department to avoid a "provocation" of the Soviet Union, Captain Eustis, his crew, and several others watched the savagery of the Soviets as they pursued the screaming Kudirka. Halfway through the ordeal, the Soviet party was reinforced. After several escapes by Kudirka and an extensive search in which it was thought for a time that he had jumped overboard, the ordeal ended. At 11:55 P.M., the bloody and bruised body of Kudirka was loaded into a U.S. Coast Guard boat by six Soviet sailors and was taken to the Soviet ship.

Assistant Secretary of State William B. Macomber, Jr., placed major blame on the Coast Guard because it indicated in its report to the State Department at 7:45 P.M. that the defecting Lithuanian sailor was "being returned" to the Soviet ship, or "has been returned." Macomber said that as a result of that report the State Department had assumed that the matter was settled and had been unaware of the bloody four-hour struggle that had followed. Having returned Kudirka to the Soviet ship, the United States had given up its legal right to obtain his release.

The official report of the House Foreign Affairs Subcommittee indicated that decisions had been made by Coast Guard and State Department officials without consultation with the government's policy-makers or with the experts on Soviet-American relations. This was despite the fact that Edward L. Killham, Jr., head of the Soviet Affairs desk at the State Department, received a telephone call from Coast Guard headquarters at 2:30 P.M. stating that a Russian seaman had indicated to the Coast Guard that he wanted to defect. Killham told the Coast Guard that the United States did not want to encourage defections that might cause a provocation, but he made no effort to contact his superiors at the State Department or the White House.

Although a report on the Kudirka incident went immediately from the State Department to the National Security Council, the foul-up of Coast Guard and State Department communications did not come to the attention of President Nixon until November 29—six days after it happened. When Mr. Nixon came across the report in his weekend reading on Sunday, November 29, he found the incident "outrageous" and said he wanted to get to the bottom of it. Though the muddled communication between the State Department and the Coast Guard was blamed for the incident itself, there was no outward indication that the president recognized the still greater problem of communication at the top. In a day of emphasis on "hot lines" between Washington and Moscow and of studied efforts to avoid "misunderstandings" with the Soviets, why wasn't there a clear system for communication within the top levels of the Nixon administration?

But the manner in which Dr. Kissinger conducted the NSC and controlled communications with the president, and his adroitness in wrapping "national security" secrecy around his actions, made it unlikely that Congress would ever be able to pinpoint the responsibility for the NSC delay of six days in alerting President Nixon to the Kudirka incident. If Dr. Kissinger was to received credit when programs were successful, he should manfully accept the blame when his plaything—the National Security Council—had a responsibility and failed to fulfill it. Unfortunately, the report on the Kudirka affair would go to President Nixon through Dr. Kissinger, and it was safe to speculate that responsibility would be placed on officials in the lower ranks of the Coast Guard and the State Department rather than in the upper echelons of government.

When the House Foreign Affairs Subcommittee hearing concluded, Chairman Wayne Hays, an Ohio Democrat, declared that "the man responsible for ordering the return of this defector should be court-martialed, dismissed from service, and, preferably, sent to Siberia." But the subcommittee was never able to penetrate the maze of State Department double-talk and "executive privilege" that shielded the highest officials from responsibility for their actions.

Months later, it was reported that Simas Kudirka was returned to the Soviet Union, where he was prosecuted, convicted, and sentenced to ten years' imprisonment at hard labor for treason.* Official reports of the House subcommittee charged that U.S. officials actually violated international law and other international agreements when they permitted Soviet sailors to board the Coast Guard vessel to forcibly remove the Lithuanian defector. A report by the State Department to the House subcommittee stated that "there is no provision of international law which required that the seaman be delivered by the Coast Guard vessel's commanding officer to the Soviet authorities. A defector may be retained in the United States' custody for a sufficient time to determine whether he is entitled to refugee status." The State Department's report was too late to be helpful to the Coast Guard officers who had wept at what they considered to be responsible orders from the very top of the government.

In my "Watch on Washington" column for Sunday, December 13, 1970, I wrote:

> If the president settled for simply pinning the responsibility for poor communications between the State Department and Coast Guard, he will have dealt with only a part of the problem.
>
> The fact that he did not learn about the incident for six days is fully as serious as the interdepartmental communications problem. To be successful, an administration must be able to learn of pending problems, get the facts together quickly, get the warning to the president, and get effective response from the government agencies with responsibility.
>
> The president, and others high in the administration, must be constantly pre-

---

* On July 18, 1974, the U.S. State Department ruled that Kudirka was in fact an American citizen. In August 1974 he was released from the Soviet prison camp, and on November 5, 1974, he arrived in New York with his mother, Marija Sulsience; his wife; and their two children.

pared to assess the facts of an emergency nature and respond in a manner that does not permit the situation to deteriorate.

Excessive secrecy, poor communications, and an ignorant and unseemly fear of provoking the Soviet Union had made it impossible to cope with the problem of saving Simas Kudirka. "But there still may be time to correct the larger weakness that could be fatal," I wrote in a futile effort to warn Mr. Nixon of deep troubles in his White House organization, including the National Security Council. Had Mr. Nixon heeded the warnings, there would have been no need for a "Houston plan" and no need for a "plumbers unit."

*Chapter Twenty*

# POWER PLOYS THAT CORRUPT

THE STINGING REPORT criticizing Robert S. McNamara that was filed by the Senate's Permanent Investigating Subcommittee on December 18, 1970 should have been a warning to every high-level official in the Nixon administration that the truth always emerges eventually. The ninety-three-page report, concluding one of the longest investigations in the history of the Senate, charged that McNamara, as defense secretary, gave untruthful testimony under oath on the price and performance of the F-111 warplane built by General Dynamics Corporation.

McNamara, supported by President Kennedy and President Johnson, had been able to use "executive privilege," unjustified "national security" classifications, and a broad range of equally devious secrecy devices to stall Chairman John L. McClellan's inquiry into the highly questionable award of the multi-billion-dollar contract to the Texas firm. Brilliant and articulate, McNamara had been able to stonewall the McClellan committee because of his shining public image as the patron saint of "cost effectiveness" studies of Pentagon expenditures, which theoretically saved the taxpayers billions of dollars on Defense Department programs. For several years, the former Ford Motor Company president got by with the biggest public relations show Washington had ever seen before it collapsed in the face of several investigations of the conduct of the Vietnam War and of defense procurement contracts.

The report charged, moreover, that former Deputy Defense Secretary Roswell Gilpatric had been involved in a "flagrant conflict of interest" in his role in the award. Prior to joining the Defense Department as deputy secretary— the Number Two post—Gilpatric had been a lawyer for General Dynamics and was deeply involved in a project to rescue it from financial ruin. It was also charged that former Navy Secretary Fred Korth was involved in conflicts of interest and other improprieties when he wrote letters on Navy stationery to promote the business of the Continental National Bank of Fort Worth, Texas. Korth had been president of the bank, which numbered General Dynamics among its best customers. Since McNamara, as Defense boss, had defended both Gilpatric and Korth, the critical report was a severe triple blow to the man who a few years earlier had been hailed as a "human computer" and a kind of ultra-super public official. McNamara's stature prior to 1965 and 1966 was greater than that of Dr. Henry Kissinger in the first years of the Nixon administration, and his reputation for efficiency and effectiveness made him head and shoulders above H. R. Haldeman or John Ehrlichman.

The charge that McNamara had falsified records and have given untruthful testimony before committees of Congress was among the harshest judgments ever rendered against a Cabinet officer up to that point, and should have been a warning to President Nixon, his Cabinet, and his White House aides that they too might be brought before Congress and made accountable. Had Nixon's top assistants bothered to look closely, they would have noted the significant fact that there was no defense of McNamara by either Senator Jacob Javits, the New York Republican, or Senator Edmund Muskie, the Maine Democrat, who in 1963 and 1964 had carried the major burden of defending McNamara's decision to give the contract to General Dynamics. But the lessons of McNamara's serious blunders on the F-111 contract went unheeded by President Nixon, Haldeman, Ehrlichman, and a few Cabinet officers who should have known better. They had the awesome power of the presidency at their disposal and believed that this situation would last forever. I do not believe that the use and gross misuse of "executive privilege" was a conspiracy to corrupt federal government agencies for either private gain or political advantage. Certainly, a few individuals were interested in personal financial gain, and there was a widespread desire to use all of the powers of the federal government to insure Nixon's election in 1972. But Nixon's cohorts lacked the experience to construct a conspiracy, although they understood early that a sweeping doctrine permitting arbitrary secrecy could be a devastating political tool.

Initially, "executive privilege" was simply a convenient instrument for concealing amateurish bungling or minor political favoritism. Occasionally, it was a device to avoid the inconvenience of making a responsible accounting to Congress or the public.

But as the device proved successful, it became a precedent not to be overlooked by the corrupt or the corruptible. The insidious poison of secrecy spread throughout the government. Errant or venal lower-level bureaucrats relied on secrecy to mislead Cabinet officers and the White House about internal bureaucratic dishonesty or errors. Frequently, it covered up scandalous conditions that had been present long before the Nixon administration took power.

For example, the Federal Aviation Administration (FAA) tried to block an inquiry into laxity on air safety regulations for charter flights, which in October 1970 had resulted in a crash in Colorado which killed thirty-one

Wichita State University football players. Philip Ryther, a senior safety evaluator for FAA, told me that a panel he headed had urgently recommended
tightening of air safety regulations at the conclusion of a four-month study in
March 1970. Ryther's report recommended increasing the frequency of aircraft inspection, tightening pilot-training restrictions, and requiring pilots to
be familiar with the specific aircraft they were flying. Ryther made his report
in April 1970—six months before the crash that killed the Kansas athletes.
Between April and October, the deeply concerned Ryther had gone outside of
the chain of command in the Department of Transportation to try to force
speedy action on the safety recommendations his panel had unanimously supported. For such "insubordination," Ryther was forced to resign on September 15, 1970—just fifteen days before the crash.

Twenty-five days after the tragic crash, the FAA bureaucrats who had
brought charges against Ryther for insubordination approved new restrictions
on chartered aircraft in line with the recommendations Ryther had made in
April. The new FAA standards for charter flights were printed in the Federal
Register on October 27 with the following preamble: "A recent accident has
highlighted the need to regulate more strictly the leasing of large airplanes by
educational institutions for the carriage of student groups, as for example football teams and choral groups."

It was impossible for me to get a straight answer from FAA about the
long delay or about the vindictive actions against Ryther. To me, this case
seemed comparable to the firing of cost expert A. Ernest Fitzgerald by the
Air Force after he called attention to cost overruns on the C-5A aircraft, or
to the State Department's firing of security evaluator Otto F. Otepka for calling attention to lax security.

The White House had no direct responsibility for the laxity at FAA; thus,
I hoped for a positive response when White House speech-writer Patrick
Buchanan, White House Press Secretary Ronald Ziegler, and Special Assistant John D. Ehrlichman were informed. Buchanan saw the need for swift
White House action to pin the responsibility on those officials who had caused
the delays while firing Ryther, and he said he would call my news columns
on the subject to the attention of President Nixon. Ehrlichman said he would
have his chief deputy, Egil (Bud) Krogh, look into the matter. What I did
not know at the time was that Ehrlichman and Nixon had Krogh deeply involved in directing the so-called "White House Plumbers Unit" and had placed
the highest priority on obtaining information for a "psychiatric profile" of Dr.
Daniel Ellsberg, charged with responsibility for leaking the "Pentagon Papers"
to the *New York Times*.

In late August, after eight months had passed with no indication that
Ryther's complaints were being followed up, I wrote a "Watch on Washington" column that sharply criticized the administration. "A review of the record of the experience of Philip Ryther, a former employee of the Federal
Aviation Agency, is not something that gives confidence in the responsiveness
of the Nixon administration," I said. I reviewed Ryther's complaints and the

abortive investigation by a Senate Commerce Subcommittee headed by Senator Howard Cannon, a Nevada Democrat, that was requested by Senator James Pearson, a mild, moderate Republican from Kansas. The Department of Transportation and the FAA were not required to produce internal documents and were permitted to make inadequate, self-serving explanations of the air tragedy. Ryther was not allowed to testify on the manner in which he had been reprimanded, threatened, and, finally, forced to resign, and Chairman Cannon would not even promise a report on the tragedy. It was the kind of congressional ineffectiveness that promotes arrogance among bureaucrats and at the White House.

I revealed that in July Ryther had written to President Nixon and had gone to the White House to meet with Ehrlichman. Instead, he saw Krogh. Ryther had written Nixon: "I have personally brought this subject to the attention of high officials on your White House staff as well as to top officials at FAA and the Department of Transportation. Notwithstanding the series of aviation disasters in our country over the last few months, our reports and recommendations are still being covered up. Effective steps have not been taken to correct the hazardous conditions which exist and the public is not being dealt with candidly and forthrightly by the federal officials responsible for aviation safety."

Ryther had asked for the strongest corrective action—replacement of the seven men in FAA and the Department of Transportation who have key responsibility for aviation safety. Senator Pearson agreed with Ryther about the negligence of the FAA and the injustice of Ryther's superiors in ousting him rather than correcting the regulations. "I had been of the opinion that it would not be necessary to do any more than call the facts to the attention of the administration to get some action," Pearson said with mild concern. "I'm afraid I was over-optimistic." Senator Vance Hartke (D., Ind.) another member of the Senate Commerce Committee, declared that he did not know why "it is so difficult to get action from the executive branch when the facts are as clear as this." Said Hartke: "Ryther, who wrote those recommendations, is being treated as if he is the culprit. It shouldn't be necessary for a man with a documented case to have all of these frustrations in getting a full hearing and the report he is demanding." But few in the press were concerned about this tragic accident, the FAA negligence that had contributed to it, or the serious weaknesses in government that it indicated. And Congress, like the executive branch, seldom takes a risk unless forced to by press and public interest. John Ehrlichman couldn't find the time or manpower to delve into serious mismanagement at FAA, but my column appeared on the same Labor Day weekend that White House lawyer G. Gordon Liddy and White House consultant E. Howard Hunt went to Los Angeles to supervise the team that burglarized the office of Dr. Lewis J. Fielding in search of papers dealing with his treatment of Daniel Ellsberg. White House action on Ryther's complaints could have stimulated a much-needed cleanup of FAA. But, the press largely lost interest after the initial reports of the accident, exerting no force on Congress to act, and the White House ignored a careful documentation of derelict government action even though it involved an inexcusable loss of life.

A review of my experience with the Nixon White House, from the outside, indicated rather consistent application of these general rules:

1. If partisan political gain may result from exposure of questionable activity on the part of Democrats, there is no limit to what measures will be approved and even initiated.

2. If the problem involves merely improper or wasteful practices by venal or incompetent bureaucrats, do not risk involvement in the controversy but permit it to be handled through normal channels, unless it represents a threat to the presidential image.

3. If the problem involves questionable activity by any Nixon appointee or others who might be helpful in re-electing the president, impose all the force of government to try to conceal the evidence of culpability.

Certainly the first rule applied to White House approval of cooperation with William Lambert of *Life* magazine in his critical article on Senator Joseph Tydings, the Maryland Democrat who was given priority status as a target for political extinction in the 1970 race. Lambert's investigation of the charge that Senator Tydings used "his personal and senatorial prestige" to promote the interests of a Florida realty finance company was probably justified, and the Nixon administration had an obligation to make government records available unless there were "national security" or other clear statutory prohibitions against it. However, the timing of the government investigation and the release of the report were clearly political, and contributed to the defeat of Senator Tydings by Republican Glenn Beall, Jr., in November 1970. (In the realm of conflict-of-interest investigations most administrations are probably negligent, particularly if United States senators or congressmen, or high-level political appointees, are involved.)

The State Department investigation of Tydings' actions in connection with a $7 million loan guaranty for a housing project in Nicaragua was announced in August 1970—after publication of Lambert's article, and less than eight weeks before the general election. The State Department Inspector General's report clearing Senator Tydings of any illegality in visiting Agency for International Development (AID) officials was not released until a week *after* the election in which Tydings was defeated. Tydings' friends contended that the report "cleared" him of any improprieties, but Lambert insisted that it "supports and strengthens the point I was trying to make" about the dangers of possible conflicts of interest when there is no violation of the law. Lambert had quoted an AID official as saying that Tydings, then a senator-elect, "was there to make a pitch on a project, and he made the pitch." Tydings claimed that his meeting with the AID official was "an innocent and innocuous visit," a general discussion of foreign aid programs, and that there was no mention of the project in which he had a beneficial interest. Tydings was keenly aware of the fine line between "making a pitch" for the loan in which he had an interest and the general conversation about his views on foreign aid. As United States attorney in Maryland, Tydings had prosecuted two congressmen—Representative Thomas Johnson, a Maryland Democrat, and Representative Frank W. Boykin, an Alabama Democrat—for criminally misusing their public offices by calling a government agency without revealing their personal interest. Conflicts of interest laws often present close questions, and, in hindsight, Tydings admitted that it had been "a mistake" to have accompanied his business associate to the AID office. But the quick follow-through by the Nixon White House was not characteristic behavior.

By contrast, the administration ignored massive evidence of brutal mismanagement of personnel in the State Department, as the vindictive personnel office permitted destruction of documents, falsification of records, and perjury to go unpunished. Because of the risk of offending the State Department establishment and its friends in Congress, the Nixon White House refused to insist on fair play and public hearings for John D. Hemenway, an able foreign service career officer who was favorably disposed toward the administration. Obsession with re-election obscured all other issues, and only a scheme to wound a political "enemy" or to insure the continuation of the Nixon administration was certain to be regarded as worthy of the most urgent attention. A loyal government servant destroyed by false documents and perjured testimony had virtually no chance of receiving attention or support in seeking redress against those responsible for a criminal obstruction of justice.

Hemenway, a graduate of the U.S. Naval Academy and a Rhodes Scholar, had made spectacular strides up the foreign service ladder until the Kennedy administration came into power. Fluent in German and Russian, he continued to receive good ratings but was not promoted because of disagreements with some of his superiors on Soviet-American policy. When the Nixon administration came into power, Hemenway expected to have greater rapport with the policy-makers and believed he would receive at least routine support when he produced evidence of perjury and falsification of documents in connection with his case. But the Nixon White House had no enthusiasm for any cause unless it could be directly tied to the 1972 election, and would institute no action to right the wrongs perpetrated by an entrenched bureaucracy.

I tried to appeal to a sense of decency and fair play on a half dozen cases, and it was useless, even when a veteran foreign service officer who had been passed over for promotion committed suicide. Charles W. Thomas, who killed himself on April 12, 1971, was "selected out" of the foreign service despite a brilliant record. His failure to win promotion to a higher grade within a proscribed period was a result of one low rating by a superior with whom Thomas disagreed. A subsequent investigation of that rating resulted in an inspector general report, by Ambassador Robert McClintock, recommending Thomas for immediate promotion to FSO-3 and assignment to the National War College. But the McClintock report was misfiled in the personnel record of another foreign service official with the same name and was not discovered until Thomas had been passed over for promotion again. For five years,

Thomas tried to get the personnel office to admit its error and to grant him the promotion he needed to continue as a foreign service officer.

The Nixon White House was insensitive to the pleas of Thomas, and Secretary of State William P. Rogers and Under Secretary Elliot L. Richardson rejected the personal appeals of Thomas. Obsessed with being reinstated, unable to find employment and faced with White House indifference, the forty-eight-year-old foreign service officer shot himself. It took a determined bipartisan effort by Senator Birch Bayh, a liberal Indiana Democrat, and Representative Ross Adair, a conservative Indiana Republican, to force the State Department to hire Thomas' widow and reluctantly grant him a posthumous promotion more than three years after his death in April 1971.*

Even in the face of the Thomas suicide and a number of other cases spotlighting the injustices of the foreign service system, the White House refused to support bipartisan reform legislation sponsored by Senator Bayh and Senator John Sherman Cooper, Republican of Kentucky, and supported by others such as Republican Representative John Ashbrook, an Ohio conservative. The White House and Secretary of State Rogers wanted no part of a fight with ruling forces in the State Department personnel office. By contrast, a political deal that promised to bring big money and votes to President Nixon in 1972 was certain to occupy the attention of the president and his most trusted advisors. The long scramble to spring Teamster boss James R. Hoffa from prison was a case in point.

*Chapter Twenty-one*

# NIXON SPRINGS HOFFA

I REALIZED how much political heat was on to spring Jimmy Hoffa from prison when it was revealed that Senator Norris Cotton had hand-delivered a petition with 250,000 signatures to White House Counsel John W. Dean III. The senior senator from New Hampshire was an arch-conservative Republican with little sympathy for organized labor, certainly not someone one might expect to carry water for a man recognized as one of the most corrupt figures among organized labor's leaders. Only serious political considerations could have convinced him to front for Hoffa. I suspected, as many reported, that William Loeb, publisher of the *Manchester* (New Hampshire)

---

* Representative Edward Mezvinsky (D., Iowa) gave the Charles W. Thomas bill the final push to clear the House Judiciary Committee and the House in December 1974. On January 2, 1975, President Ford signed the bill granting Thomas reinstatement and posthumous promotion. Thomas' widow and children were to receive the benefits they would have been entitled to if he had died on active duty as a foreign service officer.

*Union Leader* and a long-time supporter of Hoffa, was the force behind Cotton. Six years earlier, the Teamsters Central States Pension Fund had lent Loeb $2,000,000, payable in twenty years at 6½ percent interest. Loeb very actively worked for parole or executive clemency for Hoffa in 1969 and 1970, when I was able to sidetrack those efforts by Attorney General Mitchell and John Ehrlichman. I thought I had been successful in persuading the Nixon White House of the political dangers associated with doing favors for Hoffa. Ehrlichman had barred me from talking to President Nixon on the Hoffa matter at that time, so I did not know Nixon's attitude. I assumed from the reports of others and the lack of any reprimand that he approved my actions. The new moves by Senator Cotton seemed to me a good omen, for I judged that if Loeb felt compelled to bring out such big artillery he was not getting favorable soundings regarding the possibility of a parole for Hoffa when he became eligible in March 1971.

In November 1970, I had written a column about the renewed activity of a "Free Hoffa" group pressing for a Christmas-season presidential pardon, but really aimed at springing Jimmy from the federal prison at Lewisburg before July 5, 1971—the date set for the next Teamsters convention, when his term as general president would expire. In the wake of Senator Cotton's visit to the White House, I made some new inquiries in preparation for an article in the *Commercial Car Journal*. I was told that President Nixon still opposed pardon or parole and that Ehrlichman and Haldeman were not convinced of the political advantage that would flow to Mr. Nixon in return for favorable action. I wrote:

> Hoffa will not be free by the July 5, 1971, Teamsters convention for the very good reason that the record is against him.
> In the end, the Nixon administration can be expected to make its decision on the basis of the Hoffa record, and not on the basis of the propaganda that is flowing out of the typewriters of the lobbyists and columnists who are engaged in a massive 'free Hoffa' movement.
> To do other than keep Hoffa tucked safely in the Lewisburg federal prison would be political suicide for an administration that has tried to make a point of being a law enforcement administration. It would be totally at odds with the Nixon administration's drive against organized crime in New Jersey, New York, and other large cities to free James R. Hoffa, who has worked hand-in-glove with some of the worst elements in the underworld in those areas.

The January issue of the Teamsters magazine carried a picture of the union's vice president, Frank E. Fitzsimmons, with President Nixon at a bill-signing ceremony at the White House on December 23. That occasion had been the signing of tax legislation with special application to the Teamsters' over-the-road drivers, who had been subjected to double taxation in some instances. "It was significant that Fitzsimmons did not mention imprisoned General President Hoffa and the issue of a parole or a pardon that has been the subject of thousands of words each month in the organization magazine," I wrote, basing my comments on information from a White House source.

Pointing to the role of Senator Cotton, I explained that "within the White House it was accepted as a political act that Senator Cotton was required to perform" for Loeb, publisher of the largest daily newspaper in New Hampshire. "While there is some White House sympathy for Loeb's push for Hoffa's release, there is an inclination to give only lip service to the freeing of Hoffa while talking about the pardon as a kind of 'political disaster' that President Nixon must avoid."

On March 31, 1971, the United States Board of Parole announced that it had denied Hoffa's request for parole, after receiving a special report from representatives of the Organized Crime Division of the Department of Justice. This meant Hoffa would remain in prison for another year before again being eligible to apply for parole, unless, in the meantime, the president stepped in to commute his sentence or grant him a pardon. I believed that Richard Nixon was too savvy politically to give his critics direct evidence of favoritism toward Hoffa, even if he had some secret commitment. The parole board announced on June 25, however, that it had received an application for a rehearing on Hoffa's parole and had set a July 7 date for the hearing—two days after the start of the Teamsters convention in Miami Beach. As a result of the hearing, George J. Reed, parole board chairman, announced that the board had found "sufficient new and substantial information" to warrant an *en banc* appellate review of the Hoffa case and had set August 20, 1971, for a rehearing. Walter Sheridan, former special assistant to Attorney General Robert Kennedy, called me to report that "a deal was on" for Hoffa at the White House and the Board of Parole.

In a July 18, 1971, column, I wrote:

Those who advised President Nixon to sit down with the executive board of the International Teamsters Union and write that 'Dear Frank' letter to Teamsters President Frank Fitzsimmons have done Nixon a disservice.

The Teamsters' executive board contains at least two vice presidents currently under indictment—William (Big Bill) Presser, of Cleveland, and Sam Provenzano, of Newark. This is hardly the sort of a group President Nixon should be associating with even if he is hunting for labor support.

Before he commented that "Fitz is my kind of a labor leader," he should have had a better idea of the full background of Frank Fitzsimmons, who has been operating the Teamsters as the handpicked successor to the imprisoned Teamsters boss James R. Hoffa.

Frank Fitzsimmons may be a step up from Jimma Hoffa . . . but a close reading of the McClellan committee hearings would indicate that it is a small step indeed.

On July 28, 1971, I wrote to President Nixon to warn him again of the dangers in showing favoritism toward Hoffa. I hand-carried the letter to Ronald Ziegler in the West Wing of the White House and was later assured that it had been delivered to President Nixon. I had not seen him privately since May 1970, just before I left the White House. On November 7, 1970—immediately after the off-year congressional elections—I had been one of a group of columnists who interviewed him about his reactions to the election results.* White House Chief of Staff Haldeman had coldly rejected my several requests to see President Nixon personally in order to discuss matters I had dealt with in my column. I had not attempted to reach him by personal letter prior to the July 28 letter dealing with the Hoffa matter and the Joseph Hirshhorn Museum and Sculpture Garden.** Although Patrick Buchanan had assured me that he was calling my mildly critical columns to President Nixon's attention, I knew that Haldeman could short-circuit the trusted Buchanan if he disapproved of my material being included in the daily summary of the news. I knew the ever-watchful Haldeman would undoubtedly read my letter before it was delivered to President Nixon, so I would have nothing but Ziegler's word that it had in fact been received by the president.

In the opening paragraph of my letter I stated that I had made a number of unsuccessful efforts to see him about the Hoffa matter and the Joseph Hirshhorn Museum and Sculpture Garden. The letter went on: "It would be unwise from the standpoint of good government as well as your own political fortune to free James R. Hoffa on some promise that he will not run the Teamsters Union. Anyone familiar with the background knows this is wishful thinking. It is particularly bad to provide Hoffa with a parole at this stage in the light of the testimony before the McClellan committee and other places on the harm done by early release of big figures in organized crime."

I described the Hirshhorn project as "filled with so many illegal and irregular activities by Dillon Ripley, [secretary] of the Smithsonian, and others that I doubt if it could get a handful of votes in Congress at this stage."

I am sure you have not been given the full details on these matters and realize that these cases may lack the earmarks of high-priority projects. However, I regard them as vital from a standpoint of demonstrating an active interest in promoting honest government.

* Others present were *Newsweek* columnist Stewart Alsop, *Chicago Tribune* columnist Willard Edwards, and syndicated columnists James Jackson Kilpatrick, Nick Thimmesch, Richard L. Wilson, William S. White, and Roscoe and Geoffrey Drummond.
** President Lyndon B. Johnson made the controversial decision to bypass the required congressional procedures and approve expenditure of nearly $20 million in tax money to construct a gallery on the mall to house the art purchases of Joseph Hirshhorn, a wealthy international uranium speculator who had been convicted of illegal international money transactions. What Hirshhorn demanded and got for his collection of paintings and sculpture, for which he was reported to have paid about $4 million, included the government-financed home for his art works, with the government paying more than $2 million a year for staff and maintenance costs in perpetuity. It was also agreed that the monument—between the Washington Monument and the Capitol—would carry his name, and that he would get more than $40 million as a write-off for his "gift" to the federal government. It was a good deal for Hirshhorn, urged on Johnson by then Supreme Court Justice Abe Fortas and S. Dillon Ripley, secretary of the Smithsonian Institution. It was an LBJ deal, but there was little reason for President Nixon to be saddled with the responsibility for the construction and dedication to Hirshhorn, and several efforts had been made in Congress to at least remove Hirshhorn's name and control from this national art gallery.

I believe that your moves in Vietnam and with regard to meeting with the Red Chinese put you in a position of having little to fear on the international issues. There is a great deal of danger with regard to domestic issues and this is likely to become worse before it gets better.

I know that you are interested in doing what is best for the country. I believe that in any crisis the strongest thing a president has going for him is belief in his integrity. I believe that proceeding with a parole for Jimmy Hoffa or continuing the building for Hirshhorn (a man with two criminal convictions) would seriously undermine your record.

I have just completed a book on organized crime and the Strike Forces, and believe that the Strike Forces' accomplishments (in convicting organized crime figures) represent one of the strongest forces for your 1972 campaign. Any relaxing on Hoffa, who has been convicted of pension fraud and jury tampering, could seriously undermine your efforts to project a strong law enforcement image.

I have tried to present in this letter the same nonpartisan advice I would have given to you as presidential ombudsman. Respectfully yours.

I recognized that the letter was probably an exercise in futility, but I wanted to assure myself that I had done everything I could do to ensure that those making the decision had all of the facts from every perspective.

I also called chairman of the Board of Parole, George Reed, suggesting that he seek information from specific individuals in the Organized Crime Division of the Justice Department who were knowledgeable about Hoffa's background and connections, and agreed to hand-deliver a copy of my book *Tentacles of Power,* on Hoffa's hoodlum empire. In addition, I wrote the following letter to Reed on August 6:

I hope you have had an opportunity to read *Tentacles of Power.* I believe reading it is essential to having any real understanding of James R. Hoffa and the Teamsters Union.

I have had conversations with White House people and they inform me that you are an independent body operating on your own responsibility. I know there have been some periods in the past where this was not the fact, but a fiction. I would call specific attention to the record dealing with the much-criticized decision to spring the Capone mobsters in the late 1940's.

However, the White House has made it clear that you and your board have the full responsibility on this particular matter. It is for that reason that I urge you to ask for the comments of the Organized Crime Section in the Justice Department, where I am sure there is a realistic understanding of what release of Jimmy Hoffa might do.

I would call your attention to the fact that Hoffa's wife will have a key role in the political organization, that his son will be a $50,000-a-year counsel to the Teamsters Union, and that his life-long friend, Frank Fitzsimmons, will continue as general president.

I am sure that regardless of his resignation from miscellaneous Teamsters offices Jimmy Hoffa will run the Teamsters Union if he is released, and that agreements to the contrary will not be worth the paper upon which they are written.

In concluding, I suggested that he "contact Senator John J. McClellan for his comments," adding, "Please feel free to contact me on any matter where there is any confusion."

On August 20, the Board of Parole announced that it had "affirmed its previous decision to deny him [Hoffa] a parole." Reed announced that Hoffa's case would be considered again in June 1972 and that "his entire record will be reviewed, including his relationship, if any, with the International Brotherhood of Teamsters Union." Significantly, the board noted that "no new testimony was introduced by the Department of Justice," a fact which coincided with Sheridan's reports to me that Attorney General Mitchell had blocked the efforts of the Organized Crime section to submit a critical report on Hoffa's continuing connections with major organized crime figures.

I believed the Hoffa matter dead at least for another year, until I received a telephone call from Charles W. Colson, special counsel to the president, on November 4, 1971. Colson said he wished to meet with me, that it was "important, at the request of the president," and that he could not even mention the subject on the telephone. When I met Colson at his office, it wasn't until I had agreed that this was to be a secret conference with "no news stories" before an unspecified event was announced publicly that he told me the subject was "possible executive clemency for Jimmy Hoffa." Prior to that moment I had hoped President Nixon was engaged in political shadow-boxing and had no serious intention of taking the risk of direct action to free Hoffa. Colson said that the president had instructed him to take the Hoffa matter up with me and to seek my advice. I told Colson that I had given my advice in a letter to President Nixon and in countless columns and articles over a period of months. My view hadn't changed. I felt Hoffa had betrayed the union membership, tried to subvert our system of justice, and misused millions of dollars in pension funds, thus jeopardizing the security of aging members and their families. I said I thought it would be foolhardy for President Nixon to take the responsibility for freeing Hoffa only a few months after the parole board refused to do so.

Colson said that Hoffa had failed to win a parole in August because of "a technicality" involving the fact that Hoffa had not resigned from Detroit Teamsters Local 299 but had indicated to the parole board that he had resigned. "It is inevitable that Hoffa will be free next summer," Colson said and explained "all of the disadvantages of it appearing that the administration has done something for him (in an election year) without the political advantage of having Hoffa and Hoffa's supporters grateful." Colson revealed that he had suggested the alternative of executive clemency on the Christmas weekend, which could be viewed as "an act of compassion." He said he believed, as did President Nixon, that the brief criticism that would accompany Hoffa's release "would blow over by next summer." Colson said that he and John Mitchell had favored giving Hoffa a parole in March 1971, but had avoided any intervention at that time because of the risk of being charged with interfering with an independent agency of the government. Although he insisted that no firm decision had yet been made, it was apparent that he leaned heavily toward a commutation of Hoffa's sentence in time for Christmas, and I assumed he was reflecting the president's view. But he asked my opinion of the relative risks involved and said that such recommendations would weigh heavily with the president—clumsy flattery which I recognized as having no merit. I pointed out that executive clemency meant that "the president must go on the line for Hoffa" and that this made him "a sitting duck" for critics who would see the link with a convicted labor racketeer as one more reason for distrust.

Colson mentioned that Frank Fitzsimmons, now president of the Teamsters Union in his own right, had been most helpful in keeping President Nixon's Pay Board labor members in line. "He is the only one who will stand up to George Meany," Colson said, and quoted Fitzsimmons as saying in a speech in California that he would stay with the Pay Board regardless of what other labor members did. I asked Colson whether the reason for springing Hoffa was to show some gratitude to Fitzsimmons for his support of the president's economic programs. Colson said that this was not the reason, and admitted that there was some question about whether Fitzsimmons actually wanted Hoffa out of prison. Fitzsimmons had made no pitch on the subject, Colson said, and he had concluded that Fitzsimmons would be content to run the Teamsters Union with Hoffa safely in prison. The objective, as Colson spelled it out, was simply to bow to the inevitable release of Hoffa and to try to gain some political advantage from Hoffa supporters in the Teamsters Union, including the executive board members who overwhelmingly favored Hoffa's release.

I asked whether this entailed arrangements for political contributions of any kind. Colson said it did not, and that the administration would simply want an endorsement. He said he had specifically rejected the idea of any type of arrangement for campaign funds. I emphasized the political criticism that would certainly accompany any evidence that even small Teamsters Union contributions went into the president's 1972 campaign. Colson agreed but said that there would probably be some worker participation in the campaign. He stressed that AFL-CIO President Meany and others in organized labor would be in the Democratic camp regardless of their candidate, and that Nixon needed labor support. In response, I questioned the wisdom of wooing or accepting any labor support if the corrupt Teamsters Union was the best source of support that could be found. Colson shrugged this problem off as something I was giving an undue amount of consideration. He said that nothing was settled but that he would convey my views to President Nixon. Colson also said that he hoped I would not try to make too big an issue of it if Hoffa was granted executive clemency. I said that I knew I would write critically about it and that I believed that many others would too. "We expect a couple of bad stories from you, and wouldn't try to have it otherwise," Colson said. "We just don't want you to drag it out if no one else does."

While I had Colson's ear, I mentioned that I believed the administration was heading for serious trouble over the Civil Service Commission's denial of a public hearing for A. Ernest Fitzgerald in his dispute with the Air Force. I also mentioned that the State Department would be involved in a case comparable to the Dreyfus case if there were ever full public exposure of the perjury, false statements, distortion of records, and cover-up by its personnel division. Colson said that he shared my concern over these problems but that he avoided getting into problems that were Bill Rogers' responsibility because of the special relationship between Rogers and Nixon, which went back more than twenty years.

I was depressed, angry, and then sadly disappointed with Richard Nixon as I walked out of the Executive Office Building to return to the National Press Building. That night I jotted down notes, and the next morning I dictated a memorandum of the conversation, which I recognized as a prelude to the release of Hoffa. By my promise to Colson I had bound myself not to write about the decision until either I learned about it from another source or an official announcement was made. In the following weeks I did not even acknowledge to Walter Sheridan that I had any personal corroborative knowledge when he told me of reports of a deal to spring Hoffa sometime before Christmas. His sources were within the Teamsters Union, but they were not specific as to the date of the release.

On December 19, 1971, at a party in the home of William O. Bittman, one of the lawyers who had prosecuted Hoffa in Chicago, I received specific confirmation that Hoffa was to be freed during the next week. Although I had expected it, I experienced a wave of disappointment as I immediately called the *Des Moines Register* with an exclusive story that Hoffa would be released before Christmas.

On December 23, Colson called to suggest that I go to John Dean's office at 4:00 P.M. to get a background briefing on the Hoffa release. The bare facts were bad enough. Nixon had personally approved a commutation of sentence for Hoffa only a few months after the parole board had rejected his application for parole. It was the first time President Nixon had commuted a sentence after clemency had been denied by the parole board, and it seemed to me that the whole Hoffa-Nixon relationship, dating from the 1960 campaign, would be back in the 1972 campaign, and that all the old Hoffa-Nixon ties would be fair game for political commentary.

When I arrived at John Dean's office, the news of Hoffa's release had already come over the United Press International ticker in my office. Dean handed me a prepared statement being distributed at the Justice Department at the same time and said he had been instructed to answer all my questions. It was quickly apparent that Dean was not informed on the background of the case and that I was receiving the special "stroking" that Haldeman and Ehrlichman employed to beguile and cajole. I was not angry with Dean, for he was a pleasant and naïve young man carrying out a nasty chore without understanding fully just how odious it was. The prepared statement glossed over Hoffa's crimes and did not mention his links with organized crime and the nature of the crimes still being committed against the pension funds of the Teamsters Union.

Dean said that the commutation by President Nixon had been made on the recommendations of the pardon attorney and of Attorney General John Mitchell, and that Hoffa had been "a model prisoner." The young lawyer said Colson had suggested that I would be particularly interested in the condition requiring that Hoffa "not engage in the direct or indirect management of any labor organization prior to March 6, 1980, and if the . . . condition is not fulfilled this commutation will be null and void in its entirety." This was cited by Dean, and later by Colson, as "a tough provision" because without it Hoffa would have been able to get back into the union business in 1976—five years after his release from prison. I was not impressed. It was a political deal with Hoffa any way you looked at it. They would all live to regret dealing with this labor racketeer, perhaps even before the 1972 election.

*Chapter Twenty-two*

# LOCKHEED AIRCRAFT––
# BAIL-OUT AND COVER-UP

THE NIXON WHITE HOUSE, which in 1970 had resisted my pleas for direct involvement in the fight for justice for Air Force cost analyst A. Ernest Fitzgerald, in early 1971 suddenly showed great concern about the operations of Fitzgerald's nemesis—the Lockheed Aircraft Corporation. But that concern was not to order the reinstatement of Fitzgerald, who had been wrongfully discharged after testifying on the C-5A overruns. Nor was it to assure Fitzgerald an open Civil Service hearing in his dispute with the Air Force hierarchy, as Fitzgerald's lawyers argued was his basic right as an American citizen. And certainly it was not to censure the Number One defense contractor for shoddy work and deceptive financial reports in connection with the C-5A or any of its other military contracts, as demanded by Senator William Proxmire of Wisconsin and Senator William Moorhead, the Pennsylvania Democrat who headed the House Government Operations Subcommittee on Government Information. Senate and House committees, assisted by the General Accounting Office (GAO), had been trying to stimulate presidential concern over those problems for months. The fact is, the White House was concerned about the best means to solve Lockheed's financial woes.

In early 1971, beset by economic troubles, Lockheed requested a $200 million bail-out by the Defense Department in connection with its C-5A contract. The request was rejected by Defense Secretary Melvin Laird, but Laird suggested that if Lockheed could establish that it was in the public interest for the taxpayers to come to its rescue, special legislation could be passed by Congress. Lockheed officials then found an attentive ear at the Treasury Department, where Democrat John B. Connally had been appointed secretary as part of President Nixon's southern strategy for 1972. The former Texas governor, anxious to make a good impression on the Georgia-based firm, accepted the argument that without government help the ailing corporation would go bankrupt, with a resulting loss of 25,000 to 30,000 jobs. Prodded by Connally, President Nixon on May 4 recommended that the government guarantee a loan of $250 million to Lockheed. The specific loan guaranty related to a $1.2 billion investment in the L-1011 Tristar jet airbus, a commercial contract. It was the alternative to direct Defense Department help on the bungled C-5A contract, under heavy criticism in Congress for months. Under the program President Nixon and Connally recommended to Congress, the private banking sector would make the $250 million in loans to Lockheed but the government would guarantee repayment if Lockheed defaulted.

Majority Leader Mike Mansfield (D., Mont.) was not impressed with the need to extricate the giant corporation from its financial difficulties. "It is time to call a halt to bailing these companies out from the consequences of their own mismanagement," the Montana Democrat told the Senate. Senator William Proxmire (D., Wis.), who had had a leading role in exposing Lockheed's defense contract deceptions, said:

> The administration's decision to guarantee this . . . loan is a serious mistake. If the government does not step in, the Lockheed management would have to pay the price of failure by leaving the company. Lockheed stockholders would lose. The bankers who had loaned Lockheed funds would have to take their losses, but that is what the American free enterprise system is all about. The responsibility for business management and those who benefit from the success must bear the cost of failure as well as the benefits of success.

Representative Moorhead said that the Nixon administration was taking "a large step toward socializing the aircraft industry," and pointed to criticism from William Allen, chairman of the board of the Boeing Company, and from other business executives who said the government guaranty of a loan to Lockheed would amount to an unfair competitive advantage. John Connally, the most outspoken proponent of the Lockheed rescue, said: "The failure of major business enterprise can have serious national and regional consequences, including the causing of substantial unemployment, as well as other business failures."

But though the Lockheed Corporation was asking for government help, it refused Senator Proxmire's requests for details on its financial plight. Surprisingly, Defense Department officials also refused Proxmire's request for this data on the grounds that it was "confidential information" and that Lockheed classed it as "proprietary data." When Assistant Secretary of Defense Barry J. Shillito appeared before Proxmire's Joint Economic Committee, Proxmire told him, "It seems to me the taxpayers have a right to this information if they are to put up the money to guarantee the loan." Proxmire declared that "defense contracting is a disaster area," and added: "It is ironic that those who are responsible for bringing the procurement system and a large sector of the industrial community to the brink of fiscal chaos have done so in the name of national security." Gordon Rule, an outspoken Navy expert on defense contracting, insisted that the government should reject Lockheed's request for the loan guarantee. "If their management has been lousy, I say let 'em go broke. I don't see why we should take this action."

But despite the protests, the Nixon administration, with Connally leading the way, won narrow approval by Congress. The vote was 192 to 189 in the House on July 30, and 49 to 48 in the Senate on August 2. On August 9 President Nixon signed the bill, which provided for a three-member Emergency Loan Guarantee Board to supervise details of the loan. Treasury Secretary Connally, who served as chairman of the loan board, immediately clamped a tight lid on access to records under a general claim of "executive privilege," in order to bar from Congress details of how the loan was being supervised. Comptroller General Elmer Staats and the auditors of his watchdog agency, GAO, complained that this lack of access to financial records made it impossible for them to determine whether the assets pledged by the company as security complied with the law's requirement that Lockheed loans be "fully collateralized." Connally and Treasury Counsel Samuel R. Pierce, Jr., argued that the law establishing the Lockheed loan board had no provision requiring access by the GAO. Staats responded that GAO access to all government records was established firmly in the Budgeting and Accounting Act of 1921, which provided for a constant independent audit of government agencies as a safeguard against waste, mismanagement, and corruption. But Connally remained firm, even after the House and Senate Banking Committees agreed with Staats' interpretation that the "intent of Congress" is that GAO is authorized to have access to "all records" unless there is a specific congressional denial of access in the law.

The House committee reports took issue with Connally:

There are certain overriding questions of public policy which transcend the legal arguments involved. In view of the highly controversial nature of the Lockheed loan guarantee and the size of the U.S. financial commitment, the committee believed the Emergency Loan Guarantee Board should cooperate fully with GAO in making its records available. In passing the Emergency Loan Guarantee Act, the committee does not believe that Congress intended to deny to the GAO any information of a type which it has customarily collected. . . .

Senator Stuart Symington of Missouri went even further when he said:

The GAO has often been called the watchdog of Congress. It would now appear that the executive branch desires the watchdog to be not only toothless, but blind. If the position of the loan board were correct, in all future legislation Congress would be required to state specifically, in each and every case where a new government entity is created, that GAO had the right to examine the records and review the operations of the agency in question, an agency whose efficient performance is often vital for the Congress to know about prior to additional commitment of taxpayers money.

The GAO wanted to determine:

1. What basis there was for a board waiver of the law's prohibition against Lockheed making any payments on its other indebtedness to any lender whose loan is guaranteed under the act, as long as any portion of the guaranteed loan is outstanding.

2. What standards were applied by the board in deciding that the inability of the Lockheed Corporation to obtain credit did not result from the failure of Lockheed management to exercise "reasonable business prudence."

3. Whether the board had received the audited financial statements from the borrower prior to approval of the arrangements as required by law.

4. Whether the board had received appropriate notice and certifications from the bank that was making the loan and whether the board had received a financing plan from Lockheed, as required by law to provide each pay-out on the loan guarantee.

Ernie Fitzgerald assured me that the records the GAO was seeking from Connally were the minimum records that should have been available in order to properly account to Congress. The preferential treatment for Lockheed by the government was well documented, and there seemed no reasonable argument for continuing secrecy. But Connally, an expert at stonewalling, disregarded the complaints from the GAO and Congress. By June 12, 1972, when he resigned as Treasury secretary to head a Democrats-for-Nixon organization in the presidential campaign, he still had not permitted access to the records. Connally's arrogant defiance of Congress and the GAO had not damaged his image with the public or the press. Instead, there was more than a touch of admiration for the confidence with which he had handled congressional complaints. President Nixon, who had long had trouble handling the press, obviously admired the manner in which the articulate and self-assured Texas Democrat alternately criticized and cajoled the press and got away with it. Reports circulated that President Nixon was considering dropping Vice President Spiro T. Agnew for the more sophisticated, more clever Connally.

George P. Shultz, who succeeded Connally as President Nixon's third secretary of the Treasury, rejected GAO appeals to open the board records on the Lockheed loans on the grounds that he was unfamiliar with the issue and did not want to suddenly reverse a policy that obviously had the approval of President Nixon. That stall worked until after Nixon's landslide victory in November 1972, when there was no need, political or otherwise, for opening the records. The use of "executive privilege" had been successful in the face of well-documented complaints from influential members of Congress, and there seemed no reason it couldn't go on forever.

In the midst of Connally's success in barring GAO from the Lockheed loan records, Fitzgerald commented philosophically: "Guys like Connally have probably got it figured about right with the Congress and the press. There is no real consistent follow-through necessary to get to the bottom of these

things, and the cover-up works more often than it doesn't. A few, like Proxmire or Congressman Gross, will stay with something over the months and
years necessary to get something done. But most of them have a very short
attention span, and the bureaucrats or politicians can stall them until they
lose interest. The same is true of the press. They have to be off to some new,
hot story, and they forget all about the secrecy and the unanswered questions
that are frequently a better story than what they are chasing."

Fitzgerald cited the erratic congressional and press interest in his own case,
which involved a major weapon system, billions of dollars in overruns, and
easily documented injustices, as an example of this short attention span. The
Air Force cost expert commented on "the great flurry" of front-page stories
and editorials when he testified on the nearly $2 billion in cost overruns, and
the protests when his job was abolished for "economy reasons." "Contrast
that with the little attention given to the Air Force efforts to block me from
getting an open hearing," Fitzgerald said, adding that there had been virtually
no attention to the Civil Service Commision's support of secret hearings. "Although open hearings are an essential part of due process of law, there was
practically no coverage of Proxmire's charge that I was being subjected to an
unjustified star chamber proceeding," Fitzgerald told me. If the American
Civil Liberties Union hadn't furnished me with two damned good lawyers
[John Bodner and William Sollee], I wouldn't have been able to afford to
challenge the Air Force."

During the same period that the Nixon administration was bailing out
Lockheed and Connally was concealing records, the administration permitted
the Air Force and the Civil Service Commission to trample on Fitzgerald's
rights to a public hearing. "The Civil Service Commission members have
made it clear that they are a part of this effort to cover-up the bungling
on the C-5A," Senator Proxmire commented. "Unless national security is
involved, or unless the man involved wants the hearing closed to protect
his reputation, there should be an open hearing." Herman D. Staiman, the
Civil Service Commission hearing examiner, had granted the Air Force's request for a closed hearing on the Fitzgerald matter with the support of the
Civil Service Commission's general counsel, Anthony Mondello. Mondello
defended secret hearings thus: "It resulted in a better atmosphere for personnel actions." Representative H. R. Gross, the fiesty ranking Republican
member of the House Post Office Service Committee, declared: "This is
the kind of ruling that makes me reluctant to give the Civil Service Commission any discretionary power."

"There is no excuse for a secret hearing for this case," Gross said. "Fitzgerald went before a Senate subcommittee and he told the truth about the
costs of the C-5A, and the Air Force superiors didn't like it. Fitzgerald is
entitled to a public hearing on the merits of whether he was forced out because of his testimony, or was simply dropped because of a reduction in
force." The Iowa Republican added: "I have an idea that the Air Force is
trying to hide or confuse the record in this instance."

The basic logic of the Proxmire and Gross statements was later laid down as the law by United States District Judge William Bryant in a decision upheld unanimously by a United States Appeals Court panel in the District of Columbia. But Judge Bryant's order supporting Fitzgerald's right to an open hearing as basic due process did not come down until late 1971. The Justice Department then contrived to further delay the hearings by challenging the order in the United States Court of Appeals, where it was possible to defer a decision until 1972. Further procedural delays by the Justice Department in determining whether it would appeal to the United States Supreme Court prevented Fitzgerald from starting his open hearing until January 1973—well after the 1972 election.

But Fitzgerald and his two young attorneys were philosophical about their fight against government's bureaucracy secrecy. "I've got a good case, and they aren't going to wear me down by stalling," Fitzgerald said. Although he was out of a steady job, he was able to keep a reasonably satisfactory flow of income from speaking engagements, writing, and contract consultant work for two committees of Congress. Although he was determined to see the fight through until he was reinstated in his Air Force job, Fitzgerald commented bitterly on the manner in which the Nixon administration had rejected his pleas to be restored to his job, yet rushed to provide a $250 million loan to the Lockheed Corporation, whose deplorable mismanagement had cheated the American people in terms of additional cost and defective military equipment.

*Chapter Twenty-three*

# THE POISON OF SECRECY SPREADS

The Nixon White House created a milieu in which the insidious poison of secrecy permeated virtually all departments and agencies of the federal government. The press was "the enemy," and appointees of the president were not to fraternize with the enemy except to leak a story in order to test public reaction or to hurt an opponent. Even then it was dangerous, for an unfavorable political reaction required a scapegoat. The most heinous crime of all was to be identified as the source of a news story embarrassing to President Nixon, Haldeman, Ehrlichman, or Kissinger. Under these circumstances, the safest thing was to ignore all questions from the press or Congress. It might be personally embarrassing to refuse to answer a question or return a call, but to many it was a better alternative than to risk the scathing criticism of Haldeman or political death from the silent treatment.

Secretary of the Interior Walter Hickel was the victim of a vehement denunciation from Ehrlichman because of comments to the press that were out of step with the White House line. The firing of Secretary Hickel on November 25, 1971, was the first clear notice of the extent to which President Nixon would go to back Haldeman and Ehrlichman. The fiesty former governor of Alaska, a self-made millionaire and former boxer, was unaccustomed to being ordered around—especially by the young and inexperienced White House aides who carried messages from Haldeman and Ehrlichman. Hickel believed his cabinet post assured him automatic access to President Nixon for discussion of government problems. Instead, he seldom saw the president except at cabinet meetings, where the formal structure and a strict agenda barred informal discussions of many of the problems the administration faced. His efforts to see President Nixon privately were blocked by Ehrlichman's nondiscriminatory rudeness, which he applied equally to cabinet officers, sub-cabinet officers, congressmen, senators, and all but a few members of the White House staff.

On May 6, 1970, Secretary Hickel tried to reach the president by sending Mr. Nixon a private letter urging him to establish communication with the nation's youth and recommending that he consult with members of his cabinet on such matters. The Hickel letter was "leaked" to the press, and its implied criticism of President Nixon caused an uproar. While the letter centered on the lack of communication with protesters, the secretary of the interior was speaking for virtually the whole cabinet when he appealed to Mr. Nixon to meet with members "on an individual and conversational basis. Perhaps then we can gain greater insight into the problems confronting us all." It was reported in May 1970 that Hickel had talked privately with the president only twice since the inauguration, when Mr. Nixon had told the American people how much he was going to depend on the men he selected for the cabinet. I was still on the White House staff at the time, and the Executive Office Building and White House mess buzzed with discussion; everyone understood why Hickel had spoken out. We hoped his letter and the resulting furor would make it perfectly clear to Mr. Nixon that he had a serious problem within his government, as well as with the protesters and the press.

When he was asked about the Hickel matter at his news conference on May 8, the president declared that Hickel held "very strong views" but that he was "outspoken" and "courageous." This, he said, was why Hickel was his secretary of the interior and why he had defended the Alaska Republican when he was under attack by conservationists when he was first nominated. Although Hickel accepted this praise from the president and joined in the effort to elect Republicans to the Senate and House, there was no substantial change for the cabinet or the White House staff in their access to President Nixon. But Haldeman and Ehrlichman harbored deep resentment because the Hickel letter had so critically called attention to what they believed was their strength—their vigilance at the entrance to the Oval Office.

Their strength was demonstrated on November 25, when President Nixon, in consultation with Haldeman and Ehrlichman, summoned Hickel to the White House and fired him. He emphasized his displeasure by naming Interior Under Secretary Fred Russell to serve as acting secretary immediately, pending confirmation of Representative Rogers Morton, who was then chairman of the Republican National Committee.

Hickel announced to newsmen at the Interior Department two hours later that the president "personally terminated me" and gave a one-sentence summation of the problem of "trying to do the job for the president and all Americans and still somehow survive—as an individual." Said Hickel: "I had to do it my way." Under fire by environmentalists at the time of his appointment, Hickel was praised by his earlier critics as an excellent conservationist in his handling of extremely difficult problems like the oil blowouts in Santa Barbara and the Gulf of Mexico.

Press Secretary Ronald Ziegler spoke for the White House: "The president feels that the required elements for a good and continued relationship which must exist between the president and his cabinet members simply did not exist in this case." Stories were leaked to the press through anonymous sources that Hickel was "a poor administrator" and "was not a good policymaker," without mention of what particular actions had displeased President Nixon. Others who were considering dissent got the message: They risked being fired and discredited if they balked at carrying out orders or made public their frustration.

On November 27, abrupt dismissal orders were issued to six of Hickel's top aides at the Interior Department by Frederic V. Malek, whom Haldeman had installed as special assistant to the president to handle personnel matters. Those fired were individuals who had displeased Ehrlichman in his dealing with the Hickel problem: Charles Meacham, U.S. commissioner for fish and wildlife and deputy assistant secretary for fish, wildlife and parks; Dr. Leslie Glasgow, assistant secretary for fish, wildlife and parks; Josef Holbert, deputy director of information; Tom Holley, director of congressional liaison; Pat Ryan, executive assistant to Hickel; and Dr. Donald Dunlop, Hickel's science adviser. Ryan and Holbert had submitted their resignations on November 26.

Hickel declared on the nationally televised CBS program "Face the Nation" on December 6 that it was "incredible" that his six aides had been fired with orders to clear out their desks before the end of the working day. He said he did not know whether this was the president's decision. Hickel told how Malek had used the term "purge" in telling him of the decision and said that the White House had made the change at the time it did in order "to take the heat" right after the election so that the affair would be forgotten by 1972. The deposed secretary of the interior declined to elaborate on the oil policy disputes that were a part of his conflict with the White House, but reports circulated that the White House was considering a proposal to sell Navy petroleum reserves in Alaska, Wyoming, and California, a step reportedly favored by private oil companies.

I knew that the Ehrlichman-Haldeman barrier had created equally unsatisfactory conditions for many other cabinet officers, but the firing of Hickel strikingly demonstrated that Nixon appointees had to accept the yoke of obedience and not make public their frustration when Haldeman or Ehrlichman barred the president's door. George Romney, secretary of the Department of Housing and Urban Development (HUD), was particularly restive because of his inability to confer with President Nixon and the constant meddling in his department by Ehrlichman and Ehrlichman's White House aides. Romney realized that the White House–directed reversal of his decision on the Austin Geriatric Center was a Nixon decision made under the influence of former President Johnson. But he chafed at the constant, day-by-day incursions on his department by Ehrlichman and his assistants, who tried to give the impression that their suggestions and directions were "the president's wish" or "what the president wants done."

Most of this was too petty to merit creating an issue by demanding to see President Nixon, even if that were possible. But Ehrlichman and Haldeman stated clearly that they considered it the responsibility of cabinet officers to expedite the decisions the president wanted made and to "take the heat" if there was public criticism. Cabinet officers were on notice that they would be held strictly accountable for statements to the press, press conferences, or information leaked from their departments that proved embarrassing to President Nixon. Combine this with Ehrlichman's broad thesis that "executive privilege" could cover essentially any communication within the White House or between the departments and the White House, and it was easy to understand why few cabinet officers would risk regular press conferences or open policies.

To Secretary Romney, an unusually forthright, honest, and independent man, this atmosphere was particularly difficult because he had been president of American Motors, governor of the State of Michigan, and a front-running contender for the Republican presidential nomination in early 1968. He was accustomed to working hard, thinking his problems through, arriving at a practical solution, and then discussing his plans publicly to test them for flaws. As a businessman, a governor, and a candidate, he was recognized as open, decent, and willing to modify his views, but strongly opposed to making decisions based on partisan political arguments or back-room pressures. But he also recognized that no administration could have all of its cabinet officers going off in different directions, even though each should be the major force with the president in his own area of responsibility.

But Romney's experience with a frank, open policy had been disappointing in early 1968 when he had to give up his quest for the Republican nomination because of the political and journalistic ridicule he was subjected to after his forthright admission that he had been "brainwashed" on Vietnam policies by the Johnson administration. Although he was laughed out of politics because he was considered naïve on the subject of "truth in politics," Romney subsequently saw Richard Nixon emerge with the Republican nomination and the presidency by the clever contrivance of announcing a secret plan to end the Vietnam War. That, plus the firing of Hickel, was enough to raise serious doubts about the practical value of forthright politics, and it caused Secretary Romney to be less available to the press. Inevitably it led to the acceptance of a policy that prohibited disclosure of the names of fee appraisers employed by the Federal Housing Administration (FHA) in connection with its loan programs. The appraisers placed valuations on individual pieces of property for the government before federal loans were made, so these appraisals were at the heart of the whole loan program.

George Romney did not initiate the secrecy at FHA which brought him in conflict with Representative William Moorhead of Pennsylvania and Representative John Moss of California—two avid congressional fighters for open government. However, Romney did sign a letter on November 11, 1971, which the House Government Operations Subcommittee on Government Information Policy interpreted as the broadest possible defense of HUD policies and as an assumption by him of personal responsibility for any questionable appraisals in the agency as a whole. In all good faith, apparently, Romney accepted the bureaucrats' legal thesis that the identity of the appraisers was protected by "executive privilege" and that once the FHA accepted an appraisal by the experts as fair, those figures became the official position of the FHA and had to be defended all the way to the top of the agency. HUD lawyers cited a ruling by United States District Judge L. Clure Morton in Nashville, Tennessee, as the precedent, even though all of the law and logic of other courts and the House Government Operations Subcommittee challenged that precedent.

Representative Moss, a long-time leader in the fight against excessive government secrecy, declared: "Romney has taken a bad legal precedent in Tennessee and has expanded it into an extensive argument for a secrecy principle that could corrupt HUD from coast to coast. It would appear that George Romney has been brainwashed by the bureaucrats and the lawyers in his agency who have something to hide." Representative Moorhead, who succeeded Moss as chairman of the government information subcommittee, said, "If the Romney logic is followed there won't be a single appraisal in any agency that is available for public inspection." Moorhead told me: "The whole point of the Freedom of Information Act would be lost. If Romney and his agency can bar newspapers from access to the names of appraisers who make the specific appraisals in Pennsylvania, it is only logical that the same policies will apply in Illinois, Iowa, Florida, or Massachusetts."

The specific case before Moorhead's subcommittee involved a suit that John Siegenthaler, editor of the *Nashville Tennessean,* had filed against Romney's agency for access to the name of the man who had appraised the home of a Mr. and Mrs. Hugh James for $10,850. The *Tennessean* had information from two separate, independent appraisers that the house was worth $4,000 to $5,000. A small amount of money was involved, but Siegenthaler was a knowledgeable editor who understood that the principle of secret government decisions was far greater than the $10,850 Mr. and Mrs. James had paid for a dilapidated home near Nashville. The astute editor also realized that the case had a particular appeal to public sympathy and understanding because the Jameses were both blind and appeared to have been fleeced by a real estate man in collusion with local FHA officials. Siegenthaler and I had served on the National Sigma Delta Chi journalism society's Freedom of Information Committee, and he called me to discuss the suit at the time it was filed. Later I agreed to appear as a witness on government information policies, if his lawyers felt they needed the testimony.

When Siegenthaler first told me of the lawsuit, I called George Romney. The $10,850 evaluation of a house in Tennessee seemed a niggling thing to discuss with a cabinet officer who was responsible for billions. I apologized to Secretary Romney but explained that as a friend I wished to warn him that he should examine the case closely before putting his good name to the corrupting policy of venal bureaucrats. Romney agreed to take my call only because he trusted me not to quote him and thus create problems with Ehrlichman and Haldeman. From our association in the Nixon administration, we had developed a rapport based on our experience of the difficulties created by the obsessive secrecy and the lack of access to President Nixon.

I told Romney that I did not wish to quote him or even press him to take a position on access to FHA appraisal reports and the names of appraisers. "I do intend to write critically about these policies, and I want to be sure you have an opportunity to study the problem and not get trapped by simply defending the actions of subordinates," I said.

Romney thanked me profusely, saying he wished to be warned about potential problems, and with his characteristic candor said: "If we were doing something wrong around here, we want to know about it. It's a big agency, and sometimes the only way we know what is wrong is when we read it in the press." He promised "to take a close look at" the Nashville appraiser problem, but, as he later told me, he got tied up in other things and failed to examine the total problem.

The House Government Operations Subcommittee, true to form, pursued its inquiry into the Nashville matter and similar secrecy policies in Philadelphia, where inflated housing appraisals appeared to be responsible for scandalous conditions. Secretary Romney was persuaded to defend his agency against sharp criticism by the *Philadelphia Inquirer* in a well-documented series of articles dealing with federal housing loans in Philadelphia.

In a November 11, 1971, letter to the editor of the *Inquirer,* Romney cited the highly questionable ruling by Judge Morton in Tennessee and then expanded upon it. The letter, written by the HUD legal office, put Romney in the position of taking the blame for everything that went wrong in HUD, on the theory that "appraisals . . . prepared in the first instance by individuals, were adopted by HUD and became actions of HUD."

Therefore, if any appraisals are wrong, it is appropriate to criticize HUD and HUD's executives, including me, but it is neither relevant nor appropriate to criticize the individual who made them.

The decision not to name individuals who made specific appraisals is not a cover-up of HUD's action. The names of those individuals who had some part in making appraisals, accepting it, and acting on it are not related to the fact that HUD has adopted it. The press does not need to know those names in order to criticize HUD's actions.

I could not believe that Romney understood what he had signed, and I made inquiry at HUD to determine whether the letter was really Romney's letter and whether he really wished to stand behind its distorted logic. An effort to talk to Romney failed, but I was told that he stood solidly behind the contents of the letter. There was no other choice but to directly criticize the HUD secretary, who was supporting, and even expanding, the corruptive secrecy policies. Representative Moss struck at the heart of the issue when he declared: "At the time that the Freedom of Information Act was passed, we believed that we were ending the need for making any kind of showing of wrongdoing or possible wrongdoing in connection with requests for information." Said Moss: "Romney appears to have picked up a lot of unmitigated nonsense that has been used to justify secrecy over the years. Romney suggests the names are not needed to pursue the investigation and that it would be a disservice to the public to publish the names. The fact that such appraisals are subjected to public second-guessing keeps our road programs and our housing programs as clean as they are."

Moss said that the House Government Operations Subcommittee investigation indicated that the *Philadelphia Inquirer* knew of the housing racket in the Philadelphia area through which hundreds—perhaps thousands—of dilapidated houses have been nominally rehabilitated under FHA programs and sold to unsuspecting and often poor and ignorant slum dwellers. The mark-ups appeared to be as much as 1,000 percent too high, Moss said. He charged that the immense profits were made possible entirely through the FHA's appraisal system, since the houses were bought for next to nothing. Then, after a quick patch-up for a few hundred dollars, mortgage funding was guaranteed by FHA on the basis of a post-patch-up appraisal, Moss said. The fact that many of these appraisals are by so-called "fee appraisers," who are often real estate brokers paid on a job basis, had led the *Philadelphia Inquirer* to conclude that some fee appraisers have intimate business connections with some of the speculators. "Mr. Romney now would trust only his agency to dig out the evidence of scandals and call a spade a spade despite a record of less than vigorous activity [by HUD] in the past," Moss said.

I wrote a stinging column accusing Romney of responsibility for spreading "a poisonous secrecy precedent" that was published on December 4 and 5, 1971—the weekend of the winter Gridiron Dinner at which Romney was one of the guests. The winter Gridiron Dinner is a more intimate affair than the lavish white-tie bash that the organization of veteran Washington newsmen stage for more than five hundred guests each spring. Romney was among the dozen guests—all high officials of the Nixon administration—who were entertained less formally each December in the Federal Room at the Statler Hilton.

I had been unable to reach him while writing the column, but at the dinner he greeted me warmly and said he was sorry he had not been able to return my call. I accepted his excuse that he had been "busy as the devil" and told him I had written a column denouncing his secrecy policies. I said I had wanted to talk to him about the "unwise" letter he had written to the *Inquirer* but felt I had expressed my critical view in earlier conversations. I explained that I considered it foolhardy for him to put his good name on the line by taking personal responsibility for all of the crookedness and mismanagement in HUD. "Did I do that?" he asked, and his sincerity convinced me he did not associate the letter to the *Philadelphia Inquirer* with the secrecy problem in Tennessee that we had discussed earlier. I told him that, regardless of his own honest motivations and a desire to move aggressively against infractions, small pockets of corruption and favoritism would inevitably develop. "You aren't going to be able to police the entire agency yourself, and you can't rely entirely on any inspector general in the agency who will inevitably become part of the bureaucracy," I said. "You need every bit of help from the press and the Congress to keep your agency clean."

Romney said that the HUD counsel's office had put the issue in terms of his having the responsibility for keeping HUD operations honest, and that problems should and could be handled from the inside. "We depend on these fee appraisers, and once we accept their figures we assume the responsibility that those figures are accurate, fair figures," Romney said. "We shouldn't release the name of the little appraiser and make him take the blame." George Romney, the perpetual Boy Scout, was thinking in terms of protecting lower-level fee appraisers from second-guessing and occasional unjust criticism, and was overlooking the fact that major scandals appeared to have developed as a result of rackets based on manipulation of hundreds and perhaps thousands of these appraisals.

"Your only protection from your own agency is keeping everything on the public record," I advised. "Don't accept the arguments of the bureaucrats, the lawyers, and the White House on 'executive privilege.'" He said his lawyers cited Judge Morton's decision in Tennessee as supportive of their policy of not revealing the appraisers' names. I told him that there was no law and no court precedent for the arbitrary, all-embracing "executive privilege" theories espoused by Ehrlichman to cover all "internal executive branch" documents and conversations. Romney said that he agreed with me on the general principles that open government was self-policing and that secrecy fostered corruption but that he had to live within the policies laid down by John Mitchell at the Justice Department and the White House. I predicted that Judge Morton's decision would be upset by the Sixth Circuit or by the U.S. Supreme Court. Romney was skeptical, and he was troubled by my belief that he was unwittingly covering up housing scandals.

Within six months, my prediction was fulfilled. Three different federal court decisions largely nullified the broad secrecy policies HUD lawyers had sold to Secretary Romney. On May 5, 1972, the Sixth Circuit Court of Appeals declared that Judge Morton had been wrong when he had declared "no possible purpose would be served by releasing the identity of the appraiser." In ruling that HUD had to provide the names of its appraisers to the *Nashville Tennessean,* the court said:

The appraisal in this case is an analysis of facts involving a professional opinion. The name of the author is a relevant and necessary part of that [appraisal] opinion. One of the reasons for the First Amendment, as well as the Freedom of Information Act, is to promote honesty of government by seeing to it that public business functions under the hard light of full public scrutiny. The very name of an appraiser could be sufficient to establish a motivation sufficient to trigger an investigation.

Although the district judge [Morton] apparently felt that equitable considerations required a withholding of the appraiser's name, it is my opinion that the exact opposite is true. . . . Generally, anonymity is not the privilege of individuals charged with the responsibility of transacting the business of government.

Major federal housing scandals had been concealed by HUD secrecy policies in the Philadelphia area, including the old dodge of taking various records to a federal grand jury and then claiming they can't be made public because they are part of a grand jury proceeding. That practice was slapped down by one of the United States District Court rulings in the Eastern District of Pennsylvania that dealt with HUD's obstructionist tactics. Those two United States District Court rulings in Philadelphia quoted from a Supreme Court decision written by Chief Justice Charles Evans Hughes that was probably more applicable to the major operations of a $250 billion-a-year government in 1971 than when it was written in 1931. "The administration of government has become more complex, the opportunities for malfeasance and corruption have multiplied," Chief Justice Hughes wrote. "Crime has grown to most serious proportions, and the danger of its protection by unfaithful officials and of the impairment of the fundamental security of life and property by criminal alliances and official neglect, emphasize the primary need for a vigilant and courageous press, especially in great cities."

In Philadelphia and Nashville, where the newspapers were deeply involved in the hard work of exposing and eradicating corruption in the federal housing programs, the court decisions were regarded as highly significant. Most of the Washington press corps treated the decisions as "local stories," but I regarded them as significant, with broader applications than simply the housing scandals in Detroit; New York City; Camden, N.J.; St. Louis; Chicago; and Washington, D.C. What should have been clear to Romney and other top government officials is that housing programs and other programs, both federal and local, designed to aid the poor can be subject to parasitic money grabs by speculators. These speculators may work in collusion with government officials in bilking the poor. In a column on June 4, 1972, I wrote:

Illegal schemes are one of the constant hazards to social programs. The corruption not only robs the poor and the blind, as well as the federal taxpayers, but causes the public to have an attitude that can jeopardize entire programs.

It is difficult for any administration to keep the thieves out. It is impossible to defend the programs for the poor in which there is substantial corruption or gross mismanagement.

As HUD's recent experience shows, the department heads can't keep the programs clean from Washington, although they may be run by experienced men with the best intentions.

Secrecy in these domestic social programs only obstructs legitimate public inquiries, which may be the best allies of the honest public official. That is the real lesson of Secretary Romney's experience with secrecy at HUD and the corruption it has hidden in cities from coast to coast.

But while that column was being written, the Senate was making final preparations to compromise its right to a full explanation of the controversial ITT affair. It agreed to limit sharply the questioning of Peter Flanigan, special assistant to President Nixon, who had initially claimed "executive privilege" in his refusal to testify before the Senate Judiciary Committee. The compromise with the White House on Flanigan's testimony took place in the hearings on the nomination of Richard Kleindienst as attorney general. On June 8, 1972, the Senate agreed to settle for less than the whole truth by confirming Kleindienst by a roll-call vote of 64 to 19.

*Chapter Twenty-four*

# THE ITT COVER-UP

PRESIDENT NIXON'S desire to have two of his cabinet officers head his 1972 re-election campaign set the stage for a congressional inquiry of the Justice Department's controversial settlement of an anti-trust case against International Telephone and Telegraph Corporation. Although the investigation of the ITT affair was terminated inconclusively, the false and misleading testimony given by a number of witnesses—including Attorney General Mitchell and the then deputy attorney general, Kleindienst—was a highly vulnerable point. That vulnerability made both Mitchell and Kleindienst uneasy, and eventually resulted in Kleindienst's entering a plea of guilty to a criminal charge of giving misleading testimony before the Senate Judiciary Committee.

On February 15, 1972, President Nixon nominated Deputy Attorney General Kleindienst to succeed Mitchell, who was resigning to become director of the Committee to Re-elect the President. Maurice Stans, Nixon's leading fund-raiser in the 1968 campaign, resigned as secretary of commerce in January to serve as Chairman of the Finance Committee to Re-elect the President. To succeed Kleindienst as deputy attorney general, President Nixon turned to L. Patrick Gray III, a retired Navy Captain who had practiced law in New

London, Connecticut, and had served in the Nixon administration as executive assistant to the secretary of health, education, and welfare, Robert Finch, and as an assistant attorney general in charge of the Justice Department's Civil Division. I took a dim view of Kleindienst's nomination because he had supported the most extreme White House interpretations of "executive privilege" in order to withhold documents from Congress. But Assistant Attorney General Henry E. Peterson, whom I regarded as one of the most honest career law enforcement men I had known, assured me that "Kleindienst is honest." Said Peterson, "He has never asked me to make any decision for political purposes, and I have reason to know he has shielded me from some of those political pressures." With no facts to the contrary, I accepted this.

Kleindienst was a conservative and although he was associated with many of Mitchell's controversial policies, there was no evidence of personal dishonesty. The liberal opposition to his nomination, led by Senator Edward M. Kennedy, centered on such questions as Justice Department policies on wiretapping, legislation to control handguns, and the question of whether the Justice Department had shut off a federal grand jury investigation of the killing of four students at Kent State University.

On February 29, the Senate Judiciary Committee unanimously approved the Kleindienst nomination, and it appeared that the Arizona Republican was set to receive overwhelming approval from the Senate. But columnist Jack Anderson on the same day printed his first report on the Dita Beard memorandum, which he said was "evidence that the settlement of the Nixon administration's biggest anti-trust case was privately arranged between Attorney General John Mitchell and the top lobbyist for the company involved"—ITT. Anderson did not mention Kleindienst's name in his syndicated column, which appeared in the *Washington Post,* but directed his fire to Mrs. Beard's secret memorandum charging that the anti-trust case had been fixed and indicating that "the fix was a pay-off for ITT's pledge of up to $400,000 for the upcoming Republican convention in San Diego."

The column was met with denials from ITT officials, the Justice Department, and the White House. The ITT statement concluded: "The San Diego contribution of the Sheraton Hotels [an ITT firm] was made as a non-partisan joint effort on the San Diego community and was purely support of a local situation. Sheraton has two hotels in San Diego and a third is under construction which would be completed in time for the convention. There was no tie-in of any kind between this local joint participation and any other aspects of ITT's business."

But the March 1 Anderson column zeroed in on Kleindienst with the charge that he "told an outright lie" about the Justice Department's sudden settlement of the ITT anti-trust case. The lie, it was charged, was contained in a letter to Democratic National Chairman Lawrence F. O'Brien in which Kleindienst denied any role in the settlement. "The settlement between the Department of Justice and ITT was handled and negotiated exclusively by Assistant Attorney General Richard W. McLaren [then head of the anti-trust division]," Kleindienst had written. Anderson said that his associate, Brit Hume, had been told by Felix Rohatyn, a director of ITT, that he (Rohatyn) had met privately with Kleindienst several times during the period of the negotiations. The column quoted from the Dita Beard memorandum, identifying those knowledgeable about the political deal on the Republican convention as including John Mitchell, H. R. Haldeman, and California Lieutenant Governor Ed Reinecke.

On March 2, Kleindienst was back before the Senate Judiciary Committee at his own request to clear his clouded credibility as a result of the Anderson column. He admitted that he had met at least three times with Rohatyn and that at Rohatyn's suggestion he urged McLaren to call a meeting in which directors and other ITT representatives were permitted to make another plea of financial hardship to Justice and Treasury Department officials. Although he admitted meeting with ITT officials in the summer of 1971, Kleindienst denied having any knowledge of the $400,000 political contribution in connection with the Republican convention until December, 1971. Rohatyn and McLaren corroborated Kleindienst, but in so doing they established that Kleindienst had also been present at meetings between McLaren and ITT officials. In fact, McLaren testified that following one of these meetings, he arranged on April 29, 1971, through White House aide Peter Flanigan, for an outside consultant to study the ITT case. On May 17, 1971, the independent consultant chosen by Flanigan, Richard J. Ramsden, submitted a report to the Justice Department through the White House that was generally favorable to the ITT position.

When Mrs. Dita Beard was spirited out of Washington and hospitalized in Denver, reportedly too ill to testify before the committee or answer questions for committee investigators, the committee focused on Flanigan who declared himself unavailable because of his executive privilege as a member of President Nixon's staff. The White House press office gave no immediate verification of Flanigan's authority to claim executive privilege, but critics recalled that President Nixon on April 7, 1969, had assured the House Government Operations Subcommittee on Information Policy that "under this administration, executive privilege will not be asserted without specific presidential approval." In the letter to Representative John Moss, then chairman of the subcommittee, President Nixon had said: ". . . this administration is dedicated to insuring a free flow of information to the Congress and the news media—and, thus, to the citizens." As Mr. Nixon stated, three months after his first inauguration: "I want open government to be a reality in every way possible. . . . I am committed to ensuring that both the letter and the spirit of the Pubilc Records Law will be implemented throughout the executive branch of government."

Flanigan remained unavailable to the press, but Press Secretary Ronald Ziegler said, "There is no concern that he [Flanigan] conducted himself improperly." In answer to the question of whether Flanigan or other White House aides would testify, Ziegler said it was his "personal opinion that under the executive privilege process members of the White House staff would not testify." McLaren insisted that Flanigan was "simply a conduit for my request to Ramsden" for advice, and that this did not constitute White House political tampering with the decision. The administration had a difficult decision to make in determining whether President Nixon should specifically approve Flanigan's use of executive privilege in refusing to testify. By supporting Flanigan's refusal he would immediately be vulnerable in an election year to a charge of refusing to deal frankly with the public and Congress. However, if he did not back him, it would open up the possibility of even more embarrassing questions on the curious chain of events suggesting White House involvement in the controversial ITT settlement.

It was apparent by this time that Ramsden's brief study of the ITT case had been used as an "independent" economic verification of Rohatyn's arguments for a settlement. Senator John Tunney, a California Democrat who was a member of the Senate Judiciary Committee, noted for the record that Ramsden had said, "Peter Flanigan contacted me and I returned the report to him." He said that Flanigan "relayed the questions to me that I was supposed to focus on." Ramsden said Flanigan was aware that Ramsden's New York investment firm of Brokaw, Schanen, Clancy and Company controlled a pension fund that owned 3,240 shares of ITT stock worth $208,800. Ramsden, who had served as a White House fellow, was paid $242 plus expenses of $80 for the two-day job of compiling the so-called "independent report" on the multi-billion-dollar ITT conglomerate.

Flanigan refused to testify but offered to submit an affidavit to answer the questions raised by the Judiciary Committee about his role in the ITT case. The Democratic Senators, including Kennedy, Tunney, Philip Hart of Michigan, and Birch Bayh of Indiana, immediately rejected the idea of settling for an affidavit. The Democrats drew the unflattering comparison between Flanigan's refusal to testify and President Eisenhower's insistence that presidential aide Sherman Adams go before a congressional committee to answer charges that he accepted favors from Boston millionaire industrialist Bernard Goldfine and made calls to government agencies on Goldfine's behalf. Senator Thomas Eagleton, Missouri Democrat, stirred the White House with the charge that "the real missing witness" was Peter Flanigan and not Mrs. Dita Beard, who remained hospitalized in Denver. Eagleton described Flanigan as "a man who works in the shadows" and chided him about his reluctance to answer questions about his mysterious duties as Mr. Nixon's ambassador to the world of business. White House Press Secretary Ron Ziegler bristled in describing the charges as "absurd." He characterized Flanigan as "an honest man who is doing a fine job." But in his thirty-minute session with the press Ziegler failed to provide any explanations of substance.

On March 14, former Attorney General Mitchell admitted under oath that he had met with the head of ITT but denied being personally involved in the settlement. Mitchell said that his thirty-five-minute meeting with ITT President Harold Geneen in August, 1970, dealt only with Geneen's arguments that the Nixon administration was too vigorous in its anti-trust policy, not with the ITT problem. In response to questions, the former attorney general declined to say whether he would advise President Nixon to claim executive privilege for Flanigan but launched a counter-attack against the Democratic committee members for a "scurrilous attack" upon "three outstanding people—Kleindienst, McLaren, and Solicitor General Edwin N. Griswold." He charged that "their integrity, honesty and ability have been impugned" by what he said were irresponsible attacks on the ITT settlement. By linking Solicitor General Griswold to those he contended were maligned, Mitchell tried to give the whole ITT matter respectability. Griswold and McLaren defended the actual settlement of the ITT matter as reasonable, but Griswold, a former dean of the Harvard Law School, said he knew nothing about White House pressures or political arrangements made around the time of the anti-trust settlement.

Senators Robert Byrd (D., W. Va.), Sam Ervin (D., N.C.), and John L. McClellan (D., Ark.), and other Democratic conservatives, joined the liberal Democrats on the Senate Judiciary Committee to notify the White House that the committee would not report the Kleindienst nomination until Flanigan had come before the committee to answer questions. At this point, the White House and the conservative Democrats negotiated to restrict the questioning of Flanigan to certain specific aspects of the ITT affair covered in the hearing. Since Senator Ervin was not displeased with Kleindienst, he reluctantly agreed that if Flanigan would appear to be questioned that he would support a sharp restriction on the questioning. With liberal Democrats protesting the restrictions, Flanigan testified before the committee on April 20 but shed no new light on the controversy or on any role President Nixon may have had in the ITT settlement. Flanigan maintained that he had had no part in the decision and had acted only as a conduit to obtain for the Justice Department an independent analysis of the validity of ITT's economic plea.

On April 24, Flanigan sent a letter to the committee touching on some points he had refused to discuss when he testified. He said that twice he had discussed the ITT case with Kleindienst, which was in direct conflict with Kleindienst's earlier testimony that he had at no time discussed the case with Flanigan, or could not remember any such conversation. Recalled to clear up this point on April 27, Kleindienst admitted that his earlier testimony had been inaccurate but blamed a hazy memory. Kleindienst also testified that he had not discussed the case with President Nixon, which he later admitted was a misrepresentation. In fact, he subsequently divulged that President Nixon bluntly ordered him to drop Justice Department plans to appeal one of the ITT cases in a stormy conversation during which he informed the president that he would resign if Nixon insisted he drop the appeal. Had Kleindienst testified truthfully on April 27 it would have created an explosive political issue before the 1972 election and probably would have barred his confirmation.

Although the liberals on the committee, and the perceptive and persistent Senator Byrd, were not satisfied with Kleindienst's testimony or the administration's attitude toward the inquiry, the administration had been cooperative enough to make it difficult for some Democrats to remain in opposition to the Kleindienst nomination without appearing to be obstructionists.

On May 2, 1972, J. Edgar Hoover, director of the Federal Bureau of Investigation, died. The seventy-seven-year-old Hoover had dominated the FBI as its only director. President Nixon praised Hoover as a "legend in his own lifetime" and as the symbol and embodiment of the values he cherished most: "courage, patriotism, dedication to his country and a granite-like honesty and integrity." The next day he appointed his close friend and long-time political supporter L. Patrick Gray III as acting director of the FBI. President Nixon said he would not nominate Hoover's replacement until after the November 7 election because he wanted to keep Senate consideration of the nomination out of election-year politics. At Hoover's funeral President Nixon eulogized the veteran law enforcement officer as "a giant."

"His powerful leadership by example helped to keep steel in America's backbone, and the flame of freedom in America's soul," the president said. "He personified integrity; he personified honor; he personified principle; he personified courage; he personified discipline; he personified dedication; he personified loyalty; he personified patriotism."

"Each of us stands forever in his debt," Mr. Nixon said. "In the years ahead, let us cherish his memory. Let us be true to his legacy. Let us honor him as he would surely want us to do, by honoring all the men and women who carry on in the noble profession of helping to keep the peace in our society."

"Great peace have they which love the law," said President Nixon, quoting from the Psalms, and returned to the White House, where Haldeman kept the "Gemstone" file of reports on lawyer G. Gordon Liddy's covert operations to wiretap and burglarize National Democrat Party headquarters.

Pat Gray had good relations with Haldeman and former Attorney General Mitchell. After a period at HEW as executive assistant to Secretary Robert Finch, Gray had moved to the Justice Department as an assistant attorney general in charge of the Civil Division. He had been nominated to be deputy attorney general under Kleindienst, but the long hearings that delayed the Kleindienst confirmation also held up action on Pat Gray's nomination to succeed him in the Number Two post at Justice. The fact that the Kleindienst nomination was in trouble meant Gray was delegated the chore of smoothing over the ITT affair and related problems for the Nixon White House. The low-key fifty-five-year-old Navy bureaucrat had handled the problem well enough so that Kleindienst's confirmation seemed certain unless liberal opponents engaged in a filibuster.

The misrepresentation by Kleindienst and the failure to require Flanigan to testify fully regarding President Nixon's role set the stage for favorable action by the Senate on June 8. An overwhelming 69 to 19 vote confirmed the nomination of Kleindienst. Eighteen of the nineteen opposition votes were from the Democratic liberal clique, making it appear only partisan opposition.

But to me the no vote of Senator Robert Byrd was most significant, for I regarded the moderately conservative West Virginian as one of the most decent and knowledgeable men in the Senate. Byrd liked Kleindienst personally and had no sharp ideological disputes with President Nixon on the Vietnam War, domestic social programs, or law enforcement.

I visited with Byrd in the ornate President's Room, just off the Senate floor, a few days after the vote. He said he didn't "like the feel of it" but couldn't put his finger on any falsification of testimony or violation of law. It was a combination of things. Byrd had a hard time accepting Kleindienst's excuse that a vague memory accounted for his inaccurate testimony in denying he had talked with Peter Flanigan. Byrd resented the appearance of White House collusion with ITT officials in coordinating a defense against the Dita Beard memorandum. And despite administration and ITT charges that the memorandum was irresponsible, it seemed to Byrd that every new bit of testimony elicited from the administration or ITT officials corroborated allegations in the memorandum that had earlier been denied. "I hope that I'm wrong," Byrd said, "but it just didn't seem to me to be the kind of atmosphere that should surround the nomination of the attorney general, who is supposed to be the Number One law enforcement official in the nation."

I didn't like the looks of it either, and I was particularly concerned about the manner in which the Judiciary Committee had agreed to the White House demand that it restrict its questioning of Peter Flanigan. Such a response only supported the arguments of Haldeman and Ehrlichman that the power of the presidency made it possible to shut off any investigation of White House actions by simply refusing to produce documents or to permit White House officials to testify either in court or before congressional committees. They leaned on the precedents set out in the discredited memorandum that William P. Rogers had used during the Eisenhower administration. Had they followed the history of investigations closely, they would have seen that arbitrary secrecy justified by executive privilege worked only when the White House was on reasonable sound political ground. When I was at the White House I had argued that executive privilege claims always collapsed when the issue was hot and the president's position was untenable, and I hoped I was right. But Ehrlichman and Haldeman believed blindly that the power of the presidency and the impenetrable secrecy of executive privilege made them invulnerable to inquiries by Congress, the GAO, the press, or even federal grand juries.

For the moment they could gloat. An attorney general compromised by his testimony before the Senate Judiciary Committee wouldn't be as independent of White House wishes as he might wish. And Pat Gray, anxious to be permanent director of the FBI, knew that political loyalty in an election year compensated in great part for his lack of qualifications in law enforcement at a White House where loyalty was the name of the game.

*Chapter Twenty-five*

# GAME PLAN AT CREP

THE NEARLY four-month delay in getting Senate approval of Richard Kleindienst as attorney general upset the game plan at the Committee to Re-elect the President. The tightly knit group, known as CREP, had been organized to raise millions and make major plans for Richard Nixon's 1972 campaign. It had been necessary for former Attorney General John Mitchell, who had taken over as director of CREP in March 1972, to testify on the ITT affair with particular stress on some aspects of the Dita Beard memorandum. The testimony and preparation for testimony had taken a great deal of his time, as had the behind-the-scenes guidance he was giving Acting Deputy Attorney General L. Patrick Gray, who was in charge of the Kleindienst strategy in the Senate hearing.

Until Mitchell officially took charge in March, the re-election committee had been operating under Jeb S. Magruder, the aggressive protégé of H. R. Haldeman. Magruder had established the first offices at 1701 Pennsylvania Avenue in the spring of 1971 with a small planning staff that included Rob Odle, Bart Porter, and Bob Marik. Haldeman had tested Magruder as a White House assistant with the title of special assistant to the president, and then as deputy director of communication. Magruder had been Haldeman's man in both jobs, although Herb Klein held the title of director of communications, a $42,000-a-year post. While inside the White House I had known that Magruder was one of Haldeman's men, and I was aware of the speculative comments when Haldeman moved Magruder to the communications office to usurp most of Klein's operation. Klein, a long-time friend of President Nixon, was permitted to retain his title and draw his salary while deciding whether to accept this massive interference with his independence or to resign.

When Magruder was moved from the Executive Office Building to the suite of offices in the First National Bank Building at 1701 Pennsylvania Avenue, it was apparent that Haldeman intended to run the Nixon re-election committee from the West Wing of the White House. The First National Bank Building was no more than a five-minute walk from the West Wing. The CREP offices were housed in the same building as the law firm of Mudge, Rose, Guthrie, and Alexander, to which Mitchell had returned. Conveniently, in a corner suite of the same building was Murray Chotiner, an old Nixon campaign strategist Haldeman had admiringly described to me on one occasion as "having the guts of a burglar." Chotiner was associated in the practice of law with Marion Harrison, a fast-rising Republican lawyer with close personal ties to Kleindienst, Mitchell, and virtually every assistant attorney general in the Nixon administration.

Alabama Governor George Wallace's removal from the race had been a plus, but the Kleindienst fuss had been disconcerting, to say the least, and had marred President Nixon's two great historic firsts—the trip to the People's Republic of China in February and the visit to the Soviet Union in May. The trip to Peking was an exotic Oriental venture that captivated the nation and the world with its dazzle and political daring as an unprecedented presidential journey. Mr. Nixon's trip to Moscow culminated in the Soviet grain deals and the Strategic Arms Limitation (SALT) talks and agreements—both hailed as administration triumphs.

By mid-June, all systems were go. Mitchell was operational director of the Nixon re-election committee, Stans was in charge of fund-raising, Kleindienst had been confirmed as attorney general, and Pat Gray was acting head of the FBI. Senator Edmund Muskie, the Maine Democrat who had led President Nixon in the polls only a few months earlier, had faded. Senator Hubert Humphrey of Minnesota was dwindling as a Democratic political force, and Senator Henry M. Jackson of Washington was experiencing difficulties building an effective campaign apparatus. The Democratic race was emerging just as Haldeman hoped, with Senator George McGovern, the liberal South Dakota Democrat, far ahead of all other Democratic contenders. The liberal leader of the peace crusades who proposed a $35 billion cut in the Pentagon budget was President Nixon's favorite for the Democratic nomination. The big game plan for the president's re-election was being guided quietly and efficiently, with little notice being taken of it except for complaints from Senator Robert Dole (R., Kans.), then chairman of the Republican National Committee, who protested that Maurice Stans and the organization he referred to as "creep" were soaking up all the political money that should have been available for congressional and senatorial campaigns.

But the early morning of June 17, 1972, brought the Nixon re-election committee into the national spotlight in a manner destined to be remembered in history as a disastrous political tragedy. Five men were arrested at the Watergate headquarters of Democratic National Chairman Lawrence F. O'Brien at 2:30 A.M.—too late for the story to appear in the *Washington Post* that Saturday morning, and with only the bare details carried in the *Washington Star-News* that afternoon. The Sunday-morning *Washington Post* of June 18 carried sufficient detail to reveal some type of political plot by Republicans or by a small group who believed they were helping Republicans. That first comprehensive story carried the byline of Alfred E. Lewis, the *Post*'s police reporter, and a note that details had been contributed by eight other reporters: Bob Woodward, Carl Bernstein, Bart Barnes, Kirk Scharfenberg, Martin Weil, Claudia Levy, Abbott Combes, and Tim O'Brien. A number of things in that three-column front-page story made it immediately apparent that this was a burglary worthy of special attention.

The facts stood out sharply, illuminated by the identity of the burglars.

One of the five men arrested, James W. McCord, identified himself as a former employee of the Central Intelligence Agency (CIA). Three of the men were native-born Cubans, and the other was reported to have trained Cuban exiles for guerrilla activity after the 1961 Bay of Pigs invasion. The *modus operandi* was not that of punks after the petty cash. They were all wearing surgical gloves when captured inside the Democratic headquarters and had in their possession a walkie-talkie short-wave receiver that could pick up police calls, two thirty-five-millimeter cameras with forty roles of unexposed film, and some sophisticated bugging devices. The burglars were reported to have had $2,400 in cash in their possession, most of it in $100 bills which would be traceable by the FBI and other federal agencies after some prodding by appropriate Democrat-controlled congressional committees. The United States Attorney's office had entered the hotel rooms of the arrested men and found another $4,200 in cash, also in $100 bills, with the serial numbers in the same sequence as the money taken from the men arrested at Democratic National Committee headquarters.

Most important, the *Washington Post* had put a lot of manpower on the story and was, at least for the moment, concentrating on the kind of detailed coverage necessary to produce results in situations involving government corruption and political conniving. A case in point was the paragraph dealing with the circumstances under which Douglas Caddy, who identified himself as a corporation lawyer, had showed up at the police station after a 3:00 A.M. call from the wife of Bernard L. Barker, one of the three Cuban-Americans, who lived in Miami, Florida. No ordinary request could rout a Washington corporation lawyer out of bed in the early morning hours to go to a police station to arrange bail for a burglar suspect he had met only casually over cocktails at the Army-Navy Club in Washington. And why wouldn't Caddy answer the *Post* reporters' questions as to why he had brought an experienced criminal lawyer, Joseph A. Rafferty, Jr., into the case to represent all of the burglars? Caddy's explanation was "She [Mrs. Barker] said that her husband told her to call me if he hadn't called her by 3:00 A.M., that it might mean he was in trouble." If the five men were arrested at 2:30 A.M., why would the signal for trouble be set in motion automatically at 3:00 A.M.? The statements by Earl Silbert, the assistant United States attorney, that the burglary was "professional" and "clandestine" were superfluous. The only explanation other than Republican intrigue was that a group of erratic and irresponsible Cuban-Americans had chosen to do President Nixon a political favor in the hope that the administration would be more amenable to their aspirations for United States government assistance in an invasion of Fidel Castro's Cuba.

I noted with special interest that a former Iowa congressman, Deputy Democratic Chairman Stanley Greigg, had been called to Democratic headquarters to coordinate facts on the burglary-bugging attempt. Greigg had told the *Post* that it was "obviously important" that several of the suspects came from the area around Miami and Miami Beach, where the Democratic National Convention was to be convened on July 10.

On Sunday, June 18, when James McCord was identified by the Associated Press as a "security coordinator" for the Committee to Re-Elect the President, the picture started to clear for me. McCord had worked for the FBI from 1948 to 1951 and for the CIA from 1951 to 1970; he now operated his own consulting firm in Rockville, Maryland, a suburb of Washington, D.C. He had joined the staff of the Nixon re-election committee in January 1972 and was on the committee's regular payroll at $1,200 a month, according to reports required under the new federal law on campaign financing. He was also a consultant for the Republican National Committee, but both it and the Committee to Re-elect the President tried to give the impression that McCord had been off on a wild project of his own.

John Mitchell, as director of the Nixon re-election campaign, issued a statement saying:

> We want to emphasize that this man [McCord] and the other people involved were not operating either in our behalf or with our consent.
> The person involved is the proprietor of a private security agency who was employed by our Committee months ago to assist with the installation of our security system. He has, as we understand it, a number of business clients and interests, and we have no knowledge of these relationships. We want to emphasize that this man and other people involved were not operating on either our behalf or with our consent. There is no place in our campaign or in the electoral process for this type of activity, and we will not permit or condone it.

The Democratic national chairman immediately responded with a statement in which he said that the incident "raised the ugliest questions about the integrity of the political process that I have encountered in a quarter of a century of political activity."

> No mere statement of innocence by Mitchell . . . will dispel these questions —especially as the individual allegedly involved remains on the payroll of the Nixon campaign organization. Only the most searching professional investigation can determine to what extent the Committee for the Re-election of the President is involved in this attempt to spy on Democratic headquarters. I call upon Attorney General Kleindienst to order an immediate and thorough investigation by the Federal Bureau of Investigation. This investigation must remain open until we know beyond a doubt what organization or individuals were behind this incredible act of political espionage.

It was apparent to me that John Mitchell was lying about McCord's involvement, as he lied so easily about essentially anything in his department when it was convenient for him to do so. What was he covering up? Obviously, the Committee to Re-elect the President was deeply involved in the burglary, and from my knowledge of White House operations that meant that White House Chief of Staff Haldeman probably had material knowledge or had intentionally left the dirty work to Mitchell or others. Washington reporters and politicians were asking: Why would anyone want to hear what was going on in Larry O'Brien's office? What did they expect to find in the safe? Who would authorize such a stupid move with such grave risks?

I had enough insight into Haldeman's insatiable curiosity about what "the enemy" was doing to expect him to devise counter-moves in his game plan. Haldeman's beaver patrol, his pry and spy system, and his admiring comments about Murray Chotiner having "the guts of a burglar" gave me some clues to his priorities. The White House chief of staff was clever enough to leave few tracks, for he rarely originated memorandums or gave signed approval for any actions. My conversations with Jeb Magruder, Rob Odle, and others had revealed that Haldeman was running the Nixon re-election committee with a tight rein from the West Wing of the White House. I could only speculate as to how much of the detail went through to President Nixon and how much of it Haldeman withheld for himself. The system operated with Haldeman, Ehrlichman, and Kissinger as the major conduits of information to the president, and they were the only ones who could clearly establish his knowledge and responsibility.

I tried unsuccessfully to get some tangible evidence of Haldeman's knowledge of the burglary-bugging from my friends and former associates at the White House and at the re-election committee. Panicky, they did not even want it known that they were talking to me. They were fearful I might write a story critical of Haldeman and that they could be identified as or suspected of being the source. I understood why they did not want me to telephone them at the office and why they refused to return my calls. Haldeman's spy system included a good many of the secretaries and inadvertently included others who simply kept lists of all incoming and outgoing telephone calls and visitors. While my own effectiveness was sharply restricted, I was pleased to see the continued interest of the *Washington Post,* the *Washington Star-News* and the *New York Times* in what Ziegler tried to brush off as a "third-rate burglary" unworthy of White House attention.

On Monday, June 19, I contacted Stan Greigg, deputy Democratic chairman, to get a first-hand account of his participation in events at Democratic headquarters immediately after the arrest of the five men and to inquire as to his precise role in the developing events. Since Greigg was a former mayor of Sioux City, Iowa, and a former Iowa congressman, I thought I could at least get a story of considerable local interest to readers of the *Des Moines Register.* It would have been difficult to find a better source of information than the forty-one-year-old deputy chairman. He had been the first man on the scene on June 17, and he had been designated by Larry O'Brien to provide liaison with the Secret Service, the FBI, and the Metropolitan Police in the District of Columbia. While I did not expect confidential information from him, Greigg was an infallible source for checking the accuracy of information in the newspapers or on the wire services. And, indeed, it was mutually beneficial to discuss the hard evidence and to speculate where it could lead. It was Greigg's job to keep on top of all facts and to prevent a whitewash, and to make some educated guesses on the involvement of White House figures and the counter-moves that could be expected. It was my judgment, after sifting the evidence and making my own projections, that Greigg was "on top of the biggest potential political bonanza the Democrats have had in the effort to unseat President Nixon in 1972," and I wrote as much. Greigg told me that initially he had thought of political espionage as the reason for the break-in but had dismissed the idea as too far out, until he learned the true identity of McCord and his connection with the re-election committee. Within a few hours after that revelation, Larry O'Brien and lawyer Joseph Califano, a former special counsel to President Johnson, agreed that there was sufficient evidence to file a $1 million civil lawsuit against the re-election committee and its officers for invasion of privacy and other damages.

In filing the suit, O'Brien had charged that "some of the lines run to the White House." Although my own knowledge of Haldeman's control over the re-election committee led me to the same conclusion, I felt that O'Brien had gone beyond the current evidence. The charge brought a denial from John Mitchell that either he himself, the White House, or the Nixon re-election committee had been involved in the burglary. At a press conference on Thursday, July 23, President Nixon was asked about the Watergate burglary but declined to comment other than to say that Mitchell and Ziegler had handled the matter correctly and had stated the facts accurately. It was not difficult to keep on top of the Republican or White House side of the Watergate affair that first week, because the president and others were sparse in their comments or simply unavailable. By contrast, the Democrats were eager—almost too eager—to pursue every lead and draw broad conclusions.

As I discussed the matter with Greigg, I told him of my own view that Haldeman controlled the re-election committee through Magruder and that he had used Magruder to undercut Klein, but I warned that proof would be hard to develop because of Haldeman's extreme caution about putting his own views or instructions in writing. After several conversations with Greigg, I put together a lengthy story on Friday, June 24, for use in the *Des Moines Register* that weekend. I wrote:

It is possible that O'Brien's comments on the "lines to the White House" represent a political poetic license more than sound evidence, but the Greigg reports to him have emphasized these facts that the White House cannot duck or minimize:

1. McCord, one of the five arrested in the Democratic headquarters office at Watergate, has now been admitted to be the top security man for two major Republican organizations dedicated to the re-election of President Nixon.

2. McCord held a federal license for use of walkie talkies and other use of air waves for "security activity" on behalf of the Republican National Committee.

3. Mitchell heads the Committee for the Re-election of the President, is recognized as one of the men closest to Mr. Nixon, and until recently was Attorney General Richard Kleindienst's boss.

4. The acting director of the FBI is L. Patrick Gray, who served as an assistant attorney general under Mitchell and had been nominated as deputy attorney general by Mr. Nixon with approval of Mitchell just prior to being named to the FBI post on the death of former Director J. Edgar Hoover.

5. The Justice Department, now responsible for the investigation of the Watergate burglary and bugging, is headed by Kleindienst.

O'Brien and Califano have noted that under their civil damage suit they will be empowered to question witnesses as a part of pre-trial fact finding, witnesses who even remotely have anything to do with the hiring, firing, or other activities of McCord.

The financially bankrupt Democrats recognize that this procedure can be used to milk $100 million worth of publicity in free television time and newspaper space in the months between now and the November election.

The depositions, then, constitute the one kind of issue that could upset the best White House planning on the Vietnam War scenario, and the political fall-out from the president's visits to Peking and Moscow.

On Monday, June 26, I tried to put the Watergate problem in perspective from the standpoint of the potential danger and the political power forces that existed at that point. From the evidence then available and a knowledge of the people involved, it was apparent that someone with money and consider-able authority in the Nixon political structure had put together the Watergate bugging-burglary. Also, it seemed clear to me that no cover-up could be totally effective in this instance, even with the Nixon White House firmly in political control of the FBI and the Justice Department. The Democrats controlled the congressional committees and, with that counterbalance, our government sys-tem was in a position to do its job eventually. Although some of the Demo-cratic committee chairmen could be bribed or conned by a coldly cynical White House, there was virtually no chance of keeping the lid on all Demo-crats. Political common sense as well as honesty dictated that President Nixon accept the fact that he had to make an honest investigation of the Watergate matter or risk serious political consequences later. The only proper and safe course for President Nixon was a bipartisan commission headed by honest men of stature. I made that suggestion in my "Watch on Washington" column for July 2:

· The potential for damaging political fall-out from the burglary and "bugging" of National Democratic Party headquarters is so great that only forceful action by President Nixon can save the Republican Party from serious consequences in the November election.

To date, the most damaging fact is the arrest of the top security man for two Republican Party organizations along with four others at gunpoint at Democratic headquarters on June 17.

So far, there are only hints of lines of responsibility that point to the White House. However, the hints are strong enough that the president should waste no time in taking a leaf from President Calvin Coolidge's book when he set up a bipartisan special counsel to handle the investigation and prosecution of the in-famous Teapot Dome scandals.

It was a precarious step for President Coolidge to take, but it was necessary to avoid political blame in the 1924 election for the crimes of the Harding ad-ministration. Eminent men, one a Republican and one a Democrat, were named to head the investigation independent of the Justice Department. The then attorney general, Harry Daugherty, was involved in improprieties on the fringe of the Teapot Dome scandals.

The fact that Coolidge won the 1924 election by a substantial margin is some indication of the worth of the bi-partisan special committee's decision absolving him from blame.

President Nixon could take a long step up the credibility ladder by naming similar men of recognized integrity to investigate the Democratic headquarters burglary independent of the Justice Department.

Former Senator John J. Williams of Delaware, whose aggressive pursuit of dishonesty and unethical conduct in both parties was the hallmark of his twenty-four years in the Senate, would be the type of Republican who should be named.

Former Senator Paul Douglas, a liberal Democrat from Illinois, is the type of man who would have the confidence of most liberal Democrats.

The fact that there have been so many questions of credibility raised around Kleindienst's confirmation is one of the reasons the public may have grave doubts about how thoroughly the Justice Department, headed by Kleindienst, will handle the investigation promised on the alleged robbery and "bugging" caper.

This is particularly sticky because the Committee for the Re-election of the President is headed by former Attorney General John N. Mitchell, Kleindienst's former boss.

Also, the acting director of the FBI is Patrick Gray, who had served as an assistant attorney general under Mitchell and had been nominated as deputy attorney general by Mitchell and Nixon prior to being named to the FBI post upon J. Edgar Hoover's death.

President Nixon cannot afford to leave unanswered questions in the investigation of the burglary at Democratic headquarters, and it is unlikely that any investigation under the direction of Kleindienst and Patrick Gray will be sufficient to stifle doubts of the Democrats as well as many Republicans.

Many Democratic political figures have taken advantage of the political bonanza and O'Brien has moved into an enviable strategic position. His $1 million damage suit can be milked for $100 million worth of publicity in the months between now and the election.

The case is in the hands of two clever lawyers—Edward Bennett Williams and Joseph Califano. This civil damage suit permits the calling and swearing of relevant witnesses in the pre-trial depositions.

There are essentially no limits on the use of the procedure, and almost anyone in the White House or the Republican National Committee or the Committee for the Re-election of the President who had dealings with McCord, would be subject to questioning.

Democrats are free to stage the depositions and time them for maximum political benefit, with full newspaper and television coverage.

Implications of "political espionage" by White House personnel is a fascinating bit of business, and even if there are very few lines to the White House, the Democrats will savor every morsel before the television cameras or in the nation's press.

Democrats control the committees of the House and Senate and many chairmen are bold and eager to get into the big act of 1972—even if only on the fringe and on a most limited jurisdictional basis.

The president, a man with considerable experience in investigations, should be the first to recognize the potential dangers in the months ahead. He also should recognize the advantages inherent in following the Coolidge pattern of seizing the initiative soon and selecting a believable bipartisan committee to look into the entire burglary and "bugging" incident.

That column appeared on July 2, and I hoped President Nixon would see the danger ahead. Unknown to me, he was knowledgeable about the involvement of two former White House aides—E. Howard Hunt and G. Gordon Liddy—and was actively engaged in trying to use the CIA to cover their role and the guilty knowledge of his more intimate advisers.

Book 3

*Chapter Twenty-six*

# STONEWALLING BEGINS

O<small>N</small> J<small>ULY</small> 1, 1972, the sudden resignation of John Mitchell as director of President Nixon's campaign for re-election corroborated my belief that the Watergate burglary was not the "caper" of a few erratic Cuban-Americans led by a former CIA official. The Mitchell resignation was too neatly packaged at the end of a series of stories about Martha Mitchell's being fed up with "politics" and demanding that John resign to save their marriage. For a man so tight-lipped about his public actions, such behavior suggested a carefully concocted alibi. On June 23—less than a week after the Watergate arrests—Martha called Helen Thomas to describe herself as "a political prisoner," to state that she loved her husband very much, but to add: "I'm not going to stand for all those dirty things that go on." The usually sphinx-like former attorney general made himself available to Helen Thomas, of United Press International, to confirm that there was a marital dispute. Mitchell was quoted by Miss Thomas as saying: "That little sweetheart. I love her so much. She gets a little upset about politics, but she loves me and I love her and that's what counts." Mitchell added that he and his wife had a compact under which "we aren't going to be in Washington after November 7. We're going to leave lock, stock, and barrel."

The whole scenario (to adopt a Haldeman phrase) that had developed since the arrests at the Watergate on June 17 smacked of a carefully contrived cover story that took advantage of Martha's erratic behavior to explain Mitchell's hasty exit as being "for personal reasons."

Senator William Proxmire (D., Wis.) was already zeroing in on a vulnerable point—the traceable $100 bills found on the burglars and in their hotel rooms. He was demanding that the Federal Reserve System and the Justice Department make a report to him on the results of the investigation, under his authority as the ranking Democratic member of the Senate Banking Committee and as chairman of its Financial Institutions Subcommittee. Proxmire's first call for a report on this mysterious cash had gone out before 10:00 A.M. on Monday, June 19—two days after the Watergate arrests. Proxmire later charged that the "Federal Reserve Board ducked, misled, hid out, avoided calls, and gave us the idiot treatment."

"I think their refusal to cooperate was both a despicable act and unworthy of them as an arm of Congress," the irate Proxmire said. He explained his request thus: "First, Federal Reserve notes were involved, they were in numerical sequence, and commercial banks keep details of transactions of this size. Those who paid for this job [the Watergate burglary] might be traced through the bills. Second, in this case the executive branch is a party of interest. One of the men caught was directly connected with the Nixon campaign. I hope that higher-ups may be innocent of these wrongdoings. But with the executive branch having a conflict of interest, it was essential that the Federal Reserve Board, which is an agent of the Congress, should give Congress the facts promptly, fully, and completely."

On the following day, June 20, Senator Proxmire had already obtained the numbers on the unexplained $100 bills, and his staff had traced them to the Miami and Philadelphia Reserve District. He reported that in the same hour Federal Reserve Board Chairman Arthur Burns wrote him that the board had "no knowledge of the Federal Reserve bank which issues those particular notes," and the Federal Reserve Bank at Philadelphia had refused to return calls to his Senate staff. Proxmire said that a short time later his staff was notified that the information on the bills would not be available and "should not be released to anyone other than the investigative authorities, namely the FBI and Justice."

Senator Proxmire told me that he regarded the Federal Reserve Board's position as "an outrageous action" which made the board a part of the cover-up. The Wisconsin Democrat had no faith in either Attorney General Kleindienst or Pat Gray being objective and thorough in an investigation involving a Nixon political committee. He declared that it was an unusual situation when "the Federal Reserve, an agent of the Congress and independent of the Executive Branch, refused to cooperate with Congress while falling all over itself to aid the executive branch." It "suggests they have something to hide," Proxmire said. "One would have to be extraordinarily naïve not to feel the Federal Reserve may be covering up for someone high in the executive branch of our government who is directly involved with the espionage action against the Democratic National Committee." Proxmire made no direct accusation against Dr. Arthur Burns, but he suggested that "Burns should re-read the Constitution. It provides that Congress, not the executive, has the money power. Under our Constitution the Federal Reserve Board is directly obligated to Congress and is independent of the executive branch. Certainly with the president of the United States and his supporters a party at interest, the Federal Reserve Board should recognize their clear constitutional obligation to Congress. In this case they have failed to do so."

Proxmire's moves on the Senate side to expose the source of the cash were coordinated with similar moves by Representative Wright Patman, chairman of the House Banking and Currency Committee. Although their initial efforts to obtain routine information were unsuccessful, both Patman and Proxmire were determined to obtain answers to those questions that were within their jurisdiction. Proxmire's administrative assistant, Howard E. Shuman, and legislative assistant Richard A. Wegman were given the job of following through. On the House side, Chairman Patman assigned the job of coordinating the inquiry to Joseph C. (Jake) Lewis, a quietly aggressive professional staff member, and Chief Investigator Curtis A. Prins.

It was apparent that the lawyers for the Democratic National Committee intended to take depositions from White House Special Counsel Charles W. Colson and former White House consultant E. Howard Hunt. Clearly some effort would be made to question Mitchell, former director of the Committee to Re-elect the President; Maurice Stans, the finance chairman; Hugh Sloan, the treasurer; Jeb S. Magruder, the deputy director; and others. The unexplained money and the identification of James McCord as a security man for the Nixon re-election committee would be a sufficient reason to request, and even demand, sworn testimony in connection with the damage suit filed by Democratic National Chairman Lawrence F. O'Brien. Mitchell, Nixon, Haldeman, and Ehrlichman were especially aware of the political danger in the FBI's initial reports on the mystery money, and they knew that there was no sound argument for refusing to turn those reports over to a properly authorized congressional committee. Unaware of the contents of the reports, I was nevertheless certain that such money could be traced because of the rules of the federal banking system about the recording of serial numbers in large cash transactions. Senator John Williams had told me years earlier that his experience with Internal Revenue investigations had demonstrated that large cash transactions are usually traceable because of carelessness in handling cash, on the general assumption that it cannot be traced.

Senator Proxmire said that he intended to keep publicly pressing the Justice Department and the Federal Reserve Board for reports on the source of the funds. He was not chairman of the Senate Banking Committee, which had the clearest jurisdiction in this matter, so he could not issue subpoenas without going through Chairman John Sparkman of Alabama and the committee, which he did not want to do. Although Proxmire was chairman of the Joint Economic Subcommittee, it did not have subpoena power and would have to go to the Senate floor to seek special authority in an area where its jurisdiction would be flimsy at best. His judgment was that his staff could keep pressure on without subpoenas and with requests for reports from the General Accounting Office.

Representative Wright Patman's Banking and Currency Committee staff had unmistakeable jurisdiction for requesting reports on large money transactions and raising questions about whether executive branch agencies were effectively administering rules and regulations. Although Patman had to approach his full committee for authority to issue subpoenas, Jake Lewis believed it best to try to develop the broad outlines of the case through interviews before making an issue of the need to call witnesses from the White House or the re-election committee.

This was the situation on July 1, at the time of John Mitchell's sudden resignation as Nixon's campaign director and his replacement by former Minnesota congressman Clark MacGregor. MacGregor had served as a counselor to the president since his defeat by Hubert Humphrey in the 1970 Senate race. I had a good relationship with MacGregor and expected the open and forthright Minnesotan to be a breath of fresh air after the chilly reticence of John Mitchell. I suggested a bipartisan investigating commission to Mac-

Gregor as the way to resolve Watergate. MacGregor replied that as the new campaign director he had enough to do and "didn't want to look back any more than was necessary." The investigation of the past would be left to the Justice Department and President Nixon, MacGregor told me. He said he was unaware of any members of the present staff at the Nixon re-election committee who were involved in the Watergate matter but that he would take action to obtain the resignation of anyone linked to the Watergate burglary by substantial evidence. He suggested that I take my idea of a bipartisan investigating committee to the White House. I didn't blame him for wanting to keep his own areas of responsibility to a minimum and to avoid the hopeless task of correcting the past.

I sent a copy of my July 2 column to White House speech-writer Pat Buchanan and suggested that he call it to the attention of President Nixon. Pat was deeply concerned about the possible implication of the White House in the Watergate affair or in an attempted cover-up, and he agreed that a bipartisan commission would prevent Haldeman from involving President Nixon in an unwise defense of Charles W. Colson, who had been identified as one of Hunt's White House contacts. At that point, the only tangible evidence of a White House connection was a story by Bob Woodward of the *Washington Post* which disclosed that two of the Watergate burglars carried address books containing the notations "W. House" and "W.H." and the name and home telephone number of E. Howard Hunt, a $100-a-day White House consultant. Hunt, a former CIA agent and novelist, had worked out of Colson's office in the Executive Office Building, Woodward reported. The White House had denied that Hunt was on the White House payroll after March 29, 1972, although Woodward wrote that he had been referred to Colson's office when he called the White House switchboard and asked to speak with Hunt in late June.

Buchanan said that he knew nothing about it and didn't want to know, that he was mainly concerned with "keeping the Old Man [Nixon] out of it." While Buchanan was a firm conservative, an ardent, long-time admirer of President Nixon, and a tough political operator, he felt it best to fight most political battles in the open. In earlier conversations we had shared our concern that Colson's daring and controversial methods, much admired by Haldeman, would get the administration in serious trouble. But I knew that Buchanan was in fact powerless to do more than make suggestions, voice mild warnings, and abide by the final decisions President Nixon made in closed conferences with Haldeman and Ehrlichman. It was obvious that Buchanan was not in on the Watergate game plan, though he complained mildly that the *Washington Post* story headline "White House Consultant Linked to Bugging Suspects" was just the kind of "guilt by association" that the *Post* deplored.

I disagreed and said that the *Post* was simply doing the aggressive job it should have done in earlier investigations, but that the Nixon White House could not register a legitimate complaint until it was completely open and honest with regard to the facts on Hunt's employment and Colson's role. "The hard fact is that Watergate is going to come unwound at some point, and the president should get on top of it," I warned. "The Democrats control the committees of Congress and some of those Democrats are going to force this investigation because it is to their political advantage to do so. And you know, as well as I do, that the press and the television networks are not going to help a Nixon administration cover up anything. This is the time for the president to stand back from the investigation and not become tarred with a cover-up."

Buchanan agreed. He said he thought that Senator John Williams would make a good member of an investigation commission, winced at Senator Paul Douglas as "too liberal" but said he believed he would be honest, and said he would "take it up with the powers."

I talked with Buchanan several times in July, constantly stressing the importance of an independent investigation because any decisions made by Kleindienst, Pat Gray, or the Nixon White House would be suspect. Buchanan was elated over the nomination of Senator McGovern as the Democratic candidate and was particularly pleased that the combined persuasiveness of Senators Jackson, Humphrey, and Muskie had not been able to convince McGovern to abandon his proposed $35 billion cut in the Pentagon budget. "It makes him a sitting duck," Buchanan chortled, and he exulted over the shambles the Democratic candidate had made of the selection of a running mate. The greatest news of all to the Nixon White House was the announcement on July 19, 1972, that the AFL-CIO Executive Council had voted twenty-seven to three to "refrain from endorsing either candidate for president." George Meany, the seventy-seven-year-old president of the AFL-CIO, hadn't changed his tune on "Tricky Dick Nixon," but he was denying McGovern the vital support of labor that all Democratic candidates had been able to count on for forty years.

In late July, Pat Buchanan told me that "the powers" had rejected my idea for a bipartisan commission to conduct the Watergate investigation. "They want no part of Senator Williams," he said.

"Doesn't the president understand that in the long run an independent, straight investigation will be for his protection?" I asked.

Buchanan said that he did not know President Nixon's precise view on this point but that Haldeman and Ehrlichman "don't want John Williams in here prying around under any circumstances." He said, "The powers feel more comfortable with John Dean handling it." While Buchanan continued to show concern over Watergate, he was euphoric about the way the "game plan" was shaping up for the election. Nixon was certain to name Vice President Spiro Agnew as his running mate and the Miami Beach convention would be presented on prime-time television so that its efficiency and control could be contrasted with the chaotic brouhaha staged by the Democrats.

Immediately after the Democratic convention I learned that an old friend of mine, William O. Bittman, had been retained by E. Howard Hunt, and a former Justice Department official told me he had heard that Bittman's retainer was $25,000 in cash.

"Was it in $100 bills?" I asked facetiously.

"I don't know anything about the details and I don't have any hard evidence that it is true, but it comes from a responsible source," my informant said.

If the fee was in cash, it meant that Hunt's survival was important to some people who had access to big money. And the use of cash meant that Hunt intended to cover the source of his defense fund. It also meant that he was more seriously involved than would appear from the few sketchy hints in the newspapers.

My source declined to reveal his source; I decided to ask Bittman directly. I had known him since 1964, when as a young prosecutor he had obtained the conviction of Teamster boss James R. Hoffa for pension fund frauds. Later he had been brought to Washington by Assistant Attorney General Herbert J. (Jack) Miller to handle the prosecution of Bobby Baker on charges of income tax fraud and misuse of political funds. After the conviction of Baker, who was defended by famed criminal lawyer Edward Bennett Williams, Bittman had left the Justice Department to join the prestigious law firm of Hogan and Hartson as a trial lawyer. His triumphs in the Hoffa and Baker cases were only the high points in a career distinguished by more than seventy straight victories as a government prosecutor. Our relationship had been very close during the prosecution of Hoffa and the investigation and prosecution of Bobby Baker, and I had the highest regard for his integrity. I knew that he had passed up offers of promotion during the Johnson administration because he regarded them insidious bribes; he refused to relinquish his role as chief prosecutor in the Baker case for a post as United States attorney in Chicago or as special assistant to Attorney General Ramsey Clark. Bittman remained my good friend now that he had changed roles and become a defense lawyer in big criminal cases, and I called him periodically to discuss a point of law or investigation strategy on cases where his clients were not involved. I knew he would not divulge evidence against Hunt unless it served his client's best interests, and I did not expect him to.

Bittman came on the line with a hearty and friendly: "Now what the hell do you want?—as if I didn't know."

After an exchange of pleasantries in which he acknowledged Hunt had retained him, I asked about the report that the fee had been paid in cash and was $25,000.

"You know I'm not going to tell you about my dealings with my clients," Bittman said. "The fees I get and the manner in which those fees are paid is a private matter."

I said that I was sure he understood why I was asking these questions and that I respected his relationship with his client but that "I had this report on the $25,000 cash fee and I figured that you could and would tell me if the report was inaccurate."

"I hope you are not going to treat my lack of comment as confirmation," Bittman said.

"No, I'm not regarding it as confirmation of a $25,000 cash fee, but I'm sure that if there were no cash involved (in your dealings with Hunt) you would tell me just to save a lot of searching around," I replied. "Many aspects of this Watergate matter are as intriguing as the Bobby Baker case."

Bittman agreed that it was "an interesting case from many standpoints" and said he hoped he would be able to tell me all about it at some later time.

I said I had an idea that the case would be a matter of intense public concern for some time and that I had a compelling interest in it. "I hope you'll give me a ring if there are any developments that you can discuss that are not inconsistent with your client's interest," I concluded.

By late July several other bits of information that I considered highly significant had dribbled into the public domain. *Newsday* reported that G. Gordon Liddy, a former White House and Treasury Department lawyer, had resigned from the re-election committee because he had refused to cooperate in the FBI investigation of the Watergate burglary. Liddy, a lawyer for the Finance Committee at CREP, was a former FBI agent and an unsuccessful candidate for the Republican nomination for a New York congressional seat in 1970. *Washington Star-News* reporters Joseph Volz and Patrick Collins wrote that Hugh W. Sloan, Jr., had resigned his post as treasurer of the re-election committee at about the same time that he was being questioned by a federal grand jury investigating the Watergate affair. Sloan's explanation that he had resigned for "purely personal reasons" was obviously a cover story. I had known Sloan when we were both members of the White House staff and had thought him to be a serious and dedicated young man who would never knowingly have done a dishonest thing. Sloan had been in Haldeman's organization in the White House, but he seemed to possess a dimension beyond the neat, polite, well-groomed advertising agency polish of White House Press Secretary Ronald Ziegler and Presidential Appointments Secretary Dwight Chapin.

I called Sloan to verify the *Star-News* story. He said the affair was upsetting to his wife, who was expecting a baby in September. He had cooperated with the FBI but declined to discuss that testimony or what it might mean about the involvement of CREP officials. He said that he had returned my call because he regarded me as a friend from our time at the White House. I remarked that he was treasurer of the Nixon re-election committee, which made him responsible for the campaign reports filed with the Office of Federal Elections at the GAO under the new campaign financing act, which had been in force since April 7, 1972. He said that he had been proud to be given that title and the responsibility, but that it had amounted to "a lot of pressure." I observed that he could be set up as fall guy if anything went wrong and he assured me that he had handled his duties properly and legally. I was sure he had, but he was noncommittal about others. "It is under investigation by the grand jury," he said, and I knew he was deeply troubled. Because he had principles, he was out of a job and was unlikely to find one in the administration, since he had demonstrated that his loyalty could not be relied on when it came into conflict with his conscience.

In July, the House Banking and Currency Committee investigation had linked two highly questionable financial transactions to the bank account of Bernard L. Barker. One was a $25,000 certified check deposited in Barker's bank account. Kenneth H. Dahlberg, a Minneapolis business executive, had delivered the check to Maurice Stans on April 11—four days after the effective date of the new federal campaign financing law. Barker's Miami bank account had also been the depository for four cashier's checks totalling $89,000, issued by the Banco Internacional in Mexico City to Manuel Ogarrio Daguerre, a prominent lawyer. They had been deposited in Barker's account on April 20—less than two months before the Watergate burglary-bugging. Walter Rugaber of the *New York Times,* working on leads in Miami and Mexico City, broke the story of the Mexican checks. Bob Woodward of the *Washington Post,* who had written the first story of the $25,000 check, identified Dahlberg as President Nixon's Midwest finance chairman and quoted Dahlberg as saying that he had turned the money over to Maurice Stans and had no idea what had happened to it. Dahlberg had given the impression that the $25,000 was collected from several individuals and said that he could not recall whether he had turned it over to the treasurer, Hugh Sloan, or to Maurice Stans.

The Rugaber and Woodward stories were the first justification for Phillip S. (Sam) Hughes, director of the Office of Federal Elections, to make direct inquiry of CREP on possible irregularities in complying with the reports required under the new federal campaign financing law. If Hughes or Comptroller General Elmer Staats had been reluctant to become embroiled in the controversy of Watergate, they could no longer justify lack of action. To make certain that the new federal election office exercised all of its authority in the investigation, Senator Proxmire in early August made a formal request for GAO to enter the politically sensitive inquiry and conduct a complete audit of the origin of the unidentified funds and the date they were received by the Nixon re-election committee.

Proxmire said that his own investigations indicated that the contribution of $25,000 had not been reported, as it should have been under the new law. Mitchell and Stans admitted that they had collected an estimated $10 million before April 7, the effective date of the new law, and had not included it in public reports. "The committee has complied with the law," Mitchell declared, and refused to elaborate. Proxmire said that GAO auditors had been unable to find any report of the $25,000 Dahlberg check delivered to Stans on April 11, and that it was a possible violation of the law. However, he conceded that Dahlberg, the wealthy president of a Minneapolis electronics firm, might have collected the money from others prior to April 7. But, Proxmire said, even if the committee effectively produced proof of delivery before the April 7 deadline, it still had to report disbursement of the funds to Barker and to explain why one of the Watergate burglars was the recipient of this sum of money.

It was a sensitive spot for GAO, and particularly so for Staats and Hughes, who had both worked in government with Maurice Stans in earlier years. Hughes had worked for the Bureau of the Budget while Stans was director during the Eisenhower administration. At that time, Stans had been instrumental in obtaining a substantial promotion for Hughes, But Staats and Hughes assured me that they intended to treat Stans in the same manner as they would any other person. The fact that the whole Washington press corps was watching would have discouraged any urge to favor an old friend and benefactor.

In calling the matter to the attention of GAO, Proxmire specified that G. Gordon Liddy had refused to answer questions for the FBI and that the Justice Department was representing Charles Colson in his refusal to give his deposition in the civil damage suit involving Watergate. "I am asking that the GAO audit the books and investigate this matter because the Justice Department has a direct conflict of interest in this matter, both as a part of the administration and particularly because they are representing Mr. Colson on the White House staff in a civil suit connected with the Watergate incident," Proxmire said.

Even after the $25,000 in Nixon re-election committee funds had been traced to Barker, and even though James McCord, a Nixon re-election committee security man, was one of those arrested, the White House and the press office at CREP continued to deny any involvement by responsible officials. The break-in was laughed off as a "caper." White House officials and Stans told Republican senators and congressmen that the $25,000 had been put into Barker's account not as payment for the burglary, but only because Barker's bank account was being used to obtain cash. DeVan Shumway, press officer of the Nixon re-election committee, said that the transaction had been handled by Liddy but didn't know why it had been handled that way. He pictured Liddy as doing many strange things, hinting that the Watergate affair had been Liddy's idea and that he would probably be indicted. This was roughly the same explanation given by MacGregor and Stans to various Republican congressmen and senators.

When Buchanan informed me that "the powers" in the White House had rejected my suggestion of a bipartisan investigation of Watergate, I mentioned it to Senator Proxmire. He was enthusiastic and said that if President Nixon didn't have anything to hide he should accept it. Proxmire accepted my choice of Senator John Williams and former Senator Paul Douglas as "a fine, credible team" but said Douglas would not be available because of ill health. In a Senate speech on August 10 he suggested Senator Williams and former Supreme Court Justice Arthur Goldberg. However, Majority Leader Mike Mansfield (D., Mont.) declared that he had such high regard for the nonpartisan integrity of Senator Williams that he would be satisfied if President Nixon appointed him to investigate Watergate.

On the same day, August 10, Clark MacGregor, who for more than a month had been director of CREP, told a National Press Club audience that he did not know how the baffling $89,000 in checks from a Mexico City bank that had been identified as Nixon campaign funds had ended up in the account of one of the Watergate burglars. He did say, in a carefully worded statement, "I'm satisfied from my examination of the facts that the $25,000 [from Dahlberg] was lawfully and properly contributed before April 7."

Surprisingly, Senate Republican Leader Hugh Scott of Pennsylvania also approved the idea of an independent commission to investigate the Watergate matter, but he objected to Senator Proxmire's requirement that the commission complete its study and make its report in thirty days. He said he would support the idea only if the investigators' findings were withheld until after the election was over. "That would take the issue out of the field of politics," Scott said, but Senator Frank Church, an Idaho Democrat, responded: "The American people are entitled to know the facts before they pass judgment on whether this administration should continue in office." Both Senator Williams and Justice Goldberg indicated they would be pleased to serve, if asked.

On the same day that Proxmire discussed the bipartisan commission on the Senate floor, United States District Judge Charles R. Richey entered an order rejecting a Republican request for a delay in the Democrats' damage suit until after the November 7 general election. Judge Richey, a Nixon appointee and a friend of Vice President Spiro Agnew, also ruled that the Justice Department could not represent the two White House aides in the civil suit because that same department was conducting a criminal investigation of the same burglary.

Democratic presidential candidate George McGovern and his running mate, R. Sargent Shriver, sharply criticized the Nixon administration's handling of the Watergate investigation in early August. But both went a step beyond the available evidence by charging that President Nixon had direct knowledge of the cover-up. McGovern thus destroyed a good political issue, and I so told Frank Mankiewicz, one of his top advisers, when I asked for McGovern's proof that Nixon had knowledge of the cover-up. With the focus of the nation on him, McGovern ignored a carefully written speech on the blatant conflicts of interest and wildly charged the president with an obstruction of justice he could not prove then or at any point during the campaign. He further accused President Nixon of being "at least indirectly responsible" for the Watergate burglary. "Now this is the kind of thing that you expect from a person like Hitler. You would not expect it from a country like this, that is supposed to be a free society," McGovern said in Lordstown, Ohio, on August 16.

The McGovern attack gave the Nixon campaign group just what they had hoped for: they now could disregard even the responsible complaints of Senator Proxmire, Representative Patman, and others. The White House even dared to give its blessing to Teamsters President Frank Fitzsimmons in a star-studded attempt to restore the image of that racket-ridden union. Charles Colson and six of President Nixon's cabinet members appeared at a cocktail reception at the palatial Teamsters building. In attendance were Labor Secretary James Hodgson, Treasury Secretary George Shultz, Transportation Secretary

John Volpe, Attorney General Richard Kleindienst, Interior Secretary Rogers Morton, and Commerce Secretary Peter Peterson. White House Press Secretary Ronald Ziegler said, "I don't think the question of the administration supporting the Teamsters union came before the president. I am assuming that each of the cabinet officers and Mr. Colson received invitations to attend this function, and made independent decisions to attend. I see nothing wrong with them attending if it served a good cause. It is my understanding that the Teamsters is now cleaned up."

To mark the opening of the Republican convention on August 21, 1972, I wrote a story focusing on H. R. Haldeman as the person most responsible for the well-disciplined convention and the organization at CREP.

Since January, 1969, Haldeman has been at President Nixon's side, with full knowledge of everyone the president has seen and with control over whom the president sees and what matters are worthy of the president's time. It is a power far greater than Sherman Adams exerted in the Eisenhower administration.

Haldeman has acquired this power through his position as head of the White House secretariat and through his dominant role in most White House appointments. Someone had to screen government communications to the president, and Haldeman assumed or was given this role, which he exercised through a host of neat and bright young men—most of whom had complete loyalty to and dependence upon the man most responsible for their being on the White House staff.

It is these young men who have been the functionaries who established, staffed, and ran the Committee for the Re-election of the President, the well-financed organization that dominated planning for the Republican convention.

I wrote of Jeb Magruder's role in establishing CREP and the fact that this Haldeman protégé, with Frederic Malek, another deputy director of CREP, had directed the committee after John Mitchell resigned. "Although former Representative Clark MacGregor of Minnesota took over the chairman title when Mitchell left for family reasons, it was as a name front and as a spokesman," I wrote. "Magruder and Malek will be running the show—Magruder in the office and Malek as deputy director in charge of field operations."

On August 29, 1972, in a press conference at the Western White House at San Clemente, President Nixon rejected Democratic appeals for a special prosecutor or an independent investigation. He listed at least five investigations of the Watergate matter in progress and said: "Now, with all of these investigations that are being conducted, I don't believe that adding another special prosecutor would serve any useful purpose." He then spoke of another White House investigation that he had requested his White House Counsel John W. Dean III to undertake: "I can say categorically that his [Dean's] investigation indicates that no one in the White House staff, no one in this administration, presently employed, was involved in this very bizarre incident," Mr. Nixon said. "What really hurts is if you try to cover it up."

During the next few days, in conversations with Pat Buchanan and with various Republican congressmen and senators from Iowa, including Senator Jack Miller and Representatives Wiley Mayne, William Scherle, H. R. Gross,

I received the same message: The grand jury report would not be a white-wash limited to the five men arrested at the Watergate; others responsible for the "caper" would also be indicted. That assurance was articulated by Republican House Leader Gerald Ford and Senate Republican Leader Hugh Scott, as well as through White House congressional liaison channels. The White House apparently had things under control and would approve indictments in time to avoid being hurt by Democratic charges of a cover-up. Rumor said that those named might include Mitchell, Magruder, and Stans.

On September 15, 1972, a federal grand jury returned an eight-count indictment against seven men, and the "big fish" we had been promised turned out to be the two former White House aides, G. Gordon Liddy and E. Howard Hunt. The others were the five arrested at gunpoint at Democratic headquarters:

James W. McCord, fifty-three, president of McCord Associates and former security coordinator for CREP.

Bernard L. Barker, fifty-five, president of a Miami real estate firm known as Barker Associates, whose bank account had been the depository of $114,000 in checks representing contributions to CREP.

Eugenio R. Martinez, forty-four, of Miami, an employee of Barker's firm and a former CIA employee.

Frank A. Sturgis, thirty-seven, of Miami, a soldier of fortune and an associate of Barker.

Virgilio R. Gonzales of Miami, a locksmith and an associate of Barker.

The naming of Liddy, a forty-two-year-old White House lawyer who had been financial counsel at CREP, and Hunt, fifty-four-year-old former White House consultant and a former CIA employee, was apparently supposed to demonstrate that the Nixon administration would take action against its own.

The conspiracy count covered all seven of the defendants in the period from May 1, 1972, to June 17, 1972, and the indictment revealed allegations that there had been transcripts made of wiretaps at Democratic headquarters from a monitor operating from the Howard Johnson motor lodge across the street from the Watergate. Although the indictment included much new material on the *modus operandi* of the Watergate burglars, it left unanswered many questions about the financing of the burglary-bugging and about who approved the plan. It was hard to believe that a project involving at least seven people, and transporting five of them from Miami to Washington, could have been developed and carried out over a period of forty-five days without approval from or authorization of funds by John Mitchell or Maurice Stans and without the acquiescence of the ever-watchful Haldeman.

Attorney General Kleindienst and Clark MacGregor hoped that the indictments would eliminate Watergate as an issue in the presidential campaign. "The action of the grand jury speaks for itself," MacGregor said from his office at CREP. "We now appeal to all of those who have sought political benefit from this case to discontinue saying or doing anything that will interfere with a full and fair trial either from the point of view of the defendants or of the government." Then MacGregor suggested that "those who have recklessly sought to connect others with the case should publicly apologize for their unfounded charges and formally retract their unsubstantiated accusations."

Democratic Chairman Lawrence O'Brien made it clear that he had no intention of retracting his charges or of apologizing to Maurice Stans. "The indictments confirm my own contention that the burglary and bugging were a most serious incident raising questions that go to the heart of the American political system," O'Brien said. "We can assume that the investigation will continue, since the indictments reflect only the most narrow construction of the crime committed. In particular we will continue to press for a more thorough explanation of the funding of the crime that led to these indictments."

Ron Ziegler, a few days later, asked whether the indictments involving former White House aides had convinced me that the Nixon administration had not engaged in a whitewash. "It is a cover-up," I said, "and anyone familiar with investigations can see it is, for they haven't made a serious effort to use the immunity laws to crack Liddy, Hunt, and other witnesses who could tell how it was financed." In a column written in late September I dealt with the failure to use immunity laws to compel Liddy or Hunt to testify, for they obviously could shed light on the one big unanswered question: Where did the thousands of dollars come from to finance the expensive month-long bugging of national Democratic headquarters at the Watergate? "New immunity laws, used effectively by the Nixon administration in its war on organized crime, could be used by the Justice Department to force revelation of the financing of the burglary-bugging at the Watergate," I pointed out, adding that it was "unlikely that Liddy would have been putting up $1,600 of his own money to bug telephones at Democratic headquarters. And James W. McCord, Jr., would hardly have purchased a $3,500 interception and recording system for his own amusement while serving as chief security coordinator of the Nixon re-election committee."

Indictments were returned to the court of Chief United States District Judge John J. Sirica in mid-September, late enough to stall the trials until after the election. Pending the trial, President Nixon and other Republicans could echo MacGregor's plea that Watergate not be allowed to become an election issue so that a fair trial would be possible for the defendants and for the government. There was still one slight chance of getting an open hearing of such crucial witnesses as Mitchell, Stans, Colson, and Magruder before the November 7 election. It was already apparent that Chairman Patman's investigation represented the best practical possibility of forcing testimony from a number of key witnesses before the election, and Republican House Leader Gerald R. Ford was hard at work trying to shut off that investigation.

*Chapter Twenty-seven*

# PULLING PATMAN'S PUNCH

FROM THE BEGINNING, Congressman Wright Patman and Senator William Proxmire set their sights on Maurice Stans as a possible key to the financing of the Watergate burglary. The former secretary of commerce had been Mr. Nixon's chief fund-raiser in the 1968 campaign and had assumed a similar role in 1972 as finance chairman at CREP. As such, he would have had knowledge of funds which might have been available for the use of Liddy, McCord, and the Watergate burglars. Patman's House Banking Committee investigators were convinced that questioning Stans under oath would break the case wide open. The more that was revealed about Liddy, McCord, and Hunt, and about Barker's bank accounts, the more certain they were that substantial amounts of CREP money had to have been authorized through official channels to pay for the burglary.

An informant at CREP corroborated a story I had received from an FBI source that Stans had a secret cash fund of $350,000 in his office for special projects. The new campaign financing law required Stans to keep a record of the source of all contributions and the manner in which they were disbursed. If CREP had complied with the law, records would be available in its offices or in reports made to the Office of Federal Elections at the GAO, unless the money was both received and disbursed prior to the April 7, 1972, effective date of the new legislation.

For more than two months Patman's investigators worked quietly, trying to unravel the mystery of the $114,000 in Nixon campaign money that had been traced to Barker's bank account in Miami. It was difficult to believe the official story that Liddy had used Barker's account to convert the $25,000 check into cash and had followed the same procedure with the four cashier's checks from the Mexico City bank. It sounded to me like a cover story to avoid the obvious inference that the campaign funds had been paid to Barker to finance the Watergate burglary. Jake Lewis, of Patman's staff, commented that it would be illegal for a foreign person or corporation to contribute to a presidential candidate in a United States election. If it were established that the source of the $114,000 was foreign, it was certainly a scandalous situation and a federal law violation. The only other explanation was that an American citizen was trying to avoid identification of the contribution to Nixon by "laundering" it through a Mexico City lawyer. Jake Lewis and I speculated that the money might be from organized crime, from the Teamsters Union, or from the big oil interests in Texas.

The investigators were frustrated in their efforts to get a direct explanation from Maurice Stans about these mysterious contributions, and in late August and early September Chairman Patman was threatening to seek subpoena power from his committee or to conduct a hearing in which all of the evidence his investigators had amassed would be placed before the public. But as Patman's investigators became more resolute in their efforts to question Stans or Mitchell under oath, the Nixon administration became more adamant in its insistence that Maurice Stans not be subjected to a searching interrogation that would become public before the November election. The million-dollar civil damage suit filed by Democratic Chairman Lawrence O'Brien was under the jurisdiction of United States District Judge Charles Richey, a Nixon appointee, and he had permitted depositions under a court order prohibiting publication until after the election. Lacking subpoena power, Senator Proxmire could not enforce his demands for information from the Nixon re-election committee or from the federal agencies which operated under Nixon appointees. The GAO had no independent authority to compel testimony to be given or documents produced, but had to rely on Attorney General Kleindienst to approve subpoenas for testimony or records. The nearly three months that the Justice Department had procrastinated between the Watergate burglary and the return of indictments meant that the trial on the criminal charges could not be started until after the November 7 election. Thus President Nixon and his top campaign aides recognized that stopping Patman was essential if Mitchell, Colson, Magruder, and Dean were to avoid public testimony prior to the election.

On September 12, 1972—three days before the return of the Watergate indictments—Chairman Patman circulated an eighty-page staff report to the thirty-seven members of his committee. That carefully documented report demonstrated the need for hearings and an in-depth investigation of the highly unusual manner in which $700,000 in Texas oil money—much of it in cash—had been rushed to Washington on April 5, just two days before the new campaign disclosure law took effect. The report, based on information from police sources, the GAO, and interviews conducted by the congressional committee staff, revealed for the first time how William Liedtke, president of Pennzoil Corporation of Houston, had collected cash, securities, and checks worth $700,000 in his office, cleared the transaction with Stans, and placed the money in a suitcase to be sent by private plane to CREP. Roy Winchester, a public relations man for Pennzoil, and another employee, Peter Mark, took the suitcase to a waiting Pennzoil plane in the late afternoon. They arrived at Washington National Airport at about 9:00 P.M. and within the hour delivered their parcel to the Nixon re-election committee, where Winchester found such confusion at the finance office that he decided to return the next morning to file the confidential report.

Liedtke, chairman of the Southwest Regional Finance Committee to Re-elect the President, told Patman's investigators he had no records of the contributors because "in the fund-raising business you don't deal in receipts."

The Patman committee staff reported that Stans refused to divulge the names of the contributors of any part of the $89,000 in checks that had gone through the Mexico City bank or of the remainder of the $700,000. Stans's position was that confidentiality was part of the contract between the Nixon re-election committee and the contributors and that he had no authority to unilaterally break that contract. This was stonewalling at its worst, and Chairman Patman, in a cover letter to committee members, wrote: "It appears that the Committee to Re-elect the President and its allied groups are willing to go to any lengths to conceal the identity and origin of these [Mexico City] checks. All of the mystery of the growing speculation about the sources of these funds could be cleared up if these records were made available to this committee [Banking and Currency] and to the public."

The report also identified oil interests as the contributors of the $89,000 that had been sent through the Mexico City bank. There were obvious conflicts between the story Stans told investigators about the $89,000 in checks and the statements by other witnesses, and Patman emphasized the importance of resolving these conflicts by putting Stans and the other witnesses under oath at the earliest time. In zeroing in on Stans, the report made these basic points:

1. Stans was finance chairman when more the $10 million in contributions was accumulated from sources still not revealed or reported.

2. Some of that money, including the $89,000, found its way into Barker's bank account in what appeared to be a violation of the laws that prohibit foreigners and foreign corporations from contributing to American election campaigns.

3. For a time, Stans had personal custody of the $25,000 certified check from Kenneth Dahlberg that also found its way into the account of Barker.

4. Stans had refused to reveal to the subcommittee the source of the $89,000 or of any part of the $700,000 delivered to his office at Nixon re-election committee headquarters.

Liedtke had told investigators that he had had two separate telephone conversations with Stans on April 3 to determine whether there were any legal problems in putting the money through the account of a Mexico City lawyer, Manuel Ogarrio Daguerre. Later in the day, Liedtke said, he had received a telephone call in which Stans cleared the checks from the Mexico City bank with the comment, "Okay, bring the money to Washington."

The Patman report also revealed that the $25,000 certified check from Dahlberg was actually a contribution from Minneapolis financier Dwayne Andreas, a friend of Hubert H. Humphrey who had helped provide financial backing for Humphrey's various races for senator, vice president, and president. Andreas had explained that he had sought to hide the $25,000 contribution to Richard Nixon because he thought his Democratic political friends might not understand why he was making large contributions to both Richard Nixon's and Hubert Humphrey's primary campaigns.

The Patman report, though still technically secret, was leaked to me and a few other Washington reporters, but Patman made a public pitch to sub-poena Stans and Mitchell.

From mid-July on I had tried to interview Maurice Stans, but he had not returned my calls. My relations with him had always been good and I was sure that if he had a credible story he would have seen me. I needled DeVan Shumway and Powell Moore of the Nixon re-election committee press office because of Stans's unavailability, which I referred to by Haldeman's term, "stonewalling." "Stans just isn't seeing anyone," Shumway said. "I'm sure that he will see you as soon as he sees anyone, but this Watergate matter is extremely sensitive and he doesn't want to take a chance of upsetting things." Shumway said that he was certain Stans wasn't the kind who would have any part of financing a burglary and that he was confident Stans had a good ex-planation for the mysterious money.

In late August and early September I increased the frequency of my calls to Stans's office, but I had nearly given up, despite assurances that he would see me "at the right time." Suddenly, on September 12, I was told that Stans hoped to be able to see me within a few days. An appointment was initially made for 8:00 A.M. on Wednesday, September 14, but it was cancelled on the evening before, and I was told he hoped to schedule it for a later time the next day. The interview was ultimately set for that afternoon.

In preparation, I reviewed my copy of the still-secret report by the Patman committee staff to establish firmly the history of the $25,000 Dahlberg check and to review the intricate legal problems connected with the $89,000 in Texas oil money. But most important from my standpoint were these ques-tions: Had Stans had any conversations with President Nixon on these con-troversial transactions? Had Stans made any kind of verbal or written report to President Nixon or anyone in the White House on the legal problems in-volving the cash contributions and the money traced to Barker's bank ac-count? The General Accounting Office had questioned the legality of CREP's failure to report the $25,000 Dahlberg check. I wanted to know whether Stans accepted this judgment and, if he rejected it, on what basis he did so. The Patman committee had also made charges of conflicts between his story and the stories told by other witnesses. The major question was what legal advice he had relied on in following the controversial policy of pressing for cash contributions before April 7 in order to avoid the necessity of reporting them. Even if it was technically legal, I wanted to ask Stans whether he had discussed with President Nixon the ethical questions involved in such a de-liberate violation of the spirit of the new law.

Those were a few of the questions that were in my mind as I walked from the National Press Building and turned west on Pennsylvania Avenue to the new First National Bank building, which housed the Committee to Re-elect the President. As I walked by the imposing iron fence of the White House, I felt especially free and was happy to be on the outside, with no responsibility as an apologist for Watergate. The sight of the Executive Office Building evoked memories of the huge first-floor office I had occupied, with its plush gold carpet, ornate fireplace, twenty-foot ceiling, and television set that gave a quick play-back of essentially any network or local public affairs program. I had returned to that office only twice after leaving the White House staff. The first time was shortly after I left, when it was occupied by Robert P. Mayo, director of the Bureau of the Budget. The second time, I dropped by to chat with Fred Malek, a Haldeman protégé in charge of personnel recruiting and management for the White House and for the various agencies. There weren't many changes. It still had the same painting, borrowed from the National Gallery of Art, but I didn't find it as unbearably oppressive as in my last few months there.

I crossed the street and took an elevator to the second floor of the First National Bank Building, where Stans's office was located. I was early, and chatted briefly with Dan Hofgren, an assistant to Stans whom I had known on the White House staff. The handsome young New York investment banker asked what I thought of Watergate. I told him frankly that I believed it could be a serious weapon against President Nixon if Senator McGovern understood how to use it and was even reasonably effective in changing some other aspects of his campaign. When Stans's secretary said he was ready to see me, gray-haired, fatherly Dick Moore strolled in to ask whether I would mind if he sat in. Moore, a California public relations man and lawyer, was on the White House staff. I got the impression that President Nixon wanted him present during my interview with Stans. Moore explained that while President Nixon wanted Stans to tell me all of the facts, there must be due regard for "executive privilege" in order to protect the presidency.

The absurdity of trying to use executive privilege, at best a flimsy doctrine, to clothe discussions of President Nixon's purely political operations annoyed me, but with an attempt at good-humored acceptance I said I hoped it wouldn't mean too much coaching of the witness, and we all laughed. In interviewing Stans personally, I wanted to see his reactions as much as to record his responses, for I had difficulty imagining how he could logically explain the tangled financial operations of CREP. But it made little difference what explanation he gave; the interview was important because it would be his first interview on the Watergate matter, except for secret Justice Department questioning and the unsatisfactory explanations given to the Patman investigators. If his responses were the same as he had given Patman's investigators, I would continue the questions until he stopped answering, for I was certain that the questions he did not answer would be as revealing as those he did.

At this point my musings were interrupted by Dick Moore, who insisted that the interview be on a "background only" basis. I scowled for this meant that I could not quote Stans directly. I would have to present whatever he told me as "the story Stans is telling his intimates," or in some other way disguise the fact that I had actually talked to Stans. Now I understood the game. They were trying to use me to determine what questions Stans might face from an aggressive questioner but also wanted to be free to deny my version at any subsequent time. I did not like their conditions, but my only alternative was to walk out. Under normal circumstances I probably would have taken a walk, but I was intrigued by the prospect of asking questions for an hour or so and watching Stans and Moore scramble for a safe public posture.

After some general questions about Stans's difficulties and how he was standing up under the strain, I burrowed into his failure to answer questions or appear under oath before Patman's committee. "It makes you look like you've got something to hide," I said, and told him that if he had a credible explanation he should try to get it out quickly.

Stans assured me that he had nothing to hide but said that Patman was "political" and that Patman's investigators had treated him in a rude and inconsiderate manner. Stans said that they only wanted to make political hay out of Watergate to help George McGovern and that it was in the national interest to save the country from a McGovern presidency. He felt that any explanation he gave would be "distorted" by the Patman committee, and further distorted by the anti-Nixon press.

To establish a point of rapport, I said that I feared what McGovern's $35 billion cut in the Defense Department budget would mean to the U.S. defensive posture but that Patman's staff report was well-documented and made a persuasive argument for public hearings. Stans said that he believed Watergate indictments would be returned "within a few days" and that this would take the heat off generally. He expressed confidence that the House Republican leadership (he named House Republican Leader Gerald Ford and Representative Garry Brown, both of Michigan) could block Patman from obtaining subpoena power until after the election. Most of the Republicans would stick together and enough Democrats on the committee were opposed to McGovern's candidacy to make it possible for Patman to be defeated in his own committee, Stans said. I observed that even if Patman were stopped, the Office of Federal Elections and the GAO were still regarded as nonpartisan by the public. Dick Moore interjected that neither the Office of Federal Elections nor the GAO had subpoena power and that they "have to go through the Justice Department."

I then brought up the recent GAO report which concluded that the Nixon re-election committee had acted illegally in failing to report the $25,000 Dahlberg contribution, which had been delivered to Stans on April 9—two days after the effective date of the new law. Stans said that he believed no report was required. According to Stans, on February 9, 1972, Andreas and Dahlberg had attended a board meeting of the National City Bank of Minneapolis at the Seaview Hotel in Miami Beach. At that time Andreas had made a commitment to deliver the $25,000. On March 12 Andreas requested his secretary to have $20,000 drawn to his credit balance at the Seaview Hotel in order to have it on hand for the contribution. Three days later Andreas obtained that $20,000 in cash, added another $5,000, also in cash, and placed the money in an envelope in the Seaview Hotel safe. Andreas called Dahlberg on April 5 to tell him that the funds were on hand and that he wanted to make the contribution and to be sure it was done before April 7. "He stated that he would place the envelope in a safe-deposit box in Dahlberg's name to insure that title had passed," Stans said. "Dahlberg accepted the contribution on that basis and reported it by telephone to Stans on the same day. Andreas placed the funds in box 305 of the Seaview Hotel and the records show the issuance of that box in the name of Dahlberg." On April 7 Dahlberg went to Florida and "drove to the Seaview Hotel to pick up the money, but was unable to do so because the vault had been closed for the day." On April 8, "Dahlberg and Andreas talked on the telephone and made arrangements to meet on the ninth. Dahlberg asked Andreas to secure the envelope from the safe-deposit box for him and bring it to the place of their meeting." The ultimate delivery of the $25,000 at the Indian Creek Golf Club was simply "a technicality," Stans said, for there had been "a legal constructive contribution" from January or February.

"Did the GAO investigators have all of the facts you've gone over with me?" I asked.

Stans said that they had been given the full explanation.

"And still they disagree with your legal interpretation?" I asked. I inquired as to who in the Nixon re-election committee had given him an opinion to the contrary or whether he had obtained an opinion from any other government sources.

Stans said that he had been given a legal opinion by a CREP lawyer at the time of the receipt of the money. He winced when I asked the name of the lawyer, but finally responded that it was G. Gordon Liddy.

"Do you have any other legal opinion to back you on this interpretation?" I asked, suggesting that under present circumstances a legal opinion from Liddy was of questionable value.

Stans said that in several meetings with White House Counsel John W. Dean III on the subject during the past month Dean had assured him of the validity of Liddy's opinion.

"But have you had any opinion from Dean since the report of the GAO challenging the legality of the transaction?" I asked.

Stans assured me that he had.

I asked to examine a copy of Dean's opinion and Stans looked to Dick Moore for guidance on whether or not to allow me to see it. Moore said that he probably should not give it to me because of "executive privilege" covering White House papers .

My next question was whether Dean's legal opinion had been checked with the Justice Department, which had responsibility for following through on violations of the federal election laws.

Stans said it had not. He said that he thought "a legal opinion from the White House counsel was about as high as you could go" and saw no need to check it further. He was confident that the Justice Department would agree with Dean's opinion. I marveled at the lack of ethical sensitivity of a White House counsel who was willing to give private legal advice to a partisan political organization, advice that was at odds with the position of the GAO and the Justice Department. But I did not raise this question, which

I knew would end the interview abruptly, because I still wanted to try to determine the extent of President Nixon's personal knowledge of all these questionable actions.

"Have you discussed these matters with President Nixon?" I asked.

Stans said yes before Dick Moore could say anything about executive privilege.

I assured him that I did not want to go into the details Stans had given the president, or the president's responses, but wanted to know only whether President Nixon was reasonably well satisfied with Stans's and the re-election committee's performance, or whether there was friction between Stans and the president over his handling of these matters.

Moore said that "conversations with the president are an awfully sensitive area" and suggested that Stans say only that there had been discussions, that the president or Haldeman had been provided with details, and that there was no friction.

I said that I was particularly interested in determining the truth of rumors that President Nixon and Haldeman were irritated with Stans over what they considered bungling in the handling of financial matters involving Watergate.

Stans said that his relations with President Nixon remained warm and friendly and that Mr. Nixon had never voiced any anger with Stans's actions.

I asked whether the president knew that Dean had given Stans a legal opinion on the Dahlberg check, and Stans, looking at Dick Moore, said he did not want to get into that area because "executive privilege" might be involved.

Stans said that the only reason he had not made a public statement on all aspects of the questionable contributions was that his counsel, Kenneth Parkinson, had advised him that any comments might jeopardize the rights of those under investigation by the grand jury.

I next turned to the $89,000 "laundered" in Mexico City.

Stans cringed at the term "laundered," complaining that it sounded like an illegal act by the Mafia. He hurriedly assured me that his investigation showed that the $89,000 did not constitute illegal gifts from foreign nationals or foreign corporations. "They were legal contributions from Americans with funds in Mexico," Stans said. "The funds were simply put through the Mexico City lawyer's account to be delivered back to the Nixon re-election committee before the April 7 deadline."

"Who were the American contributors?" I asked.

Stans said that he did not know the identity of the specific donors but that he had been assured by Liedtke that they were Americans. He argued that since the money had been delivered to CREP headquarters on April 5, there was no need to report the names of the donors and thus break his word to Liedtke and donors.

But, I asked, if he did not know the identity of the contributors, how could he be so sure that they were not serving as a front for organized crime or were not persons seeking favorable government treatment?

Stans merely reiterated that he had been told the money was from Americans in Mexico and that Liddy's opinion had been that the contributions were legal.

Stans said that he had consulted Liddy for advice on the legality of the transaction when he received an inquiry from Liedtke, his chairman in charge of the Southwest Regional Finance Committee, on April 3. Stans resented the Patman staff report indicating his story was not true and that it conflicted with the stories of several other witnesses. He had handled millions of dollars in contributions, and in his interviews with Patman's staff he had simply not remembered all of the details.

Stans said that he had not tried to refresh his memory by consulting with Liddy because "on the advice of counsel" he had not seen nor spoken with Liddy since late June, when Liddy was fired for refusing to answer questions for the FBI. Stans acknowledged that he had worked with Liddy on a day-to-day basis from late March until late June but insisted that he had no knowledge of Liddy's outside activities or of his sources of money for these activities. He said he had requested "a lawyer" to interpret the new Federal Campaign Expenditures Act and that Liddy had been assigned to his staff. Liddy had attended almost every meeting of Stans's campaign finance committee, and had "a full load of work." Said Stans: "I didn't know he had any spare time for all of these other activities." After Liddy had refused to cooperate with the FBI, Stans said his lawyer advised him not to have further communication with Liddy in order to avoid inadvertently involving himself in conversations that might be used to entrap him in the Watergate affair.

During our conversation, Stans acknowledged that Liddy was one of a select few who had access to the $350,000 cash fund that was kept for a brief time in Stans's office and for a longer time in the office of Hugh Sloan, Jr., the former treasurer of the Nixon re-election committee. Stans said he had trusted both Liddy and Sloan implicitly and that he still trusted Sloan, but that Sloan had resigned because the burden of being treasurer for the Nixon committee had become too heavy for him to carry. Sloan had been "concerned with the investigation and wanted no part of" the problems just then beginning to plague the committee, Stans said, explaining that it was "the treasurer" (Sloan) who had responsibility for compliance with the new federal campaign expenditures law, not "the finance chairman" (Stans) or "the director" (Mitchell). While Stans stressed his high regard for Sloan and expressed sympathy for the fact that Sloan had no job, it was apparent to me that the eager young man had been given the title of "treasurer" to make him the fall guy if anything went wrong.

As the interview drew to a close, I asked Stans whether he had had any conversations with President Nixon about the sending of campaign funds through Mexico, and again Moore injected himself into the conversation, warning that Stans "should not discuss any conversations with the president." I pursued the question in several ways before gaining any more than a tacit acknowledgment by Stans that he had had some conversations with President Nixon on the Mexico City checks. He refused to say when these conversations had taken place or what had been said.

As I left, I asked for a copy of Stans's memorandum describing the chronology of the Dahlberg check. Stans hesitated and I pressed the issue: "I want to be sure I have it accurately, and I don't want to have you complain later that I gave a wrong impression because I wasn't precisely accurate on matters of sharply differing legal opinion." Moore said they couldn't give me a copy of the same memorandum they had refused to give the Patman committee. I retorted: "If the memorandum is accurate, there is no reason you shouldn't give it to me for use in writing my story. If you've given me an inaccurate story, I want to have something concrete to come back here and raise hell about if I've been used." Stans assured me that the memorandum was indeed accurate; Dick Moore nodded his assent. I took my copy of the memorandum, we all shook hands, and I left the office.

Returning to the National Press Building down Pennsylvania Avenue, I brooded over what I had learned:

White House Counsel John Dean, heading an investigation requested by President Nixon, was providing legal opinions to Stans and others who were responsible for the irregular and perhaps illegal handling of huge amounts of cash.

President Nixon had consulted with Stans, had some knowledge of the Mexican maneuver, and had expressed no criticism of Stans or of the manner in which the re-election committee was being run.

If Stans did not know about the planning of the Watergate burglary, he was at least in a position to give some damned devastating testimony on Liddy's access to large amounts of cash.

Stans and Moore were satisfied that the return of criminal indictments against the five arrested men, and perhaps a few others, would clamp a tight lid on discussions of Watergate until after the election. Judge Richey had wrapped the depositions in the civil suit in secrecy, which would limit the use of that information by Democrats. Stans and Moore, mirroring the White House view, regarded Patman as the only problem in keeping Watergate under cover until after November 7 and "Four More Years" of Nixon.

There was too much material for one background story, and I was seriously limited by the agreement not to attribute the information to Stans or otherwise reveal him as the source. Since there was no pressure to rush into print, I concluded I could sleep on it before making a decision as to the best way to handle the story. Clearly, the most important part of the story as I finally wrote it would be the revelation that "the White House has assured Maurice Stans . . . it agrees with his view that no public report to the General Accounting Office was required on the $25,000 contribution received from financier Dwayne Andreas of Minneapolis." I wrote that a White House legal opinion to that effect had been given to Stans by John Dean and that it contradicted a published opinion by the GAO. I had been shocked at the revelation that a White House counsel was in charge of the Watergate cover-up at the same time as President Nixon was assuring the public that Dean was the man he was depending on to make certain there was no cover-up. Such tactics had been used by the Des Moines police department long ago when a corrupt chief of police wanted to cover up a police scandal, but I had never seen it done so blatantly since.

If Dean was coordinating the cover-up, it certainly had to have the approval of Haldeman and Ehrlichman and possibly the president. Dean was a pleasant young man whose major asset was his unquestioning obedience, his dedication to accomplishing what his superiors wanted without too many questions. I had known John since the time he had been in the Justice Department as an aide to Attorney General Mitchell, who treated the young lawyer with all of the pride of a father who has a precocious son. Dean moved to the White House as counsel to the president at about the time I was resigning. Press Secretary Ziegler had said in a press briefing that John Dean would take over some of my ombudsman duties. Dean and I had a couple of conversations before I left the White House, and on a later occasion I pointed out the danger inherent in executive-branch officials claiming "executive privilege" to hide their crimes or mismanagement. Dean, probably the youngest White House counsel in history, had not moved to that position as a boat-rocker. He was ambitious, and he had learned by thoughtful observation that any daring acts should have the approval of the boss. I could not be angry with Dean, only sorry for him. He was locked into the Nixon White House by his own ambition and his willingness to perform any chore in order to survive.

On Friday, September 15—the same day the indictments were returned against seven Watergate defendants—I wrote my first story based on the interview with Stans. I also wrote the story of the indictments, so the Stans story didn't appear in the *Des Moines Register* until September 18. The wire services ignored it because it had no direct quotes of a controversial nature, but Jake Lewis of Patman's committee was amazed that a White House counsel was giving Stans legal advice contrary to GAO's position. Lewis was certain that committee members would be interested in questioning Stans extensively on this and other points if they could persuade the committee to approve subpoena power to compel him to testify. A strong case was being made for hearing the testimony of more than twenty witnesses, and it was apparent that the questioning of either Stans or Mitchell in an open session would have a devastating political impact. Obviously the White House felt the same way and had placed the highest priority on blocking Patman.

I accepted the fact that my responsibility was to report all material facts available and that my own personal conclusions on election day would have little or no impact on the passions and prejudices of millions of voters. Therefore I must give full attention to the open hearings Patman sought, disregarding any fear that it could result in a McGovern victory. I compiled all the material I needed to present the case fully in a story that appeared in the *Des Moines Register* on September 25 under the heading: "Democrats' Last Chance for 'Early' Watergate Hearing."

"The showdown will be Wednesday on the last chance for the Democrats to get the testimony on the Watergate burglary-bugging aired before the November election," I wrote, detailing what was at stake in Chairman Patman's effort to obtain formal authorization for subpoena power. I explained that although the Democrats held a 22-to-15 majority, some Democrats were expected to defect because of disenchantment with McGovern. Jake Lewis said that Patman expected some depletion in Democratic ranks but was hopeful that his case was strong enough to influence some of the more independent Republicans who would be moved by the enormity of the evidence of political corruption.

Among these Republicans Lewis mentioned Representative Margaret Heckler of Massachusetts, who had defeated former House Speaker Joe Martin in 1966. I knew Mrs. Heckler casually and had been impressed with her intelligence, independence, and interest in honest government. She had graduated from Boston College Law School in 1956—just ten years before she upset Martin in a Republican primary. The first year she was in Congress she introduced herself in the House Cloak Room and said she had admired my work on the TFX investigation and the Bobby Baker case. We had discussed briefly the integrity of Senator John Williams, the stern honesty of Representative H. R. Gross, and the sordid politics of Lyndon Johnson. She hoped to be a force for good in politics and I knew she could if her idealism was coupled with common sense. Periodically, I had seen Representative Heckler over the intervening six years in committee meetings, on the House floor, and at several Republican functions when I was in the White House as special counsel. Our conversations had been brief, with little opportunity to detect whether she had changed her attitude on the importance of integrity in government. She had been one of the guests of honor at a special Gridiron Dinner in White Sulphur Springs, West Virginia, in November 1970—a few months after I left the White House. We had an opportunity to get into a broad-ranging discussion of politics and I was pleased to find that her four years in Congress had effected no change in her belief in the necessity of good government. It was this strong idealism which Chairman Patman hoped to appeal to for one Republican vote, to give a bipartisan cast to his investigation, and I decided to talk to her to probe her thinking.

The vote initially slated for September 27 was postponed until October 3, and that week I talked to Margaret Heckler. She deplored Watergate and the indications that it was financed by Nixon campaign funds, and bitterly criticized the fact that the White House gang was ignoring the Republican National Committee and the senatorial and congressional candidates except in a few cases. When I asked her what she was going to do on the vote to give Patman subpoena power she turned her fire on Patman, characterizing him as "a tyrant" who was going to use the committee to try to elect George McGovern. "Why not let the full truth come out?" I asked. She replied that fair trials for the seven Watergate defendants had to be considered and that, in addition, Patman and his staff could be expected to distort the record. "That's the White House line being peddled by [Representative] Garry Brown to block public questioning of Stans and Mitchell," I said. "It's as bad a cover-up as the Bobby Baker case, and they are using a lot of the same tricks." I sug-

gested that she read the eighty-page report by Patman's staff for herself and
not rely on Brown, who was carrying the ball for the White House. I told her
Brown's letters to the Department Justice appeared to be an attempt to push
Assistant Attorney General Henry Petersen into fronting for a delay in House
hearings until after the election.

She told me that she had not had time to examine all of the evidence Patman's staff had accumulated but that House Republican Leader Gerald Ford
had told her it was one of the most obviously partisan investigations he had
seen in his years in Congress. Ford had told her that the White House had assured him that Watergate was simply "a caper" perpetrated by Liddy, Hunt,
and some irresponsible Cuban-Americans. He had assured her that no higher
officials at the White House or the re-election committee were involved and
that Patman was engaged in "a political witch hunt."

"I think you should read the staff report," I repeated.

She responded that Assistant Attorney General Petersen, whom she had
been told was a Democrat and a veteran career employee of the Justice Department, had written a letter asking for a delay in congressional hearings
until after the criminal trials. She asked whether I believed that Petersen
would be part of a Republican cover-up, and I had to say that I didn't believe he would willingly take any action that was political unless specifically
directed to do so by the attorney general. That Petersen letter was the Republicans' trump, and I did not want to challenge his credibility even though
I believed it a mistake in judgment to have signed the letter when he must
have known how it would be used.

On October 3, after a week of heavy Republican lobbying, Chairman Patman lost the vote for authorization for subpoena power. The vote was 20 to
14, with all Republicans, including Representative Heckler, opposed. Four
southern Democrats—Roy Stephens of Georgia, Tom Gettys of South Carolina, Charles Griffin of Mississippi, and Bill Chappell of Florida—joined the
Republicans. Other Democrats voting against Patman were Richard Hanna of
California, and Frank Brasco of New York. "Representative Garry Brown,
key figure in engineering the defeat, acknowledged in an interview that he
worked with the Justice Department and Representative Gerald R. Ford, the
House minority leader, to block the hearings," I wrote in the October 4, 1972,
*Des Moines Register*. Patman predicted that eventually "the facts will come
out, and when they do I am convinced they will reveal why the White House
was so anxious to kill the committee's investigation. The public will fully understand why this pressure was mounted." Democratic Chairman Lawrence
O'Brien said the committee action was "beyond comprehension." Said
O'Brien, "It is a victory for the [Nixon] administration . . . a victory for
secrecy, suppression, and skullduggery." It was also a victory for Gerald
Ford, who had met with Republican members of the House Banking and Currency committee jointly and individually to explain the importance of stopping Patman's "witch hunt" and protecting the rights of the seven Watergate
defendants.

*Chapter Twenty-eight*

# SCENARIO FOR A LANDSLIDE

WITH THE CURTAIN pulled down on Patman's House hearings and criminal charges pending against the Watergate seven, President Nixon was in a position to keep the lid on further revelations while taking the offensive against Democratic candidate George McGovern and other critics. President Nixon could use McGovern's intemperate charges to ridicule his critics in the press and in politics; he could answer some questions but refuse to answer others on the grounds that he was leaning over backward to assure fair play for the Watergate defendants. This strategy was comparable in many respects to that used in the 1968 campaign, when he had stressed his "secret solution" for the war in Vietnam, but would not discuss it because he did not want to interfere with President Johnson's handling of that war.

But I believed that there were a number of questions concerning the financing of the Watergate burglars by the Nixon re-election committee that President Nixon would have a tough time handling, particularly if they were pursued aggressively. I was eager for him to hold a press conference but unprepared for the spontaneous unannounced meeting with the press on October 5, which I learned about from the United Press International city wire only after it had started. Shortly after 11:00 A.M. the wire service reported that a presidential news conference was in progress in the Oval Office. I grabbed my coat, bolted from the office, and raced the four blocks to the West Gate of the White House, angry because Press Secretary Ronald Ziegler hadn't called me. (I rarely attended Ziegler's briefings, considering them a waste of time, but customary procedure is to telephone reporters before an unscheduled press conference.) I fumbled to pull my press card from my billfold as I approached the sentry box at the West Gate, and was so irritated and exhausted from my sprint that I ignored the smile of the White House policeman, who nodded as he pushed the button to unlock the gate. As I raced up the drive to the West Wing, I mulled over which of the questions I would ask when I got into the Oval Office.

I was stopped in my dash across the pressroom toward the hall to the Oval Office by one of the press office secretaries, who told me that I would not be permitted to enter because I was too late. I explained that I had not been called, and she was "sorry, but Ron and Jerry [Deputy Press Secretary Gerald Warren] are in the Oval Office, and they are the only ones who can make an exception to the hard rules about latecomers." The president's voice was coming through the speaker system into the press office and, still fuming,

I sat down to take notes. The press conference had just started. I asked if there had been anything on Watergate. I was told that there had been only one question, at the very beginning of the press conference, on how the president was planning to defend himself against the charges of corruption. It was a general question, and President Nixon had used it to heap scorn on McGovern for having compared the president of the United States to Adolph Hitler. I listened to a long series of answers on a negotiated settlement of the Vietnam War, to the president's defense of the wheat deals with the Soviet Union, and to a discussion of an Ehrlichman scheme to use federal funds to reduce property taxes by 50 percent.

Then another Watergate question was asked. It was so rambling, non-specific, and antagonistic in tone that it provided Mr. Nixon with a perfect opportunity: "Mr. President, don't you think that your administration and the public would be served considerably and the men under indictment would be treated better, if you people would come through and make a clean breast about what you were trying to get done at the Watergate?"

President Nixon ignored the unsupported personal accusation that he was involved in planning the Watergate burglary and responded in a controlled tone: "One thing that has always puzzled me about it is why anybody would have tried to get anything out of the Watergate. But be that as it may, that decision having been made at lower levels, with which I had no knowledge, and as I pointed out—"

"Surely you know now, sir," the questioner interrupted.

The president continued: "Just a minute. I certainly feel that under the circumstances that we have got to look at what has happened and to put the matter into perspective. Now, when we talk about a clean breast, let's look at what happened. The FBI assigned 133 agents to this investigation. It followed out 1,800 leads. It conducted 1,500 interviews. Incidentally, I conducted the investigation of the Hiss case. I know that is a very unpopular subject to raise in some quarters, but I conducted it. It was successful. The FBI did a magnificent job, but that investigation, involving the security of this country, was basically a Sunday school exercise compared to the amount of effort that was put into this." The president hurriedly said that he agreed with the amount of effort put into the case, adding: "I wanted every lead carried out to the end because I wanted to be sure that no member of the White House staff and no man or woman in a position of major responsibility in the Committee for Re-election had anything to do with this kind of reprehensible activity."

Then President Nixon made his first effort to put Watergate behind and leave it to the courts: "Now, the grand jury has handed down indictments. It has indicted, incidentally, two who were with the Committee for the Re-election . . . one who refused to cooperate and another who was apprehended. Under these circumstances, the grand jury now having acted, it is now time to have the judicial process go forward and for the evidence to be presented." It was the same scenario played by Stans two weeks earlier. Then he subtly performed the double job of taking a sharp jab at the press and attempting to justify his refusal to comment further on the case: "I would say finally, with regard to commenting on any of those who have been indicted, with regard to saying anything about the judicial process, I am going to follow the good advice, which I appreciate, of the members of the press corps, my constant, and I trust will always continue to be, very responsible critics." He made reference to his well-publicized blunder in commenting at a press conference that Charles Manson was guilty of murder before the trial was concluded: "I stepped into one on that when you recall I made, inadvertently, a comment in Denver about an individual who had been indicted in California, the Manson case. I was vigorously criticized for making any comment about the case, and so, of course, I know you would want me to follow the same single standard by not commenting on this case."

The president avoided a question as to whether he would have any more press conferences before the November 7 election. "I would plan to try to find ways to be available for purposes of presenting my position," Mr. Nixon said, but he indicated that this would be largely in prepared speeches and through surrogates. He ended on a condescending note: "To come precisely now to your question, I think that the format of questions and answers, for members of the press can be useful. Certainly, I will consider the possibility of using that format. Maybe not just here [in Washington], maybe in other places as well."

I was doubly angry at Ron Ziegler. I had had several questions, backed by law and fact, which were very much to the point of the Watergate burglary and which the president should have answered for the American voters before their ballots were cast. Now it appeared that there would not be another press conference in Washington before the election—the ultimate in a cover-up, and, it seemed, one he was going to get away with. I was frustrated and inwardly seething when Ziegler came out of the Oval Office, but I managed to be restrained as I told him I wished to speak with him alone. In his office, I asked why I had not been called. "Didn't you make it?" he responded.

"No, I didn't make it, and I want to know why I wasn't called," I said, and accused him of deliberately failing to call on instructions from Haldeman.

"I assure you it wasn't intentional and that it won't happen again," Ziegler said.

"I believe I was not called intentionally because you knew I would have some tough Watergate questions," I responded.

"There were some Watergate questions, and the president answered them," Ziegler replied. "The transcript of the press conference will be available to you as to everyone else."

I said that I had heard the rambling, inept queries but that I had had specific questions regarding the evidence indicating the Nixon re-election committee had financed at least a part of the Watergate burglary. "They weren't asked, and now it doesn't appear there will be an opportunity between now and the election," I said.

"Maybe I can answer them for you," Ziegler said.

"I don't think you know any real answers, and I don't believe you know where to get them," I snapped. "You forget that I used to work around here and know your game."

This slur on his competence brought a defensive response: "Things aren't like they were when you were here. I have a lot of input and a lot to do with policy."

The thought of Ziegler making policy or being anything other than Haldeman's errand boy was ludicrous, but I held my tongue and turned to the financing of the Watergate burglars and the evidence that two employees of the Nixon re-election committee, Liddy and McCord, had made substantial outlays of cash. The indictment stated that McCord had spent $3,500 for electronic devices used in the Watergate burglary and that Liddy had spent at least $1,600 in connection with the burglary. I asked Ziegler whether he or anyone in the White House really expected the press to believe that McCord and Liddy had used their own money on these expenditures. In response to his "no," I asked him where he thought the money had come from.

"Why, I didn't think there was any question but that the money came from the committee," Ziegler said. I was astonished to hear the White House press spokesman admit that the burglary had been financed at least in part by the Nixon re-election committee, when the committee's press office had denied any knowledge that the money came from its funds. I asked the question again, being careful to make clear reference to the Nixon re-election committee and the Watergate burglary funds, and again Ziegler repeated: "There is no question but that the money came from the committee."

Then I said that I had wanted to ask the president about the conflict of interest posed by the participation of Attorney General Kleindienst and Acting FBI Director Gray in an investigation involving a Nixon campaign committee.

"Don't you think Dick Kleindienst is honest?" he asked.

I replied that it wasn't a matter of the inherent honesty or dishonesty of either Kleindienst or Pat Gray, but that their political positions made it impossible to be objective in their assessment of political crimes which might reflect on President Nixon.

"You heard the president say what a thorough investigation had been conducted," Ziegler said. "I can get you all of the statistics, and probably more from the Justice Department and the FBI."

I assured him I didn't quarrel with the accuracy of the statistics, but that it didn't make any difference how many miles you traveled, how many people were interviewed, or how many leads were run out if the investigative agency was so encumbered by political loyalty that it neglected to ask the right question of only one witness.

Ziegler said that President Nixon was personally making sure that the investigation was being followed up properly and that it was being handled by John Dean. "You like John Dean, don't you?" Ziegler asked.

I said that it didn't make any difference whether I liked John Dean or not, that he was a part of the Nixon team investigating a Nixon problem. I am sure Ziegler could not fathom the "conflict of interest" concept. I left with his assurance that there would be "no mistakes in the future" in regard to my being notified of a press conference.

As I walked back to the National Press Building, I pondered Ziegler's success with "the White House regulars"—those reporters who spent most of their time waiting in the press lounge, attended all of his press briefings and traveled on most presidential trips. Ziegler was the greatest stonewaller of all because he had no sense of shame when he was caught misleading the press or was called upon to stand firm on an absurd inconsistency or an unconscionable suppression or distortion of fact or law. If it satisfied Haldeman and the president (and probably in that order) it was good enough for the young advertising executive, who was accustomed to tossing aside last month's PR gimmicks as "inoperative."

Most presidential press secretaries had some newspaper experience, and, even though they were trying to do a public relations job for their particular president, they felt a sense of public responsibility and some obligation to be truthful. Most press secretaries took pride in being "technically accurate" and consistent even though they may have withheld part of the facts. If the full truth surfaced later, they wanted the record to demonstrate that they had handled the information competently and with an understanding of the people's right to know about their government. But that was not what Haldeman wanted. Ziegler was to do or say whatever would best serve the interests of Richard Nixon for the moment, even if a little thought would demonstrate that candor and honesty would be better in the long run.

The former Disneyland guide had to trot out to the press briefing room and recite precisely what he had been told by the president, Haldeman, Kissinger, or Ehrlichman, and to say no more. Under these circumstances, his lack of in-depth comprehension was an asset, as was his lack of interest in what the members of the press corps thought collectively or individually. I saw Ziegler's admission that CREP had financed the burglary as one of those unthinking slips of the truth that occasionally occur even in the careful grilling of a press functionary. But when I got back to the office, the thought struck me that perhaps Haldeman had changed the White House story on the financing of the burglars. Perhaps a change in tactics was necessary now that indictments had been handed down.

In any case, Ziegler's admission was a good story, and I quickly called Van Shumway at the Nixon re-election committee to ask him if CREP was still denying that any of the financing of the burglars came from Nixon campaign money. He said that was still the position at CREP. Without disclosing my talk with Ziegler, I said that it was important to be sure because I had some indication that the position might have changed. Shumway said that he had no information that the position had changed or would change. I asked him to call me immediately if there were such a change. He insisted that he couldn't visualize any circumstances under which there would be such an admission and said that he did not have to detail the political reverberations of a headline that read: "Nixon Re-election Committee Admits Financing Burglary."

I felt my story would crack the stone wall. I wrote it for the October 6, 1972, *Des Moines Register,* quoting Ziegler as saying, "There isn't any question but that the money [to finance the burglary-bugging at Watergate] came from the committee." In the same story I quoted a spokesman for CREP as saying that there had never been any admission from any official of that organization that Nixon campaign funds had financed the burglary. As soon as the story appeared in the morning *Register,* I called several friends in the Washington press corps, including Dan Thomasson of the Scripps-Howard Washington Bureau and Jack Nelson of the *Los Angeles Times.* Up to that time I had never met Bob Woodward and Carl Bernstein of the *Washington Post,* but I knew of their work. During the next few days I talked to both of them several times. Thomasson, Nelson, Bernstein, and Woodward all saw the significance of a White House admission on the financing of the burglary, and I hoped they would follow through, for I had great confidence in their ability to deal with stonewalling.

Thomasson called the White House immediately, but Nelson was deeply involved in some then undisclosed Watergate-related project and Woodward and Bernstein were working hard on what I learned later was the Donald Segretti "dirty tricks" story. They said they would alert the regular White House reporters. Later that day Thomasson called to tell me that Ziegler was giving "a kind of half-assed denial" of my story but that he regarded it as confirmation. Thomasson said Ziegler alleged that the quotation I had used was a "misinterpretation" of what he had told me. Ziegler was now saying: "I have no personal knowledge of any aspect of this [Watergate financing] matter other than what I have read in the press. Therefore, I am not in a position to draw any conclusion or to make any comment, and the reporter for the *Des Moines Register* was so informed." This was indeed "a half-assed denial." Ziegler did not challenge the accuracy of the quote but simply stated that as White House press secretary he had no knowledge of the Watergate financing and was not in a position to draw a conclusion. His statement that he had told me he was not informed on Watergate was a flat, outright lie; actually, he had been trying to impress me with how knowledgeable he was. To declare that he was not authorized to speak on Watergate was preposterous when he had been pushed forward as the official source of all White House statements on Watergate.

When Ziegler returned my call late in the afternoon, I told him that it was absurd for the White House spokesman on Watergate to say he knows only what he has read in the papers. I reminded him of his boast to me that he now knew what went on in the White House and had a policy role. "Now you are saying you weren't authorized to make the statement you made to me," I said.

"I thought our talk was confidential and off the record," Ziegler quibbled.

I reminded him that there had been nothing said or hinted about con-fidentiality because I had been protesting my lack of an opportunity to ask the question at a public presidential press conference. I asked him if he were challenging the accuracy of my quotation because, if so, I intended to make an issue of it. I reviewed the sequence of our conversation and asked: "Do you deny that conversation took place in your office?"

He said that he did not deny it, and had not denied it in the statement he had read to the reporters.

"As long as it isn't a denial of the accuracy of my quotation, it is fine with me," I said, but added I would be scrutinizing his statements on the subject very carefully.

Many newspapers treated Ziegler's statement as a denial of my quotation, which I believed was as much a fault of their superficiality as it was Ziegler's fault. But over the next few days several reporters told me that Ziegler was treating it as a denial of my quotation. It irritated me to see that he had gone back on his word.

I went to the White House press briefing the next week to have it out with Ziegler. This time there would be a transcript, so there could be no later mis-interpretation of the background for my story. I arrived early and seated my-self a few feet away from the briefing podium. Ziegler entered with a smile which vanished when he saw me within ten feet of where he would be stand-ing, but then he mustered a weak smile and said, "Hi, Clark, what brings you over?" I nodded coldly in response and sat through a series of routine an-nouncements, questions on the Paris peace talks, and, ironically, questions about a speech on crime which President Nixon would give the next Sunday. When the questioning lagged a bit, I broke in: "Ron, there has been some dis-pute about our conversation as of last Thursday, and I wanted to go over that with you here to make sure there is no misunderstanding about what you are denying." Then, slowly and precisely, I continued: "You are not denying the quote itself, 'there is no question but that the money came from the commit-tee'; is that right?"

Ziegler dodged: "I have issued a statement on that, Clark. I will stand by it."

"My story has been questioned on this," I said. "That is important to me. It is an important point relative to the Watergate investigation. I want to go over this. I want a confrontation out here where we have witnesses, where the question of accuracy can be settled."

Then Ziegler put up the stone wall: "I have issued a statement and I stand by it."

I answered: "I don't want you to get away that way. I want to go over the context in which this was said."

In detail, I went over the manner in which the questions had come up, how "we had gone over the $1,600 that Liddy had in his possession," and "the $3,500 that was spent for the electronic devices by McCord in connec-tion with the Watergate bugging. I raised the question about the source of this money, and we had agreed that it was absurd that they would spend their own money for this—and at that point you said, 'There is no question but that the money came from the committee.' There was not any question about what money or what committee we were discussing." I asked, "Do you challenge that?"

Again Ziegler stonewalled: "I have issued a statement and stand by it."

By now I was thoroughly frustrated, and I was disgusted with the lack of support from the other reporters. "That is the kind of crap we have been getting out of this White House all along," I snapped. "You may not know about this, but you have been denying implication of the White House and the committee people . . . for the last two months. I was not aware that you were unauthorized to speak on the subject [of Watergate], because certainly the press conferences up to now have indicated that you were."

Ziegler turned from me without responding and asked: "Any other questions?"

The questioning turned to the bombing in Vietnam and other cosmic subjects, with other reporters unconcerned that Ziegler had brushed off a highly relevant series of questions. Later, from the back of the room, I got an assist when a reporter asked: "Did Clark Mollenhoff quote you accurately in that story?" but Ziegler again avoided answering by simply stating that he had given his response on that point. A comment that President Nixon was giving a speech on crime that Sunday left me an opening for a last parting shot at Ziegler: "The Sunday speech on crime—will that include Watergate?" Ziegler's responses had been unsatisfactory, but at least the press briefings were transcribed. At some point this permanent record could be used to demonstrate just how incompetent the press briefings were.

As I left the briefing room, several reporters patted me on the back and commented: "That's the way to do it, Clark." Another commented, "It sure is good to see someone take on Ziegler," but others stayed clear of me until we were outside of the briefing room and far outside of the hearing of anyone who could tattle to Ziegler before they felt free to commend me for my questioning. Some meant it, but they had been noticeably quiet when I was trying to force something other than a non-answer from Ziegler.

After the press conference, Dan Thomasson called to tell me that he had heard I had "climbed all over Ziegler." He said that he wished he had been there to help me. But Dan, like Jack Nelson, Bob Woodward, Carl Bernstein, and a handful of excellent investigators, had been out on other leads, unaware that I had intended to confront Ziegler that day. I vowed that the next time I would let a couple of them know, to make certain I had adequate support, but I didn't know how quickly the next confrontation would roll around or that it would be with an old friend, Clark MacGregor.

On Sunday, October 15, the *Washington Post* carried a story by Woodward and Bernstein linking President Nixon's appointments secretary, Dwight Chapin, to the hiring of lawyer Donald Segretti. It quoted anonymous sources and identified Chapin as someone who met almost daily with the president.

The *Post* said that Gordon Strachan, a young lawyer of Haldeman's White House staff, had a role in hiring Segretti for political sabotage against the Democrats and that Segretti was paid by Herbert W. Kalmbach, President Nixon's personal attorney. I knew that if Chapin was involved there was a 90 percent chance that Haldeman knew of it or even had a major hand in directing it. Chapin, Haldeman's protégé at the J. Walter Thompson advertising agency, had been brought to the White House by Haldeman and rarely made a move without consulting his mentor.

The angry response from the White House was what I had expected when the conflagration got that close to Haldeman and the Oval Office. The story was written to protect sources, which made it vulnerable to attacks. Chapin called the charges that he was Segretti's contact "fundamentally inaccurate," "hearsay," and a "collection of absurdities." Ehrlichman, appearing on ABC's "Issues and Answers" the next Sunday, commented that the *Post*'s report linking Chapin to Segretti was "hearsay about four times removed." President Nixon's special assistant characterized acts of political sabotage as a part of the "folklore" of America and said that October of an election year was expected to be "mud month." He dismissed the *Post* story as "not having any proof, but a lot of charges." Ziegler took the offensive early Monday morning by saying that the *Post* story and an even more comprehensive account in *Time* were "a raft" of stories which he would not "dignify with comment." When asked whether President Nixon was concerned about the charges, Ziegler replied: "I think I would say the president is concerned about the techniques being employed by the opposition. . . . Some of the sources . . . are known Democratic Party participants." Senator Robert Dole, then the Republican national chairman, followed with a stinging denunciation of the *Post* and of Senator McGovern. He declared that for a week, "the Republican Party has been the victim of a barrage of unfounded and unsubstantiated allegations by George McGovern and his partner-in-mud-slinging, the *Washington Post*." The Ziegler and Dole counterattacks did not deny specific facts but relied on name-calling that I had found was usually associated with a weak defense. I called the White House press office and the Republican National Committee to determine whether there was any specific denial of the facts set forth. The fact that my questions were not answered convinced me that Chapin, Strachan, Kalmbach, and Segretti were indeed deeply involved.

In mid-afternoon the CREP press office called to alert me to a press conference Clark MacGregor had scheduled at 5:00 P.M. to discuss the stories linking Chapin and Kalmbach to Segretti. As I came in, I talked briefly with Carl Bernstein about the lack of specific denials of the *Post*'s stories. Then I moved to a seat near the front of the room. If MacGregor were to engage in denials, I was going to try to pin down any evidence he might have to discredit the Chapin stories. The president had said that MacGregor was instituting an investigation of Watergate and related matters independent of the Justice Department and the White House investigation by John Dean. It was conceivable that the *Post,* in its enthusiasm to keep the Watergate story alive, had gone out on a weak limb.

MacGregor was an open and forthright man, and I had had a high regard for his integrity and independence in the past. But shortly after we entered the room it was announced that no questions would be permitted. MacGregor was to read a prepared statement for the television cameras and leave. I protested to Shumway that we had been told this would be a press conference, not a television production with questions barred. He was apologetic as he said that "the signals were changed" after we had been called and that initially MacGregor had intended to submit to questions. "Who changed the signals?" I asked. Shumway said he did not know. When MacGregor's statement was circulated, it was apparent why he did not want to answer questions, for it was the same type of name-calling retort we had heard earlier from Ehrlichman, Ziegler, and Dole. It was totally uncharacteristic of MacGregor, and I was sorry he was letting himself be used. I knew by instinct that Haldeman was calling the shots. MacGregor's most vulnerable paragraph read: "Using innuendo, third-person hearsay, unsubstantiated charges, anonymous sources, and scare headlines . . . the *Post* has maliciously sought to give the appearance of a direct connection between the White House and the Watergate . . . a charge which the *Post* knows—and a half dozen investigations have found —to be false." I read through the statement while waiting for MacGregor to appear and tried to find even a single reference to specific findings of other investigations that were contrary to the *Post* stories. Finding none, I was determined to challenge MacGregor's credibility and credentials unless he could state that he had access to the results of an investigation that specifically disproved any substantial point in the *Post* story.

MacGregor was uneasy and smiled weakly as he walked to the lectern. He began by saying that due to "unusual developments of the past few days" he would not be able to respond to questions. I protested the lack of questions and asked: "What credibility do you have?" Other reporters fell silent, and MacGregor squirmed uneasily as I pressed on. "What documents have you seen? If you can't tell us, you have no right to stand there." To silence me, MacGregor indicated that when he completed his statement he would hear me out and respond to my questions. But instead, after reading it, he dashed from the room with my demand for the right to ask just one question ringing in his ears. Bernstein and other reporters joined in the shouted disapproval of his hurried departure, but the usually genial MacGregor ignored the derisive comments as he bolted out the door.

I called Van Shumway after the press conference and said that I was sorry it had been necessary to challenge MacGregor publicly but that I resented the press being used as props for a television show designed to get over a one-sided story. Shumway said it had not been his decision nor MacGregor's. "Haldeman?" I asked. He responded, "I can't say." (Months later, MacGregor confirmed that the orders had come from Haldeman. He said he had been embarrassed to let himself be used but had scheduled the press conference with every intention of answering questions. The script had been dictated by the White House.)

It was an exercise in futility. Television that night dutifully carried film clips of MacGregor's charges against the *Post*. Since there was substantial evidence of press bias against President Nixon on other issues, a large number of voters would probably conclude that Watergate was just another political fuss of no real importance to the average citizen. How wrong they were! The scenario designed to discredit McGovern was being played out. Military men and labor leaders were used to promote fear of the South Dakota senator's proposed defense spending cuts. Then, in the last week of the campaign, the administration trotted out Dr. Henry A. Kissinger to defuse the peace issue, which had been the central theme of McGovern's appeal. "Peace is at hand," said Dr. Kissinger, pronouncing his benediction from his position as a nonpartisan statesman. The "most admired" man in America allowed himself to be used.

I knew that the resulting Nixon landslide on November 7, 1972, would increase the arrogance of the president's men who had managed to keep the story of the White House involvement in Watergate from emerging. The Nixon-Agnew ticket won in forty-nine states, losing only in Massachusetts and the District of Columbia. Haldeman and Ehrlichman would consider this a mandate to escalate their concept of the ultimate in secret government— "executive privilege." They would suppress the truth again and again to screen their abuses of power. They would continue to administer the government by rewarding their friends and punishing their "enemies." I feared for my country and knew that I was marked for retaliation.

*Chapter Twenty-nine*

# A JUDGE NAMED SIRICA

IN THE AFTERMATH of the 1972 Nixon landslide, only one man stood in the way of a complete cover-up of the Watergate affair and of the continuation and expansion of the corruptive doctrine of executive privilege. That man was my long-time friend United States District Judge John J. Sirica, who was chief judge of the United States District Court in the District of Columbia. Standing in the path of the Nixon political juggernaut, the sixty-eight-year-old Sirica, son of Italian immigrants, seemed a frail and futile figure. What could one man do when the Democratic leadership in Congress had failed, when the Democratic Party's presidential candidate had failed, when the press had failed, and when confused voters appeared to have endorsed the oppressive and corrupting secrecy of the Watergate cover-up?

President Nixon, buoyed by the unprecedented victory, demonstrated in the weeks immediately following the election that he was eager to challenge the Congress and the courts. Nixon, Haldeman, and Ehrlichman interpreted the success of their game plan as "a mandate of the people" for "four more years" in which to manipulate the power levers of government as they pleased. Nothing seemed impossible as one reviewed the maneuvers used to keep the lid on the Watergate affair. The ultimate in executive privilege had been shoved down the throat of the Senate Judiciary Committee in the ITT affair and it had worked. Although Attorney General Richard Kleindienst was balky about following some orders, in the end he had collaborated in stopping the Patman committee's Watergate hearings. The incorruptible Henry Petersen, a Democrat who was assistant attorney general in charge of the Criminal Division, had been persuaded of the wisdom of Ehrlichman's suggestion that Maurice Stans be excused from appearing before the federal grand jury. Petersen had also been prevailed upon to send a letter to Chairman Patman arguing for a delay in his planned hearings. Petersen had thus helped give a nonpartisan appearance to the vital power play managed by House Republican Leader Gerald Ford. Watergate had also proved a good testing ground for the loyalty of the young men in the White House and the Committee to Re-elect the President, and Haldeman and Ehrlichman were moving them into the various government agencies to exert an even tighter White House control over agency operations and decisions.

From the White House standpoint there was little to fear from the independence of one federal judge when they had performed the miracle of politicizing the Federal Bureau of Investigation through the appointment of the fumbling, tractable L. Patrick Gray. The death of the independent J. Edgar Hoover had given the White House unusual access to reports of FBI agents and an element of control over use of those reports.

Gray, a retired Navy bureaucrat ambitious for the permanent appointment as Hoover's successor, was amenable to White House machinations. He had corroborated Nixon's assertion about the thoroughness of the Watergate investigation and had coordinated attacks on Democratic candidate George McGovern with the White House game plan. Haldeman and Ehrlichman were also aware that Gray had aided the Watergate cover-up by questionable disposition of documents.

The White House regarded Judge Sirica as a loyal, rock-ribbed Republican, and if he remained independent of political pressures the worst they expected was a tough trial for the seven Watergate defendants and prison terms in line with his reputation as "Maximum John." Neither President Nixon nor his top aides believed that Sirica would go beyond the immediate charges and seek the whole truth. If the defendants received long sentences, political control of Justice Department and Parole Board appointments could temper Sirica's stern justice with mercy. Ultimately, there was the president's constitutional power to grant full and unconditional pardons. The situation existing in October and November, 1972, gave little reason for believing that Judge Sirica would do more than a routine job of presiding at the trial. The White House controlled the FBI, the Justice Department, and the United States Attorney's office. The White House had resisted all suggestions for a special prosecutor. What could a trial judge do against these odds, particularly a life-long Republican, a supporter and admirer of Richard Nixon, and an appointee of President Dwight D. Eisenhower?

An image such as Judge Sirica's, under most circumstances, would have made me wary of the success of this politically sensitive investigation. My deep involvement in stories revealing political corruption in the federal judiciary in several midwestern states had taught me that even federal judges are often politicians in robes, retaining many of their partisan and ideological biases and the loyalties that resulted in their selection as judges. Although lifetime appointments to the federal bench were supposed to free federal judges of the need to keep their political fences mended, too many used the insulated judicial power to become temperamental tyrants. Many of my colleagues in the press pointed to Judge Sirica's ties with the Republican organization and jumped to the conclusion that under the stern law-and-order face of "Maximum John" lurked another highly partisan Nixon Republican.

I had known John Sirica well since 1957, when he was the presiding judge in the trial of Seattle Teamsters Union boss Frank Brewster. I had visited with him in his chambers during that trial, had seen him socially, and had followed his conduct of the trial of one of Bobby Baker's associates, Fred B. Black, Jr., on an income tax evasion charge. During those fifteen years, we had discussed his 1944 resignation as counsel for a House investigating committee in a stormy public hearing rather than be a party to a cover-up, and the House investigation of the operations of the FCC and other regulatory agencies in 1958, when the Eisenhower administration's invoked executive privilege to hide political tampering at the regulatory agencies. (Bernard Schwartz, a young New York University law professor, was fired by the House Legislative Oversight Committee in a 1958 incident that was not unlike the cover-up that John Sirica had faced in 1944.)

I knew from those conversations that Judge Sirica understood in great depth the need for both the Congress and the courts to contain the great power of the executive branch within the bounds set by Congress. I knew he recognized the corrupting influence of secret government decisions and of the over-use of the phrases "national security" and "executive privilege" to hide evidence of crimes. But I also knew he was an admirer of Richard Nixon, having actively worked for the Eisenhower-Nixon ticket in 1952 and 1956, prior to his appointment to the bench. He had voted for Nixon in 1968 and was impressed with what President Nixon and Vice President Agnew professed to believe about firm and fair law enforcement.

Judge Sirica had been pleased when I invited him to be my guest at the White House Mess on April 21, 1970; he said it was his first meal at the White House. We had discussed my job as special counsel to President Nixon and the idea that I had been hired to help keep the government honest. Judge

Sirica thought it was a good idea, but I told him that it didn't always work out as well in practice as it did on paper. That was my way of hinting at the problem I was having in getting access to President Nixon. Judge Sirica smiled in acknowledgment and made reference to his similar problem with the FCC investigation. When he resigned as counsel for the House Commerce Committee, Judge Sirica told me, he had declared: "I don't want it on my conscience that anyone can say John Sirica is a party to a whitewash."

That declaration of conscience by Judge Sirica came through in essentially every situation he was involved in. He believed that it was the role of the trial judge to elicit all of the truth as well as only the truth in his courtroom, to exercise his power to that end and not to be overly concerned about whether he would be upheld by judgments of the United States Court of Appeals, as long as he believed that he was doing "what is right." Such emphasis on conscience can be skillful public relations, but I had known him well enough to be convinced he was pretty much what he appeared to be on the surface. Born to poverty, he was proud of his hard-earned law degree and sensitive of the need to avoid any appearance of leniency toward organized crime or political figures. An early career as a welterweight boxer had abolished physical fear, and long experience as a prosecutor, defense lawyer, and judge had taught him that a completely honest man has no reason to fear the truth or any process that ensures the emergence of the truth. Since I had been burned badly because of my faith in Richard M. Nixon, I hesitated to write or speak of my conviction that Judge Sirica would be a trustworthy and aggressive judge. This reluctance endured despite long conversations with him in the fall of 1972 in which we talked of the importance of honest government and I expressed a belief in the eventual triumph of right over wrong. We did not speak of the merits of the cases before him, but I was sure that he was lonely and in need of assurance that if he did precisely what he believed to be right, at least one individual would remember it and record it in historic perspective.

Throughout the fall, Judge Sirica's rulings had contained hints that he would be no part of a Republican cover-up. By the first of December I had decided to go out on a limb with a column favorable to Sirica, in order to balance the skepticism of the left. Written on December 3, 1972, for publication on December 9 and 10, the column began with the assertion that the Watergate trial was not "his first venture into the hot political waters of the nation's capital." I wrote: The public record of the sixty-eight-year-old trial judge has marked him as tough and non-partisan through his career as an assistant U.S. attorney prosecuting the toughest cases, a few tumultuous months as chief counsel for a congressional investigating subcommittee, and fifteen years on the federal bench. He has been a lifelong Republican, but his reputation for independence and non-partisanship was established as early as 1944 when he was named chief counsel by the Democratic chairman of a House investigating subcommittee looking into charges of political tampering and favoritism at the Federal Communications Commission.

I described how the Roosevelt White House abused its power by retaliating against the committee chairman, Gene Cox, a Georgia Democrat, who had accepted a $2,500 fee from a radio station while a member of Congress. Cox was forced to resign the chairmanship rather than pursue the investigation, which might have involved some members of the Roosevelt family. "Representative Clarence F. Lee, a California Democrat, was named to take over the investigation of the FCC," I wrote. "He wanted a tough, experienced, nonpartisan prosecutor. Sirica was the man Lee called, but before the then forty-year-old prosecutor would take the job, he extracted a promise from the chairman that he had to be permitted to follow out all leads regardless of who was involved." White House interference continued to the point where it was impossible for Chairman Lee to keep his promise. "Sirica," I related, "took the unprecedented action of resigning as chief counsel in a public hearing and of denouncing the investigation as the 'whitewash' that it was." I also declared: "Judge Sirica has an understanding of the political chicanery that can take place with big political slush funds through his work as an assistant defense attorney in the criminal trial in 1940 of Frank Boehm, president of Union Electric Company of St. Louis, Missouri. Boehm was on trial for perjury in connection with testimony he had given dealing with a $500,000 slush fund for use at Missouri's capital city of Jefferson City for influencing and entertaining both Democratic and Republican legislators. Boehm was convicted."

In reviewing the facts in those cases with Judge Sirica prior to writing my column, I sensed the same pride in honest, nonpartisan action that I had felt throughout our association. It made me more confident as I wrote: "If the seven men indicted in connection with the burglary and bugging at Democratic headquarters in the Watergate complex expect to have an easy time because Sirica is a lifelong Republican appointed in a Republican administration, they should give more study to Sirica's background." I noted that one ambiguous order by Sirica limiting public statements had been interpreted as an effort to muzzle the Congress and the press. I explained it in this way: "Judge Sirica signed one controversial order early in the court proceedings dealing with the Watergate Seven which was interpreted by critics as barring further comments by the press and further political comments or congressional investigation until the conclusion of the criminal trial. However, within a day after Judge Sirica saw how his ruling was being interpreted, he issued a clarifying order stating clearly that it was not his intent to interfere with congressional comment or investigations, political criticism, or prodding by the media."

Even before this column appeared, Judge Sirica had made a statement in open court indicating that he planned to insist that the search for the truth in the Watergate trial be broader than the narrow limits indicated by the prosecutors. "This jury is going to want to know: What did these men go into that headquarters for?" Judge Sirica said. "Was their sole purpose political espionage? Were they paid? Was there financial gain? Who hired them? Who started this?"

The White House showed no concern that Judge Sirica wanted to know

"Who hired them?" "Who started this?" Although President Nixon was avoiding press conferences because he might be questioned about the Watergate investigation, reports from Republican senators and congressmen who saw him at various functions at the White House in December 1972 indicated that he was "euphoric," convinced that the Watergate investigation was dead and would be buried at the conclusion of the criminal trial in January. Haldeman and Ehrlichman were moving ahead with plans to reorganize the entire structure of the federal government and to make dozens of personnel changes to insure a tighter rein over the departments, even though some independence in cabinet officers had to be tolerated for a few months. In December I wrote in a column:

Those who displease Haldeman, show an unwanted independence, or even represent an unspoken challenge to his authority are moved aside, dropped, promoted up and out, or fired."

The decision of George Romney to resign as secretary of housing and urban development was tied to his independent spirit and his frustration in being treated like a puppet by the White House staff.

A decision not to continue Commerce Secretary Peter G. Peterson in a cabinet post was due in part to his independence and a flair for personal publicity that Haldeman and other White House staffers considered too pushy.

The high degree of competency in international trading matters that Peterson, a forty-six-year-old former board chairman and chief executive officer of the Bell & Howell Company, brought to the Commerce Department did not weigh as heavily as White House staff resentment of his independence.

Senator Robert Dole (R., Kans.) carried out the overwhelming majority of his chores as Republican National Chairman according to a script and tone approved by Haldeman, but occasionally balked at taking instructions through White House staff members and expressed dissatisfaction at his lack of access to the president.

That was enough for him to be dumped almost as unceremoniously as the Democratic chairman, Jean Westwood, who presided at McGovern's disastrous campaign. Dole's stout partisan stand on issues was regarded as a minus by the same White House staffers who wrote or approved the script.

One important appointment last week was viewed as a prime example of Haldeman's efforts to keep tight White House control over federal agencies. Presidential advance-man and travel-arranger Ronald H. Walker was named director of the National Park Service, succeeding career park official George H. Hartzog.

Conservationists, who had urged selection of an experienced parks man, were dismayed. The Sierra Club said Walker, thirty-five, who co-ordinated President Nixon's journeys to China and Russia as well as his domestic trips, is not the kind of appointee the public has a right to expect.

My own experiences, as well as the outward signs, led to my conclusion that the landslide victory over McGovern had "solidified and increased" Haldeman's hold on the federal government. It already was a power greater than presidential assistant Sherman Adams wielded in the Eisenhower administration, and it may have been unprecedented. The only possible exception is the influence of Col. Edward M. House during the last years Woodrow Wilson was in the White House and ailing. There were reports that Haldeman was dissatisfied with the cooperation of Attorney General Kleindienst during the Watergate investigation and was planning to replace him with John Ehrlichman. The game plan for the second Nixon administration called for moving Egil (Bud) Krogh, Ehrlichman's Number One assistant, to the job of under secretary in the Department of Transportation.

Jeb Magruder was serving as a director of the inaugural committee. The White House was looking for a high government post for him where confirmation wouldn't be necessary because of some touchy questions which might be asked about the $350,000 cash fund and the financing of G. Gordon Liddy. One former White House aide, resentful of Haldeman's lack of concern about finding him a job, told me that Magruder was "being taken care of because he had lied to the Watergate grand jury. He should have been indicted, and they all know it. It is a sad state of affairs when the guys who do the dirty work and lie about it are getting the big jobs and those of us who try to be honest are still left hanging at Christmas time." Two months later Magruder was placed in a $36,000-a-year job as an assistant to the secretary of commerce. It was clear that Magruder, as deputy director of the Nixon re-election committee, would have to testify in the Watergate burglary trial and might have to be sacrificed if his perjured testimony developed any substantial cracks.

With control of the Justice Department, the Nixon White House was confident that not even independent Judge Sirica could penetrate the stone wall of silence created by the prosecution's theory that Gordon Liddy was the mastermind and that there was no criminal responsibility at a higher level. But Judge Sirica was to demonstrate that he was hardly an average judge in his aggressive search for the truth.

*Chapter Thirty*

# THE ELUSIVE TRUTH

On December 8, 1972, the body of the wife of E. Howard Hunt was recovered from the wreckage of a jetliner which had crashed near Midway Airport in Chicago. The discovery that Dorothy Hunt was carrying $10,000 in $100 bills at the time of her death stirred speculation that the money was in some manner linked to the Watergate burglary. It was reported a week later in the *Washington Star-News* by Joseph Volz and James R. Polk that Mrs. Hunt was insured for $250,000 under three insurance policies issued at Washington National Airport, where the United Airlines flight had originated. Hunt said that the $10,000 his wife had been carrying was to be invested in a real estate venture with a relative in the Chicago area and that the only reason he had not made the trip was that "I would have to get a court order to leave Washington." Apparently he would not have wanted to explain to the court the need to deliver $10,000 in cash to a relative for a normal real estate transaction.

From the outset, Hunt's background had intrigued me. As a former CIA official, he was undoubtedly the link with the Cuban-Americans who were arrested at Democratic headquarters. The admitted fact that he was a White House consultant working out of the office of Special Counsel Charles W. Colson conjured up many new theories, for Colson was Haldeman's political operations man. Periodically, since the summer of 1972, I had raised questions with William O. Bittman, Hunt's attorney, about reports that he had been paid a $25,000 retainer fee in cash. Each time he refused to discuss the size of his fee or even whether it had been in cash. However, each time it became more apparent to me that the rumors I received from sources close to the other defendants contained more than a fragment of truth.

In the pre-trial period of December 1972, Bittman argued vehemently against Judge Sirica's attempt to explore the connections between the $100 bills found on the Watergate burglars and the Nixon campaign checks deposited in the Miami bank account of Bernard Barker. The indictment, Bittman argued, made no reference to the $25,000 check from Kenneth Dahlberg or the $89,000 in checks from the Mexico City bank. Assistant United States Attorney Earl J. Silbert, the chief prosecutor in the case, countered that the government would offer evidence on the $25,000 check and would trace the $89,000, but "not necessarily from its source" because that would involve calling an alien to testify.

The jury was selected, and Silbert had made his opening statement on January 7, 1973. He said that the prosecution would prove that the Watergate burglary was a part of an "intelligence operation" financed with $235,000 in Nixon re-election committee campaign funds. The evidence, he said, would show that Hunt and Liddy were the principal directors of a wide-ranging political spying effort which originated in December 1971. The chief prosecutor said Liddy had been paid a total of $235,000—mostly in $100 bills—by Jeb Stuart Magruder; Herbert L. Porter, one of Magruder's assistants; and CREP Treasurer Hugh W. Sloan, Jr. But Silbert indicated that the government had no evidence linking Magruder, Porter, or Sloan to the planning of the Watergate burglary or to efforts to engage in a similar illegal entry at the presidential campaign headquarters of Senator George McGovern or Senator Edmund Muskie. He said Sloan would testify that he gave $235,000 in cash to Liddy on instructions from Magruder.

At the conclusion of Silbert's remarks, Bittman suddenly told the court that Hunt wished to plead guilty to three major counts of the eight-count indictment. He explained that the tragic death of Hunt's wife a month earlier had left Hunt with the care of four children ranging in age from nine to twenty-two and pleaded that Hunt not be imprisoned. Judge Sirica took Hunt's guilty plea under advisement and four days later, with the jury out of the room, said he would reject a plea on only three counts, insisting on Hunt's entering a plea of guilty on all of the six counts with which he was charged. Judge Sirica told the lawyers for all of the defendants that he considered the Watergate affair "a most serious crime" and that he would not permit guilty pleas to interfere with complete disclosure of all evidence against all seven defendants and any others who happened to be involved. He called Hunt and Bittman before the bench and told Hunt that he would read each of the six counts to him and ask specific questions as to whether he was guilty of the acts charged. When Bittman objected to this unusual procedure, Judge Sirica declared: "I don't want Mr. Hunt to come back someday and contend that he didn't do some of these things." Then he served notice on the other six defendants that he would follow the same procedure if any of them wished to change their pleas to guilty, but all sat nervous and unsmiling at the front of the huge courtroom while Hunt methodically answered that he was indeed guilty of all of the acts charged in the indictment.

Judge Sirica ordered Hunt held, then released on a $100,000 bond, pending sentence and cooperation with the federal grand jury. Again Bittman protested the amount of the bond, pleading that Hunt had served his country for more than twenty years as a CIA agent, had four children and property in the Washington area, and was not likely to flee. In reply, Judge Sirica said Hunt had put up only $1,000 with the surety company for the $10,000 personal bond on the initial arrest and that, in reviewing Hunt's CIA background, he had concluded that he might have friends in any part of the world. He also reminded Bittman that Hunt had disappeared from Washington in the days immediately following the June 17 burglary and arrests and had not reappeared until several weeks later. Sirica said that he did not believe the $100,000 bond excessive in light of "the serious crimes" involved. In questioning Hunt, the judge emphasized that the charges could mean "more than thirty years in prison" and more than $40,000 fines. Coming as it did from "Maximum John" Sirica, Hunt and the other defendants knew that this was not an idle threat.

Outside the court, before the television cameras, Hunt said that "anything I may have done, I believed to be in the best interests of my country." Asked if he could testify on the possible involvement of "higher-ups" Hunt said: "To my personal knowledge there was none."

The next day, Martin Schram, Washington Bureau Chief for *Newsday,* reported that persons close to the four Cuban-Americans had told him that each of them had been offered $1,000 a month for as long as they had to stay in prison. Speculation increased that Hunt was the conduit for the payoff money and that he had urged them to enter pleas of guilty. Attorney Henry B. Rothblatt, who represented the four Miami men, said, "There will be no change of pleas as long as I am on the case."

A few hours later, the four Miamians discharged Rothblatt as their attorney; the following Monday they entered guilty pleas. Judge Sirica questioned them intensively before accepting their pleas. As the guilty pleas were entered by Bernard L. Barker, Frank A. Sturgis, Eugenio R. Martinez, and Virgilio R. Gonzales, each was asked whether he had been coerced or induced by payments of money to plead guilty to the charges of conspiracy, burglary, and illegal wiretapping and bugging. Each denied that he had been paid or coerced and swore that he had received only expense money. Barker was questioned closely by Sirica about the source of the cash he had received to pay for hotels, travel, food, and equipment. Barker insisted that he didn't know. After listening to him repeat several times that he "got that money in the mail in blank envelopes," Sirica snapped, "I'm sorry, I don't believe that."

The judge then went beyond the specific acts charged against the defendants in the indictment and asked each man if he knew of "any higher-ups who were involved." Each denied any knowledge of such involvement, denied that money was his motivation, and explained that, as good soldiers in the effort to liberate Cuba from Premier Fidel Castro, they "did not ask questions" but simply carried out orders. The plan was to burglarize and bug Democratic headquarters at the Watergate and to burglarize and bug McGovern's office, the four men told Sirica. But they were vague as to how this would help the "free Cuba movement" to which they were dedicated. Chief prosecutor Silbert had pictured the four as men of modest incomes and had indicated that their motivation was financial; their own attorney, Rothblatt, had entered a plea of poverty in seeking his clients' release prior to trial on $10,000 bond each. However, reporters noted that all four were well dressed and that they had lived well throughout the early stages of the trial in a suite at the Arlington Towers apartments, a luxury high-rise building in the nearby Virginia suburbs. They had returned to Miami several times and had no problem raising legal fees for Rothblatt, a big-name civil rights attorney from New York City.

With the number of defendants cut from seven to two—G. Gordon Liddy and James McCord, Jr.—the trial moved forward, with lawyers for both men protesting that the sudden elimination of Hunt and the four Cuban-Americans would raise questions in the minds of the jurors that would make it impossible for their clients to receive a fair trial. On January 17, 1973, the jury heard testimony from Alfred C. Baldwin III, a former FBI agent who said he had been hired by McCord to monitor telephone conversations from Democratic headquarters. He had listened in from Room 723 in the Howard Johnson Motor Lodge, across the street from the Watergate. He said that on May 2, 1972, McCord had cleared his employment with Fred LaRue, then an assistant to campaign director John Mitchell. Baldwin said his employment was terminated on June 17—a short time after the arrest of the five men at Democratic headquarters. He identified McCord and Liddy as the men he had dealt with in monitoring the telephone calls and in meetings to discuss the burglarizing and bugging of McGovern's campaign headquarters. Baldwin testified that over a period of several weeks he overheard about two hundred telephone conversations, typed logs describing the conversations, and passed them to McCord. He said that he had destroyed his own handwritten notes on those conversations and that he did not know what McCord had done with the logs. On one occasion, Baldwin testified, he was instructed to deliver a report on the conversations to a guard at the Nixon re-election committee, but he could not remember the name of the man to whom he delivered the report. Baldwin admitted that he was a co-conspirator in the burglary-bugging but contended that he had been unaware that the interception of telephone conversations was illegal.

Hugh Sloan, former treasurer of CREP, put at least a part of the responsibility on John Mitchell and Maurice Stans when he testified that he had been troubled by the huge cash payments he was making to Gordon Liddy at the direction of Jeb Magruder. Sloan said that before he had doled out the last of the $235,000 in cash to Liddy he "verified" the arrangement with Maurice Stans, who, according to Sloan, said he had "verified" the arrangement with Mitchell. Sloan said that he had been unaware of the nature of Liddy's assignment, other than that it was "intelligence-gathering." He said that his first suspicion that Liddy might be engaged in illegal political espionage came on the morning of June 17 when he passed Liddy in the hall of the Nixon re-election committee offices and Liddy commented: "My boys were caught and I made a mistake of using someone from here [the re-election committee]. I said I wouldn't do it. I'll probably be fired."

After excusing the jury, Judge Sirica questioned Sloan extensively on his professed lack of knowledge of the illegal nature of the activities he was financing. "Didn't anyone indicate to you the nature of Liddy's activity?" Judge Sirica asked.

Sloan answered, "No."

"You are a college graduate, aren't you?" Judge Sirica asked.

Sloan answered that he had a degree from Princeton.

"What was your major?" Sirica asked.

"History," Sloan replied.

The judge shook his head in disbelief as Sloan answered in the negative to a series of questions dealing with the amounts he had disbursed ($3,000 to $5,000 at a time) and the lack of reports from Liddy on how the money was being spent. Sloan said that he had kept a record of the cash he had disbursed to Liddy and also through Herbert (Bart) Porter, the director of committee scheduling. He said he had "destroyed" that cash book on instructions after making a summary of the cash disbursements which he gave to Maurice Stans.

I had known Hugh Sloan at the White House, had liked him, and was saddened by the tragedy that Watergate had brought to his life. Only a few months earlier he had been on the White House staff, a well-paid and trusted aide to President Nixon. There seemed no limit on his future; he probably would have been in line for a sub-cabinet post. When Haldeman shifted him to the Nixon re-election committee in March 1971, his disappointment at leaving the White House was outweighed by the assurance that it was a promotion in recognition of his loyal and effective work for President Nixon.

When we visited briefly in the hall outside Judge Sirica's courtroom and later talked on the telephone, Sloan told me that Haldeman had assured him that if he did a conscientious and effective job for the campaign committee he would be given an even better government position later. The title of "treasurer" was an impressive one, and Sloan said he hadn't recognized until too late that it made him responsible under the new federal laws for the accuracy and completeness of campaign records. What happened to Hugh Sloan could have happened to any young man who was energetic and ambitious but slightly naïve about the hazards of handling mysterious political funds and "intelligence-gathering." He had been concerned about Magruder's instructions to make large amounts of cash available to Liddy, but those fears had been quieted by personal assurances from Stans and John Mitchell. Certainly, Sloan assumed, they were honorable men and would not permit any activities that violated the law. Sloan said his first real suspicion that the law had been violated was Liddy's comment about his "boys" being caught at Watergate, followed by a demand for access to a large paper shredder on the third floor of the committee's offices.

Contrary to suggestions from Magruder, Sloan had cooperated with the FBI and told the full story to the federal grand jury without so much as requesting a promise of immunity from criminal prosecution, which he could have done. After that, he had resigned; his wife was pregnant and he was out of work for months before accepting a part-time job as a "consultant" at the Nixon re-election committee to help in establishing some order in the financial records after the trauma of the Watergate investigations. Sloan told me that his job as a consultant had resulted in an uneasy relationship with his former colleagues, who knew that he had already testified freely before the grand jury. That he was back on the committee's payroll in any capacity made Judge Sirica suspicious of his testimony, which was at odds with the testimony of Magruder and Porter on the amount of cash which had been disbursed to Liddy.

On January 30, 1972, the jury returned a verdict of guilty on all counts against Liddy and McCord. The jury had been sequestered in the federal courthouse since January 9, and it returned the verdict within two hours after receiving instructions from Judge Sirica. Both Liddy and McCord heard the verdict without emotion; they did not seem surprised. Both stood before the jury with slight smiles on their faces, and Liddy had his arms folded. McCord was convicted of conspiracy, two counts of second-degree burglary, attempting to intercept oral and wire communications, possession of bugging equipment, possession of wiretapping equipment, and actually intercepting conversations. Liddy was convicted on the same counts, with the except of the two involving possession of bugging and wiretap equipment. The maximum sentence for Liddy could have been fifty years in prison and $40,000 in fines; McCord faced a possible sixty years in prison and $60,000 in fines. Though Judge Sirica had a reputation for giving heavy sentences, they appeared calm and certain of rescue. Would Nixon dare use executive clemency to spring the convicted Watergate burglars before his term ended in January 1977? I was convinced that he and his White House gang would contrive a phony reason for "compassion," deny that there had been a deal, and stonewall all questions.

Though Judge Sirica had tried harder than most judges would have to establish whether "higher-ups" were involved, the trial was over without that question being directly answered. Most of the testimony at the trial did not go far beyond the specific charges of burglary and bugging at the Watergate, and testimony about the participation of others was limited to those who had approved the expenditure of more than $235,000 in cash. President Nixon and White House Secretary Ronald Ziegler still insisted that no present White House or administration officials had any knowledge of what they called "a bizarre affair." However, Senate Majority Leader Mike Mansfield (D., Mont.) believed that it was a serious crime worthy of a much deeper investigation than the executive branch had given it at that point. He designated Senator Sam Ervin, a canny North Carolina Democrat who was constitutional law expert, to head an inquiry to be started as soon as the Watergate trial was concluded.

Judge Sirica gave added stimulus to the Senate inquiry on February 2 by saying that he hoped Congress, by a broad enough resolution, would grant the Senate committee enough power to get to the bottom of the case. He was "not satisfied that all of the pertinent facts that might be available had been produced before an American jury." This was an informed, direct criticism of the FBI investigation and of the handling of the prosecution by the Justice Department. Judge Sirica also declared that he was not satisfied that "somebody else doesn't know anything about what the $199,000 Mr. Liddy got [directly from Sloan] was going to be used for." At a bail hearing for Liddy and McCord, Sirica expressed a "great doubt" about whether Hugh Sloan "has told us the entire truth in the case." He was alluding to inconsistencies in testimony by Sloan and Magruder, and in this instance incorrectly suggesting that it was Sloan who had lied. (It was later established that Sloan had told the truth clumsily and that Magruder had cleverly falsified his story and persuaded his assistant, Bart Porter, to corroborate it with a false account of the cash transaction.)

But the impetus from Judge Sirica was all that was needed to get seventy-to-zero support for a resolution establishing a seven-member select committee to probe all aspects of the Watergate case and other reported attempts at political espionage in the 1972 campaign. The committee was to be chaired by Senator Ervin; the vice chairman was to be Senator Howard Baker (R., Tenn.). Other members of the committee were Senator Joseph M. Montoya (D., N. Mex.), Senator Herman E. Talmadge (D., Ga.), Senator Daniel K. Inouye (D., Hawaii), Senator Edward J. Gurney (R., Fla.), and Senator Lowell P. Weicker, Jr. (R., Conn.). As the investigation was launched, Chairman Ervin recognized that the Nixon White House might try to claim executive privilege to thwart his inquiry. He served notice that he "would not tolerate witnesses ducking behind the stone wall of executive privilege to avoid giving us the truth."

*Chapter Thirty-one*

# THE EXECUTIVE PRIVILEGE CLOUD

As PRESIDENT NIXON's second term got underway in January 1973, the problem of executive privilege widened beyond the cover-up of the responsibility for the Watergate burglary and the concealment of fraud in the federal housing program. Executive privilege was the major instrument used by the Defense Department and the White House to bar a congressional inquiry into the demotion and reassignment of Gordon Rule, a veteran Navy procurement specialist, after he had criticized President Nixon's appointment of Roy Ash as director of the Office of Management and Budget. Testifying before Senator Proxmire's Joint Committee on the Economy, Rule charged that the appointment of Ash, former president of the financially troubled Litton Industries, was "a mistake" because of potential conflicts of interest involving an earlier effort to obtain a $1 billion to $2 billion government bailout for Litton in the form of a Navy contract. Within a few days after Rule's testimony, Rule was transferred from his job as director of the Procurement Control and Clearance Section to a post as consultant at the Navy's logistics management school at Anacostia, Maryland. Senator William Proxmire called the action "a heartless and cruel reprisal against a witness who has told us the truth and given us his best judgments for the benefit of the taxpayers." The furor over the Navy's action against Rule resulted in his reinstatement within a few days, but the administration pulled the secrecy curtain on inquiries as to who in the White House had directed the retaliation against Rule.

At the same time, the Air Force resorted to executive privilege as a final barrier to the efforts of Air Force cost expert A. Ernest Fitzgerald to obtain the testimony of top Air Force civilians and military officials he accused of conspiring to fire him because of his truthful testimony on the huge cost overruns on the C-5A program. In the Fitzgerald case, the Civil Service Commission, which in theory protects the right of career government employees, was emerging as a major vehicle for punishing employees who answered congressional committees truthfully. Initially, the Civil Service Commission had joined with the Air Force to deny Fitzgerald the open hearing he sought in order to press his charges against the Air Force. The hearing was opened only after Fitzgerald's lawyers obtained a court order and a ruling that an open hearing was a basic due process of law to which he was entitled. But the order by United States District Court Judge William Bryant, which was endorsed unanimously by a three-judge panel of the U.S. Court of Appeals for the District of Columbia, did not assure Fitzgerald and his lawyers that the truth about his dismissal would be revealed. Air Force Secretary Robert C. Seamans and several other witnesses claimed that their conversations and communications with White House officials could not be used as testimony. The Air Force officials' refusals were upheld and approved by Chief Civil Service Hearing Examiner Herman Staiman, the same man who had initially consented to Air Force requests to keep the hearing closed.

Fitzgerald's lawyers were unable to find out from the White House or the Air Force whether this invocation of executive privilege had the president's personal approval. President Nixon had assured Congressman John Moss and the members of his House Subcommittee on Government Information Policies that he would not use executive privilege loosely and would personally examine and authorize each use. I made several efforts to learn from the Air Force and the White House whether Mr. Nixon had been consulted in this case. White House Press Secretary Ronald Ziegler said that he didn't know and wouldn't request the information. My only alternative was to wait for a presidential press conference so that I could ask President Nixon whether he had had any role in what appeared to be a criminal obstruction of justice involving the Air Force, with an assist from the Civil Service Commission.

I hurried to the White House briefing room on January 31 in response to a call telling me that President Nixon was due to appear for a press conference shortly after 11:00 A.M. Midway through the press conference I was recognized. "Mr. President," I said. "Did you approve the use of executive privilege by Air Force Secretary Seamans in refusing to disclose the White House role in the firing of Air Force cost analyst Fitzgerald?" Then, to refresh his mind in case he did not immediately recall the case, I explained: "It came up yesterday in the Civil Service hearings. He [Seamans] used executive privilege. You stated earlier that you would approve all of these uses of executive privilege, as I understand it, and I wondered whether your view still prevails in this area or whether others are now entitled to use executive privilege on their own in this type of case."

"Mr. Mollenhoff, your first assumption is correct," President Nixon began, seemingly endorsing the idea that he should have personal control over the use of executive privilege, but then he continued in a disjointed and confusing manner: "In my dealings with the Congress . . . I do not want to abuse the executive privilege proposition where the matter does not have a direct conference with or discussion within the administration, particularly where the president is involved." He mentioned Peter Flanigan's forced appearance in the ITT investigation as an example of "an extraneous matter as far as the White House is concerned. . . . we waived executive privilege for Mr. Flanigan last year, you will recall; we are not going to assert it." Then, on the Fitzgerald case, he continued: "In this case, and I understand it—and I did not approve this directly, but it was approved at my direction by those who have the responsibility within the White House—in this case it was a proper area in which the executive privilege should have been used."

Clearly, he was trying to make distinctions which did not exist, but he had also admitted that he had not personally approved the use of executive privilege by Seamans. He went on: "On the other hand, I can assure you that all of these cases will be handled on a case-by-case basis, and we are going to be in a position where the individual, when he gets under heat from a congressional committee, can say, 'Look I am going to assert executive privilege.'" He then explained procedures under which, it appeared, John Dean would actually be making decisions for the White House as to the use of executive privilege. "He [the executive branch witness] will call down here, and Mr. Dean, the White House counsel, will then advise him as to whether or not we approve it." The president's imprecise and inarticulate discussion was at odds with the law, and certainly with his own past comments on executive privilege.

"I want to follow [up with] one question on this," I said.

Mr. Nixon injected a good-natured "Sure." "This seems to be an expansion of what executive privilege was in the past, and you were quite critical of executive privilege in 1948, when you were in the Congress. . . ." I started to review his own violent opposition to executive secrecy when President Truman blocked his investigations.

"I certainly was."

"You seem to have expanded it [executive privilege] from conversations with the president himself to conversations with anyone in the executive branch of Government, and I wonder, can you cite any law or decision of the court which supports that view?"

President Nixon bristled slightly as he responded: "Well, Mr. Mollenhoff, I don't want to leave the impression that I am expanding it beyond that. I perhaps have not been as precise as I should have been." Then he tried to soothe me: "And I think yours is a very legitimate question because you have been one who has not had a double standard on this." Admitting, perhaps inadvertently, that he had a double standard on the issue of executive secrecy, he went on: "Let me suggest that I would like to have a precise statement prepared which I will personally approve so that you will know exactly what it is. . . . I understand that. But I would rather, at this point, not like to have just an off-the-top-of-my-head press conference statement delineate what executive privilege will be." When he suddenly realized what an imprecise mess he had made of the difficult executive privilege discussion, he commented: "I will simply say the general attitude I have is to be as liberal as possible in terms of making people available to testify before Congress, and we are not going to use executive privilege as a shield for conversations that might be just embarrassing to us, but that really don't deserve executive privilege."

Even in trying to extricate himself from the discussion gracefully, the president had inserted a limitation that seemed to me to disqualify the Air Force's use of executive privilege in the Fitzgerald hearings, so I asked an unprecedented fourth question: "The specific situation with regard to Fitzgerald, I would like to explore that. That deals with a conversation Seamans had with someone in the White House relative to the firing of Fitzgerald and justification or explanations. I wonder if you feel that that is covered [by executive privilege], and did you have this explained to you in detail before you made the decision?" Recognizing that he was cornered by his rambling, illogical comments, President Nixon's eyes flashed angrily and he disregarded the need for caution: "Let me explain to you. I was totally aware that Mr. Fitzgerald would be fired or discharged or asked to resign. I approved it and Mr. Seamans must have been talking to someone who had discussed the matter with me. I approved it. . . . No, this was not a case of some person down the line deciding he should go." With an air of finality, he concluded: "It was a decision that was submitted to me. I made it and I stick by it."

To a casual observer this might have seemed the *coup de grâce* to Fitzgerald's long and valiant struggle to prove that he was wrongfully discharged by the Air Force. An angry president had blazed defiance and vowed to "stick by" the decision. Who was above the president? But it was immediately apparent to me that that lawyer-President Richard Nixon had committed another monstrous blunder in a major case. In his anger he had apparently confused the Fitzgerald and Rule cases. Had Fitzgerald's lawyers written the script for that press conference they could not have done a better job of destroying the Air Force's contention that Fitzgerald was discharged as the result of a routine reorganization which had abolished his $30,000-a-year job. President Nixon had said, in effect, that Secretary Seamans had contacted the White House for approval of a decision to get rid of Fitzgerald and that Mr. Nixon had personally approved dismissal of the cost analyst who had told the truth to Congress. Upon reading the press conference transcript, Fitzgerald's lawyers commented to me that the president's unwitting legal blunder gave them proof that Fitzgerald had been deliberately discharged and that President Nixon was a part of an illegal conspiracy and cover-up. The Air Force was certain to recognize that the President's statement undercut its legal position, and would urge the White House to correct the record.

"The president misspoke himself," was Ziegler's euphemistic admission at a press briefing the next day that Mr. Nixon simply didn't know what he was talking about on the Fitzgerald case. Ziegler had not yet conjured up the practice of declaring unpardonable *faux pas* or knowingly false statements to be simply "inoperative." Ziegler told us that the president had noted his own error in reviewing the press conference transcript and wanted it corrected as early as possible. Ziegler said only that the president had had another case in mind when he so firmly assumed personal responsibility for disposition of the Fitzgerald case. "The president requested that a check be made. We have [made a check] . . . and find no record of the matter [the Fitzgerald case] ever being brought to the president's attention for a decision." From my own experience as special counsel in 1969 and 1970 I knew this to be untrue. I had investigated the Fitzgerald matter in the late fall of 1969 and had written memoranda to President Nixon, Bryce Harlow, John Ehrlichman, and Bob Haldeman, as well as others, with recommendations that Fitzgerald be retained and promoted in view of his efforts to eliminate waste from defense spending.

The press conference confrontation on the Fitzgerald case was effective in several ways. It demonstrated to the Air Force and the White House press office that stonewalling on information was not always successful and that it could occasionally be embarrassing to the president. It forced President Nixon to take specific notice of the Fitzgerald case so as to avoid future embarrassment on that subject. It put the spotlight of public attention on the misuse of executive privilege in a case with which most of the press was only vaguely familiar. Perhaps it was most important because President Nixon had promised that his counsel, John Dean, would draw up a definitive statement on Nixon's stand on executive privilege. I was assured privately that Mr. Nixon had asked Dean to get into the Fitzgerald case "and straighten it out." I was still hopeful that when John Dean and President Nixon recognized the full corruptive influence of executive privilege they would steer toward a legally defensible course. I knew that the upcoming Senate Watergate investigation would revolve about congressional access to White House and other executive branch documents, and that claims of executive privilege would be used by the White House to try to shut off or limit that investigation.

I talked with John Dean on executive privilege and told him of the great injustice to Fitzgerald. I also advised him that unless the White House took action quickly on the Fitzgerald case I would inform Fitzgerald and his lawyers of information I possessed about White House knowledge of the conspiracy against Fitzgerald. He retorted that because I had received this information as special counsel to the president, executive privilege would bar its disclosure. He also warned that there might be some ethical questions about my disclosure to Fitzgerald since I had been a lawyer for the president. Dean's warning was low-key. He said that he had not explored the question deeply but that Ehrlichman had suggested that he discuss it with me. I replied that I had examined the question of executive privilege thoroughly and did not believe that I could be barred in any way from testifying for Fitzgerald or giving him information as long as that information was accurate and did not violate national security. I mentioned my book on the history of executive privilege, *Washington Cover-Up*. Dean raised the question of lawyer-client ethics. I responded that if he examined the law on lawyer-client confidentiality he would find that it was sharply limited. "I did not receive any confidential information from President Nixon on the Fitzgerald case, and there would be no ethical barrier to my giving truthful testimony in any forum that will hear me," I said. Dean did not argue the point further but said that he was simply passing along the views of Ehrlichman. He said that he was sympathetic with my view of the Fitzgerald case and hoped to be able to convince the Air Force and the White House that Fitzgerald should be reinstated.

I did not know at that time that Dean was deeply involved as a co-conspirator in the Watergate cover-up. He was troubled by that role, anxious to extricate himself, but sinking deeper into the mire of a criminal obstruction of justice each passing week. Entangled with his own problems, he was only half-informed on executive privilege. He was fearful that his superiors could prevent him from telling the truth or could discredit and destroy him if he did so. Dean was searching for a way to escape even while dutifully cautioning me against testifying on behalf of Fitzgerald.

The evil of executive privilege loomed large in the Fitzgerald Civil Service hearings and was destined to play an even larger role in the Watergate investigation. But though the insidious doctrine was contaminating the whole government, with the encouragement of the White House, it was amazing how many legislators, reporters, and editors were unconscious that this was at the root of the moral decay they criticized in defense contracts, in foreign aid, in housing programs, in welfare programs, and in the so-called independent regulatory agencies. Many accepted the executive branch fiat as an established, proper use of presidential power to prevent disclosure of official actions. This dictatorial doctrine was defended on some of our best editorial pages, in the speeches of some of our most highly respected senators and congressmen, and in discussions among supposedly scholarly and knowledgeable members of the academic community. It was shocking to hear respected members of the Washington press corps speak of "the well-established doctrine of executive privilege," with precedents that "went all the way back to George Washington and Thomas Jefferson." I was distressed that they had been so easily brainwashed by the propaganda of the Nixon administration and prior administrations and that they were unaware of the research that had been done by a number of congressional committees which demonstrated the lack of support for arbitrary executive secrecy in the United States Constitution, in the laws made by Congress, or in the rulings of the United States Supreme Court. The Supreme Court, in fact, had consistently rejected the doctrine.

In 1962 I had carefully researched the subject for my book *Washington Cover-Up*, a history of executive branch secrecy which was well received by a wide range of congressmen and senators. The political spectrum varied from Senator John McClellan, the conservative Arkansas Democrat, to Senator William Proxmire, the liberal Wisconsin Democrat. Other supporters included Senator Barry Goldwater, Senator Estes Kefauver, Senator Margaret Chase Smith, Senator Wayne Morse, and Senator Sam Ervin. Such diverse political figures as Representative John Moss, a liberal California Democrat, and Representative H. R. Gross, a conservative Iowa Republican, had applauded my exploding the myth of executive privilege. Professor Raoul Berger, who later was recognized as the foremost scholarly authority on executive privilege and impeachment, characterized it as the pioneer study on the subject.

But the book had been published in 1962 and its warnings had been forgotten by the time the murky cloud of executive privilege menaced the Washington scene during the Nixon administration. The world of journalism was then so concerned over the threatened jailing of a couple of reporters—William Farr of Los Angeles and Peter Bridge of Newark—for refusing to testify about confidential sources that it couldn't see the larger and more ominous issue. And in over-reacting to an imagined threat to freedom of the press the media were demanding that Congress pass a federal law giving reporters, editors, and publishers the right to refuse to testify as to the sources of their information. Floods of publicity were unleashed as professional newspaper organizations launched a campaign to force Congress to confer upon editors and investigative reporters the absolute right to refuse to cooperate with police, the courts, or federal grand juries, even if violations of criminal law were involved.

In early February 1973, frustration with the superficiality of the press on the question of executive privilege prompted me to write:

The press is creating a full-scale fuss for Congress to pass a highly questionable newsmen's shield law, but at the same time is virtually ignoring the greatest threat to press freedom in our history—President Nixon's expanded interpretation of "executive privilege."

If the press does not heed the warning of a few members of Congress who have tried to call attention to the executive privilege problem, the losers could well be the American people, who will have unwittingly endorsed Mr. Nixon's greatly expanded claims of privilege.

In brief, Mr. Nixon now claims the president has the right to refuse to comply with congressional subpoenas for any "internal working papers" of the executive branch and to refuse to make available for questioning any White House officials or any other executive branch official carrying out an assignment for the White House.

Prior to his landslide victory in November, Mr. Nixon had indicated to Representative John Moss that he would personally examine and approve each instance of officials invoking "executive privilege," but since the election he has said White House Counsel John Dean and others have discretion to invoke it.

It was apparent to me that Nixon planned to use the record of past endorsement of executive privilege by some newspapers to justify his own withholding of documents and testimony from the Ervin committee. Some newspapers and some Democratic political figures were vulnerable to a charge of having a double standard if they were critical of Nixon for his cover-up, because they had certainly given approval to this arbitrary secrecy doctrine during the Eisenhower, Kennedy, and Johnson administrations. And those who were endorsing absolute shield laws to protect confidential news sources were in a poor position to criticize a president for asserting the right to cover up evidence of crime "in the national interest."

*Chapter Thirty-two*

# GOOD OLD PAT GRAY

WHEN I LEARNED that the FBI was involved in the Watergate investigation, I pointed out in my column how ludicrous it was to believe that L. Patrick Gray III, a long-time Nixon supporter, could be objective in an investigation involving possible wrongdoing by a Nixon political committee. President Nixon and his administrative aides had the retired Navy captain where they wanted him. Gray was acting director of the FBI, and, while he had no law enforcement experience, he was ambitious for the post of permanent director. However, that decision would not be made until after the November 1972 election. If Nixon won, Gray had a reasonably good chance for the appointment. If Nixon were defeated, Gray's dream would go up in smoke.

I wrote of Gray's conflict of interest in late June, in July, in August, in September, and in November—a few days before the election. I quoted from his political speeches and called attention to his slavish parroting of the White House line on the thoroughness of the Watergate investigation, but my column was not heeded in the turmoil created by unsupported charges Senator George McGovern was making. Though Gray and Attorney General Kleindienst had rejected Democratic charges that the Watergate investigation had been a whitewash, both had simply echoed the statistics Nixon had quoted. Gray had even assured the United Press International editors in early October that he had taken the Watergate case "under my own wing. The acting FBI director scorned critics who questioned the propriety of the Nixon administration investigating itself and said that raising the question of propriety "is really leveling a general indictment against all public officials." Gray said that a cover-up of the Watergate case would require the president to issue specific orders to the attorney general, who would transmit them to the assistant attorney general in charge of the criminal division and the acting director of the FBI, who would have to order twelve hundred agents to cover up relevant evidence. "He [the president] would have to control the U.S. attorney for the District of Columbia and the men and women of the grand jury," Gray said in as absurd a statement as I had ever heard by a law enforcement official. "Even if some of us are crooked, there aren't that many that are. I don't believe everyone is a Sir Galahad . . . but there's not been one single bit of pressure put on me or any of my special agents." That was a damned lie, but I did not know it at the time, when I wrote: "Acting Director Gray may still be so new on the job that he does not understand the subtle pressures that can be used to discourage effective inquiries involving high-level political functionaries. If he doesn't know, the old investigator Richard Nixon could probably tell him all about the Hiss case and the Kansas City vote frauds."

On November 5—two days before the election—I wrote: "The new politically responsive Federal Bureau of Investigation emerging under the guidance of Acting Director L. Patrick Gray III is causing grave concern among senior FBI officials and former FBI agents. Since his appointment in May . . . the genial new boss of the nation's Number One investigative agency has launched one reform after another. He seems eager to show that Pat Gray is not going to be another J. Edgar Hoover." I observed that Gray was to be a speaker at the November 9 convention of the Society of Former Special Agents of the FBI, Inc. at the Roosevelt Hotel in New Orleans. "It is unlikely that he will run into much criticism of the new rules granting FBI agents more discretion as to hair length, mustaches, and wearing apparel," I wrote. "Nor is he likely to have much criticism on his policies that now permit the hiring of women as special agents and accelerate the hiring of minority groups for special agents." Those public relations gimmicks had stilled criticism in segments of the press which should have been expected to be highly critical of Gray's Watergate role.

As I reported in my November 5 column, the former FBI agents centered their criticism on these points:

1. The large number of speeches that Pat Gray has given, many of them in the heat of the political campaign. In timing and tone, they are in sharp contrast to Hoover's rare speeches and his avoidance of any appearance of being political.

2. Pat Gray's participation in the direction of the investigation of the Watergate burglary-bugging and events flowing out of that investigation. This has been widely interpreted as a Nixon administration investigation of crimes involving personnel of a Nixon political committee.

3. Pat Gray's defense of the thoroughness of the Watergate investigation and related matters at a time when it is a major issue being stressed by Democratic political figures.

4. Pat Gray's orders to twenty-one FBI field officers in fourteen states to supply information in order for John Ehrlichman . . . to give the president maximum support during campaign trips over the next several weeks.

But the criticism of the former agents and of a large number of agents still serving failed to quash the big public relations campaign Gray was conducting to win public approval and guarantee being named permanent director. It was sickening to read the saccharine essays asking: "Can a Nice Guy Head the FBI?" and the equally naïve bunk about how morale had improved in the FBI without the iron hand of J. Edgar Hoover. Editorial pages that had carried blistering criticism of President Nixon for Watergate crimes overlooked the incompetence and political venality of Pat Gray because he was hiring more women and blacks. These reforms were overdue and should have been applauded, but certainly not at the expense of permitting a fumbling bureaucrat to destroy a competent and thorough investigative agency.

When the Senate hearings on Gray's confirmation opened on February 28, only a scattering of newspapers and a handful of senators were opposed to the nomination. At first glance the opposition consisted of the little band of liberal Democrats on the Judiciary Committee, led by Senator Edward M. Kennedy of Massachusetts and including Senators John V. Tunney of California, Philip A. Hart of Michigan, Birch Bayh of Indiana, and Quentin Burdick of North Dakota. Chairman James O. Eastland of Mississippi, was certain to vote with the Republicans, as was Senator John L. McClellan of Arkansas. Senator Sam Ervin of North Carolina seemed to be leaning toward the nomination; but Senator Robert C. Byrd of West Virginia was raising questions about the thoroughness of the Watergate investigation under the direction of Pat Gray. Seated in the Judiciary Committee hearing room in the Dirksen Senate Office Building, flanked by the two United States senators from Connecticut—Abraham Ribicoff, a Democrat, and Lowel Weicker, a Republican—Pat Gray seemed certain of confirmation. Senator Ribicoff praised Gray as "completely nonpartisan" and a man of "outstanding ability, character, and integrity." Senator Weicker criticized a *Time* story questioning Gray's law enforcement experience and his experience as a lawyer. 'I believe he is a man of absolute integrity, and I believe he is a man of intellectual capacity," Senator Weicker told the Judiciary Committee. At that time the Connecticut senators did not know that the acting FBI director had deliberately destroyed evidence that the FBI had taken from E. Howard Hunt's White House safe.

Pat Gray was only a short way into his prepared statement when he described himself as "determined that the FBI will remain completely and absolutely non-political. . . . This is one of the pillars of its historic strength. This is a policy that enables the FBI to perform efficiently, regardless of which great political party holds the reins of government, a policy that enables the FBI to carry out its responsibilities without the pull of political allegiance or the thrust of political influence." Then, hypocritically, Gray continued: "When I met with President Nixon last May, at the time of my appointment as acting director, he gave me only one instruction, and he reiterated it on the sixteenth of this month [February]: that the FBI and its director continue to stay out of politics and to remain free of politics." Before that first day was over, Pat Gray was to admit making a number of speeches during the 1972 campaign which Democratic senators labeled political. Of those sixteen speeches between July 13, 1972, and the general election, he said: "The theme of those speeches is that America is a great and good land and a land populated by good people. I can say to this committee under oath that I did not design, write, plan or intend any one of those speeches to be political speeches."

Senator Ervin said, "I infer that the speeches you made during the time might be designated as patriotic speeches, extolling the virtues of America, and speeches dealing with law enforcement problems."

Gray responded: "That is correct, sir."

Then Ervin read from a speech made before the City Club of Cleveland, Ohio, on August 11, in which he quoted Gray as commenting on the national economy, increased earnings and a rising gross national product, the rate of inflation, and the export of foodstuffs, medicines, technology around the world. "Now a person might place an interpretation on that message, in view of the particular issues that had been joined between President Nixon and Senator George McGovern, that it was calculated to help President Nixon and hurt Senator McGovern, could he not?" Senator Ervin asked.

"I think someone could draw that conclusion but I think properly to interpret it and place it in perspective, you have to see what came before it," Gray responded, insisting that the speech was not intended to have political consequences.

Senator Bayh next asked Gray whether he had been aware that the Cleveland City Club had been addressed by George McGovern only a few weeks earlier and that the Democratic vice presidential candidate, R. Sargent Shriver, had spoken there only a week or so later. Gray said that he had been unaware of these facts and of a White House memorandum which had set a priority on getting an administration spokesman into that forum, "with Ohio being crucially vital to our hopes in November." Bayh introduced the text of the memorandum from White House aide Patrick E. O'Donnell, written on June 13, 1972, to L. Patrick Gray on the subject of "Freedoms Forum—The City Club, Cleveland." Gray said that he could recall having seen the White House memorandum but that he "didn't attach any weight to that" (the political factor). "I said this morning . . . that I believe in personal dialogue, and I believe this was a good forum to take the FBI's message and try to talk about the FBI and try to let the people see the acting director of the FBI," Gray explained.

Gray's major problem on the first day of testimony involved his admission that FBI reports might have been improperly leaked to Donald Segretti, who had been engaged in "dirty tricks" for the Nixon re-election committee. Equally damaging was Gray's admission that although he didn't know how the FBI reports had been leaked to Segretti he had made no effort to find out. Gray told the committee that his investigative effort on the leak consisted of one telephone call to White House Counsel John Dean to ask Dean whether he had shown Segretti the FBI reports at the Republican convention. When Dean replied that he had not, and that he had not even had the reports at the convention, that ended his inquiry, Gray said. Under questioning by Senator Hart as to why he hadn't pursued his inquiry of Dean, Gray responded: "The presumption is one of regularity when you are dealing with the White House." Gray said that the investigation of Segretti, a friend of Dwight Chapin, who had only recently departed from a job as White House appointments secretary, was aimed only at the question of whether Segretti had engaged in illegal wiretapping or had otherwise been involved in the Watergate burglary. When the investigation failed to show any involvement in the Watergate affair, the investigation was dropped because Segretti's "dirty tricks" seemed to be "just political activity."

When Senator Robert Byrd resumed the questioning late that day, I was certain the Gray nomination was in trouble. Byrd expressed his "fear that the FBI could, under a politically oriented director, become the political arm of the White House. I think this would be a danger to the protection of the constitutional liberties of all of our people. I think the politicization of the FBI could—I am not saying it will happen at all—but it could be the first step toward the conversion of the FBI into a sort of American Gestapo."

Although the intense and methodical Byrd told me that he did not have his mind made up, it was obvious that he was deeply troubled by Pat Gray's speeches, his subservient attitude toward Haldeman and Ehrlichman, and, particularly, his giving FBI reports on Watergate investigation interviews to John Dean. The evidence indicated that one memorandum had been leaked and that the FBI reports or information based on those reports had been leaked to lawyers at the Nixon re-election committee for their use in defense strategy. It was particularly important for Senator Byrd to carry the aggressive questioning, because he was a moderate Democrat not usually identified with the more liberal group that looked to Senator Kennedy for direction. Thus, his questions could not be discounted as "anti-Nixon" or "anti-conservative."

Under the probing of Senator Byrd, Gray admitted that he had limited the scope of the initial investigation to criminal violations of the intercepted communications statutes, but that he had consulted with Attorney General Kleindienst and Assistant Attorney General Petersen in making the decision. After the limited scope of the investigation had been defined, Gray said, he did not consult or seek direction or guidance from either Kleindienst or Petersen. "I pushed the FBI button and said, 'Go, give it a full court press,' and they know exactly what to do."

"Did any FBI agent on the case feel there were leads which should be pursued and which were necessary in the case but which you or the Justice Department did not pursue?" Senator Byrd asked.

"If they did I do not know about it," Gray responded.

"So the committee is to understand that no agent at any time wished to pursue any lead which was turned down by you or the Justice Department?" Byrd asked.

Gray answered: "I can recollect none. But before I answer that under oath so categorically, I would want to check because that is a pretty broad question. I testified earlier this morning that there were instances in which I stopped the investigation for a couple of days until I could get something clarified with regard to particular people. I think it was in response to questions from Senator Hart involving the Central Intelligence Agency."

"But when it came to higher-ups in the White House were they to follow leads?" Byrd asked.

"I know of no restrictions that were placed upon them but the agents know, Senator, just as operating practice—and any president, I feel sure, would want to be accorded the same treatment by his subordinates—when you get that close, let us be real sure we want to go there," Gray answered.

"So when the clearance was sought the green light was given?" Byrd asked.

"That is right," Gray responded.

"In every instance?" Byrd shot back.

"I am not going to answer that question that categorically because there may be some instance, even in my intensive review of this case . . . where I could make an error."

Byrd questioned Gray about the transfer of a number of FBI agents who had been working on the Watergate case, including Robert G. Kunkel, the special agent in charge of the Washington, D.C., field office who had moved the FBI into the investigation even before Gray was notified at 3:45 A.M. on June 17—an hour and fifteen minutes after the arrests at Watergate. Gray insisted that all of the transfers were normal reassignments except for that of Kunkel, who was transferred to St. Louis because of "a personal and disciplinary matter . . . I do not want to air. . . ." Under questioning by Byrd, Gray said that at the time he was notified of the Watergate entry the FBI had already identified James McCord as "an ex-FBI agent and security officer for the Committee to Re-elect the President" and that before the end of that day the FBI had identified E. Howard Hunt as a possible suspect and had notified Alexander P. Butterfield, a deputy assistant to Haldeman. This revealed that Haldeman, Ehrlichman, and Colson were aware of the problem with Hunt within twenty-four hours of the Watergate burglary. Gray said that Colson and Ehrlichman were interviewed by FBI agents but that Haldeman had not been interviewed, despite published reports that he had authority over a $350,000 cash fund at the Nixon re-election committee.

"You do not think it would be worthwhile to question Mr. Haldeman?" Byrd asked in disbelief.

"No, sir," Gray replied, "because we in our interviews and our total investigation had no indication that Mr. Haldeman was involved."

"Why would it not be appropriate to try to determine who authorized the payment from the fund?" Byrd asked.

"We think we did determine who authorized the payment from the fund," Gray replied.

Byrd asked: "Who was it?"

"We feel, from the interviews we got, that Jeb Magruder was the individual who allocated $250,000 [for the Watergate burglary]," Gray replied.

"Did you go beyond Magruder?" Byrd asked.

Gray responded, "We talked to other people . . . and the grand jury did, but I do not have access to the grand jury testimony." This was a most unsatisfactory reason for not questioning Haldeman, but Byrd pressed for the identity of the White House officials Gray had discussed the investigation with. "John Wesley Dean, counsel to the president, and I think on maybe a half dozen occasions with John Ehrlichman," Gray said, and Byrd ended his questioning at 6:30 P.M.

The next day, I talked with various members of the committee, including Senator Byrd, who was now gravely disturbed over the inadequacy or political venality of Gray. He said he believed that the White House had "used Gray" for the purpose of a cover-up and that Gray, out of deference to requests from representatives of the president, had unwittingly permitted himself to be used. Dean, under the guise of conducting an investigation for President Nixon, appeared to have been the conduit by which the White House received FBI reports. With access to the reports he was in an excellent position to direct and control the cover-up. Senator Byrd said that he had already concluded that Dean's testimony would be essential to determine the damage done by Gray's blundering, obsequious cooperation with the White House.

Senator John Tunney, the liberal California Democrat, stated that he was deeply concerned about the Gray nomination but "might have to vote for it" because of the tremendous support it had on the editorial pages of some important newspapers. Tunney said that although Gray left much to be desired as a law enforcement official, he had managed a great public relations job with his hiring of more women, more members of minority groups, and relaxation of dress regulations. "As a liberal, I have to be particularly careful to avoid being classed as automatically anti-Nixon," Tunney said. "It is good that Bob Byrd is taking the lead on a lot of questions that must be asked." When Tunney took up the questioning, he inquired: "Would it be appropriate under any circumstances for anyone to take an FBI file which was given to them in confidence for their eyes only and turn it over to a third party, one who was a subject of the investigation?"

Gray replied: "Segretti was not a subject of an investigation. He was one of the many people who were being interviewed in connection with Watergate." Then, turning to the "serious breach of trust" in dissemination of files to unauthorized persons, Gray said. "Those files are sacred so far as we are concerned. But we are plagued with this problem and we have been plagued with this problem for as long as the FBI has existed."

Tunney followed by asking whether FBI files are made available to White House personnel as "surrogates" of the president.

"I am not going to make those available to everybody who works in the White House, but if you are talking about counsel to the president, if you are talking about Mr. Haldeman and Mr. Ehrlichman, the answer to your question is yes."

"Do you make any file available to them that the FBI has?" Tunney asked.

Gray responded: "Upon specific request from one of those individuals acting as agent of the United States, I would, and I engage in the presumption of regularity which I think all of us have to engage in."

In that second day of testimony, the newest revelation was Gray's admission that he had permitted former Attorney General Mitchell to block an FBI effort to interview Mrs. Mitchell. Gray said that he had initially approved a request from FBI agents to interview Mrs. Mitchell but had not insisted on a follow-through when Mitchell refused to let his wife be interviewed. He said that this was "a matter of courtesy"; Senator Bayh characterized it as "a double standard" of justice, with high officials and former high officials being accorded privileges that would be denied to others.

White House Press Secretary Ronald Ziegler called me on the morning of

Friday, March 2, to tell me that President Nixon would have a press conference at 11:00 A.M. He said that the president had asked him to call and
request that I not ask any question on executive privilege because John Dean
was still working on the comprehensive position paper and it would be ready
in about a week. I agreed not to initiate questioning on executive privilege but
said that I could not say I would not follow up if the subject were raised by
someone else. John Dean had told me that he was almost through with the
executive privilege statement, and it was a simple courtesy to agree to wait for
it to be released.

But I had not agreed to forego questions dealing with the Gray nomination, and I asked: "Mr. President, Mr. Gray has been up before the Senate
Judiciary Committee, and he has been under attack for political speeches in
1972, and there is a controversy about whether those are or are not political
speeches. I wonder if you have looked at those [speeches], and whether you
have a view on that." I further explained: "It seemed to me the most vulnerable point was a memo from Patrick O'Donnell from the White House that
was distributed to all the surrogates for the president that went to Pat Gray on
the Cleveland situation, and it involved a setting out of how crucial Ohio was
in the campaign in 1972. I wonder if you felt that was a breach of your instructions relative to the politics of Pat Gray and whether you had investigated
this."

"Well, Mr. Mollenhoff," the president replied, "that is a very proper question. I mean I would not suggest other questions are improper, but it is a
very proper question because when I appointed Mr. Gray, as you remember,
I said I was not going to send his name last year because I felt that we should
wait until we got past the political campaign so that the Senate could consider
it in a nonpolitical and nonpartisan atmosphere, and the Senate is now doing
that." President Nixon declared that Gray "must be, as Mr. Hoover was before
him, a nonpartisan figure. If there was anything indicating that during the
campaign we were trying to enlist him in that, it certainly didn't have my
support and would not have it now. I would also say, too, that the current
Senate investigation or hearing, I should say of Mr. Gray, is altogether proper.
They ask him all of these questions. I want the people of this country to have
confidence in the director of the FBI. I had confidence in him when I
nominated him. I believe that the Senate will find, based on his record since
he was nominated, that he has been fair, he has been efficient, and that he
will be a good, shall we say, lawman in the tradition of J. Edgar Hoover, and
I am sure that the Senate will overwhelmingly approve him."

Toward the end of the press conference President Nixon said that it would
be improper for him to comment on the Watergate case since it was still in
the courts, but he again asserted that no one on the White House staff at the
time the investigation was conducted was involved in "or had knowledge of
the Watergate matter." He was asked whether he would object to John Dean's
going before the Judiciary Committee or the Senate Watergate committee to
explain the relationship between the FBI and the White House in the investigation.

"Of course," the president said.

"Why?" he was asked.

"Well, because it is executive privilege," he replied. "No president could ever agree to allow the counsel to the president to go down and testify before a committee. . . . Where information is requested that a member of the White House staff may have, we will make arrangements to provide that information, but members of the White House staff, in that position at least, cannot be brought before a congressional committee in a formal hearing for testimony. I stand on the same position there that every president has stood."

As the president was starting to leave the briefing room, I fired one last question: "Mr. President, on that particular point . . . if counsel was involved in an illegal or improper act and the *prima facie* case came to light, then would you change the rules relative to the White House counsel?"

He hesitated for a moment and then replied: "I do not expect that to happen, and if it should happen I would have to answer that question at that point." Then he added, as an afterthought to close the press conference: "Let me say, too, that I know that, since you are on your feet, Clark, that you had asked about the executive privilege statement, and we will have that available toward the end of the next week or the first of the following week, for sure. Obviously, the Ervin committee is interested in that statement, and that will answer, I think, some of the questions with regard to how information can be obtained from a member of the White House staff, but consistent with executive privilege."

Within an hour after the press conference I received a call from John Dean. The pretext was a question about the Fitzgerald case and executive privilege, but he finally got to the point of his call: "I heard your question at the press conference and it intrigued me. Did you have any specific illegal act by the counsel in mind?"

Dean was curious about information I might have, and I decided to avoid dealing with my suspicions but to let him worry a little: "I didn't have any particular thing in mind, John, so you can relax." We both laughed, and I added: "—not at this time." Dean was bothered by the demands for his appearance and he was concerned over my continued insistence that executive privilege would collapse if a *prima facie* case of crime were involved.

By the time the hearings resumed on March 6, it was apparent that the Gray nomination was in serious trouble. Nice guy Gray had emerged as being as careless with the truth as he was with FBI files. This was apparent to many members of the Judiciary Committee, although Chairman Eastland and most of the Republicans were standing firm behind President Nixon's choice. But even the White House was concerned. The White House tapes later revealed that John Dean, who had read the transcript of Gray's testimony, told Ehrlichman, "It [Gray's testimony] just makes me gag."

"It's awful, John," Dean said. He suggested that the White House staff use executive privilege to avoid giving testimony on the Watergate matter.

Ehrlichman commented: "Well, I think we ought to let him hang there. Let him twist slowly, slowly in the wind."

Dean quoted President Nixon as telling him that very morning: "I'm not sure that Gray's smart enough to run the Bureau the way he's handling himself." That was the day that Gray put the noose more firmly around Dean's neck by acknowledging that FBI interviews of White House personnel had taken place with the White House counsel present. Gray had conceded that this was "not normal" procedure. He said that FBI officials had expressed their displeasure but had later informed him that Dean had not interfered with the questioning of White House personnel by the FBI agents. Gray told the committee that if "mistakes" had been made they were "honest mistakes" not intended to thwart the investigation. Senator Tunney commented that he regarded Dean's testimony as vital with regard to the handling of a number of FBI files alleged to have been in the hands of those under investigation.

The official White House statement on executive privilege was issued by Dean on March 12. It started with the usual fallacious statement that it was a "well-established" doctrine "first invoked by President Washington, and . . . recognized and utilized by our Presidents for almost two hundred years since that time." Obviously, Dean had not listened when I explained that there was no law or court case to sustain executive privilege and that it had never been anything but a cover-up for wrongdoing and mismanagement. There was one encouraging sentence: "Executive privilege will not be used as a shield to prevent embarrassing information from being made available but will be exercised only in those particular instances in which disclosure would harm the public interest." Then Dean resorted to the statistical bunk about the "thousands of hours" officials of the Nixon administration had spent testifying, claiming that "there were only three occasions . . . when executive privilege was invoked anywhere in the executive branch in response to a Congressional request for information."

These facts speak not of a closed Administration but of one that is pledged to openness and is proud to stand on its record.

Under the doctrine of separation of powers, the manner in which the President personally exercises his assigned executive powers is not subject to questioning by another branch of government. If the President is not subject to such questioning, it is equally inappropriate [sic] that members of his staff not be so questioned, for their roles are in effect an extension of the President. Otherwise, the candor with which advice is rendered and the quality of such assistance will inevitably be compromised and weakened.

What is at stake, therefore, is not simply a question of confidentiality but the integrity of the decision-making process at the very highest levels of our government.

So said the president who in those same weeks was privately advising his aides to stonewall, to falsify, to misrepresent the facts on Watergate.

The very next day the Judiciary Committee challenged President Nixon by voting unanimously to "invite" Dean to testify in the hearings on the Gray nomination. Senator Tunney, who sponsored the proposal, said that he thought it "quite improbable" that the committee would vote confirmation of

Gray unless Dean testified on his handling of FBI files given to him by Gray.

On March 14 Dean wrote to the Judiciary Committee stating he would not appear to testify but offering to reply to written questions directly related to the Gray nomination. He cited the president's March 12 statement, which he had written. White House Press Secretary Ziegler said that he did not consider Dean's refusal to be an invocation of executive privilege but rather adherence to the constitutional doctrine of separation of powers. To the PR men in the White House, "separation of powers" may have sounded less dictatorial than "executive privilege," but it was just another euphemism.

The president refused to recognize me at his March 15, 1973, press conference because "you had three questions last time." He reaffirmed his refusal to send Dean or other White House aides before the Judiciary Committee or the Senate Select Watergate Committee and said that he would welcome a court challenge to his position. Referring to speculation that the Senate "might hold Mr. Gray as hostage to a decision on [testimony by] Mr. Dean," President Nixon said that he could not believe that "responsible members" of the Senate would engage in such a political act. He said that perhaps Dean had a kind of "double privilege" because of his lawyer-client relationship with the president as well as his position on the White House staff.

By mid-March of 1973 it was apparent that the members of the Judiciary Committee, led by Senators Byrd, Ervin, and Kennedy, were going to insist on testimony from Dean. Pat Gray was a worn and torn hostage in a battle over executive privilege which was but a prelude to a bigger battle on the same issue when the Senate Watergate Committee started its hearings. It was now obvious to anyone watching the political tug of war that John Dean was being pulled into the whirlpool of the raging political flood of Watergate.

*Chapter Thirty-three*

# JOHN DEAN AND EXECUTIVE PRIVILEGE

JOHN DEAN HAD REPEATEDLY assured me that he wanted to resolve the Fitzgerald case and restore Fitzgerald to duty with the Air Force. On March 1, 1973, he told me that he had an okay from President Nixon to bring the case to a close. He seemed sincerely concerned by the injustice done to the Air Force cost analyst and anxious to demonstrate that he could right the wrong. At Dean's request, I sent him a copy of one of the memoranda I had written to President Nixon in November 1969, when I was special counsel to the president. This memorandum of my conversation with two Air Force officials corroborated Fitzgerald's contention that the Air Force had spread false stories as a part of the conspiracy to oust him for informing Congress of the C-5A jetliner cost overruns. I sent the memorandum to Dean with the clear and specific understanding that it and the accompanying letter would not be given to the Air Force but would be used by Dean's office to elicit the truth from Air Force officials.

Four days later, an Air Force source told me that Dean's assistant, David Wilson, had given the Air Force both the letter and the memorandum. I called Dean to protest this breach of our agreement. "I thought you were a man of your word," I admonished him. "We had a firm agreement that those letters were to be used by you to seek the truth, and not be given to the Air Force." Dean professed ignorance of what had happened, but a few minutes later he called back to say that David Wilson, unaware of our agreement, had indeed given the letter and memorandum to the Air Force legal office. "I hope you realize what this has done," I exploded. "You have given the Air Force your case, and you have given me no choice but to make the same material available to Fitzgerald. This is also to put you and the White House on notice that I intend to testify for Fitzgerald and to make my entire file of White House memoranda available to him unless the case is straightened out."

Dean continued to protest that it had been a mistake and asked me to believe that he had not intentionally leaked the memorandum to the Air Force. I told him that it was impossible to determine the truth or to trust in his sincerity and warned him not to permit the Air Force to fabricate some new story in the mistaken belief that this constituted Fitzgerald's best evidence. "I wasn't born yesterday, and I've dealt with deceptive government officials before," I warned. "Just keep in mind that I still have other memoranda and corroborative evidence to compel them to be honest." I told Dean that I was sorry to have this experience with him because I had liked him and had trusted him to shoot straight with me, even though I knew that as counsel to the president he had to be ever-mindful of his responsibility to President Nixon. The right and decent thing for President Nixon, I said, would be to restore Fitzgerald to his job; it would also be best politically. By rewarding honesty, he would demonstrate that fixers and crooks would not be tolerated. I assured Dean that I was going to stay on the Fitzgerald case until I dropped and that it would continue to be a problem until it was corrected.

Dean said he agreed with me completely but that the final decisions were not his to make. "You know what the situation is around here," he said. "You know where the power is, and I'm just trying to do the best I can within that system." I pitied him and the other young men in the White House who wanted to do what was right but were trapped by their own ambition and the necessity to please Haldeman, Ehrlichman, and the president.

I still felt sorry for Dean a few days later when he told me that the White House had decided to wait until the Civil Service hearing was concluded before taking any action. While giving me that message, he said Ehrlichman had raised the question of whether I could testify for Fitzgerald or provide him with my memoranda without permission from President Nixon. Dean said that Ehrlichman had told him to ask me whether I had given sufficient thought to the ethical problems involved because of my lawyer-client relationship with President Nixon and because of executive privilege. "I haven't looked into these ethical questions deeply, but they did seem worth mentioning to you," Dean said in his low-key manner. "Have you thought about that?"

Indeed I had thought about it before going to the White House. I reminded him that I had researched the material on executive privilege very carefully, that it was a constitutional myth not supported by law or court decision. The lawyer-client relationship would not apply unless I had learned something on a confidential basis from President Nixon or had given him personal legal advice. I told Dean that I was aware of Ehrlichman's belief that he had an ethical club over every lawyer who worked at the White House who might be called to testify on any White House action before Congress or any other forum. "Ehrlichman and Haldeman gave me that lecture when I was leaving," I told him, and explained that I had not bothered to argue with them on the subject because there is no law to sustain such an umbrella of secrecy and it is naïve to believe that such an authoritarian doctrine could be enforced in Washington. "There is no ethical barrier to telling the truth in any official forum," I said, except for true national security considerations and true lawyer-client confidences. "It isn't fear of law violations or fear of breaching ethical standards that has kept me from writing about my White House experiences. It is simply a matter of waiting to have my judgments in perspective."

At the time of these conversations, the first three weeks of March 1973, I did not know that Dean was suffering his own inner tug of war over his personal involvement in the crime of obstruction of justice, as he became mired in the problem of paying blackmail money to former White House consultant E. Howard Hunt and the other convicted Watergate burglars, who were due for sentencing by Chief Judge John J. Sirica on Friday, March 23. But it was clear when I sat down to write my column on March 18, 1973, that Dean was coordinating the Watergate cover-up. It was equally clear that he didn't want to but was following orders. Personal experience told me the person giving the orders had to be Haldeman or Ehrlichman, or conceivably President Nixon, for Dean was too cautious to undertake the obviously dangerous mission unless he believed President Nixon wanted it. Personal experience also told me that President Nixon had not necessarily given the order. He might not even be aware of what was specifically being done. The bridle Haldeman and Ehrlichman had on communications with the president meant that only they would know the extent of the president's knowledge of Dean's project.

My conclusion that the White House was directing the cover-up was a result of my interview with Maurice Stans, testimony by Hugh Sloan and his private comments to me, Ron Ziegler's constant reference to the "John Dean investigation," and information from White House sources that Dean personally had escorted Liddy to the Nixon re-election committee to introduce him to Magruder. By mid-March, Pat Gray's testimony had verified information I had received from friends in the White House and at the Nixon re-election committee months earlier. It confirmed reports that John Dean sat in on nearly all FBI interviews with White House personnel, over objections from career FBI officials, and that the FBI was supplying the White House with reports on the progress of the investigation. Some accounts reported suspicious delays in handling the contents of Howard Hunt's safe in the Executive Office Building. These were rumors, a mixture of second-hand reports and informed guesses from inside sources who were highly vulnerable to political pressure because they held jobs at the White House or with the Nixon re-election committee and wanted better jobs. Most of them were shaky on facts, uncertain on corroborative detail, or had no access to firm documentation which could be protected against destruction in the shredders. Gray's testimony, as well as his willingness to make political speeches, made it clear that he would have taken any risk to assure the continued good will of Haldeman and Ehrlichman he needed in order to become permanent FBI director.

The best corroboration that the White House was in charge was a criticism of Haldeman and Ehrlichman "for picking John Dean to run the cover-up." This was from a canny political operator who worried that Dean was "too inexperienced and too naïve to run the kind of cover-up that Lyndon Johnson ran in the Bobby Baker case." What my source knew about the cover-up he never told me, and I refrained from asking because it would only shut off our periodic discussions.

Another equally knowledgeable White House official had commented during the same period: "Jeb Magruder should be going to jail, but Haldeman is trying to find a spot for him where he doesn't have to go to the Senate for confirmation until this Watergate thing dies down."

At a cocktail party during the Christmas season and in a couple of street-corner conversations, an official of the Nixon re-election committee had commented: "I know Jeb Magruder should have been indicted with the Watergate burglars. Some evidence that he knew about it ahead of time has the White House worried." This source didn't like Magruder or the way he had run the Nixon re-election committee and the 1973 Nixon inaugural committee. He didn't tell me what he knew, but he wasn't one who shot from the hip, even though I knew he would be unlikely to give Magruder the benefit of the doubt on a question of guilt.

This was the background against which I wrote about John Dean on that Sunday afternoon in mid-March 1973—a week on which the attention of the nation and the world would be focused within a few months. I was trying to give President Nixon the benefit of every doubt as I wrote:

President Nixon made a grave tactical error in assigning Presidential Counsel John W. Dean III the task of investigating the possible White House involvement in the bugging and burglary on Democratic headquarters at the Watergate.

Unless there was something to hide, President Nixon should have recognized the political danger in naming a number of the White House inner circle to investigate the possible involvement of other members of that same inner circle.

Dean had an insurmountable problem in trying to deal at arm's distance with several key White House staffers and with officials at the Committee to Re-elect the President, who were friends and associates at the White House only a few months earlier.

In that later category were Deputy Campaign Director Jeb. S. Magruder, Treasurer Hugh Sloan, Jr., and Administrative Officer Robin Odle. All had varying degrees of responsibility in accumulation and disbursement of the mysterious $300,000 cash fund kept in the office safe of Finance Chairman Maurice C. Stans, the former secretary of commerce.

In addition, Dean faced problems in his relationship with G. Gordon Liddy, former White House lawyer now convicted of burglary and illegal eavesdropping at the Watergate. Dean escorted Liddy to the Nixon committee headquarters to introduce him to Magruder, who later testified he approved "security" projects for which Liddy received $235,000, mostly in $100 bills.

In vouching for Liddy's ability and integrity, Dean observed that Liddy's FBI background would be of special value for "security work" the committee planned. Throughout the Watergate investigation and trial, it has been difficult to separate Liddy's legitimate "security work" from his illegal activities.

Little wonder that Senator John Tunney (D., Calif.), Senator Robert Byrd (D., W.Va.), and Senator Sam Ervin (D., N.C.) have questioned Dean's role in sitting in on all FBI interviews with White House staff members.

Acting FBI Director L. Patrick Gray III, a Nixon appointee, has testified that the FBI would have preferred that Dean not be present, but that it was one of the conditions laid down by the White House for FBI interviews of staff members. Dean was not present as legal counsel for the staff members interviewed, but as counsel to President Nixon, Gray explained.

Gray also admitted that at the request of the White House he turned over more than eighty FBI files on the Watergate investigation to Dean's office. He said he had once stopped the flow of such information to the office of White House Chief of Staff H. B. (Bob) Haldeman.

Members of the Judiciary Committee considering President Nixon's nomination of Pat Gray as permanent director of the FBI have been critical of Gray for his willing distribution of FBI reports on the Watergate to Dean. They have noted there is evidence indicating that material from these reports was "leaked" to the officials of the Committee to Re-elect the President and to Donald Segretti, the young California lawyer alleged to have been hired for political sabotage by the Republicans.

Segretti was initially contacted for the job by former White House Appointments Secretary Dwight L. Chapin and was paid $30,000 to $40,000 from the cash funds of the Committee to Re-elect by Herbert Kalmbach, President Nixon's personal lawyer, according to FBI reports Gray turned over to the Judiciary Committee.

President Nixon had to know that Dean, the man he selected as investigator, monitor, and screening judge of the Watergate case, had been an assistant to former Attorney General John Mitchell at the Justice Department. Reliable sources report that Mitchell personally pushed Dean for the White House counsel job.

That placed Dean in the position of investigating activities at the Committee to Re-elect in the period when his former boss and benefactor, Mitchell, was director of the Nixon re-election effort.

Another incident indicating Dean's close relationship to the re-election committee involved legal opinions he gave to Finance Chairman Maurice Stans on several controversial contributions that had not been reported to the General Accounting Office (GAO). Those legal opinions to Stans were directly contrary to the views of the GAO's Office of Federal Elections, which said the contributions had to be reported and the records kept.

If President Nixon was unaware of the relationship between Liddy and Dean at the time he assigned Dean to the Watergate probe, he should have been mindful of the other facts that would cause political critics to question the sincerity of the investigation of White House staffers.

It was unrealistic for Nixon to believe that Dean would be regarded as any more objective than Pat Gray, who had a permanent appointment as FBI director riding on retaining good relations with the White House.

With all of those factors present, the president also assigned the job of writing the most recent and most controversial paper on executive privilege to Dean —the man who will be the most immediate beneficiary of this expanded White House secrecy cloak.

But Dean's treatment of executive privilege cited no law and no court cases to support the expanded privilege and relied upon what experts call a "flimsy" constitutional claim which Mr. Nixon criticized himself in 1948 as a device that would have permitted the cover-up of President Harding's White House gang during the notorious Teapot Dome scandals.

Mr. Nixon's critics now charge it is "a power grab" to cover up White House involvement in the Watergate. The president and John Dean are in a most untenable position, even though the president may be able to convince the public that his actions are motivated by a deep desire to defend the sacred "separation of powers" doctrine.

On the same day I wrote that column, Senator Sam Ervin, on "Face the Nation," declared that the Senate Judiciary Committee would hold up action on the Gray nomination until it had testimony from Dean. On the CBS television show, Ervin declared that if confrontation with the White House was necessary, the Senate would send the sergeant-at-arms to arrest Dean or any other White House aides who refused to testify. Ervin rejected President Nixon's suggestion that it would be irresponsible of the Senate to hold the Gray nomination hostage to break the executive privilege claim. "It would not be fair to Mr. Gray or to the Senate" to take action without hearing Dean's explanation of the serious charges, Ervin said. He declared that the president "has stretched beyond any precedent on the subject" his claim that Dean and other White House aides need not testify on the handling of the Watergate investigation because of executive privilege. The wily Senator Ervin threw out a warning to White House aides against following Mr. Nixon's advice by observing that if there are jail terms to be served "it will not be the president who will go to jail. It will be the White House aides."

The senator rejected President Nixon's offer to have Dean answer questions in writing. Ervin, veteran of many courtroom battles, declared that as a practicing lawyer the president should know that "you can't administer an oath to a piece of paper" and "you can't cross-examine a piece of paper." There is only one way that Dean or any other White House aide could avoid giving testimony, Ervin said—by availing themselves of the protection of the Fifth Amendment on the ground that to be required to give testimony might be incriminating. With a smile, Senator Ervin said that he was sure the congressional committees would respect the right of White House aides to take the Fifth Amendment.

On Monday, March 19, things started to come apart for the Nixon White House. It began when Senate Democratic Whip Robert Byrd declared in a floor speech that "the integrity of the Senate" was at stake in connection with requests that John Dean appear. "The Senate should not deviate from its insistence upon the appearance of Mr. Dean," Byrd said, adding that it was "almost impossible to avoid the suspicion . . . that someone at the White House, in preparing the statement [on executive privilege] for Mr. Nixon, was trying to cover up White House involvement in . . . political sabotage and espionage." Byrd supported Senator Ervin's suggestion that the sergeant-at-arms be sent to arrest Dean if he did not appear at the Gray hearing or before the Senate Watergate committee. "If the president wants to close the door on the supply of information," Byrd said, "the Senate ought to close the door on the president's nominee [Gray]."

The West Virginia Democrat scoffed at President Nixon's interpretation of executive privilege as "a well-established doctrine" and said that he did not know "of any precedent which would allow the president to lay down a blanket immunity for members of his present White House staff from being required to appear in a formal session of a congressional committee." He declared that there was "total inconsistency" in the president's stating that the privilege would not be used to cover up either criminal activity or embarrassing information and then using it to prevent questioning of Dean on the serious problems raised in the Gray hearing. "There is no question involving military security in such an appearance by Mr. Dean. There is no question involving sensitive relations with other countries. . . . It boggles the imagination," Byrd said, to see how the public interest could possibly be harmed by sworn testimony on the Watergate affair.

Senate Republican Leader Hugh Scott, persistent White House defender, characterized Ervin's threat to jail Dean as "bombast" about a crisis that will never arise. "I can't imagine someone walking into the White House and putting handcuffs on a White House aide," Scott said. "The public reaction would be terribly adverse." But Scott's support was of little solace to Dean and other White House aides as the Judiciary Committee members simply chewed Gray up on Tuesday, Wednesday, and Thursday.

On Tuesday, Gray was led through the inadequacies of the FBI investigation and the bold favoritism it had shown toward the Nixon White House and the Nixon re-election committee. On Wednesday, under questioning by

Senator Edward Kennedy and Senator Tunney, he admitted that he had delivered raw FBI files to John Dean in a secret arrangement not known even to Attorney General Kleindienst. Why did he take this unusual step without notifying Kleindienst? Gray fumbled for an explanation before stating dispairingly that he had no explanation "except that I just did it," adding, "He was counsel to the president of the United States and he requested them."

Senator Kennedy asked whether "by hindsight" he would have made the files available. When Gray said that he could see no reason for caution in dealing with Dean, Kennedy called attention to the information in the FBI reports about Dean's relationship with C. Gordon Liddy. Kennedy recalled that Jeb Magruder had testified that it was Dean who recommended Liddy to the re-election committee and that Dean had made special mention of Liddy's FBI background as important in connection with any "intelligence-gathering" at the committee.

It was on Thursday, March 22, that Gray's bumbling effort to defend his subservience produced a crisis for himself, Dean, and the White House. Under Byrd's persistent probing, Gray had revealed a damaging chronology in Dean's handling of the Hunt investigation. Hunt, who had entered a plea of guilty to all counts, was due for sentencing the next day, and, unknown to Byrd or other members of the Judiciary Committee, was the subject of much concern in the Oval Office at the White House. Byrd recounted earlier testimony from Gray that two of Dean's aides had searched Hunt's office in the Executive Office Building, just west of the White House, and that material from the search, including the contents of Hunt's safe, had been turned over to Dean on June 20. During the FBI interview with White House Special Counsel Charles Colson on June 22, which Dean attended, Dean had commented, in reply to a remark by one of the FBI agents, that he did not know whether Hunt had an office at the White House and would "check it out."

Byrd asked Gray whether he believed that Dean had "lied to the agents" about his knowledge of whether Hunt had an office in the White House complex. Gray responded that he "would have to conclude that judgment is probably correct." The news stories centered on the fact that Gray had acknowledged that Dean "probably lied" to the FBI, and the White House responded angrily, calling Byrd's charge "reprehensible, unfortunate, unfair, and incorrect." White House Press Secretary Ziegler said, "Mr. Dean flatly denies that he ever misled or lied to an agent of the FBI." Dean's recollection was that he had been asked by the agents whether or not they could visit Hunt's office, not whether or not Hunt had an office there. The furor over whether Dean had lied to the FBI faded into obscurity on Friday, March 23, when the seven convicted Watergate defendants appeared before United States District Judge John Sirica to be sentenced.

About a week before the sentencing, I had sent Judge Sirica a copy of my March 11 column, in which I explained the delayed sentencing procedure used by United States District Judge Warren J. Ferguson of Los Angeles. Judge Ferguson had used delayed sentencing to persuade former Army

Sergeant Major William Wooldridge and other members of the "Khaki Mafia" to testify truthfully and to cooperate fully with Senator John L. McClellan's Permanent Investigating Subcommittee. Judge Ferguson "had accepted pleas of guilty from Wooldridge, Sergeant Sam Bass, and Sergeant William Higdon on charges of conspiracy, fraud, and conspiracy to defraud the government," I had written.

In an unusual move, Judge Ferguson had delayed sentencing until after he received a report on how well they cooperated with the Senate Permanent Investigating Subcommittee.

This is almost certain to lift the secrecy curtain on the identity of higher-ups who have been protected since 1969 by the fact that Wooldridge, Bass, and Higdon had all claimed the Fifth Amendment privilege.

Having entered pleas of guilty, all can now be granted immunity to testify before the Senate subcommittee and undoubtedly will testify fully to lessen the penalties, which could be $10,000 in fines and up and from two to five years in federal prison."

It seemed to me that Judge Ferguson's problem had been similar to the one Judge Sirica now faced in getting to the "higher-ups" in the Watergate matter. Within a few hours after he received the column, Judge Sirica called Judge Ferguson in Los Angeles.

Five of the Watergate defendants received "provisional" sentences of maximum terms—thirty-five years for E. Howard Hunt, Jr., and forty years each for Bernard L. Barker, Frank A. Sturgis, Eugenio R. Martinez, and Virgilio R. Gonzales. All five had entered pleas of guilty, and, in sentencing them, Sirica pointedly said, "I recommend your full cooperation" with the federal grand jury and the Senate Watergate committee investigating the Watergate case. "You must understand that I hold out no promise or hopes of any kind," Judge Sirica said sternly, "but I do say that should you decide to speak freely I would have to weigh that factor in appraising what sentence will be finally imposed in each case." Liddy, who with James McCord had been convicted by a jury, was sentenced to the maximum term—six to twenty years in prison and a fine of $40,000. Judge Sirica called his role "sordid, despicable, and thoroughly reprehensible."

McCord's sentencing was put off until March 30 as a result of a letter from McCord to Judge Sirica charging political pressure, perjury, obstruction of justice, and threats of retaliation by the administration. The letter gave substance to what everyone believed but most were afraid to write. It did not go into evidentiary detail as to his knowledge of the roles of those who had planned and financed the Watergate burglary, but it was obvious to anyone familiar with the investigation that cooperation by McCord would open up wide new avenues of evidence. The letter was shattering for the Nixon administration because McCord, former chief security officer for the Nixon re-election committee, had been identified in the trials as the recipient of wiretap reports on the telephones at Democratic headquarters. McCord would have knowledge of who had received those reports at headquarters and who had paid the expenses. In my March 24 column I wrote: "McCord's request for an opportunity to talk to Sirica privately in chambers was accompanied by the explanation that 'I cannot feel confident in talking with an FBI agent, in testifying before a grand jury whose U.S. attorneys work for the Department of Justice, or in talking with other government representatives.' "

Over that weekend, McCord talked with Sam Dash, the chief counsel for the Senate Select Watergate Committee, and over the next few days appeared in closed sessions with Senate committee members. On Sunday, March 25, a Senate committee source and a Washington lawyer told me that McCord had named John Dean, Jeb Magruder, and John Mitchell as being among the persons who had "prior knowledge" of the burglary and bugging at the Watergate. The *Los Angeles Times* reported the next day that McCord had implicated Dean and Magruder in having advance knowledge of the Watergate burglary.

White House Press Secretary Ziegler flatly denied that Dean had prior knowledge. "The president has complete confidence in Mr. Dean and wanted me again here this morning to publicly express President Nixon's absolute and total confidence in Mr. Dean in this regard," Ziegler said. He told reporters that President Nixon had telephoned Dean from his office in Key Biscayne to discuss his possible involvement in Watergate and that, on the basis of that conversation, the president had authorized the expression of "absolute and total" confidence in his White House counsel. Ziegler avoided such sweeping denials in regard to Magruder's possible involvement, simply calling attention to Magruder's prior denials of the charges. The White House press secretary said that a response to the charges on Magruder was "not relevant to this particular podium."

This indicated to me that the White House was going to try to save John Dean but would cut Magruder loose because of the vast amount of evidence that he was a part of the Watergate conspiracy. He had admitted authorizing payment of large amounts of cash to Liddy, it was clear that he had committed perjury in the January trial, and now McCord had provided other evidence based on his work at the Nixon re-election committee. The weakest link in the conspiracy was Jeb Stuart Magruder.

*Chapter Thirty-four*

# JEB MAGRUDER'S SWITCH

JEB MAGRUDER HAD REACHED the point of no return, and it was obvious that the White House was trying to dump him. I tried to reach him several times during the week after McCord's letter was read by Judge Sirica, but he was either not in his office or not responding to my calls. I finally contacted him late in the first week of April. I said that I was sorry about the bind he was in "because of the McCord development" and would like to talk with him. He asked what I knew about McCord's testimony to the Ervin committee and I said that I didn't have to know McCord's story to know that it was bad for him (Magruder). He said that he wanted to talk to others first but that he could see me the following Monday, April 9.

Immediately after talking to Magruder, I called Bernard (Bud) Fensterwald, who had become McCord's attorney. I had known Fensterwald since he had been counsel for a Senate Judiciary Subcommittee headed by the late Senator Estes Kefauver. Fensterwald had declined to go into the specific evidence McCord had, except to verify that McCord would indeed link Mitchell, Dean, and Magruder to advance knowledge of the Watergate burglary. He added that McCord had sufficient corroboration to involve them in the conspiracy. "We've really got it on them this time," Fensterwald said, "and with a little luck we will prove that the president has been involved in an obstruction of justice." It was his opinion that Magruder was the most vulnerable of the group, and he had heard reports that Dean was getting wobbly and was looking for a good criminal lawyer. His analysis of the evidence against Magruder tallied with mine, and I was aware that he knew still unrevealed information from McCord which I did not. "How well do you know Magruder?" he asked.

When I responded, "Pretty well," he suggested that I try to talk to him about his case. "You might be doing him a big favor and also get yourself a hell of a story if he's ready to talk," Fensterwald said. I said that I had just caught up with Magruder and planned to see him the next week.

By the time I saw Magruder, President Nixon had been forced to withdraw the Gray nomination in the face of Republican demands that John Dean appear before the Senate Judiciary Committee. Senator Charles Mathias, an independent Maryland Republican, said that the "poisoned public ethical behavior" of Watergate was hurting the Republican Party and that he could not vote for the Gray nomination unless Dean appeared. Senator Marlow W. Cook, a Kentucky Republican who had been an ardent supporter of Pat Gray, said that Watergate was a "rather severe stigma on the Republican Party" and indicated he would have difficulty supporting the Gray nomination. Even Senator Edward Gurney of Florida and Senate Republican Leader Hugh Scott were reported to be deeply disturbed. Although Chairman James O. Eastland of Mississippi and Senator Roman Hruska of Nebraska stayed firmly behind the Gray nomination publicly, Eastland told me privately that he was thoroughly disgusted with Gray's performance and remained firm only "because I told the president I would stand behind the nomination until he was ready to withdraw it." On Thursday, April 5, the president withdrew the nomination. He did not admit that Gray had been exposed but said that the Democrats on the Judiciary Committee had made it impossible for Gray to effectively run the FBI.

Justice Department sources confirmed that President Nixon was considering nominating Assistant Attorney General Henry E. Petersen for the post of FBI director. Other potential candidates were said to be John E. Ingersoll, director of the department's Bureau of Narcotics and Dangerous Drugs; Richard B. Ogilvie, former Illinois governor; Jerry Wilson, police chief of Washington, D.C.; and United States District Judge William Matthew Byrne of California. Judge Byrne was said to be included on the list because he was a former FBI agent. What wasn't stated at the time was that he was the sitting judge in the trial of Dr. Daniel Ellsberg on charges of having leaked the highly classified "Pentagon Papers" and that John Ehrlichman had called him to San Clemente that day to ask if he were interested in the appointment.

Magruder's office was in the huge Commerce Department building. Haldeman had installed him there in a $38,000-a-year job as director of the Office of Program Development. I arrived a few minutes early and waited in the colorful outer office where Magruder's two secretaries were seated, wondering whether they realized how temporary Magruder's Commerce Department tenure would probably be. It was possible that they saw his big job with the Nixon re-election committee, his heading of the 1973 Inaugural Committee, and his links with Haldeman as "Four More Years" of security. That was probably what Magruder hoped for, although I assumed he had seen the handwriting on the wall indicating that he had been nominated to walk the plank for the good of the Nixon team. Pat Gray had suddenly been dropped after weeks of praise and support from the president. Magruder couldn't have missed the new White House line on executive privilege as laid out by Ziegler in the face of Republican complaints. White House and administration officials would be required to go before the federal grand jury still investigating Watergate and the cover-up.

Magruder came out of the inner office as I finished a last-minute review of the criminal case against him as outlined on an index card I was carrying in my shirt pocket. He gave me a broad smile and a hearty handshake as I rose to meet him. When we entered his large inner office, he instructed one of the secretaries not to disturb him "unless . . ."—I did not catch the exception. Once the door closed, there was an awkward silence which he broke by saying, with a self-conscious smile, that it had been a long time since he'd seen me. I agreed and said that I was sorry our meeting was taking place under these circumstances because I liked him and was disappointed to see him in such serious trouble.

Magruder replied that he believed he "could ride it out," that his lawyers had told him McCord's testimony wasn't corroborated and that Liddy wasn't going to talk.

I told him that that wasn't the way I assessed the case and that I planned "to write a column indicting you in connection with the Watergate affair."

"I'm not here to get new evidence or to trick you into admissions," I said. "I know, and I think you know, you could have been indicted for conspiracy in the original Watergate case, and the federal grand jury could indict you now for perjury in connection with your testimony before the grand jury and in the Watergate trial."

"How do you figure that?" he asked. "My lawyers say McCord can't be corroborated, and that Liddy won't talk."

"Corroboration for McCord may be needed in connection with Dean, or Mitchell, or some of the others," I replied. "But they don't need corroboration to make a case on you, because you have already made the admissions against interest of the overt acts necessary to tie you to the conspiracy."

"But," he protested, "I'm told that [Assistant United States Attorney Earl] Silbert isn't going to push it."

"It may be a weak case, but the United States attorney's office is on the spot, along with the FBI and Justice Department, because of the Gray hearing," I explained. "The White House has lost its punch, and everyone now is going to protect himself from the Senate Watergate committee."

When Magruder declared that he did not have advance knowledge of the break-in, I replied that his denials were flying in the face of a lot of hard evidence. "I don't want to get any new evidence from you," I repeated. "I just want to go over the hard case against you and give you an opportunity to explain or clarify any point that I'm using. I'm not going to say anything to you that I wouldn't say to my son if he were in this kind of a mess." In that spirit, I covered the case against him point by point as I had prepared it for use in a column:

1. Magruder had admitted under oath that he personally approved the hiring of Gordon Liddy as financial counsel to the Nixon re-election committee, and Liddy stood convicted of being the mastermind of the Watergate burglary.

2. Magruder, in his capacity as deputy director of the compaign, met with Liddy, McCord, and others to approve general-intelligence gathering on Democratic candidates.

3. Magruder, in the Watergate trials, admitted giving personal approval to the payment of $235,000 in cash in $100 bills to Liddy with no accounting by Liddy of how the money was used.

4. Magruder had admitted meeting privately with McCord on several occasions, and, in the light of other evidence, he would be ill-prepared to deny any testimony that McCord might give as to what he had told Magruder.

5. McCord was reported to have told Senate investigators and a federal grand jury that Liddy had told him that Magruder and Dean had prior knowledge of the Watergate burglary's planning and financing.

I acknowledged that McCord's testimony as to what Liddy had told him might be largely hearsay evidence, particularly where it was neither verified nor denied by Liddy. But I explained that there was a strong pattern of corroboration in Magruder's admission of his role in hiring Liddy, in giving general approval to the surveillance of Democrats, and in paying out huge sums of money under a loose accounting system. "Will a jury believe that Jeb Magruder, a management expert, would pay out more than $200,000 in cash without demanding an accounting of some sort unless he knew it was an illegal activity?" I asked. Magruder acknowledged my point with a weak smile and a shake of his head.

He acknowledged that his authority in the Nixon re-election committee had come directly from Haldeman and Mitchell. And he conceded that he would inevitably have to give a more detailed explanation of why he had dealt with Liddy and disbursed such huge sums of cash, when he had already testified that he did not like or trust the former White House lawyer. Magruder also acknowledged that eventually he would be asked whether he had really acted on his own in conducting financial transactions in such a loose manner or whether he was following the instructions of a superior.

When I entered his office, at 2:00 P.M., Magruder had been reasonably confident that he could "ride it out," but when I left, at 2:30, he was nervous and uncertain, making frequent reference to assurances his lawyers had been giving him for some months. As a parting shot, I tossed another ingredient into his stew: "I don't know who your lawyers are and I don't want to know, but if they are paid for by the Nixon re-election committee, you had better ask yourself whether they are really looking out for your interests or whether they are using you to protect some higher-ups." As I left the office, I suggested that if he had anything he wanted to tell me about the Watergate matter, I would be pleased to receive a call from him. I was sympathetic with his position and believed that it would be in his best interests to seek immunity and to tell his full story to the federal grand jury or the Senate Watergate committee.

I felt that he genuinely appreciated the advice.

On Saturday, April 7—two days before his meeting with me—Magruder had met for the first time with his personal attorneys, James Bierbower and James Sharp. Up to that time, he had been receiving legal advice from lawyers for the Nixon re-election committee. Bierbower and Sharp had told him that they doubted his cover story but had been unable to persuade him to change it. I learned later that within a few minutes after his meeting with me, Magruder contacted his former assistant, Bart Porter, and his lawyer, James Sharp, for the first exploratory conversations about changing his story and telling the truth. Since I had assured Magruder that I would not quote him directly for a news story and would confine myself to material in the public record, I did not write the story for several days. Before moving ahead with it, I tried to reach him several times, hoping he could be persuaded to give me an exclusive on his true Watergate role.

I was still waiting for a call from Magruder a week later when I learned from a lawyer for one of the Watergate defendants and from a Justice Department source that Magruder and his lawyers had talked with Assistant United States Attorney Silbert in an effort to bargain for a guilty plea on a one-count felony indictment. On Tuesday morning, April 10, the morning after his discussion with me, Magruder went to Sharp's office and told him the truth about Watergate. The next day, April 11, he told Porter he was going to tell the truth and suggested that Porter volunteer to tell the prosecution all he knew. Thursday, Bierbower and Sharp had their first meeting with Silbert. The next day, at Bierbower's office, Magruder apologized to Silbert for having lied to him during the first Watergate investigation in 1972. The prosecutors had already been contacted by Dean's lawyer, Charles N. Shaffer, and were negotiating with him for a possible plea of guilty in return for cooperation.

Silbert's negotiations that week with lawyers for Dean and Magruder precipitated a Saturday-night crisis at the Justice Department and the White House. Magruder had told Haldeman and Ehrlichman that he had decided to tell the truth, which might implicate one or both in an obstruction of justice. The two of them, as well as President Nixon, were aware that Dean was seriously considering a plea of guilty and were trying to devise a strategy to minimize the damage to Haldeman and Ehrlichman. The seriousness of the crisis was emphasized as Attorney General Kleindienst sped to the White House to inform Nixon of the possible involvement of Dean, Magruder, Mitchell, Haldeman, Ehrlichman, Colson, and Strachan in a criminal obstruction of justice. Because of his long friendship and political association with former Attorney General Mitchell, Kleindienst told President Nixon that he wished to stand aside from the decision-making process in favor of Assistant Attorney General Petersen, who headed the Criminal Division. As he was briefed by Kleindienst and then Petersen on the general scope of the evidence, the president indicated surprise, even though he had already been informed of the involvement of all of these people in his March 21, 1973, meeting with Dean and Haldeman.

Simultaneous with the crisis created by the Magruder and Dean developments, a furious political storm had developed over testimony by Kleindienst on executive privilege. On April 10—the day after my talk with Magruder—the attorney general of the United States had shocked a Senate subcommittee by stating that military force could implement the exercise of executive privilege—the ultimate claim of presidential power. Kleindienst asserted that the president could bar Congress or the courts from any document in the executive branch and could order any executive branch official to refuse to testify even if criminal acts were involved. The attorney general had added that the president could invoke this arbitrary secrecy doctrine even in an impeachment hearing and that the Congress or the courts could do nothing except impeach him. Kleindienst observed that the United States marshals, the sergeant-at-arms, and the Capitol police were a puny physical force against the military might at the disposal of the commander in chief. I listened in disbelief as the nation's top law enforcement officer set forth the thesis that the Congress and the courts, in challenging a president's authority, must take into account the military power at his disposal.

Kleindienst's statements were shocking to Republicans as well as Democrats, and Senator Barry Goldwater was among the first to denounce the "hiding of evidence from Congress." Representative John Anderson, a senior

Illinois congressman who headed the House Republican Conference Committee, accused Kleindienst of making an "unnecessarily provocative and contemptuous statement that contained such an alarming and dangerous notion of executive privilege" that Congress could not ignore the challenge.

Anderson told the same Senate subcommittee the day after Kleindienst's appearance, "The attorney general has thrown down the gauntlet. If this Congress is to preserve even a semblance of integrity and independence, it must act immediately to nullify the sweeping claim of executive power asserted by the attorney general." Anderson said that he wondered whether "the chief lawyer for the government [Kleindienst] has ever heard of the Freedom of Information Act. The Act requires disclosing to the general public information that the attorney general has now said the president could unilaterally deny even to Congress. That proposition is simply incredible and, I might add, borders on contempt for the established law of the land."

Representative William Scherle, an outspoken Iowa conservative, declared that the president, in putting the cloak of executive privilege around the White House staff, had "endowed them with the arrogance of nobility or royalty." Said Scherle: "If the president does not wish himself and his entire government to be tarred with the same brush, he must immediately direct his entire staff to cooperate fully with the congressional committee as well as the grand jury investigating the [Watergate] case. Nothing less will satisfy the aroused conscience of the people and their Congress."

Senator Goldwater said, "The Watergate . . . is beginning to smell like the Teapot Dome." Although he was still supporting the president, he stopped short of saying that he would continue to support him. "I might not support him if it turns out he knew about all this and kept his mouth shut," Goldwater said, "but I don't think he knew about it."

On Monday, April 16, the seven members of the Senate Select Committee on Watergate agreed unanimously on procedures for requiring White House aides to testify in the hearings scheduled for mid-May. That day Senator Jacob Javits, the liberal New York Republican, joined with those condemning the Nixon administration for its extreme position on executive privilege. Javits declared that it had all the earmarks of "a cover-up" of Watergate. "Executive privilege cannot be used to cover up criminal wrongdoing," he said, a position that had nearly unanimous support in the Senate.

Aware of the possible defection of Dean and Magruder, and under pressure from an outraged Congress, President Nixon grabbed the offensive. After weeks and months of heel-dragging and cover-up, Mr. Nixon on April 17 announced at the White House briefing room a "major development" in the Watergate investigation and asserted that real progress was being made under his direct supervision. "No individual holding, in the past or at present, a position of major importance in the administration should be given immunity from prosecution," President Nixon said. "I condemn any attempt to cover up in this case no matter who is involved." This was an obvious effort to bar Dean and Magruder from seeking immunity from prosecution. Faced with the opposition of a unanimous Senate committee, President Nixon yielded, declaring that no White House staff member would be excused from testifying by claiming executive privilege. "I should point out that this arrangement is one that covers this hearing only, in which wrongdoing has been charged," Mr. Nixon said. "This kind of an arrangement, of course, would not apply to other hearings."

In addition, President Nixon tried to establish in the public mind the idea that he knew little about the Watergate cover-up prior to March 21. "On March 21, as a result of serious charges which came to my attention, some of which were publicly reported, I began intensive new inquiries into this whole matter," Mr. Nixon said. "Last Sunday afternoon the attorney general [Kleindienst], the assistant attorney general [Petersen] and I met at length in the Executive Office Building to review the facts which had come to me in my investigation and also to review the progress of the Department of Justice investigation. I can report today that there have been major developments in the case concerning which it would be improper to be more specific now, except to say that real progress has been made in finding the truth."

When the president had completed reading his statement, he left without answering questions. At this point Press Secretary Ziegler declared that all previous White House statements were now "inoperative" since they had been based on investigations conducted prior to the recent statements by several of the Watergate defendants. This was an outrageous effort to prohibit inquiry on the false and erroneous statements which had been issued from the time shortly after the Watergate burglary on June 17, 1972, up to and including Mr. Nixon's March 15, 1973, press conference, in which he had expressed confidence in all White House staff members, including John Dean.

At Ziegler's press briefing on April 18, after several futile efforts to get an explanation as to why the false and misleading statements had been made, I lashed into Ziegler: "Do you feel free to stand up there and lie and put out misinformation and then come around later and say it's all 'inoperative'?" Ziegler made no comment as I continued: "That's what you're doing. You're not entitled to any credibility at all."

Finally Ziegler said that he was "not in a position to answer any questions, no matter how they are phrased, on the subject because it could very well prejudice the prosecution or the rights of innocent individuals or indeed the judicial process itself."

That day John Dean issued a brief statement from his office:

To date I have refrained from making any public comments whatsoever about the Watergate case. I shall continue that policy in the future because I believe that the case will be fully and justly handled by the grand jury and the Ervin Select Committee. It is my hope, however, that those truly interested in seeing that the Watergate case is completely aired and that justice is done will be careful in drawing any conclusions as to the guilt or involvement of any persons until all the facts are known and until each person has had an opportunity to justify under oath in his own behalf.

Finally, some may hope or think that I will become a scapegoat in the Watergate case. Anyone who believes this does not know me, know the true facts, nor understand our system of justice.

Significantly, that statement was not cleared through the White House press office. Dean was serving public notice on Haldeman, Ehrlichman, and the president that he did not intend to walk the plank alone. Dean had told the president earlier that week that he would resign and face prosecution for obstruction of justice, but he wanted Mr. Nixon's assurance that resignations would also be signed by the men whose instructions he had followed—Haldeman and Ehrlichman.

*Chapter Thirty-five*

# TWO OF THE FINEST PUBLIC SERVANTS

THE FIRST firm evidence of the involvement of Mitchell, Haldeman, and Ehrlichman in an obstruction of justice was the statement Magruder made to the prosecutors about the Watergate cover-up. The *Washington Post,* on April 19, reported that Magruder had implicated Mitchell, and a day later William Hundley, Mitchell's attorney, acknowledged that Mitchell had been present at three meetings in which plans to wiretap the Democrats were discussed. But Hundley quoted his client as saying that he had never approved the plans, that he had, in fact, vetoed the idea.

Deeply concerned about the defection of Magruder, and realizing that desertion by Dean would be even more devastating, the Nixon team tried to soothe Dean with a telephone call from the president wishing him "Happy Easter." The White House also issued another denial that President Nixon had any prior knowledge of the Watergate burglary.

Ziegler reported that Nixon had told Dean, "You're still my counsel," and he assured me there was no change in Dean's status in spite of his unauthorized press statement that he would not be a scapegoat. Within a week, Ziegler suddenly changed his tune and warned White House reporters, including me, to be careful of "John Dean type statements" implicating Haldeman and Ehrlichman. "Those stories simply are not true," Ziegler said. "Dean is trying to save himself because he may be implicated in the cover-up." The shift in Ziegler's pitch conveyed a clear message: they had tried to protect Dean, had tried to keep him under control, but now they were abandoning him.

Charles Shaffer, a friend of mine since the days when he was prosecuting Jimmy Hoffa and Bobby Baker, had been negotiating with the United States attorney's office for complete immunity for Dean in return for his testimony.

While Shaffer declined to discuss the substance of Dean's testimony, he did confirm that no solid agreement had been reached in the last week of April; he believed that the Justice Department was under pressure from the White House not to grant immunity to Dean.

On April 27, with no advance warning, L. Patrick Gray III announced his resignation as acting director of the FBI and admitted that he had burned certain files removed from the Executive Office Building safe of E. Howard Hunt, Jr. The *New York Times* unraveled part of the story about Gray's destruction of records and, in the process, implicated Ehrlichman and Dean in the suggestion that the documents be destroyed.

Republican pressure to dump both Ehrlichman and Haldeman increased and Senator Dole, the Kansas Republican who had headed the Republican National Committee a few months earlier, said that President Nixon's only chance of retaining credibility was to fire his two top aides. "Right now the credibility of the administration is zilch, zero," Dole declared.

On April 24, I reported that White House sources revealed that Haldeman would submit his resignation and that his departure would probably signal the departure of Ehrlichman and Dean as well. In the late afternoon of Monday, April 30, the White House announced the resignations of Haldeman, Ehrlichman, Dean, and Kleindienst. Later, in a television address, Mr. Nixon went to great lengths to explain the long delays. Claiming that he had been unable to get at the truth, he said that he had taken the initiative in seeing that his White House staff went before the Senate Watergate committee. "I was determined that we should get to the bottom of the matter," the president said, "and that the truth should be fully brought out no matter who was involved. At the same time, I was determined not to take precipitous action and to avoid if at all possible any action that would appear to reflect on innocent people. I wanted to be fair, but I knew that in the final analysis the integrity of this office—public faith in the integrity of this office—would have to take priority over all personal considerations."

He described as "one of the most difficult decisions of my presidency" his acceptance of the resignations of "two of my closest associates in the White House—Bob Haldeman, John Ehrlichman—two of the finest public servants it has been my privilege to know."

Although he should have been outraged that they had deceived him, he stressed that in accepting their resignations he meant "to leave no implication whatever of personal wrongdoing on their part." Kleindienst's resignation was necessary, the president explained, because he was "a close personal and professional associate of some of those who are involved in this case." He did not name them, but I knew that he was speaking of Mitchell, Dean, and former Assistant Attorney General Robert Mardian. The president took pains to absolve Kleindienst of any "personal involvement whatever," but dismissed Dean with a curt: "The counsel to the president, John Dean, has also resigned."

The president sought to portray himself as a man so caught up in the search for peace in Peking and Moscow, and so weary from it, that he could not personally direct his 1972 campaign as he had in earlier years.

"Who then is to blame for what happened in this case?"

For specific criminal actions by specific individuals, those who committed those actions must of course bear the liability and pay the penalty. For the fact that alleged improper actions took place within the White House or within my campaign organization, the easiest course would be for me to blame those I delegated the responsibility to run the campaign. But that would be a cowardly thing to do.

I will not place the blame of subordinates, on people whose zeal exceeded their judgment and who may have done wrong in a cause they deeply believed to be right.

In any organization the man at the top must bear the responsibility. That responsibility, therefore, belongs here in this office. I accept it.

I pledge to you tonight from this office that I will do everything in my power to insure that the guilty are brought to justice and that such abuses are purged from our political processes in the years to come long after I have left this office.

Mr. Nixon paid tribute to the system that had kept the Watergate from being covered up, "a system that in this case had included a determined grand jury, honest prosecutors, a courageous judge—John Sirica—and a vigorous free press. It is essential now that we place our faith in that system and especially in the judicial system." Later he declared: "We must maintain the integrity of the White House. And that integrity must be real, not transparent. There can be no whitewash at the White House."

The president had turned many a clever phrase, and his performance had a genuine ring to many who watched it on television. But when his words were measured against his inaction and his persistent tightening of executive privilege, they emerged as hollow and faithless.

The president proposed Elliot Richardson, then secretary of defense, to be the new attorney general, replacing Kleindienst. He pledged that Richardson would be both "fair and fearless in pursuing the case wherever it leads." Although I had no doubt about Richardson's ability or his basic integrity, I believed him too ambitious and too crafty to be permitted to handle the Watergate investigation as an appointee of Richard Nixon. By now, I felt, it had been obvious to everyone that a special prosecutor should be appointed, as I had suggested ten months earlier.

On May 1, Senator Charles H. Percy of Illinois earned the undying wrath of President Nixon by introducing a resolution calling upon the president to appoint a special Watergate prosecutor from outside the executive branch. The resolution, co-sponsored by twelve other Republicans and six Democrats, called for the president to grant the special prosecutor all authority necessary and proper for the effective performance of his duties, and stipulated: "The president should submit the name of such designee to the Senate, requesting a resolution of approval."

"A simple and very basic question is at issue," Senator Percy said.

"Should the executive branch investigate itself? I do not think so." President Nixon was reported to have responded to Percy's resolution in anger at a cabinet meeting on May 1, vowing that Percy, a man of recognized presidential ambitions, would never be president "as long as I have anything to say about it."

Confirmation hearings for Elliot Richardson centered on the fact that the same conflict of interest which had caused Kleindienst to resign would represent a barrier to Richardson's objectivity. Senators John Tunney (D., Calif.), Marlow Cook (R., Ky.), and Robert Byrd (D., W.V.) called attention to the fact that Richardson was "certainly a close friend" of John Ehrlichman. It was also pointed out that Richardson was an old friend and political associate of White House Special Counsel Charles W. Colson. Both Ehrlichman and Colson were believed to have been involved in the Watergate affair.

Senator Sam Ervin opened the Senate Watergate hearing on May 17 with comments on the "atmosphere of . . . utmost gravity" as he launched a "probe into assertions that the very [political] system itself has been subverted and its foundations shaken." Said Ervin: "Our citizens do not know whom to believe, and many of them have concluded that all the processes of government have become so compromised that honest government has been rendered impossible."

The next day, as James McCord was testifying about offers of "executive clemency" and political pressures to remain silent from "the very highest levels of the White House," Elliot Richardson announced his selection of Harvard Law School professor Archibald Cox as special Watergate prosecutor. The appointment of the sixty-one-year-old Cox, who had been solicitor general during the Kennedy administration, quieted the Democratic opposition to Richardson as attorney general. On May 23 the Senate confirmed him after assurances that he would not interfere with the independent decisions of Cox unless there were indications of "gross impropriety."

McCord poured out a well-documented story of the manner in which he was hired by the Nixon re-election committee and was told by Liddy of the role of Mitchell, Dean, and Magruder. McCord also related that he had discussions of executive clemency with John J. Caulfield, a former Ehrlichman aide in the White House. He testified about a number of clandestine meetings with Caulfield and said Caulfield had told him that he was "carrying the message of executive clemency to me 'from the very highest levels of the White House.' He stated that the president of the United States in Key Biscayne, Florida, that weekend, had been told of the forthcoming meeting with me, and would be immediately told of the results of the meeting." According to McCord, Caulfield had told him that at their next meeting he might have a message for McCord "from the president himself." In a third meeting with Caulfield on January 25, McCord said, he had complained of "the massive injustice of the whole trial" while declaring that he "would fight it every way I know." McCord said that Caulfield had accused him of "fouling up the game plan" and warned: "You know that if the administration gets its back to the wall, it will have to take steps to defend itself." Said McCord: "I took that as a personal threat and I told him in response that I had a good life, that my will was made out and that I had thought through the risks and would take them when I was ready. He said that if I had to go off to jail the administration would help with the bail premiums."

Caulfield corroborated McCord's testimony on the clandestine meetings and the discussions of executive clemency. However, he identified John Dean as the originator of the clemency talk, which he assumed came from President Nixon or "at least from Mr. Ehrlichman." He said that Dean had told him to impress upon McCord the fact that "the offer of executive clemency was a sincere offer which comes from the very highest level of the White House." Dean had cautioned him not to use the president's name but to say in effect "that it comes from way up at the top." Caulfield told the committee: "At the meeting with Mr. Dean he also impressed upon me that this was a very grave situation which might someday threaten the president, that it had the potential of becoming a national scandal and that many people in the White House were concerned over it."

On May 21, a Senate Foreign Relations Subcommittee became embroiled in the Watergate controversy when Senator Stuart Symington (D., Mo.) revealed a "memorandum of conversation by Deputy CIA Director Vernon A. Walters relating to a meeting with Haldeman, Ehrlichman, and Walters and then CIA Director Richard Helms on June 23, 1972—six days after the Watergate burglary." Walters was told by Haldeman that "it is the president's wish" that he ask Pat Gray to stop the FBI investigation of the laundering of campaign funds through a bank in Mexico City. Haldeman issued a statement shortly after Symington's: "I can flatly say the president was not involved in any cover-up of anything at any time." Another Walters memorandum revealed that Gray told Nixon during a telephone conversation in early July 1972 that the Watergate case could not be covered up and that the president "should get rid of the people who were involved." Gray had given no names to Walters, except to say that "the matter would lead quite high." He had also told the president, "Any attempt to involve the FBI or the CIA in this case could only prove a mortal wound and would achieve nothing."

The White House press office announced that President Nixon would give a full and definitive speech on Watergate that would answer all of the questions being raised by the public and by Congress. Most of that May 22, 1973, speech was clever rhetoric designed to give the impression that all actions taken to restrain the FBI and CIA were necessary to preserve national security. "I wanted justice done with regard to Watergate," President Nixon said. "I also had to be deeply concerned with insuring that neither the cover operations of the CIA nor the operations of the special investigations unit should be compromised. Therefore, I instructed Mr. Haldeman and Mr. Ehrlichman to insure that the investigation of the break-in not expose either an unrelated covert operation of the CIA or the activities of the White House investigative unit (the so-called Pumbers)—and to see that this was personally coordinated between General Walters, the deputy director of the CIA, and Mr. Gray of the FBI." Mr. Nixon made the admission that he was forced to make in light of the Walters memorandum, and then explained glibly: "It was certainly not my intent, nor my wish, that the investigation of the Watergate break-in or of related acts be impeded in any way."

Nixon related that he had telephoned Pat Gray to compliment him on the successful handling of the hijacking of a Pacific Southwest Airlines plane and that Gray had discussed the progress of the Watergate investigation. "Mr. Gray suggested that the matter of Watergate might lead higher," President Nixon admitted. "I told him to press ahead."

Although, as the White House tapes later showed, he had full knowledge of the effort to use the CIA to cover up Watergate, President Nixon told the American people that the motivations of his various aides were "complex" and that there had been "possible misunderstandings."

I was not aware of any such efforts [at concealment] at the time. Neither, until after I began my own investigation, was I aware of any fund-raising for defendants convicted at the break-in at Democratic headquarters, much less authorize any such fund-raising. Nor did I authorize any offer of executive clemency for any of the defendants.

In the weeks and months that followed Watergate, I asked for, and received, repeated assurances that Mr. Dean's own investigation (which included reviewing files and sitting in on FBI interviews with White House personnel) had cleared everyone then employed by the White House of involvement. With hindsight, it is apparent that I should have given more heed to the warning signals I received along the way about a Watergate cover-up and less to the reassurances.

The truth about Watergate should be brought out in an orderly way, recognizing that the safeguards of judicial procedure are designed to find the truth, not to hide the truth. With his selection of Archibald Cox—who served both President Kennedy and President Johnson as solicitor general—as the special supervisory prosecutor for matters related to the case, Attorney General–designate Richardson has demonstrated his own determination to see the truth brought out. In this effort he has my full support.

Considering the number of persons involved in this case whose testimony might be subject to a claim of executive privilege, I recognize that a clear definition of that claim has become central to the effort to arrive at the truth.

Accordingly, executive privilege will not be invoked as to any testimony concerning possible criminal conduct or discussions of possible criminal conduct, in the matters presently under investigation, including the Watergate affair and the alleged cover-up.

With the president's assurance that executive privilege would not be used as a cover-up for crime, and with his affirmation that Richardson and Cox would be backed all the way in a search for the truth, the Senate confirmed Elliot Richardson as attorney general. Three members of the Senate— Joseph R. Biden (D., Del.), Mike Gravel (D., Alaska), and Harold Hughes (D., Iowa)—voted against confirmation, and Senator Robert Byrd gave "reluctant" support to the nomination. "There has already been too long a delay in the full and thorough prosecution of all the crimes suspected to have been committed in the context of what has become a generic term for infamy —Watergate," Byrd said, prodding Richardson and Cox to move quickly.

On May 29, Press Secretary Ziegler said that President Nixon would not give oral or written testimony to the grand jury or the Senate under any condition. "It would be constitutionally inappropriate. It would do violence to the separation of powers."

John Dean had not yet testified, but the evidence of White House crimes had been documented to my satisfaction when I wrote in my May 27, 1973, column:

> Although the Senate hearings on the Watergate affair are only beginning, it is already firmly established that there was a White House conspiracy to obstruct justice.
>
> There already are enough admissions by those engaged in the operation to indicate the framework of conspiracy evidence. The only point not yet firmly established is the degree of culpability of President Nixon himself.
>
> A strong circumstantial case is being made that the president knew, or should have known, the role his most trusted aides had in planning and execution of the Watergate burglary and the subsequent White House conspiracy to obstruct justice through a cover-up.
>
> The president must understand that he will be accountable, at least to the degree of any reasonably prudent man under the same or similar circumstances.
>
> Certainly, the first days of hearings have placed the burden of proof upon President Nixon to explain why he did not know those things that were in the public domain. That would be the minimum standard he should expect to be held to when we rely upon our president to have available the most complete information of any person in the world.
>
> To be convincing, an explanation will have to go beyond the contention that he was so busy with the massive details of the Russian wheat sales and disarmament talks that the "third-rate burglary" at the Watergate was unworthy of his attention.
>
> It was no surprise to me to see evidence emerging on the efforts of . . . Haldeman and . . . Ehrlichman to misuse the power of the president, to corrupt the FBI, to illegally misuse the Central Intelligence Agency . . . and to try to buy the silence of witnesses with promises of executive clemency.
>
> Ehrlichman and Haldeman don't dispute that they took part in certain meetings with top officials of the FBI, CIA, White House staff and officials of the Committee to Re-elect the President. They only disagree on the words they are reported to have used and, of course, both conclude they have committed no crimes.
>
> Corroboration is so deep that the only real question at issue is whether Haldeman and Ehrlichman informed the president of their activities, as they had a responsibility to do, or whether they were acting on their own.
>
> Regardless of the answer, serious questions are raised about the integrity or competency of the man in the Oval Office who must be trusted to look out for the best interests of the nation.

I reviewed my efforts in July 1972 to get the White House to appoint a bipartisan commission to investigate the Watergate affair and the rejection of my suggestion at that time. Still trying to avoid the conclusion that President Nixon had guilty knowledge of the cover-up and was in fact a participant in a criminal obstruction of justice, I wrote: "The dictatorial rule of Haldeman and Ehrlichman was imposed so cleverly that the identity of the forces of secrecy were not apparent from outside the White House. They also were difficult to cope with and impossible to conquer from the inside. From the president's continued praise of Haldeman and Ehrlichman, I must assume at this stage that he wanted it that way."

Picking a phrase from an earlier period when Mr. Nixon had been bitterly critical of Secretary of State Dean Acheson for saying that he "would not turn his back on Alger Hiss," I wrote: "President Nixon 'has not turned his back on' Haldeman and Ehrlichman, and, until he does, the public is free to draw logical conclusions from that posture."

I hoped Richard Nixon was not involved in the crimes, for this would mean that Haldeman and Ehrlichman could compel him to defend them with all of the power of the presidency, and this would inevitably mean a long and arduous effort to impeach the president. It was chilling to contemplate the steps an embattled president might take to defend himself, his position in history, and the authoritarian duo he still referred to as "two of the finest public servants it has been my privilege to know." The chilling possibility of the ultimate game plan for the commander in chief had been spelled out by Kleindienst in his Senate testimony. I didn't really think that military defiance of the courts and Congress would take place, but a desperate president might give it more than a passing thought. It couldn't happen here. The American people would not stand for it. But were Americans so different from the citizens of many other countries who had accommodated themselves to various brands of authoritarianism?

*Chapter Thirty-six*

# NIXON'S THE ONE

UNTIL JOHN DEAN testified, in the last week of June 1973, there was no direct evidence in public forums that President Nixon had knowledge of the Watergate cover-up. Rumors abounded, but the "informed sources" were of questionable reliability. As the direct evidence accumulated against Haldeman and Ehrlichman, and as the circumstantial evidence made it increasingly likely that Mr. Nixon must know, I continued to hope that the president of the United States was not using the power of his office to direct a criminal conspiracy to obstruct justice. One had to conclude that a massive conspiracy did exist and that it had some central direction from the White House. I knew that John Dean had been coordinating some aspects of that conspiracy, but from my own experience I knew that he had neither the authority nor the motivation to engage in such a serious crime unless he believed it had the approval of President Nixon. I also knew that Haldeman and Ehrlichman were clever and ruthless in manipulating and controlling President Nixon's contacts with others. It was thus possible that Dean believed that President Nixon was involved in the crime but that President Nixon did not have the guilty knowledge of those actions which makes the difference between a hard-nosed, ruthless political operation and a criminal conspiracy.

From the first day Dean testified there existed a *prima facie* case that President Nixon had knowledge of and encouraged criminal acts from the Oval Office and from his hideaway office in the Executive Office Building. The former presidential counsel, in a firm voice, refrained from charging President Nixon with crime but simply testified about conversations with the president, Haldeman, Ehrlichman, Mitchell, and Colson which established beyond any reasonable doubt that Richard Nixon was a participant in the conspiracy. Could John Dean be believed, or would his testimony fall apart in the withering fire of personal attacks from the White House press office? Could his statements withstand assaults from Republican leaders in the House and Senate who willingly accepted the characterization of John Dean as a liar and a perjurer trying to save his own skin by testifying in order to obtain immunity from criminal prosecution? While I liked John Dean, I was uncertain about his reliability as a witness or his understanding of criminal law, executive privilege, and the need for corroboration by documents and witnesses if his story was to stand up under attack. In my conversations with him about the Ernest Fitzgerald case in February and March, he seemed superficial in his understanding of evidence and with no grasp of the history or practical political realities involved in invoking executive privilege.

A few days before Dean's appearance I had talked to his lawyer, Charles N. Shaffer, whom I regarded as one of the best criminal lawyers I had known in thirty years of covering trials. I knew that he was particularly aware of the necessity to fully corroborate a co-conspirator because this had been a major problem in the Hoffa and Baker investigations, during which he had served as a Justice Department lawyer. Shaffer would have quite properly declined to discussed the details of corroboration had I asked, but I knew that he would give me the benefit of his judgment as long as it did not disclose a weakness in his client's position.

"Is Dean well corroborated?" I asked. "You know he is going to face an unprecedented attack on his credibility."

"We know our business," Shaffer said, speaking for himself and for the other counsel, Robert C. McCandless. "Dean will tell the truth. He will be corroborated by witnesses and documents." This opinion carried weight with me because I knew of Shaffer's thoroughness. Had he had any doubts, he would simply have indicated that he wasn't sure. However, he said that Dean had a large number of documents in a bank safe deposit box to support some important aspects of his case and that nearly every witness who had testified up to that point was corroborative of the story Dean would tell.

When he testified, Dean avoided any effort to excuse himself or to blame others for his own involvement:

It is a very difficult thing for me to testify about other people. It is far more easy for me to explain my own involvement in this matter, the fact that I was involved in obstructing justice, the fact that I assisted another in perjured testimony, that I made personal use of funds that were in my custody.

Some of these people I will be referring to are friends, some are men I greatly admire and respect and particularly with reference to the president of the United States, I would like to say this. It is my honest belief that while the president was involved that he did not realize or appreciate at any time the implications of his involvement.

"When the facts come out I hope the president is forgiven," Dean said, showing a magnanimous attitude which prevailed even during White House–directed efforts to discredit him. His testimony suggested that President Nixon had been the victim of a great deception.

Dean testified about three meetings in early 1972—two at the Justice Department and one at Key Biscayne—to develop plans to spy on the Democrats. It was in the office of Attorney General Mitchell that Liddy proposed and discussed "a mind-boggling" plan for the Nixon re-election committee to use "mugging squads, kidnapping teams, prostitutes to compromise the opposition, and electronic surveillance," to learn Democratic campaign strategy. Potential targets were Democratic Chairman Lawrence F. O'Brien and the leading Democratic candidates. Dean related that when Liddy's presentation was completed Mitchell "took a few puffs on his pipe and told Liddy that the plan he had developed was not quite what he had in mind and the [million-dollar] cost was out of the question." Dean told the committee that Liddy and Magruder returned with a revised plan on February 4, which Dean said he squelched with the comment that "these discussions [of criminal acts] could not go on in the office of the attorney general of the United States and that the meeting should terminate immediately." That was Dean's last direct contact with the Liddy plan, and he believed it was dead until it was revived by Magruder in March in response to the prodding of Haldeman and Colson.

Dean said that he had no knowledge of any illegal actions until a day after the June 17, 1972, arrests at the Watergate. He had been out of the country, and when he arrived in San Francisco on June 18 and called his assistant, Fred Fielding, he was advised of the burglary and advised to return to Washington immediately. In the next twenty-four hours, on John Ehrlichman's instructions, he talked to Liddy, Caulfield, Colson, Strachan, Haldeman, and Kleindienst, and learned of the involvement of Liddy and Hunt. Dean recalled a meeting with Ehrlichman and Colson on the afternoon of Monday, June 19, in which "Ehrlichman instructed me to call Liddy and to have him tell Hunt to get out of the country."

"I did this, without even thinking," Dean testified. "Shortly after I made the call, however, I realized no one in the White House should give such an instruction, and raised the matter. . . . Ehrlichman said that he [Hunt] was not a fugitive from justice so why not. I said that I did not think it was very wise. At this point Colson chimed in that he also thought it unwise and Ehrlichman agreed. I immediately called Liddy again to retract the request but he informed me that he had already passed the message and it might be too late to retract."

Hunt's status in the White House became the subject of discussion, Dean said, with a dispute about records kept by Bruce Kehrli, one of Dean's legal assistants, that were inconsistent with Colson's contention that Hunt should have been removed from the White House payroll as of March 31, 1972. The matter was eventually resolved as Colson wanted it. "I always assumed that this required some alteration of the records, but I do not know this for a fact," Dean said cautiously. He then related his and Kehrli's roles in opening Hunt's safe and making an inventory of its contents. Dean testified that Strachan, a legal aide to Haldeman, "told me that he had been instructed by Haldeman to go through all of Mr. Haldeman's files over the weekend [of June 17–18] and remove and destroy damaging material. He [Strachan] told me that this material included such matters as memoranda from the re-election committee, documents relating to wiretap information from the DNC [Democratic National Committee], notes of meetings with Haldeman, and a document which reflected that Haldeman had instructed Magruder to transfer his intelligence-gathering from Senator Muskie to Senator McGovern." Dean said that Haldeman's aide "told me his files were completely clean."

Dean testified that he met with Kleindienst on June 19 or June 20 at Ehrlichman's suggestion.

When I went to Kleindienst's office I found him totally dismayed and angered that such a stupid thing could occur. He then told me that over the previous weekend, while at the Burning Tree Country Club, Liddy sought him out. He [Kleindienst] said he was incredulous when Liddy stated that John Mitchell had instructed him [Liddy] to tell Kleindienst to get the men who had been arrested out of jail. He told me that Liddy was rattled and upset and wanted to alk about the entire matter, but Kleindienst told me that he cut Liddy off and told him he would not talk with him.

Dean's testimony was worse than I could have imagined. One attorney general—the nation's chief law enforcement officer—sitting in on the planning of a crime, and his successor so compromised politically that he refused to be apprised of the crime by one of the admitted participants. A bizarre proliferation of felonies had resulted from the effort to hide the original crime—destruction and alteration of records, subornation of perjury, perjury, misuse of the FBI and the CIA, payoffs to the Watergate burglars and their lawyers to keep them quiet, and the favoritism shown by permitting Maurice Stans to escape testifying before a federal grand jury.

Dean admitted that all the evidence of President Nixon's involvement was circumstantial until September 15, 1972—the day the federal grand jury returned the indictment against the five Watergate burglars, Liddy, and Hunt.

Late that afternoon I received a call requesting me to come to the president's Oval Office. When I arrived at the Oval Office I found Haldeman and the president. . . . The president then told me that Bob—referring to Haldeman—had kept him posted on my handling of the Watergate case. The president told me I had done a good job and he appreciated how difficult a task it had been and the President was pleased the case had stopped with Liddy.

I responded that I could not take credit because others had done much more difficult things than I had done. As the president discussed the present status of the situation I told him that all that I had been able to do was to contain the case and assist in keeping it out of the White House. I also told him that there was a long way to go before this matter would end and that I certainly could make no assurance that the day would not come when this matter would start to unravel.

Dean recalled that President Nixon said "he certainly hoped that the [criminal] case would not come to trial before the election" and asked about the status of a civil damage suit brought by the Democratic National Committee. "I then told the president that the lawyers at the re-election committee were very hopeful of slowing down the civil suit filed by the Democratic National Committee because they had been making *ex parte* contacts with the judge handling the case and the judge was very understanding and trying to accommodate their problem," Dean testified. "The president was pleased to hear this and responded, 'Well, that's helpful.' "

Dean related that there was a "brief discussion" of the House Banking and Currency Committee, led by Wright Patman, and the possibility of hearings before the election. "The president indicated that [Special Assistant] Bill Timmons should stay on top of the . . . [Patman committee], that we did not need the hearings before the election," Dean testified. He then told of his role in stopping the Patman committee and in discussions of payoffs to the Watergate burglars, of the problems with Howard Hunt after his wife's death, and of discussions of executive clemency with Colson, Ehrlichman, Caulfield, and President Nixon.

Dean testified about White House plans to pull political strings and use executive privilege to continue covering up its responsibility for the Watergate burglary. Dean said that in late February 1973 he started meeting more frequently with President Nixon in order to make a claim of executive privilege more credible and that in several of these meetings, starting on February 28, he told President Nixon that he [Dean] might be involved in a criminal obstruction of justice. "He [President Nixon] would not accept my analysis and did not want to get into it in any detail other than what I had just related," Dean said, referring to the February 28 meeting. "He reassured me not to worry, that I had no legal problems." Again, on March 1, the subject of executive privilege came up. Dean said that President Nixon had asked him about the timing of the release of the executive privilege statement which had been promised to me at his January 31 press conference.

Dean testified that executive privilege, as a cover-up device, was discussed at a number of meetings with the president in early March and was explored in detail at a March 13 meeting. There were demands for Dean to appear before the Senate Judiciary Committee hearings on the Gray nomination at the time, and Dean testified that he and the president "discussed the potential of litigating the matter of executive privilege," thus stalling the appearance of any White House witnesses before that committee until it had been resolved in the court. "The president liked the idea very much, particularly when I mentioned to him that it might be possible that he could also claim attorney-client privilege on me so that the strongest potential case on executive privilege would probably rest on the counsel to the president," Dean said. "He [the president] told me that he did not want Haldeman and Ehrlichman to go before the Ervin hearings and that if we were litigating the matter on Dean, that no one would have to appear." Dean said that the conversation then swung to the demands for money being made by the convicted Watergate burglars, and that there was no money to meet their demands.

He [Nixon] asked me how much it would cost. I told him that I could only make an estimate that it might be as high as $1 million or more. He told me that was no problem, and he looked over at Haldeman and repeated the same statement. He then asked me who was demanding this money and I told him it was principally coming from Hunt through his attorney.

The president then referred to the fact that Hunt had been promised executive clemency. He said that he had discussed the matter with Ehrlichman and, contrary to instructions that Ehrlichman had given Colson not to talk to the President about it, that Colson had also discussed it with him later. He expressed some annoyance at the fact that Colson had also discussed this matter with him.

The conversation then returned to the question of providing money to the convicted Watergate burglars and "how this was done." Dean testified, "I told him I didn't know much about it other than the fact that the money was laundered so it could not be traced and then there were secret deliveries." He said that there was further rambling conversation around it but that "the matter was left hanging" as he left the March 13 meeting.

After a number of meetings with the president to discuss Watergate, Dean said, he became concerned that the president did not understand that he had implicated himself in a criminal obstruction of justice by promising executive clemency to Hunt. On March 21 Dean opened the meeting "by telling the president that there was a cancer growing on the presidency and that if the cancer was not removed the president himself would be killed by it." Dean's testimony on that meeting was to be the focal point of heated debate and denials, as was the question of whether, at the meeting, President Nixon gave approval to pay $75,000 in "hush money" to Hunt.

John Dean was in the witness chair for five days, from June 25 through June 29. When it was over, Chairman Sam Ervin and most other members of the committee kept a neutral stance and said they wanted to hear President Nixon's side. Senator Joseph M. Montoya (D., N. Mex.) stated that he believed the young lawyer had been "a very credible witness." Senator Edward J. Gurney, a Florida Republican who was bitterly critical of Dean's testimony, called the former Nixon counsel "a shoddy turncoat" and declared that it would be "absolutely demeaning" for President Nixon to defend himself against Dean's testimony. Gurney and other defenders of the president seized on Dean's admission that he had "borrowed" $4,200 in cash from campaign money for a honeymoon in the fall of 1972 and had waited to repay it until early April 1973, after a conference with his lawyer, Charles N. Shaffer, prior to entering into negotiations with the prosecutors from the United States attorney's office. Dean defended his action by saying that he had exchanged his personal check for the cash when he borrowed the money and that he had never intended to keep it, but Gurney and other Republicans continued to refer to it as an "embezzlement." *

During Dean's appearance at the hearing, I chatted with him several times about the problems of conscience he must have been having in regard to the Watergate cover-up at the same time as he was trying to convince me not to testify for Fitzgerald. I also made a light reference to his call after the press conference at which I had asked President Nixon if he would use executive privilege if there was a *prima facie* case that his counsel was involved in crime. Dean admitted that he had called because he was curious to know whether I had uncovered evidence of his obstruction of justice. I acknowledged that I had had no concrete evidence but said that all signs had pointed in his direction. I told him that I was impressed with his excellence as a witness and that his discussion of the problem of getting through Haldeman and Ehrlichman was consistent with my own difficulty in communicating directly with President Nixon. We briefly discussed what I had written about executive privilege in *Washington Cover-Up,* and Dean said that he agreed completely with my thesis that excessive secrecy is corruptive and should not be tolerated.

Dean's testimony assumed greater credence when it was corroborated by other major witnesses—former Attorney General Mitchell; Richard A. Moore, special counsel to President Nixon; and Herbert Kalmbach, personal lawyer for President Nixon and a major collector of funds for the Nixon re-election committee. But it was Alexander P. Butterfield, former deputy assistant to President Nixon and top aide to Haldeman, whose testimony eventually provided John Dean with the ultimate in corroboration—verbatim recordings of his conversations with President Nixon in the Oval Office and in the Executive Office Building. Butterfield had installed and supervised the taping system under orders from Haldeman and the president.** A former Air Force colonel,

* Senator Gurney, a consistent defender of President Nixon, was indicted by a county grand jury in Tallahassee, Florida, on a state misdemeanor charge of having violated the state election laws. That indictment was dismissed by a state judge, Charles McClure, on May 17, 1974, as being technically "defective." On July 10, 1974, a federal grand jury in Florida indicted Gurney on charges of bribery, conspiracy, and lying to the grand jury in connection with a scheme of influence peddling and extortion to raise campaign funds. Gurney and six others were accused of having conspired to demand money from Florida contractors and developers with "matters pending" before the Department of Housing and Urban Development. It was alleged that Gurney extorted $223,160 for personal and political use in a 3½-year period starting in December 1970. The trial of Gurney, who did not seek re-election in 1974, took place in early 1975, and resulted in a hung jury on the conspiracy charge and acquittal on six other counts.
** See note on p. 368.

Butterfield had been named administrator of the Federal Aviation Administration a few months prior to July 16, 1973, when he was called to testify as to the existence of the White House tapes. All of Mr. Nixon's conversations in the Oval Office, the Executive Office Building, and several other key places had been recorded since the summer of 1971.

Although the White House used executive privilege to bar the Senate committee from access to the tapes, I believed that even the knowledge of their existence would keep the witnesses honest. If the tapes contained conversations relevant to the issues being investigated by the Senate Select Committee or the special prosecutor, I was certain that they would eventually become public even though President Nixon vowed that they would never be released to the courts or the Congress. As President Nixon defied the subpoenas of the Ervin committee and Special Prosecutor Archibald Cox to produce the tapes of his key conversations with Dean, testimony from Haldeman almost entirely corroborated Dean's testimony on the conversations of September 15, 1972, and March 21, 1973. Haldeman had been given permission by President Nixon to listen to a number of the tapes, and he was permitted to testify as to the conversations on those tapes in a manner which was intended to discredit Dean. Haldeman's ploy successfully misled most of the news writers and television commentators, who stressed his very general denial of President Nixon's guilty knowledge of the Watergate cover-up, but they overlooked these important points of Haldeman's testimony:

1. There were conversations in the Oval Office between President Nixon and Dean on September 15, 1972, and on March 21, 1973. Haldeman was present during significant parts of those conversations, and both dealt with Watergate.

2. The September 15 conversation covered the Watergate indictments, which had been returned that day, and President Nixon's congratulations to Dean for having handled those investigations well and keeping them contained.

3. The September 15 conversation had covered a discussion of ways of stopping hearings by Patman's House Banking and Currency Committee and an assessment of the problem posed by the Democratic National Committee's damage suit against the Nixon re-election committee.

4. The March 21 conversations included Dean's warning about a cancer on the presidency and about obstruction of justice, as well as Hunt's demand for additional money and for executive clemency.

5. The March 21 conversation, as Dean had testified, included his estimate that it could cost more than a $1 million for payments to the seven Watergate defendants and their attorneys, and President Nixon's comments that it would not be difficult to raise that much money.

The only significant difference between Dean's and Haldeman's testimony were opinions and conclusions by Haldeman that Dean had arrived at "erroneous conclusions" about the president's involvement in the cover-up. Haldeman said that Nixon's comments on the million-dollar payoff were not approval but just his way of drawing Dean out. "The rest of us relied on Dean and thought that what was being done was legal and proper," Haldeman testified. He said that he, the president, and Ehrlichman had not become aware of the illegal nature of some of the things Dean had done until mid-March 1973, and that Nixon then immediately started "intensifying pressure on Dean to find a way to get the full story out."

I checked with Chairman Sam Ervin, Senator Daniel Inouye (D., Hawaii), and Senator Lowell Weicker (R., Conn.), and all agreed that Haldeman's testimony established the accuracy of Dean's. Charles Shaffer said that he considered that "Haldeman actually corroborated Dean about 95 percent of the way," substantiating his own belief that Dean was conscientiously trying to tell the truth. Haldeman had challenged Dean on one factual point— whether a specific conversation took place on March 13 or March 21. Shaffer noted that even if Dean were in error as to whether a specific phrase was used in the March 13 or March 21 meeting, it was really immaterial, since both conversations had dealt with Hunt's demands for more money.

Sam Dash, the chief counsel for the Senate Select Committee, also considered Haldeman's testimony largely corroborative of Dean's and said that Dean's testimony was so well corroborated that it made a firm *prima facie* case of President Nixon's involvement in a criminal obstruction of justice. In August, Dash made his first court arguments for release of the White House tapes, declaring that a *prima facie* case of obstruction of justice existed against President Nixon. Dash argued that only through the tapes could the meaning of President Nixon's words in the conversations with Dean, Haldeman, and others be firmly established.

Senator Sam Ervin declared that the committee was entitled to hear the tapes and should not be required to accept Haldeman's interpretation of the conversations. Senator Ervin and Senator Inouye expressed concern that Haldeman had taken several of the tapes to his home and kept them overnight with President Nixon's permission. It was the president's responsibility to keep those tapes where they would be safe from any erasure or tampering, Ervin said. "If those tapes would prove that John Dean is a liar, and that the president is telling the truth, I am sure that there wouldn't be this reluctance to produce them."

Inouye declared, "If a private citizen of the U.S. can get permission to listen to the tapes in private at home, the Senate Select Committee should be able to hear them," a view which was eventually supported by all seven members of the committee.

The American people agreed that the simple way to reveal the truth would be to listen to the recordings and hear the precise words and inflection. The people weren't interested in arguments about executive privilege, separation of powers, or protecting the office of the president. They were interested in the truth as it would be disclosed on the tapes. There was no acceptable argument for not playing them. Anything less was such a blatant concealment of the truth that the overwhelming majority of the Republicans, including Senate Republican Leader Scott and House Republican Leader Ford, felt compelled to agree that the tapes should be produced.

*Chapter Thirty-seven*

# NIXON STONEWALLS

THE TELEVISED Watergate hearings had a devastating impact on President Nixon's popularity. The August 14, 1973, Gallup poll showed that public approval of him had slipped to 31 percent, while 57 percent disapproved of the way he was handling the presidency. It was the lowest rating of any president since President Truman slipped to the same low score in January 1953 after an administration punctuated by scandals. Most startling was the fact that the president's popularity had plummeted to that level only nine months after his landslide victory and only seven months after he received 68 percent approval as he was starting his second term. The Gallup organization found that 73 percent of the public believed that Nixon was involved in or had knowledge of the Watergate bugging or the alleged cover-up. Only 15 percent felt that he had no knowledge of either.

Faced with this degree of public skepticism, President Nixon appropriated prime time for a television address on August 15 to try to convince the people that "I neither took part in nor knew about any of the subsequent cover-up activities. I neither authorized nor encouraged subordinates to engage in illegal or improper campaign tactics. That was and is the simple truth."

The distorted Nixon version of the Senate Watergate hearings was encapsulated in this statement: "In all of the millions of words of testimony there is not the slightest suggestion that I had any knowledge of the planning for the Watergate break-in. As for the cover-up, my statement has been challenged by only one of the thirty-five witnesses who appeared—a witness who offered no evidence beyond his own impressions, and whose testimony has been contradicted by every other witness in a position to know the facts." The president quoted his own comments of a year earlier to demonstrate that he had repeatedly emphasized that "we should get all of the facts out first": "As I said at my August 29 press conference last year, 'What really hurts in matters of this sort is not the fact that they occur, because overzealous people in campaigns do things that are wrong. What really hurts is if you try to cover it up.' "

Then he moved to the ultimate in hypocrisy, disregarding all of the evidence: "I knew that the Justice Department and the FBI were conducting intensive investigations—as I had insisted that they should. The White House counsel, John Dean, was assigned to monitor those investigations, and particularly to check into possible White House involvement. Throughout the summer of 1972, I continued to press the questions, and I continued to get the same answer that there was no indication that any persons were involved other than the seven who were known to have planned and carried out the operation." Then, as if unaware of his own use of executive privilege, the White House Press Office's stonewalling, and the obstacles tossed in the way of the Senate Select Committee on Watergate, the Senate Judiciary Committee, House Banking and Currency Committee, and the federal grand jury, Nixon asserted: "Far from trying to hide the facts, my effort throughout has been to discover the facts—and to lay those facts before the appropriate law enforcement authorities so that justice could be done and the guilty dealt with. I relied on the best law enforcement agencies in the country to find and report the truth."

Turning to the demands of Republicans and Democrats that he make the White House tapes available, President Nixon noted: "Many have urged that in order to help prove the truth of what I have said, I should turn over to the special prosecutor and the Senate committee recordings of conversations that I had in my office or on my telephone." He contended that "a much more important principle is involved in this question than what the tapes might prove about Watergate." It was not Richard Nixon he was protecting, he would have us believe, but the office of the presidency and the rights of future presidents to a confidentiality similar to that "of lawyer and client, priest and penitant, and between husband and wife."

"It is even more important that the confidentiality of conversations between a president and his advisers be protected," President Nixon told the television audience. "This is no mere luxury, to be dispensed with whenever a particular issue raises sufficient uproar." Nimbly twisting and turning away from his defiance of the courts and Congress on the tapes, Nixon slipped in a sly hint that some "national security" factor made the whole subject too sensitive for discussion except in the Oval Office.

Referring to problems such as inflation and critical international negotiations, he declared: "We cannot let an obsession with the past destroy our hopes for the future." He left the impression that John Dean and the Senate Watergate committee were impeding progress and asked for assistance in reaching the "great goals" he had for America. "I ask for your help in reaffirming our dedication to the principles of decency, honor, and respect for the institutions that have sustained our progress through these past two centuries," he said virtuously. "I ask for your support in getting on once again with meeting your problems, improving your life, and building your future."

White House Press Secretary Ronald Ziegler indicated that President Nixon would probably have a press conference—his first since March 15—later in August at San Clemente, so I joined the traveling press on the presidential trip to a Veterans of Foreign Wars convention in New Orleans on August 20. President Nixon's general irritability and a specific hostility to the press manifested itself in a rare display of temper in New Orleans. At the Rivergate Convention Center, in full view of television cameras, Mr. Nixon suddenly grabbed Ziegler by the shoulder, spun him around, and shoved him toward an astonished press corps. "I don't want the press near me," a reporter heard him bark at Ziegler. "You take care of it." The incident, coming on the heels of the Watergate hearings, and his tense, haggard appearance on the August 15 television broadcast triggered speculation. Deputy Press Secretary Gerald L. Warren was bombarded with questions, and the press corps buzzed with rumors that the incident had dynamited the planned press conference.

On August 21, the troubles of Vice President Spiro T. Agnew momentarily took the spotlight off President Nixon and Watergate. Agnew denounced leaks to the press about the federal investigation in Baltimore concerning his possible violation of criminal laws. In a televised statement, the vice president said he could only assume from press accounts "that some Justice Department officials have decided to indict me in the press whether or not the evidence supports their position." He charged that this was "a clear and outrageous effort to influence the outcome of possible grand jury deliberations."

That day I visited White House staff offices near Nixon's Casa Pacifica estate at San Clemente, talked with Presidential Counselor Bryce Harlow, and saw the presidential office and the stretch of lawn where John Ehrlichman had strolled with United States District Judge Matthew Byrne when he was approached about being nominated as director of the FBI. Later I visited with Ronald Ziegler, who greeted me warmly in his best joy-boy advertising executive fashion, assuring me that he wanted us to get along and that he hoped our past clashes would be regarded as water under the bridge. I reminded him that he still hadn't delivered on his promise of a personal interview with the president, which he had made at the time he bumped me from the China trip in February 1972. "I didn't think you meant it when you made the promise, and I don't think you've got the clout to deliver now," I told him.

"You probably don't believe this, but I really meant that promise to make up for the China trip," Ziegler said, adding that he had "talked to the president about it many times." He asserted: "I knew you were on this trip, and I even talked to him about it today."

"I'm not going to hold my breath until it happens," I answered.

Ziegler said that "the Watergate thing has upset things a lot," and "it just hasn't been possible to do some of the things we'd planned."

I reminded him that at several points during the fall of 1972 and early 1973 I had asked to see the president to discuss Watergate and the Fitzgerald case. "I told you then it was going to fall in on you, and it has," I said. "And it is going to fall more if the president doesn't make those tapes available to the Senate committee."

"But the president has to protect the office of the presidency and future presidents," Ziegler said.

"Don't give me that bunk," I retorted. "Executive privilege is a myth, and you are going to find out I know what I'm talking about when Judge Sirica rules."

Ziegler acknowledged that the Watergate affair had fallen apart in the manner I had predicted to him as early as October 1972, but he pointed out optimistically that "the television hearings are over with," and that the president expected to improve his position in the polls "when the sensationalism is past."

I told him that he was "living in a dream world" if he thought Watergate was past—"it is just beginning in the courts." I said that I fully expected Sirica to rule against an absolute executive privilege to withhold the tapes and that I expected the United States Court of Appeals for the District of Columbia to support him by an overwhelming majority. "If and when the executive privilege issue gets to the United States Supreme Court, I expect an eight-to-one or a seven-to-two decision against President Nixon," I told Ziegler. "It is one thing for a president to defy a Senate or House committee, but a law-and-order president is going to have a difficult time defying an order of the United States Supreme Court." As I was leaving, I reminded him that our future relationship was going to depend upon whether he delivered on the interview with the president. "It is your move," I said.

In an attempt to be friendly, Ziegler told me confidentially that there would probably be something the next day—August 22—that I would be interested in and that I should plan to stay close to the Surf and Sand Motel in the morning.

"A release of the figures on federal money spent on San Clemente?" I asked.

Ziegler said that that would "probably come later."

"A press conference?" I asked. "It isn't pinned down yet," he said, "but there is a good chance. It will probably be in the morning, but don't tell anyone else." I said nothing when I returned to the *Surf and Sand,* but within a few hours the place was buzzing with rumors of a press conference the next day. Ziegler had apparently confided in all the other reporters too.

The Agnew investigation would certainly be the subject of a number of questions, and President Nixon hadn't been available for questioning on Watergate since March 15. It was hard to believe that questions would be asked about any other subject. Bryce Harlow said that the president hoped this would be a press conference to get all of the Watergate questions out of the way at once.

It was a bright sunny morning as the press arrived at the Western White House and sat down to await the president. When he arrived, he walked briskly to a position behind the microphones, smiled, and read an opening statement announcing the resignation of Secretary of State William P. Rogers. He said that he would nominate Dr. Henry Kissinger as a successor to Rogers, and turned to Frances Lewin of the Associated Press for the first question.

Miss Lewin noted his contention that disclosure of the tapes could cripple the office of the presidency, pointed out that a survey showed that three out of four Americans believed he had been wrong to make the tapes, and asked him why he had done so. President Nixon commented that both President Johnson and President Kennedy had installed equipment for taping their conversations, and said he had done it to have a completely accurate history of his conduct of the presidency because he was often too tired at night to dictate his recollections for the day. On reflection, he said, he was "just as happy" that the taping had ended.

Essentially all of the questions dealt with Watergate. They were good questions, covering Gray's warnings to Nixon about deception by his highest aides, Haldeman's access to the tapes, the testimony of Mitchell, and the efforts to contact Judge Byrne when he was presiding on the Ellsberg case. Mr. Nixon reiterated his confidence in Vice President Agnew's ability to prove himself innocent of financial irregularities.

"Mr. President, do you consider Haldeman and Ehrlichman two of the finest public servants you have ever known?" a reporter asked.

Mr. Nixon responded: "I certainly do. I look upon public servants as men who've got to be judged by their entire record—not by simply parts of it." He declared that when Haldeman and Ehrlichman "have an opportunity to have their case heard in court, not simply to be tried before a committee, and tried in the press and tried in television—they will be exonerated."

The question of whether the president would obey a Supreme Court order to disclose the tapes was still open when he finally recognized me with the comment: "I'll take the big man."

"Thank you, Mr. President," I responded.

He added, "I know my troubles if I don't take him—or if I do."

"Looking to the future on executive privilege, there are a couple of questions that come to mind," I began.

He interrupted: "I thought we just passed the point."

"Well, we speak here of the future," I explained.

"All right," he said, and I continued:

"Where is the check on authoritarianism by the executive if the president is to be the sole judge of what the executive branch makes available and suppresses? And would you obey a Supreme Court order if you are asked and directed to produce the tapes or other documents for the Senate committee or the special prosecutor? And . . . is there any limitation on the president, short of impeachment, to compel the production of evidence of a criminal nature?"

"Is there anything else?" the president said in an amused tone.

"No, I think that will be enough," I responded.

"No, I was not being facetious, but I realize it's a complicated question. The answer to the first question is that there's a limitation on the president in almost all fields like this. There's of course the limitation of public opinion, and, of course, congressional and other pressures that may arise." Mr. Nixon then mentioned the ITT case and said that "this administration has, I think gone further in terms of waiving executive privilege than any administration in my memory. Certainly a lot further than Mr. Truman was willing to go when I was on the other side, as you recall, urging that he waive executive privilege." With regard to whether he would obey a Supreme Court decision,

Mr. Nixon declined to go beyond Deputy Press Secretary Gerald Warren's comment that the president would abide by "a definitive decision."

"I won't go beyond that," Mr. Nixon said. "And particularly at this time, while the matter is still being considered by Judge Sirica. I understand his decision will come down on Wednesday and then we will make a comment."

On Wednesday, August 29, Judge Sirica ordered President Nixon to turn over to him for private examination in chambers the tape recordings of presidential conversations involving the Watergate case which had been sub-poenaed by Special Prosecutor Cox. Judge Sirica had rejected Mr. Nixon's claim of immunity from the court processes but had "attempted to walk the middle ground between a failure to decide the question of privilege at one extreme and a wholesale delivery of tapes to the grand jury on the other." Sirica's opinion, as I had expected, recognized a limited presidential privilege "based on the need to protect presidential privacy" but firmly set forth the principle that the courts must decide whether a president has properly claimed the privilege. In the case before him, Judge Sirica said, he simply could not decide whether the privilege was properly invoked "without inspecting the tapes."

Judge Sirica rejected the argument of the president's attorney, Charles Alan Wright, that "there are times when other national interests are more important even than the fullest administration of criminal justice." Wright, a University of Texas law professor, declared that it was a "simple fact of history" that no court had ever attempted to do what "Special Prosecutor Cox was asking this one to do." He argued that a decision to require President Nixon to produce the tapes would set a precedent for similar claims to be made before all of the four hundred federal district judges in the country.

"What is the public interest served in withholding these tapes?" asked Judge Sirica, cutting to the heart of the matter.

When Wright responded, "The public interest in having the president able to talk in confidence with his closest advisers," Judge Sirica asked:

"The president is the sole judge of the public interest then?"

"That has been the law," Wright said.

Sirica noted that this would mean that "the president, then, is the sole judge of executive privilege."

When Wright replied in the affirmative, Judge Sirica said, "There is potential grave abuse then, it appears to me," and commented further that such absolute power appears "contrary to the system of checks and balances."

Special Prosecutor Cox, a Harvard law professor and a solicitor general of the United States in the Kennedy and Johnson administrations, had declared: "There is strong reason to believe that the integrity of the executive offices has been corrupted. . . . Public confidence in our institutions is at stake." Cox argued that the claim of executive privilege was impeding the Watergate in-vestigation and that it should not be permitted to cover up specific evidence of discussions involving criminal activity. In concluding his argument, Cox had quoted a statement of Justice Robert H. Jackson that "with all its defects . . . men have discovered no technique for long preserving free government except that the executive be under the law."

Judge Sirica, in ordering President Nixon to produce the White House tapes for court inspection, relied heavily on a ruling by Supreme Court Chief Justice John Marshall in the 1807 treason trial of Aaron Burr in which the court ordered President Thomas Jefferson to comply with a subpoena of a letter held by Jefferson. Marshall had ruled that the president could be subpoenaed to produce the evidence essential in a criminal trial but had expressed doubt as to the process to be used to compel Jefferson to appear. The issue was resolved when Jefferson declined to go to Richmond but agreed to send the letter for court examination and to testify by deposition if necessary. In line with that decision, Judge Sirica declared: "In all candor, the court fails to perceive any reason for suspending the power of the courts to get evidence and rule on questions of privilege in criminal matters simply because it is the president of the United States who holds the evidence." The stern-faced judge said that it was incumbent upon the president to define exactly why evidence should not be produced: ". . . what distinctive quality of the presidency permits its incumbent to withhold evidence?"

On August 29, the law-and-order president issued a statement from San Clemente that he "will not comply with the order," and on August 30 he announced that he would appeal the decision. This was another application of the strategy of appeal and delay that John Dean had spelled out before the Senate Watergate committee, but there was no alternative to giving the president his day in court. Chief Judge David L. Bazelon of the U.S. Court of Appeals for the District of Columbia ordered a speed-up of the schedule to get the case to the Supreme Court when it convened on October 1.

At a news conference in the East Room of the White House on September 5, President Nixon refused to comment on the kind of Supreme Court decision he would consider "definitive." "We believe—my counsel believes—that we will prevail in the appellate courts," President Nixon said. He again asserted that there was "nothing whatever" on the tapes that would contradict his public denials of involvement in the Watergate cover-up and pictured himself as bravely accepting public condemnation to preserve the rights of future presidents.

"Can you assure us that the tapes do not reflect unfavorably on your Watergate position?" a reporter asked.

"There is nothing whatever in the tapes that is inconsistent with the statement that I made on May 22 or the statement that I made to you ladies and gentlemen in answer to several questions, rather searching questions I might say, and very polite questions two weeks ago . . . ," Mr. Nixon said. "My concern is one that I have expressed, and it just does not cover tapes, it covers the appearance of a president before a congressional committee. . . . Confidentiality once destroyed cannot in my opinion be restored."

I attended the press conference, but the president did not recognize me for a question because, he said, I had had three questions at the August 22 press conference.

On October 12, the United States Circuit Court of Appeals, in a five-to-two decision, held that Sirica had been correct in ordering President Nixon to produce the Watergate tapes for examination in chambers. In directing him to deliver the nine tapes to Sirica, the Appeals Court declared that the president is "not above the law's commands." The lengthy dissenting opinion in support of absolute privilege to be exercised at the sole discretion of the president was written by two Nixon appointees—Judges George E. MacKinnon and Malcom R. Wilkey.

I called my friend Raoul Berger, a former University of California law professor who was Charles Warren Senior Fellow at Harvard Law School, to get his view of the Appeals Court decision. He was the best-informed man in America on the subject of executive privilege and had studied the attitudes of various members of the United States Supreme Court on essentially every aspect of presidential power. Berger said that he would expect an eight-to-one or seven-to-two decision of the United States Supreme Court backing Judge Sirica. "That ought to be a definitive enough decision," he commented. He expected Chief Justice Warren E. Burger and Justice William Rehnquist to support absolute executive privilege. Though support of Sirica would be consistent with Chief Justice Burger's past decisions, Berger told me, he believed that the chief justice might line up with Rehnquist on this issue because of his friendship with and loyalty to Nixon. Rehnquist had written extensively in support of the Nixon position on executive privilege as an assistant attorney general in the Justice Department, and Berger did not think that he had changed his views. We both felt that Rehnquist should disqualify himself but saw little chance of his doing so.

The White House surprised me by failing to appeal the Appeals Court decision to the Supreme Court within the five-day period, since President Nixon had indicated earlier that he would appeal to seek a final clarification of executive privilege and his right to withhold evidence. It was my private speculation that the president and his lawyers expected the Supreme Court to affirm the Sirica order, forcing him to either produce the tapes or defy an order of the Supreme Court. Delaying by appealing to higher courts was within the court process and did not appear as defiant as actually rejecting a Supreme Court order. In line with the strategy of stall and delay, I expected White House statements promising full cooperation with Judge Sirica, followed by months of quibbling half-compliance and foot-dragging. But I did not expect the president to enlarge his strategy with direct orders to Attorney General Richardson to stop Special Prosecutor Cox. That plan, however, had been developing behind the scenes for several days before it broke into the open as the "Saturday night massacre" on October 20.

*Chapter Thirty-eight*

# I AM NOT A CROOK

PRESIDENT NIXON seemed to have no alternative under the Court of Appeals decision but to produce the tapes. He then faced the real possibility that Special Prosecutor Cox would ask for still other tapes crucial in determining which grand jury witnesses were liars. But the innovative President Nixon and his White House lawyers found another alternative. Perhaps they could persuade or force Cox to agree to a compromise. They suggested that verified summaries be substituted for the tapes or transcripts of the tapes to avoid revealing national security matters and other information they considered to be of a sensitive nature.

These summaries would be prepared by White House lawyers, acting under President Nixon's supervision, and verified by Senator John Stennis, a man with a reputation for nonpartisan fairness and integrity. But since Stennis was also known as one of President Nixon's best friends and most consistent supporters in the United States Senate, Cox resisted. The president expressed the opinion that his "compromise" would resolve "any lingering thought that the president himself might have been in a Watergate cover-up" and yet would preserve a degree of confidentiality. Cox, on Friday, October 19, flatly rejected the plan and stated that he would take his objection to court, where he would argue that "the president is refusing to comply with the court decree." Cox protested that the proposed summaries, even if verified by Senator Stennis, would not have the evidentiary value of the tapes themselves. He also called attention to the White House's lack of compliance with directions to turn over "the important notes, memoranda, and other documents the court orders require."

President Nixon's order to Attorney General Richardson for the special prosecutor to cease further legal steps to obtain presidential tapes was a violation of Richardson's word as given at his confirmation hearing, Cox said, and a violation of his own pledge to the Senate and the nation "to invoke judicial process to challenge exaggerated claims of executive privilege." Cox declared that acceptance of the president's directive would "defeat the fair administration of criminal justice. It would deprive prosecutors of admissible evidence in prosecuting wrongdoers who abuse high government office. It would also enable defendants to go free, by withholding material a judge rules necessary to a fair trial. The president's action already threatens the results in the New York prosecution of John Mitchell and Maurice Stans. I cannot be a party to such an agreement." In a nationally televised press conference at the

National Press Club, Cox explained that he would bring the noncompliance with the court's order to the attention of the court and would seek to initiate contempt proceedings against President Nixon. At that press conference I asked Cox whether it would be helpful to his cause if the American people expressed their views on the subject in telegrams or letters to the White House or to the Congress. He smiled and said he believed that it would.

At 8:24 P.M. that night, the White House announced that President Nixon had discharged Cox for refusing to obey an order and Deputy Attorney General William Ruckelshaus for refusing to fire Cox. Earlier that evening Nixon had accepted the resignation of Attorney General Elliot Richardson. White House Chief of Staff Alexander Haig later referred to the public reaction to the firing of Cox and Ruckelshaus and the resignation of Richardson as "a firestorm." Others referred to the incident itself as the "Saturday night massacre." The angry president had had to go down the line to Solicitor General Richard H. Bork before he could get someone to carry out his order to fire Cox.

That tumultuous weekend a flood of protests resulted in the first serious calls for impeachment of a president who, it was now agreed, was defying the courts and breaking his pledge to the Senate and House judiciary committees by interfering with the independence of the special prosecutor. The avalanche of letters and telegrams of protest was unprecedented, and Western Union in Washington found itself inundated with messages that had reached 220,000 by Wednesday, October 24. By that time, President Nixon had bowed to protests from House Republican leaders who said that they could not defend him against impeachment unless he made the tapes available to the court. Charles Alan Wright, chief of the president's legal defense team, went before Judge Sirica to state that "the president of the United States would comply in all respects." Declared Wright, "This president does not defy the law, and he has authorized me to say he will comply in full with the orders of the court." White House Chief of Staff Haig, who had had a major role in the Saturday night massacre, admitted at a press briefing that "we all miscalculated" the reaction to the firing of Cox.

House Judiciary Committee Chairman Peter Rodino conferred on October 24 with nineteen other Democrats on the committee, and a decision was made to "proceed full steam ahead" with an impeachment investigation, even though the committee was still deeply involved in hearings on the nomination of House Republican Leader Ford to succeed vice president Agnew, who had resigned.*

* On October 10, 1973, Vice President Spiro T. Agnew resigned and entered a *nolo contendere* (no contest) plea to one count of income tax evasion. He had been charged with failing to report $29,500 in income that he received in 1967, while governor of Maryland. In return for Agnew's plea and resignation, Attorney General Elliot Richardson agreed to drop all pending charges against him and to request leniency on the tax evasion conviction. Agnew, who had faced federal indictment for violation of bribery, conspiracy, and tax laws, thus avoided imprisonment. However, the Justice Department filed a comprehensive report on the evidence against Agnew covering the period from the time

Indecision and confusion prevailed as President Nixon scheduled a national broadcast for October 24 and then cancelled it, announced that there would be a press conference on October 25 and then rescheduled it for Friday night, October 26. Mr. Nixon opened the press conference with an opening statement dealing with the situation in the Middle East. He briefly remarked that the White House counsel had contacted Judge Sirica "and arrangements were made to . . . work out the delivery of the tapes." Then he announced that the acting attorney general, Richard Bork, would appoint a new special prosecutor. "The special prosecutor will have independence," Mr. Nixon vowed, as though he had not made the same promise to Cox when he was appointed. "He will have total cooperation from the executive branch, and he will have as a primary responsibility to bring this matter, which has so long concerned the American people, bring it to an expeditious conclusion." Mr. Nixon, who had been dragging his heels for a year to prevent the disclosure of vital evidence on the tapes, said, "We have to remember that under our constitution it has always been held that justice delayed is justice denied." He declared: "It is time for those who are guilty to be prosecuted, and for those who are innocent to be cleared. And I can assure you ladies and gentlemen, and all of our listeners tonight, that I have no greater interest than to see that the new special prosecutor has the cooperation from the executive branch and the independence that he needs to bring about that conclusion." How many times since July 1972 had we heard Mr. Nixon say that he only wanted to get the truth out in the open, to make sure the guilty were prosecuted, while he imposed the ultimate in executive privilege to withhold vital evidence?

The first question was from Frank Cormier of the Associated Press, who asked whether the new special prosecutor would have access to White House files if he felt it was necessary. "Well, Mr. Cormier," President Nixon responded, "I would anticipate that would not be necessary. I believe that as we look at the events which led to the dismissal of Mr. Cox we find that these are matters that can be worked out and should be worked out in cooperation and not by having a suit filed by a special prosecutor within the executive branch against the president of the United States." Then Mr. Nixon declared that this was not a new attitude and was the same thing that every president since George Washington had done to protect the confidentiality of presidential conversations. I knew from my talks with him that he knew this to be historically inaccurate. President Nixon obviously expected to exert control over his so-called independent special prosecutor unless the Congress intervened with legislation or won a clearly worded promise from him personally.

Other questions probed the issue of impeachment or resignation, his treatment of Cox, and a $100,000 cash fund which his friend, Charles (Bebe) Rebozo, had received from billionaire industrialist Howard Hughes. As the press conference moved on, it was obvious to me that he did not intend to

---

he was Baltimore county executive through his first term as vice president.

On October 12, President Nixon revealed that House Minority Leader Gerald Ford was his choice to succeed Agnew as vice president.

modify his use of executive privilege despite the Appeals Court decision. He avoided recognizing me a number of times because he did not wish to face a specific question on that subject. I raised my voice to shout "Mr. President" in the loud scramble for recognition. After trying for some time to ignore me, he said, with a weak smirk: "You are so loud, I will have to take you."

This was a gratuitous insult meant to put me down before I had even asked my question, and I snapped back: "I have to be, because you happen to dodge my questions all of the time."

He came back with the erroneous excuse: "You had three last time."

I let the error pass and stated my question: "Last May you went before the American people and said executive privilege will not be invoked as to any testimony concerning possible criminal conduct or discussions of possible criminal conduct, including the Watergate affair and the alleged cover-up. If you have revised or modified this position, as you seem to have done, could you explain the rationale of a law-and-order administration covering up evidence, *prima facie* evidence, of high crimes and misdemeanors?"

The president, who knew that he was using executive privilege to cover up evidence of federal crimes in defiance of the orders of the trial court, the appeals court, the special prosecutor, and the Senate committee, answered: "Well, I should point out that perhaps all of the other reporters in the room are aware of the fact that we have waived executive privilege on all individuals within the administration. It has been the greatest waiver of executive privilege in the whole history of this nation. And as far as any other matters are concerned, the matters of the tapes, the matters of presidential conversations, those are matters in which the president had a responsibility to defend this office, which I shall continue to do."

Typically evasive, he had not addressed himself to the question. I was seeking to be recognized in order to point out that omission when he suddenly turned and left the podium. Cormier got out the formal "Thank you, Mr. President" after the president had unceremoniously retreated. It was unprecedented for a president to depart from a news conference in such an abrupt manner.

When I returned to my office, George Anthan, who is also in the *Des Moines Register* Washington Bureau, had already received five telephone calls pertaining to my questioning of Nixon. "Four of them want you fired," George said, "and one fellow called to approve your question and your persistence." Within a few minutes there were a dozen more calls from viewers opposed to my question and my lack of proper respect for the president. It was depressing to find so much opposition to my question. It seemed to me that anyone paying even slight attention to the Watergate investigations and court proceedings could see that the tapes were the ultimate evidence to establish whether John Dean or Richard Nixon was telling the truth. Those early telephone calls demonstrated that there were still hard-core supporters of Richard Nixon who did not want facts but only wished to believe that he was a good president who would not lie to the American people.

But within an hour the number of telephone calls had increased sharply, and now they were running about 90 percent in my favor. By the time I left the office, I had received more than two hundred calls from people all over the country. Most of them were expressions of support in response to a broadcast by columnist Jack Anderson in which he said that he had received information that the White House was trying to have me fired as Washington Bureau chief for the *Des Moines Register*. For more than two hours the office switchboard was jammed with incoming calls, and I could not even get an outside line to call home. I finally walked out of the office at 12:30 A.M. with all the phones still ringing. My wife had been deluged with calls at home, only two or three of them critical. The next day I found out that the *Des Moines Register* switchboard had been besieged by calls asking that I not be fired. The letters and telegrams started arriving in Des Moines and Washington the following day, and within the week I received nearly one thousand. They ran about three to one in my favor, but it was an unsatisfactory victory, for about a third of my supporters showed as little understanding of the issue involved as did the overwhelming majority of my critics.

It was a dangerous business to question an American sovereign on television, even when the question was based on fact, was a proper question to raise, and was aimed at the central issue in the Watergate cover-up—abuse of presidential power to obstruct our system of justice. However, it was the last time I was to have an opportunity to question President Nixon for more than six months, for he stopped holding press conferences in Washington.

The Saturday night massacre and the tumultuous October 26 press conference had barely passed when White House Counsel J. Fred Buzhardt belatedly told the court that two of the White House tapes covered by Judge Sirica's subpoena did not exist. The public had hardly had time to assess that shocking news when it was also revealed that the missing tapes were of conversations between Mitchell and Nixon on June 20, 1972, and between Dean and Nixon on April 15, 1973. White House statements, supported by many White House witnesses, claimed that a "technical malfunctioning" of the taping system had resulted in the failure to record the crucial first meeting between Mitchell and Nixon three days after the Watergate burglary arrests and the important Dean-Nixon conversation in the Oval Office in which Dean claimed executive clemency was discussed.

There was a great deal of skepticism by both Republicans and Democrats, but none charged directly that the two tapes had been destroyed. "Coincidences, coincidences, coincidences," said Representative John Moss, a California Democrat. "It may be true, but it is regrettable that one even has to question a president's statement." Representative John Anderson, an Illinois Republican who chaired the House Republican Conference, said: "My deepest concern is, with the credibility of the White House reduced to a minimum level, the American public might not accept this explanation." Senate Republican Leader Hugh Scott tried to brush the issue aside with the comment: "This machine age isn't always perfect."

Plagued by a doubting Congress and public, the White House took the offensive with what the Administration called "Operation Candor." President Nixon decided to present his case through greater exposure to the people, more press conferences, and franker discussion of the controversial issues. It started with a question-and-answer session on November 17, 1973, before the Associated Press Managing Editors Association, fittingly staged at Disney World, near Orlando, Florida. Away from Washington reporters who were acquainted with the specific background of his many troubles, President Nixon became careless and irresponsible in his answers. Reviewing the transcript afterwards, I was unable to find one answer he had given which was not filled with major provable inaccuracies or misstatements of history or law. President Nixon ran the gamut from euphoria to self-pity on questions dealing with the mystery of the missing tapes, his role in approving Egil Krogh's participation in the Ellsberg break-in project, his tax returns, and his attitude toward Haldeman and Ehrlichman.

When asked whether he still believed Haldeman and Ehrlichman were fine public servants, Mr. Nixon said: "First, I hold that both men and others who have been charged are not guilty until we have evidence that they are guilty, and I know every newspaper man and newspaper woman in this whole audience would agree with that statement. That is our American system. Second, Mr. Haldeman and Mr. Ehrlichman had been and were dedicated fine public servants, and I believe, it is my belief based on what I know now, that when these proceedings are completed that they will come out all right."

When the questioning turned to his personal finances, Mr. Nixon commented: "Well, I should point out I wasn't a pauper when I became president. I wasn't very rich as presidents go." Then, after describing how he had acquired a net worth of just under $1 million, he concluded: "I have earned every cent. And in all my years of public life, I have never obstructed justice. And I think, too, that I could say that in my years of public life, that I welcome this kind of examination, because people have to know whether or not their president is a crook." I knew the moment he uttered it that it had been a mistake to make that statement, but he compounded it with gusto: "Well, I am not a crook. I have earned everything I have got."

To avoid congressional action to appoint a fully independent special prosecutor, President Nixon on November 1 appointed Houston lawyer Leon Jaworski to that post. Then, in the tug of war with Congress over whether legislation on the role of the special prosecutor was needed, the president and his key White House lawyers gave the House and Senate Judiciary Committees precise and clear assurances that Jaworski would not be fired without consultation with the House and Senate leadership.

Jaworski, a veteran trial lawyer, was a former president of the American Bar Association. I was certain that he was experienced enough to know that the only safe course was to play it straight, but Ronald Ziegler's remark that Jaworski was "a very respected man, a very fair man" caused me momentary concern. Ziegler lauded Jaworski at the same November 29 press briefing at which he castigated other members of the Watergate prosecution staff for having "an ingrained suspicion and visceral dislike for this president and this administration." However, within a week I began to hear favorable reports from friends on the staff about the manner in which Jaworksi was proceeding with the Watergate investigation. Many believed he would prove to be a better special prosecutor than Cox because of his long experience as a trial lawyer and because, as a conservative Democrat, he did not have to apologize for investigating the Nixon administration. Cox, who had served in the Kennedy administration and was a close friend of the Kennedy family, was constantly aware that his background made his decisions on the Nixon administration suspect.

In the last week of November 1973, still another development weakened the badly damaged credibility of the White House. First, Special Counsel Buzhardt revealed to Judge Sirica that there were some unexplained "gaps" in the subpoenaed tapes and that one tape had an eighteen-minute gap. The eighteen-minute gap was in a conversation between Nixon and Haldeman on June 20, 1972. Testimony from Haldeman's handwritten notes on the conversations indicated that the erased portion involved discussions of how to handle the Watergate burglary from a public relations standpoint. The White House's explanation came from Rose Mary Woods, Mr. Nixon's personal secretary, who testified that while transcribing the conversation between Nixon and Haldeman she by "mistake" left her foot on the pedal of the tape recorder while taking a telephone call. A panel of experts said later that the erasure of the eighteen-minute segment had taken place in at least five separate operations and that it could not have been done with the foot pedal.

In the first week of December 1973, President Nixon received another shock when the Internal Revenue Service notified him that it was reopening an investigation of his federal income tax returns for the years of his presidency. Part of the problem was the $576,000 deduction he was claiming for his "gift" of vice presidential papers to the National Archives. Also under scrutiny were his handling of capital gains on the sale of real estate and General Services Administration payments for improvements to his homes at Key Biscayne and San Clemente.

Fearing that news of the investigation might be leaked to the press, President Nixon seized the initiative and, on December 8, 1973, made public a series of documents which dealt with personal financial transactions, including his federal income tax returns for the years 1969 through 1972. He magnanimously declared that he was doing this voluntarily and that he was asking the Joint Committee on Internal Revenue Taxation to rule on whether he owed additional taxes. He promised to abide by the Committee's judgment. In his press statement, President Nixon failed to mention that the Internal Revenue Service had already notified him that it was investigating his taxes. However, he did quote from a June 1973 letter in which the district director in the Baltimore office had complimented him on the manner in which his tax return was prepared.

It was evident from that first day that a most serious problem existed in connection with the backdating of the deeds on the vice presidential papers. If the papers were backdated, this would invalidate the $576,000 "gift" and any deductions taken as a result of that gift. The income tax investigation spelled trouble not only for Mr. Nixon but for any lawyers and accountants who had had a significant role in claiming and documenting improper deductions. Even if the Joint Committee on Internal Revenue Taxation found his tax matters to be completely proper, President Nixon's reputation was already irreparably damaged with the average taxpayer, who now learned that the president of the United States paid only $792.81 in federal taxes in 1970, $873.03 in 1971, and $4,298.17 in 1972.

When I saw Nixon's federal tax returns, I suddenly realized why he had turned a deaf ear to Senator John J. Williams in 1969 when he urged the president to reject a pay raise from $100,000 to $200,000 and set a good example for the American people, who had been urged to avoid inflationary wage boosts. President Nixon had contended that the increase was not in fact a 100 percent wage raise for a man in his tax bracket, and he periodically commented on the heavy tax load that he carried along with every other American taxpayer. Now I concluded that President Nixon was not only involved in an obstruction of justice and using executive privilege to cover it up, but was probably also cheating on his income taxes.

The burden of proof was now clearly on the president to demonstrate that he was "no crook." The January 1974 polls indicated that about 70 percent of the voters agreed with my assessment, and more than 40 percent had concluded that he should resign. Chairman Peter Rodino's House Judiciary Committee was preparing to examine impeachment charges, led by a methodical chief counsel, John Doar, who was approaching his job in a quiet, workmanlike manner in heavily guarded offices located in the old Congressional Hotel, just south of the Cannon House Office Building.

*Chapter Thirty-nine*

# THE UNINDICTED CO-CONSPIRATOR

SPECIAL PROSECUTOR Leon Jaworski cautiously moved into control of the prosecution. He made his pledges of independence before the Senate and House Judiciary Committees in open session, and his authority was established clearly in communications from the White House and from the Justice Department. Jaworski moved so quietly in the first weeks that the public might have gained the impression that he was smothering the Watergate investigation for the Nixon administration. He was doubly suspect as a friend of former President Lyndon B. Johnson and former Texas Governor John B. Connally, who was reportedly involved in some aspect of the so-called dairy deals. (Because Jaworski had represented one of the organizations in the dairy industry contributions, he voluntarily removed himself from all decisions in that area and Deputy Special Prosecutor Henry Ruth was given full authority.) But the reports I received from staff members of the Senate Select Watergate Committee were encouraging, as were the reports from Sam Dash, the chief counsel, and Chairman Sam Ervin. When Judge John Sirica said that he was "impressed with the manner Leon Jaworski is handling things," I was convinced that he was not a Nixon plant.

In January 1974, Jaworski found himself pitted against President Nixon and the corruptive secrecy of executive privilege in a crucial new phase of the battle to expose Nixon's true role in the Watergate cover-up. President Nixon knew the enormity of the case which would be made against him if the Senate Select Watergate Committee or the House Judiciary Committee obtained even a few of the tapes that Judge Sirica had forced him to turn over to the grand jury. But Nixon, his lawyers, and his political supporters also recognized that presidential power would give him tremendous advantages in the legal struggle with Jaworski. In the first place, the traditional secrecy of the federal grand jury would protect the real issues from the scrutiny of the press, Congress, and the public except as they seeped into open court debates.

The special prosecutor's office could be held to the highest standards of fairness and propriety in its conduct of the investigation and could not leak information or engage in public debate to support the credibility of its key witness, John Dean. But though the special prosecutor was effectively muzzled except when he could take an issue before the court, President Nixon and his lawyers had the safeguards accorded any potential defendant, augmented by the communications facilities of the White House press office, the political power of a president and the raw governmental power to hire, fire, and otherwise exert pressure on individual citizens and businesses. Having watched various administrations invoke secrecy to shield misuse of power, I did not envy Jaworski the task he had undertaken, even though I had great confidence in the power of the truth when it is revealed to the American people.

An overwhelming amount of evidence was in the public domain as a result of the Senate Select Watergate Committee hearings during the summer of 1973. The vast majority of the American people who watched the televised hearings understood that access to the White House tapes was the best way to discover the truth. Although the public and a large segment of the press did not comprehend the full weight of the evidence against Richard Nixon which had been developed by Ervin's committee, there was an instinctive rejection of Nixon's groundless rhetoric about defending the principle of confidentiality for future presidents. Polls indicated that 70 percent of the people believed Richard Nixon was refusing to give up the White House tapes and documents to hide his involvement in the Watergate cover-up. Most of them failed to equate this concealment of evidence with a felony, even though Sam Dash, the chief counsel for the Senate Watergate Committee, had declared in open court that there was a *prima facie* criminal case against the president for his involvement in a continuing obstruction of justice.

The general public could be forgiven for not understanding the legal term *prima facie,* but it was inexcusable for editorial writers and columnists not to understand it. *Prima facie* simply means that the evidence of crime is so strong that it can be overthrown only by evidence that rebuts it. Members of "a grand jury are bound to find a true bill of indictment, if the evidence before them creates a *prima facie* case against the accused; and for this purpose, therefore, it is not necessary for them to hear the evidence for the defense," according to Black's law dictionary. In brief, a wide range of experienced lawyers believed that the evidence would warrant return of a criminal indictment against President Nixon.

On the basis of the evidence produced in the Senate Watergate hearings, I believed that a stronger criminal case existed against Richard Nixon for conspiracy and obstruction of justice than had existed against Teamster president James R. Hoffa, Washington influence-peddler Robert G. (Bobby) Baker, or New York Democratic leader Carmine De Sapio. Even so, I knew Jaworski had a tough fight on his hands against a powerful and ruthless foe who understood better than anyone else that the battle for the White House tapes was, in fact, his battle for survival.

Presidential Counsel James St. Clair, Vice President Gerald Ford, and Senate Republican Leader Hugh Scott kept up a steady drumbeat of support for Richard Nixon, interspersing it with attacks on John Dean and on groups demanding the immediate impeachment of the president. President Nixon's remarks were dutifully echoed by White House Press Secretary Ronald Ziegler and Communications Director Kenneth Clawson. President Nixon attacked Dean as a liar and perjurer. Ziegler and Clawson responded to White House directives to characterize Dean as a liar and perjurer. Scott said that he had examined documents and transcripts of some tapes which proved to his satisfaction that Dean was a liar and a perjurer. The Republican leader also began to use the phrase "a convicted felon" to describe Dean after the young lawyer entered a plea of guilty to one count of conspiracy to obstruct justice in carrying out the orders of Haldeman and Ehrlichman and what he had believed to be the will of President Nixon. Scott said that the inside information on the contents of the White House tapes had been given to him (Scott) by President Nixon and another high White House official (later identified as Chief of Staff Alexander Haig).

Vice President Ford attacked Dean with only slightly less vigor than Scott, and, on January 15, 1974, he appeared before an American Farm Bureau Federation meeting in Atlantic City and lashed out at "the powerful pressure organizations" attacking President Nixon and his policies. Ford said of the "relatively small group of activists" who wanted impeachment: "They will try to stretch out the ordeal, to cripple the president by dragging out the preliminaries to impeachment for as long as they can, and to use the whole affair for maximum political advantage." Ford identified these as the AFL-CIO and the Americans for Democratic Action (ADA). The speech was more reminiscent of Agnew than typical of Ford, but he insisted that, although the speech had been drafted in part by White House speechwriters, he had initiated and approved its substance. Ford, a Yale Law School graduate, said that he had not examined the evidence on the tapes and did not intend to do so, but was relying upon representations made to him by Nixon, Scott, and Haig. I called him and suggested that it was risky to express an opinion before he read the evidence and reviewed the elements of the *prima facie* case of a crime. Ford responded by saying that he appreciated my view and that others had expressed the same view. He said that he was relying on President Nixon's word and felt certain that Nixon would ultimately be proven right.

While the White House orchestrated the attacks on Dean, Jaworski and his aides were compelled to remain silent, for there was no means to bring the defense into an open forum. Thus, early in January 1974 it seemed that the tide might be turning in favor of Nixon. The lack of critical commentary by Chairman Rodino and the tight security which John Doar had wrapped around the impeachment investigation was mistaken by many for ineffectiveness. Doar rightly considered the impeachment inquiry a serious affair which should not be jeopardized by news leaks or careless comments.

The major legal issue was Mr. Nixon's use of executive privilege to conceal evidence of his role in planning the cover-up of the Watergate burglary, but heedless discussion could endanger the investigations of the president's abuse of power and personal financial irregularities. Other members of the forty-lawyer impeachment staff moved forward on various aspects of the investigation, but Doar and the minority counsel, Albert E. Jenner, Jr., concentrated their efforts on forcing President Nixon to give up all relevant tapes.

Essentially all members of the House Judiciary Committee—both Republicans and Democrats—agreed that in an impeachment proceeding no president could properly refuse to disclose any White House documents or recordings pertaining to the question of whether he was involved in high crimes or misdemeanors. But Rodino, Doar, and Jenner recognized that solid legal backing would not be sufficient if President Nixon and his supporters on the committee could provoke a confrontation in which the House Judiciary Committee might be portrayed as partisan or unreasonable in its demands for information. With that in mind, they limited their first requests for information to documents which would establish a solid public case without risking a charge of partisanship.

The White House announced on January 5, 1974, that James D. St. Clair, a Boston trial lawyer, would head President Nixon's legal defense team in the Watergate matter. The implication of the new appointment was that his earlier legal advisors, J. Fred Buzhardt and Charles Alan Wright, were responsible for Nixon's low credibility and bungled defense. It was apparent that President Nixon was reverting to his old trick of finding a fall guy. One could only pity Buzhardt and Wright for having been pushed out in front with an incredibly bad case. The president had concealed the facts from them and insisted on personal control of the strategy of attack, confuse, and deceive.

There is a fine line for lawyers or other presidential aides between properly carrying out their functions as defenders of the president and becoming active participants in a continuing obstruction of justice. I had discussed this problem with Buzhardt in July 1973, and he had laughed at my warnings. Now he was unsmiling and tense on the witness stand, under intensive examination about his handling of the tapes which had been erased. At no point did I believe Fred Buzhardt had engaged in illegal acts in connection with the missing tapes or the eighteen-minute gap, but he had been placed in a precarious position by President Nixon's decision to permit the tapes to be taken out of the White House by Haldeman and by Rose Mary Woods.

Buzhardt, former general counsel for the department of Defense, had been pulled into the Watergate defense by a side door and therefore had been denied the usual opportunity of a defense lawyer to demand that his client tell him everything as he embarked upon the case. Wright, a professor of constitutional law from Texas, had been understandably pleased and awed by the prospect of becoming legal adviser to the president of the United States in what was certain to be an historic case. He did what he was told and made the best possible presentation of a very bad case. Although St. Clair had a reputation for being painstakingly thorough and a brilliant courtroom tactician, I wondered whether he, too, fully realized the hazards of accepting a job as Nixon's defense lawyer. He announced that he was to be in complete control of the case, and I am sure his client had assured him that he would tell him the full truth. From my own experience with Richard Nixon I knew that there could be a vast difference between his specific personal assurances and his subsequent actions, and I did not envy St. Clair his job. I wondered whether he knew the extent of the evidence against Mr. Nixon or whether he had simply been motivated by a desire to take part in an historic case as the president's lawyer without regard for the risks.

Three days after St. Clair took over the defense, the White House released extensive reports on the International Telephone and Telegraph (ITT) dispute and on President Nixon's controversial decision to boost dairy price supports at the same time as dairy industry lobbyists were agreeing to make campaign contributions of more than $1 million to his re-election committee. Both matters were scheduled for hearings before the Senate Select Watergate Committee. The belated disclosures included facts that were at substantial variance with earlier Nixon administration statements on both subjects, putting two former cabinet officers—Secretary of Agriculture Clifford Hardin and Attorney General Richard Kleindienst—in embarrassing and possibly vulnerable positions.

Because it was now essential to President Nixon's defense, the White House revealed that President Nixon had placed a telephone call to then Deputy Attorney General Kleindienst and ordered that no appeal be filed in the ITT matter. That statement was directly contradicted by Kleindienst's testimony under oath, during his confirmation hearing, that there had been no White House pressure on him to settle the case. (He eventually pleaded guilty to having given misleading testimony to the Senate Judiciary Committee.)

Hardin had filed an affidavit in 1971, in connection with a civil suit brought by consumer advocate Ralph Nader, accepting full responsibility for the decision to boost the dairy price support level from $4.66 per hundredweight to $4.93, and stating it was based on an evaluation of new statistics, not on any political consideration. In January 1974, it suited Nixon's purpose to throw Hardin to the wolves by admitting that it had been a presidential decision based upon the "political realities" of dairy lobby activities. Hardin told me that he could not remember receiving any orders from the president to raise price supports. He denied knowledge of dairy industry offers to raise political funds of $1 million to $2 million, as was now admitted by the dairy industry and documented in White House memorandums. Hardin refused to discuss further the details of his actions, saying that he was under orders from the White House to claim "executive privilege."

Hardin's plight in January 1974 was not unlike that of a half-dozen others who found themselves embarrassed or in serious trouble for having made statements under oath in order to protect President Nixon. The game plan for early 1974 called for the sacrifice of any subordinate official or lawyer in order to save the president from impeachment. President Nixon's supporters called for the blood of messengers bearing bad news, blaming the media as they closed their eyes to the overwhelming evidence that he was involved in a criminal obstruction of justice, had permitted massive abuses of the power of the presidency, and was probably a party to the fraudulent backdating of his "gift" of vice presidential papers to the National Archives.

Some newspapers were laudatory of the strategy of Mr. Nixon's new lawyer. Many superficial editorial writers and columnists called Operation Candor a success and predicted that Mr. Nixon's stock, having reached the bottom, would start to rise. Some, in their cursory assessments, indicated that the White House statements on ITT and the dairy contributions had removed the sting of hearings by the Senate Select Watergate Committee. They predicted that the inquiry by the House Judiciary Committee under Peter Rodino would never get rolling. Duped by White House propaganda that President Nixon had some tapes which proved that John Dean was a liar, they were confident that St. Clair would release them at just the proper time.

Peter Rodino was depicted as a weak buffoon and the members of his committee—both Republicans and Democrats—were portrayed as mediocre men, weak in conviction and political motivation, lacking the courage to stand up to White House power and incapable of resisting the adroit tactics of

St. Clair. This was not the image I had of Rodino, whom I had known since he was a junior member of Congress in 1951. He had served on a House Judiciary Subcommittee headed by Representative Frank Chelf, a Kentucky Democrat, and they had effectively and courageously exposed corruption in the Justice Department during the Truman administration. On the surface, some of the members of the Judiciary Committee fitted the stereotype of genial but faltering politicians; however, a close look at their activities over the years and an examination of their credentials made me confident that they had more substance than their critics in the press. All were lawyers; they had scholarly backgrounds, were ex–FBI agents, or simply had political common sense.

The major reason for my confidence was that the staff was headed by John Doar, a serious-minded Republican lawyer who had gained prominence and favor in the Kennedy administration as assistant attorney general in charge of the Civil Rights Division. Doar had had his day in the national spotlight, handling difficult integration problems in the South, and had a full appreciation of the value of keeping quiet until you know what you are talking about. He was fortunate in the Republicans' selection of Albert E. Jenner, Jr., an experienced trial lawyer from Chicago, as minority counsel.

It was apparent to both Doar and Jenner as they embarked upon the investigation of whether President Richard Nixon should be impeached that the Senate Select Watergate Committee had already made a *prima facie* case that President Nixon was involved in a criminal obstruction of justice. Doar and Jenner knew that the job did not require any brilliant investigative coups or clever strategy. They simply needed to bring all of the evidence together in a systematic fashion and to keep steady pressure on the White House to produce the tapes which would ultimately prove whether Dean or President Nixon was telling the truth. (Although both men properly avoided direct comments on fact or law, they listened to my analysis of the evidence and the law and said that they could find no serious flaw it.) The greatest body of available evidence was in the files and hearings of the Senate committee. Chief Counsel Sam Dash and his committee had placed the information from their files into a computer system so that it was possible to obtain an immediate print-out on any testimony or information on any of the thousands of aspects of the Watergate affair.

While the "abuse of power" allegations of the impeachment investigation covered a complicated multitude of transactions, President Nixon's public statements made the "obstruction of justice" matter quite simple. The president took the position that he had been unaware that John Dean and other members of his staff were involved in illegal actions until March 21, 1973, when Dean told him that there was a cancer growing on the presidency. From that moment on, President Nixon contended, he had taken personal charge of the investigation and had made every reasonable attempt to ensure that all guilty persons were prosecuted by proper authorities. Thus, any evidence of Mr. Nixon's knowledge of illegal acts prior to March 21, 1973, would contradict his basic defense. Also, any actions after that date which were less than forthright in pursuing the prosecution and eradicating malefactors represented evidence of a continuing cover-up of serious crime.

Public opinion polls after the televised hearings in July and August 1973 indicated that no more than about 25 percent of the people believed that President Nixon had not been aware of Dean's cover-up activities until after March 21. Certainly Mr. Nixon's retention of John Dean as counsel from March 21 to April 30 demonstrated at least laxity in ridding himself of a man who had frankly told him that he (Dean), Haldeman, Ehrlichman, Colson, Magruder, and Strachan were involved in a criminal obstruction of justice. The law requires anyone with guilty knowledge of a crime to report it or become an accessory after the fact. Not only did President Nixon fail to fulfill that requirement, but his consistent use of executive privilege certainly proved that he was trying to hide the facts from Congress and the courts.

Most of the facts were in the public domain, but Doar, in assembling his staff of more than forty attorneys for the House committee, wisely established a tight security on his files and barred staff members from talking with the press. Leaks of information from the Senate Select Watergate Committee staff had hurt that committee's credibility and provided an opportunity for the White House to criticize the committee instead of dealing with the substance of the information that was leaked. The Senate committee was denounced for leaks of information as it was preparing for the last series of hearings in January. Comparable leaks from the House Judiciary Committee would have seriously damaged its effectiveness and its public image as a fair investigator of President Nixon's activities.

Doar, Jenner, Rodino, and many committee members were so confident of the strength of the evidence as the investigation started that they felt they could afford a low-key and unhurried approach, even though the White House was pressuring them to conduct early hearings "and get it over with."

The slow and careful pace set by Doar and Jenner brought charges from Republicans of foot-dragging to keep the Watergate issue alive until the election and from Democrats that the impeachment drive was losing its momentum.

To be sure, the White House and President Nixon's defenders were dominating the news with their attacks on John Dean, the staff of the special prosecutor's office, the Judiciary Committee, and the Senate Select Committee. President Nixon used his State of the Union message to convince the public he was cooperating to a reasonable extent with the special prosecutor and the federal grand jury, and that the appropriate action would be to terminate the investigation. "One year of Watergate is enough," the president said, departing from his text in a desperate appeal destined to fail as he said it. "I believe the time has come to bring that investigation and the other investigations of this matter to an end. It is time for all of us to join together in devoting our full energies to these great issues that I have discussed tonight."

Then, disregarding his serious dispute with Special Prosecutor Jaworski, Mr. Nixon said: "As you know, I have provided to the special prosecutor voluntarily a great deal of material. I believe that I have provided all the material that he needs to conclude his investigation and to proceed to prosecute the guilty and clear the innocent." Mr. Nixon indicated that if Jaworski would only be reasonable he would cooperate with the House Judiciary Committee in its investigation of whether he should be impeached.

"I recognize that the House Judiciary Committee has a special responsibility in this area," the president said, pledging cooperation "in any way I consider consistent with my responsibilities to the office of the presidency of the United States." But the limit on his cooperation was the length and breadth of executive privilege: "There is only one limitation. I will follow the precedent that has been followed by and defended by every president from George Washington to Lyndon B. Johnson of never doing anything that weakens the office of the president of the United States or impairs the ability of the presidents of the future to make the great decisions that are so essential to this nation and to the world." Throwing down the gauntlet to Congress, President Nixon declared that he had "no intention whatever of ever walking away from the job that the people elected me to do for the people of the United States."

Four days after the State of the Union address, Special Prosecutor Jaworski stated on the ABC television program "Issues and Answers" that President Nixon had not given him all of the tapes and documents he had requested and needed to complete the Watergate investigation. He said that a decision was expected from the White House on Monday, February 4. The special prosecutor also contradicted the White House and Senator Scott on the credibility of Dean. Although Scott had said that he had been given documents by Nixon and Haig demonstrating that Dean had perjured himself, Jaworski said he and his staff had reviewed all available White House tapes and documents, as well as Dean's testimony, and could find no reason to believe that Dean had lied. Jaworski, who had reviewed all of the key tapes before the federal grand jury, said that he intended to use Dean as a witness in the perjury trial of former White House Appointments Secretary Dwight Chapin. In answering Scott, Jaworski said that there "are many instances where the cause of justice required using the testimony of convicted persons." Jaworski gave more than a hint of the serious backstage struggle with White House lawyers over "relevant documents" and rejected Mr. Nixon's suggestion that he had cooperated fully. "I've had to go after it," Jaworski said, adding that "I very firmly stated" that unless the documents were produced he would resort to subpoenas or other court processes to obtain the needed information.

Vice President Ford, on the CBS television show "Face the Nation" televised the same day, modified his all-out defense of the president, declaring that all relevant tapes and documents should be made available to the House Judiciary Committee. This was his first extensive comment on the issue after the *Grand Rapids* (Michigan) *Press* had suggested that Ford should "put some distance between himself and Nixon on Watergate."

The House, on February 6, by an overwhelming 410-to-4 margin, voted to give its Judiciary Committee sweeping subpoena power, including the authority to demand the appearance of President Nixon in its impeachment investigation. It was now made perfectly clear that the State of the Union message had not hoodwinked anyone, but in fact had infuriated a lot of Republicans. The four members opposing the resolution, all Republicans, were Representatives Carlos J. Moorhead of California, David C. Treen of Louisiana, Ben B. Blackburn of Georgia, and Earl F. Landgrebe of Indiana. Chairman Rodino was pleased to be given the blanket power to gain "full and complete access to any persons, information or things in the custody or under control of any agency, officer or employe of the government of the United States, including the president." The next day, the Senate Watergate Committee voted to delay its final report for three months and to make all of its information available to the House Judiciary Committee.

On February 14, it was revealed by Jaworski in a four-page letter to the Senate Judiciary Committee that President Nixon had refused to provide additional White House tapes and documents requested by the special prosecutor. Jaworski said that this refusal was a violation of President Nixon's pledge of four months earlier. Senator Eastland, who was regarded as a friend of President Nixon, was silent. But Senator Ervin declared that there was no excuse for the refusal and that the president appeared to have "gone back on that promise." On the other hand, the House Judiciary Committee disclosed that it had received some of the information it was seeking from the White House and the promise that more would be forthcoming. "We have reached no stage of confrontation with St. Clair, have detected no element of noncooperation," Doar said.

On February 25, Herbert W. Kalmbach, President Nixon's personal lawyer and a major fund-raiser, stood before Judge Sirica and entered pleas of guilty to two criminal charges arising out of his 1970 fund-raising activities. In exchange for the guilty pleas and an offer to cooperate with the federal grand jury and congressional committee, all other criminal charges against him were to be dropped. One of the charges was a felony involving his role in funneling $2.8 million for 1970 Republican congressional candidates through secret political committees, in violation of the Corrupt Practices Act. The second was a misdemeanor arising out of an agreement with Maryland Republican J. Fife Symington, Jr., that Symington would be given an ambassadorship in Europe in exchange for a campaign contribution of $100,000. Judge Sirica postponed sentencing pending a report on Kalmbach's cooperation with the grand jury and congressional investigators.

That evening, at 7:30 P.M., President Nixon held his thirty-sixth news conference in the East Room at the White House. His opening statement was designed to couple good news on the fuel shortage with a warning that foreign affairs might be jeopardized if Richard Nixon weren't the president of the United States.

Helen Thomas, of United Press International, asked, "Mr. President, to heal the divisions in this country, would you be willing to waive executive privilege to give the Judiciary Committee what it says it needs to end any question of your involvement in Watergate?"

The non-answer was Mr. Nixon's usual promise "to cooperate with the committee in any way consistent with my constitutional responsibility to defend the office of the presidency." He avoided saying whether he would give the Judiciary Committee the tapes which had already gone to Jaworski, declared that only a serious criminal act would be impeachable, and scoffed at the suggestion that there was any evidence that he had been involved in an obstruction of justice or in federal income tax evasion.

When I finally caught his attention after several unsuccessful efforts, I strained to be polite although the question I asked was honed and precise. "Your personal lawyer, Mr. Herb Kalmbach, entered a plea of guilty today to a criminal charge of accepting $100,000 in exchange for an ambassadorial post. In your capacity as president you approve [the selection of] ambassadors and send the nominations to the Senate. Were you consulted in any manner on this engagement and this contribution by Mr. Kalmbach or anyone else in the White House, and have you done any research on this in the White House to determine who is responsible for it?"

"The answer to the first question is no," the president replied. "The answer to the second question is yes. And I would go further and say that ambassadorships have not been for sale, to my knowledge, ambassadorships cannot be purchased, and I would not approve an ambassadorship unless the man or woman was qualified clearly apart from any contributions."

Another questioner noted the lack of an inquiry about his reaction to the resignation of Vice President Agnew and then pinpointed the implication: "I would ask you if you believe that the conduct of the vice president, and particularly his conduct surrounding and leading up to his resignation, in fact brought dishonor upon his office, this administration and the country?"

President Nixon replied: "It would be very easy for me to jump on the vice president when he is down. I can only say that in his period of service he rendered dedicated service in all of the assignments that I gave to him. He went through, along with his family, a terribly difficult situation, and he resigned, as I think he thought he should because of the embarrassment that he knew that would cause the administration and also because he felt that in view of the criminal offense that was charged that he should not stay in office. Now at this point I am not going to join anybody else in kicking him when he is down." I wondered whether Mr. Nixon was anticipating the situation he might find himself in soon.

Marty Schram, Washington Bureau chief for *Newsday,* described the president's small federal tax payments, touched on the $576,000 deduction for the vice presidential papers, quoted a speech in which Nixon had charged that "special preferences in the law permit far too many Americans to pay less than their fair share of taxes," and then hit him broadside: "Now, Mr. President, do you think you paid your fair share of taxes?"

President Nixon was stopped momentarily and then blurted out his excuse: "I would point out that those who made deductions such as I made in this particular instance included John Kenneth Galbraith, Jerome Wiesner, Vice President Humphrey, President Johnson, and a number of others. I did not write the law." It was obvious that he had armed himself with a list of liberal Democrats who had taken advantage of the law permitting tax deductions for gifts of governmental papers until July 1969, but he had evaded the key issue—the alleged illegal backdating of his $576,000 gift in order to make it eligible. And the day after the press conference, Deputy Press Secretary Gerald L. Warren issued a correction: "The information that Mr. Wiesner had donated certain papers was reported in December by wire services and others, and apparently Mr. Wiesner did not take a deduction of the value of those papers. . . . The president certainly regrets the mention of Mr. Wiesner."

The following Friday, March 1, 1974, a federal grand jury returned the long-awaited indictment against seven of President Nixon's key White House advisers and political associates. Those named as defendants in the felony indictment, charging obstruction of justice, conspiracy, making false statements, and perjury, were former Attorney General John N. Mitchell, former White House Chief of Staff H. R. (Bob) Haldeman, former White House Special Assistant John D. Ehrlichman, former Special Counsel Charles W. Colson, and Gordon Strachan, a young lawyer who had served as a key aide to Haldeman. Also named for relatively minor roles in the Watergate cover-up were former Assistant Attorney General Robert C. Mardian, who had been a lawyer for the Nixon re-election committee, and Kenneth W. Parkison, a prominent Washington attorney who had served as lawyer for the Nixon re-election committee.

A sealed brown envelope which Assistant Special Prosecutor Richard Ben-Veniste also handed to Judge Sirica contained an explanation of some aspects of the case relative to President Nixon's role that Special Prosecutor Jaworski did not feel should be made public at that time. The secret report revealed that the members of the federal grand jury had wanted to name Richard Nixon as a defendant but had been dissuaded by the special prosecutor's explanation that there was serious doubt as to whether a sitting president could be compelled to come into court as a defendant in a criminal trial. The grand jury had been advised that the proper method of proceeding against President Nixon would be through the impeachment investigation of the House Judiciary Committee that was already underway. The grand jury agreed to a secret report and asked that a briefcase full of grand jury documents be sent to the House Judiciary Committee. The grand jury had also agreed to make a secret report to Judge Sirica naming Richard Nixon as an unindicted co-conspirator in the case. The report was kept secret so that the public and the members of the House Judiciary Committee would not be influenced by the conclusions of the grand jury that the White House tapes established a *prima facie* case that Richard Nixon was a knowing participant in a criminal obstruction of justice.

*Chapter Forty*

# DEFIANCE OF THE HOUSE

IMMEDIATELY AFTER the return of the indictments, it was widely rumored that the secret grand jury report dealt with President Nixon's role. But even after Judge Sirica ordered the report and the bulging briefcase of evidence delivered to the House Judiciary Committee, there was no official confirmation of the rumors.

Such confirmation would have been a critical blow to President Nixon because the federal grand jury had had access to seven hundred White House documents and nineteen of the White House tapes, including the March 21, 1973, conversations involving Nixon, Dean, and Haldeman. Obviously the federal grand jury and the special prosecutor's office did not agree with the claim by Nixon, Haldeman, Haig, and Scott that the tapes proved John Dean was a liar. In fact, all indications were that John Dean was firmly corroborated by the tapes.

Richard Nixon and his spokesmen were able to take advantage of the secrecy of the grand jury report, Judge Sirica's high regard for the rights of the defendants, and the meticulous regard for propriety shown by the House Judiciary Committee staff. Fully aware that the tapes contradicted his story, President Nixon continued to insist that he had had no knowledge of criminal acts until March 21, 1973. Even then he declared that he had rejected Dean's suggestions that they pay hush money to the burglars or provide assurances of executive clemency to convicted Watergate burglar E. Howard Hunt. Mr. Nixon did concede that some of his words might be misinterpreted as approval because of the delivery of an additional $75,000 to Hunt's lawyer the night of March 21. He told reporters at his March 6 press conference:

Now, when individuals read the entire transcript of the twenty-first meeting or hear the entire tape where we discussed these options [of clemency and payoffs], they may reach different interpretations, but I know what I meant, and I know also what I did. I mean that the whole transaction was wrong, the transaction for the purpose of keeping this whole matter covered up. That was why I directed Mr. Haldeman, Mr. Ehrlichman, Mr. Dean and Mr. Mitchell, who was then in New York, to meet in Washington that evening, if possible—it turned out that they could not meet until the next day—so that we could find what would be the best way to get the whole story out.

I also know what I did with regard to clemency and with regard to the payment of money. I never at any time authorized clemency for any of the defendants. I never at any time authorized the payment of money to any of the defendants. And after we had met on the twenty-second, I sent Mr. Dean to Camp David to write a full report of everything that he knew. That report was not forthcoming, and, consequently, on the thirtieth of August [the president meant March], a week later, I directed Mr. Ehrlichman to conduct an independent investigation, which he did conduct, and presented to me on the fourteenth of April.

As I listened to President Nixon pour out his false story to the television audience, I wondered whether he really believed that he could effectively block publication of the tapes when the March 21 tape was the central issue in one of the perjury charges against Haldeman. Certainly he knew that unless he pardoned Haldeman and the other defendants there would be a criminal trial which would necessarily unveil the still secret March 21 conversation. But to another question he responded: "I can only say that under no circumstances has any defendant or potential defendant been offered clemency, and none will be offered clemency. That would be improper, and I will not engage in that activity."

I made one effort to ask a follow-up question as to why, on March 30, he had trusted John Ehrlichman to investigate the cover-up when Dean had told him nine days earlier that Ehrlichman was one of those involved in the criminal conspiracy to obstruct justice.

"You had one last week, Clark," the president said. "In fact you had two."

It was nice to know that the president of the United States kept score on the number of questions reporters asked at his press conferences. It would have been more reassuring to believe that he was expending effort to provide accurate, responsive answers rather than engaging in a deceptive game of hiding the truth behind an avalanche of rhetoric about "cooperation." By now I had reconciled myself to the fact that, no matter what questions were asked or what answers given, Mr. Nixon would find some rationale for refusing to produce additional tapes for the special prosecutor or the House Judiciary Committee. I had no doubt that he was withholding the tapes because they clearly established that his participation in the Watergate cover-up began during the week after the June 17, 1972, arrests.

There was still no evidence that he had prior knowledge of the burglary and bugging, but he had admitted directing Haldeman and Ehrlichman on June 23, 1972, to sharply limit the FBI investigation of the mysterious $100 bills found on the Watergate burglars. President Nixon was not a naïve man, and I did not accept his explanation that he was motivated solely by concern that the FBI would uncover a CIA operation in Mexico. I did not doubt his concern for national security, but this specific worry over exposing a CIA operation seemed beyond the call of duty. This was particularly true in light of assurances by CIA Director Richard Helms and Deputy Director Vernon Walters several days earlier that there was no reason to be apprehensive about CIA involvement.

At the March 6 press conference it became apparent that President Nixon intended to limit the House Judiciary Committee to the nineteen tapes and seven hundred documents already turned over to Special Prosecutor Jaworski. His explanation of this limitation again misstated Jaworski's position on the tapes. Although Jaworski had explained several times publicly and in court that he needed more tapes and documents to proceed with the prosecution, Mr. Nixon told his press conference that "Mr. Jaworski was able to say that he knew all, and that the grand jury had all the information that it needed in order to bring to a conclusion its Watergate investigation." Although Jaworski tried to correct the record whenever it was possible to do so in a proper forum, the need for restraint prevented him and everyone on his staff from calling the president of the United States the liar and callous deceiver they believed him to be.

At the March 6 press conference Norman Kempster of the *Washington Star-News* asked about the president's expressed desire to bring the Watergate investigation to a conclusion. "You spoke of an expeditious conclusion of the impeachment hearings in the House," Kempster said. "Would it not serve the purpose of a speedy conclusion of these hearings for you to give the committee whatever materials, tapes, and documents they consider pertinent to their investigation?"

The president replied: "It would not lead to a speedy conclusion; it would delay it in my opinion. Because if all that is really involved in this instance is to cart everything that is in the White House down to a committee and to have them paw through it on a fishing expedition, it will take them not a matter of months, so that they can complete their investigation and, we trust, their decision by the first of May, which I understand is Mr. Rodino's object, but it would take them months and perhaps even as long as a year." It was now apparent that President Nixon's strategy was to delay or refuse to produce additional White House tapes and then complain that Rodino had reneged on a promise to conclude the investigation by May 1.

He added: "We will furnish the information we furnished Mr. Jaworski, the special prosecutor, all of which he considered to be relevant. We will furnish, as I have indicated, written interrogatories on any other relevant material. And we will also agree to meet with the chairman [Rodino], the ranking member [Representative Edward Hutchison of Michigan], as designated by the committee, to answer any other questions they may have. I believe that will serve the purpose." This was an effort to exclude Special Counsel Doar and Minority Counsel Jenner from any questioning session and to lure Rodino into a forum where he would be isolated and outnumbered by Nixon partisans. It was a suggestion Rodino could not accept, just as Mr. Nixon could cite it as an indication of his desire to cooperate and answer all questions.

Another questioner in that thirty-seventh and last Nixon press conference called attention to St. Clair's position that grounds for impeachment were limited to "very serious crimes committed in connection with a president's conduct of his official duties." "Would you consider the crimes returned in the indictments last week, those of perjury, obstruction of justice, and conspiracy, to be impeachable crimes if they did apply to you?" the questioner asked bluntly, without knowing that the grand jury, by a vote of nineteen to nothing, had named Mr. Nixon as an unindicted co-conspirator.

"Well, I have also quit beating my wife," the president replied, and then added: "Of course, the crime of perjury is a serious crime, and, of course, the crime of obstruction of justice is a serious crime and would be an impeachable offense, and I do not expect that the House committee will find that the president is guilty of any of these crimes to which you have referred."

At the time he answered, the president knew the federal grand jury had considered indicting him even though it lacked the knowledge that the June 23, 1972, tape contained full proof of his deep involvement in the Watergate cover-up from the start.

It was called to President Nixon's attention that he had frequently expressed a desire for complete disclosure in order to prove his innocence. "Have you ever considered the option of making that [March 21] tape and transcript public so that the American people can read it, and hear it, and make their own judgment on what happened at that meeting?"

"Yes, I have," President Nixon said, but explained that one of his concerns was that publication might "affect the rights of the defendants." He went on to say:

I think eventually the entire tape will be made available. And as far as I am concerned, when any individual who is looking at it objectively not only hears it or reads what the transcript is but also sees what was done after that particular conversation took place, [he] will conclude, first, that the president had no knowledge before the twenty-first, which Mr. Dean himself said when he came into the meeting, second, that the president never authorized clemency, in fact rejected it on several occasions in the meeting, and third, that the president never authorized the payment of money to the defendants for the purpose of hushing them up.

For the first time, on March 21, he [Dean] told me that payments had been made to defendants for the purpose of keeping them quiet, not simply for their defense. If it had been simply for their defense, that would have been proper, I understand. But if it was for the purpose of keeping them quiet—you describe it as "hush money"—that, of course, would have been an obstruction of justice.

This distinction did not explain why Mr. Nixon believed it would be proper to pay for the defense of seven persons burglarizing, eavesdropping on, and wiretapping Democratic headquarters if the Nixon re-election committee had no responsibility for planning the break-in.

The day after that last press conference, the Watergate grand jury returned indictments in the 1971 break-in at the office of Dr. Daniel Ellsberg's psychiatrist, Dr. Lewis J. Fielding. Ehrlichman, Colson, and Liddy were the three important figures among the six indicted. Convicted Watergate burglars Bernard L. Barker and Eugenio Martinez, and Felipe de Diego, all of Miami were also charged with the conspiracy to burglarize Fielding's office. Named as co-conspirators, but not indicted, were Egil Krogh, Jr., who had already entered a plea of guilty in connection with the charge and was serving a six-month prison term, E. Howard Hunt, Jr., and David R. Young, who had been granted immunity. Ehrlichman was charged with giving approval for the burglary in conversations with Krogh and Young and later lying to FBI agents and a federal grand jury investigating the incident.

The indictment of former Nixon subordinates was important to the White House now only as it might adversely influence the House impeachment investigation, for the present strategy was to shield the president. As long as Mr. Nixon could exercise the power of the presidency, he had a possibility of surviving regardless of the evidence against him. As president, he could command prime time on the television networks to deliver speeches filled with half-truths and false statements. Although digging himself into a deeper hole with each speech, he was able to keep much of the public and the press confused about the evidence. It was difficult for many to believe that the president of the United States would be so forceful in his claims of innocence if he had participated in a criminal obstruction of justice. My own analysis of the public evidence convinced me that he was a knowing liar, and yet I wondered whether he believed that it was not a serious crime for a president to direct or permit use of the power of the White House to curtail investigations, make payoffs to convicted burglars, and suggest that executive clemency would be available to those who kept silent.

The president and his aides had managed to create confusion through assaults on those singled out as enemies, but while the offensive had inflicted some damage on the Select Committee on Watergate, Dean, Cox, Jaworski, the polls showed that Nixon's personal popularity had steadily declined. He had kept only about 20 or 25 percent of his most ardent supporters loyal to him.

While criticizing and hampering Ervin, Dean, Cox, and the Jaworski staff, President Nixon constantly indicated that the House Judiciary Committee had the constitutional responsibility to investigate the actions of the president and that he would cooperate with that committee. Since a number of his strongest supporters were on that committee, he obviously believed that it would be his best battleground.

But Rodino's strategy of avoiding confrontations paid off. It was apparent in March that the Judiciary Committee was finally gaining momentum for a near-unanimous demand for White House documents was even supported by Nixon-partisan Edward Hutchison, the ranking Republican from Michigan.

In a March 15, 1974, speech before the Executive Club of Chicago, President Nixon told a cheering audience that he would not resign, for that would make him "a party to the destruction of the presidency of the United States." Although he was refusing to comply with requests for tapes from the Judiciary Committee and the special prosecutor, he insisted that he was "cooperating" as much as he could without jeopardizing confidentiality for future presidents. He declared that there was no evidence that he had committed tax fraud but conceded that he might owe more money on technical judgments as any businessman might. Two days after that speech, Representative Wilbur Mills, the Arkansas Democrat who chaired the Joint Committee on Internal Revenue

Taxation, reiterated that the public would be shocked by the report on Nixon's taxes and that it would increase the pressure on him to resign. Mills predicted that Nixon would be out of office by November.

On March 19, Senator James Buckley, Republican from New York, became the first conservative to suggest that President Nixon resign. Although other conservatives, including Senator Barry Goldwater, stopped short of demanding resignation, their comments indicated sympathy with Buckley's conclusions and concern for the welfare of the Republican Party. That evening, President Nixon went before a meeting of the National Association of Broadcasters in Houston and again declared that he would not resign. "It takes courage to stand and fight for what you believe is right," said the president. "It may be good politics [to resign] but not statesmanship."

On March 20, California Governor Ronald Reagan defended Nixon, saying that he should not resign, and Haldeman and Ehrlichman made a last-ditch effort to block Judge Sirica's order to deliver the secret grand jury report to the House committee. The former Nixon aides appealed the decision to the United States Court of Appeals.

Other Nixon partisans hoped to create confusion and find ways for Mr. Nixon to avoid disclosing the contents of the incriminating tapes. White House Counsel St. Clair demanded the right to cross-examine witnesses in the impeachment inquiry and Bryce Harlow, counselor to the president, made the absurd suggestion that the House Judiciary Committee accept tapes edited by St. Clair in lieu of the original unedited tapes. Harlow said that, to avoid a confrontation, Mr. Nixon would be willing to have St. Clair screen transcripts of forty-two tapes and turn over the edited transcripts. Having Nixon's lawyer in charge of the editing was even less acceptable than the "Stennis compromise" which had been rejected by Archibald Cox.

The attacks on Congress and the Judiciary Committee by President Nixon and White House spokesmen were causing resentment among Republicans and Democrats. House Speaker Carl Albert, Democrat of Oklahoma, said that it was a mistake for Nixon to expect to win by attacking the committee. Senator Robert Byrd, the Senate Democratic Whip, said that such attempts to provoke a confrontation and gain sympathy would backfire. On March 28, the usually mild Senate Majority Leader, Mike Mansfield, said he believed that in the House "the votes are there" to impeach Nixon. The same day, Assistant Republican Senate Leader Robert Griffin said that President Nixon had lost ground in the House but stopped just short of the conclusion that the House would impeach him. Even such a strong Nixon partisan as Senator John Tower of Texas said that the "atmosphere of confrontation" that Nixon had created had done serious damage to his cause. Vice President Ford told a meeting of midwestern Republicans in Chicago: "Never again must Americans allow an arrogant elite guard of political adolescents like CREEP to bypass the regular Republican Party organization." It was Ford's most forceful attack on the Nixon re-election committee.

On April 3, the Joint Committee on Internal Revenue Taxation issued its voluminous report stating that Nixon owed $476,431 in back taxes and interest for 1969 through 1972. The Joint Committee, without benefit of subpoenas or testimony under oath, had discovered that the deed to Nixon's vice presidential papers had been backdated; this invalidated the entire $576,000 deduction.

The detailed report avoided drawing any conclusions as to whether fraud was committed or by whom, leaving that to the Internal Revenue Service and the special prosecutor. Before the end of the day the White House said that President Nixon would pay the $432,787.13 plus interest and would not contest the claim, even though his lawyers had advised him to. Deputy White House Press Secretary Gerald Warren said that the payment of $465,000 in taxes and interest would wipe out Nixon's liquid assets.

Senator Jacob Javits, the liberal New York Republican, warned on April 3 that Nixon should not play impeachment politics by trimming his legislative program "to please a given number of senators: thirty-three plus one."

On April 5, Dwight Chapin, former Nixon appointments secretary, was found guilty of lying twice before a federal grand jury about his knowledge of Donald Segretti's "dirty tricks" in the 1972 campaign.

Commissioner of Internal Revenue Donald Alexander admitted that the Internal Revenue Service had not done a thorough job on the initial investigation of Nixon's tax returns and, a few days later, asked the special prosecutor to investigate the possible criminal conspiracy flowing from the backdating of the deed on the vice presidential papers.

On the afternoon of April 11, the House Judiciary Committee voted thirty-three to three to subpoena President Nixon to furnish the tapes and documents that had been requested. It was the first time that a president had been subpoenaed to furnish information to a committee investigating impeachment charges against him. The subpoena was issued despite frantic last-minute telephone calls from St. Clair and efforts by Vice President Ford to work out a compromise. A few days later, Special Prosecutor Jaworski went before Judge Sirica to ask for a subpoena of the sixty-four tapes he had been seeking for several months. (President Nixon had been issued a subpoena by Sirica in 1973, which was also an historic incident. That special prosecutor's subpoena was the first a court had issued to a president since Thomas Jefferson was issued one in the Aaron Burr conspiracy trial.) On April 22, Rodino said that he would request still more tapes in his impeachment investigation.

Having stalled until after the Easter recess, President Nixon was under sharp criticism from his own party, with warnings that "the first article of the bill of impeachment very well could be contempt of Congress." The long stall made it apparent that the tapes contained material Nixon believed would be highly damaging to him, and I was a little surprised when White House Counselor Dean Burch announced, on April 26, that Nixon would release "a massive body of evidence" which would "supplement charges and allegation and innuendos." Said Burch: "The body of evidence will be substantial. It will be relevant. It will be compelling and persuasive. I genuinely believe, beginning early next week, that the end of Watergate will be in sight." Burch might also have added, if he knew, that the transcripts President Nixon would release would be heavily edited, with distortions and deletions of highly relevant material.

On April 29, President Nixon went on television to tell the American people that he would deliver some, but not all, of the White House tapes and documents to the House Judiciary Committee.

It was another slick and deceptive presentation in which he again asserted that he was innocent of obstruction of justice. There were also the touches of self-pity, as he declared. "I realize these transcripts will provide grist for many sensational stories in the press." He was reluctant to make them public "not just because they will embarrass me and those with whom I have talked, which they will, [but because] they will be seized upon by political and journalistic opponents." President Nixon, knowing that John Dean had told the truth, lashed out again at his former counsel as being solely responsible for "months of rumor, insinuation, and charges . . . suggesting that the president did act improperly."

By releasing the transcripts the White House hoped to inundate the public, the press, and the Congress with so much new and distorted material that it could not be digested or understood. The strategy did not work, for the distorted editing was so obvious that it created a mass exodus of long-time supporters. Senators Scott and Javits joined with other high-ranking Republicans in criticizing the attitudes of the White House as revealed in the more than thirteen hundred pages of transcripts.

Scott, in a significant shift, said that the transcripts of key Watergate conversations reveal "a shabby, disgusting, immoral performance" by all involved. Javits criticized the "shocking lack of discussion of the public interest on what was right or fair" in the president's discussions with Haldeman, Ehrlichman, and John Dean. "There was a singular concern of people striving to save their own skins in conditions permeated by unethical and perhaps illegal behavior," Javits said. House Minority Leader John Rhodes of Arizona said, "There are areas [in the transcripts] that might possibly be brought up as impeachable offenses having to do with obstruction of justice." Representative William Scherle, an Iowa Republican, said, "There is a lot of incriminating evidence there, even though they were edited by Mr. Nixon. The release of the transcripts has not improved Mr. Nixon's chances of avoiding impeachment for he has not yet made the whole record available, and the public and the members of Congress are distrustful. The question Republicans are asking concerns what is likely to come up later that will be further embarrassment to the White House and Mr. Nixon's defenders."

The *Omaha World-Herald,* on May 8, sadly asked for Nixon's resignation. The *World-Herald* pointed to many of the administration's accomplishments in foreign affairs but concluded:

Important as these accomplishments are, they are overshadowed now by the appallingly low level of political morality in the White House, as indicated in a variety of ways in recent months and confirmed now in damning details by the White House tapes.

The transcripts have diminished the president's image from that of a moral man surrounded by underlings who had betrayed him to that of an amoral man who compounded his troubles by withholding for more than a year the shocking truth about the mess he and his administration were in.

The *Chicago Tribune,* another long-time Nixon supporter, said on May 9:

We saw the public man in his first administration, and we were impressed. Now in about 300,000 words we have seen the private man, and we are appalled.

He is preoccupied with appearance rather than substance. His aim is to find a way to sell the idea that disreputable schemes are actually good, are defensible for some trumped-up cause. He is humorless to the point of being inhumane. He is devious. He is vacillating. He is profane. He is willing to be led. He displays dismaying gaps in knowledge. He is suspicious of his staff. His loyalty is minimal. His greatest concern is to create a record that will save him and his administration. The high dedication to grand principles that Americans have a right to expect from a president is missing from the transcript record.

Although he had released an altered version of the whole truth, enough of Richard Nixon had come through to disillusion his best friends and loyal supporters. But additional tapes would tell a worse story, and Nixon was to use the power of the presidency to cling to his office for three more months. This was not the courage born of knowing he was right, but the desperate fight of a man who feared that if he gave up the protective power of the presidency he was likely to be indicted, convicted, and imprisoned.

*Chapter Forty-one*

# A DEFINITIVE DECISION

WHEN Vice President Gerald R. Ford admitted that he was "a little disappointed" by the transcripts of President Nixon's conversations with Dean, Haldeman, Ehrlichman, and others, it was probably the flabbiest reaction of any political figure who had read them. Although the Nixon-edited transcript presented a shabby picture of blatant cover-up, I was sure there was worse to come. Otherwise, the transcripts that Special Prosecutor Jaworski was seeking under a federal court subpoena and the 141 conversations sought by the House Judiciary Committee would have been made public by Mr. Nixon. I was now certain that only "a definitive decision" by the United States Supreme Court would convince President Nixon that he had to produce the transcripts or resign. I was also certain that the United States Supreme Court would rule that the president did not have an unqualified executive privilege to withhold evidence. The fact that Nixon and his lawyers did not carry their appeal of the original Sirica order beyond the United States Court of Appeals convinced me that they also believed the Supreme Court would go against them.

The only possible support President Nixon could hope for on the Supreme Court was from Chief Justice Burger and Justice William Rehnquist. Friendship is not supposed to influence members of the courts, but because of his long relationship with Nixon I thought Burger might be moved to view the president's actions in the best light possible, just as some other members of the highest court would regard him only as the political opponent Tricky Dick.

At an earlier stage, Rehnquist had said that *Washington Cover-up* had made an excellent case against arbitrary executive secrecy. I was surprised to read months later that he had become John Mitchell's leading spokesman for the ultimate in executive privilege. Before various congressional committees, Assistant Attorney General Rehnquist became recognized as the leading advocate of the Nixon administration in its refusal to make testimony and documents available to Congress. I had no way of knowing whether he had changed his personal viewpoint or was simply arguing the administration's case. Even if it was not a personal viewpoint, he had stated the administration's viewpoint with such single-minded vigor that I felt he would be inclined to support the ultimate in executive privilege rather than go against his own earlier arguments.

The president's strategy was obvious. He stressed constantly that the courts were the proper forum for deciding the guilt or innocence of the parties and the proper limits of executive privilege. As the lower court decisions went against him he bent just enough to seem to comply while avoiding the appeal which would have established the "definitive decision" that he claimed to want.

In mid-May, President Nixon, through his counsel, James St. Clair, and the White House press office, stated boldly that no more White House tapes would be produced, whether sought by the Senate Select Committee, the special prosecutor, or the House Judiciary Committee. The Judiciary Committee fretted about its lack of power to compel compliance with a subpoena, even though the committee was almost unanimous in its opinion that when sitting on an impeachment matter it had a legal right under the Constitution to demand the production of any evidence. But to force compliance in the courts represented a submission to the jurisdiction of the federal courts which House members believed would be an unwise precedent and an admission of a need to rely upon the courts. The special prosecutor, also frustrated by months of sparring with White House lawyers, moved swiftly in late May for a speedy Supreme Court decision on the president's claim that he was the final authority on evidence relevant to criminal investigations of the executive branch.

The issue of whether President Nixon could claim executive privilege on the sixty-four conversations requested by Jaworski was precisely the same point as had been the basis of the 1973 litigation on the seven White House tapes. Sirica's ruling, that President Nixon had only "a presumptive privilege" to keep confidential his conversations with his aides and that this presumption could be overcome by a strong showing that the tapes probably contained evidence of crime, had been upheld by the United States Court of Appeals. Without waiting for the Appeals Court to rule on the new case, Jaworski petitioned the United States Supreme Court for an immediate review of both cases. He argued that it was essential to expedite the ruling because he needed the additional tapes to prepare for the Watergate cover-up trial scheduled for September. The White House opposed Jaworski's petition for immediate review and St. Clair argued that the case should be handled in the proper order, without bypassing the Appeals Court, even if this meant delaying the trial until 1975. It was another stall.

On May 31, the Supreme Court agreed to speed up consideration of whether a president can withhold evidence in a criminal investigation under the claim of "executive privilege." It was announced that the case would be heard by an eight-judge court because Justice Rehnquist had disqualified himself. Chief Justice Warren Burger set oral arguments for July 8, and it was expected that the decision would be handed down within two weeks. While the special prosecutor's office prepared for arguments before the Supreme Court, the Judiciary Committee moved slowly forward, sifting the evidence against Richard Nixon.

On June 3, former Special Counsel Charles W. Colson surprised everyone by entering a plea of guilty to a charge of obstruction of justice in the trial of Dr. Daniel Ellsberg by carrying out a plan to destroy and discredit Ellsberg by spreading false information. A month later, when Colson appeared before United States District Judge Gerhard A. Gesell for sentencing, he testified that Dr. Henry A. Kissinger, as special assistant for national Security affairs, and President Nixon had asked him to disseminate derogatory information about Dr. Ellsberg following the leak of the "Pentagon papers" to the *New York Times*.

On July 8, Special Prosecutor Jaworski and one of his top aides, Philip A. Lavorac, argued before the United States Supreme Court that even the president of the United States must be subject to the processes of the law he has sworn to uphold and execute. Before a packed courtroom, Jaworski told the eight justices: "When boiled down, this case really presents one fundamental issue: Who is to be arbiter of what the Constitution says? In refusing to produce the evidence sought . . . the president invokes the provisions of the Constitution. . . . Now, the president may be right in how he reads the Constitution. But he may also be wrong. And if he is wrong, who is there to tell him so? And if there is no one, then the president is of course free to pursue his course of erroneous interpretation. What then becomes of our constitutional form of government?"

Presidential Counsel St. Clair declared that what was really at issue was whether the House of Representatives should be given the White House tapes, and not simply whether they should be available to the special prosecutor and the federal grand jury. He also argued that the Supreme Court should stand back from what was really a political battle over impeachment and not within the court's jurisdiction. "No one could stand here and argue with any candor that a decision of this court would have no impact whatsoever on the pending inquiry before the House of Representatives concerning the impeachment of the president," St. Clair said.

Justice Potter Stewart asked, "You are saying that the courts have to stop dead in their tracks from doing their ordinary business in any matter involving even tangentially the president of the United States if, as, and when a committee of the House of Representatives is investigating impeachment?"

St. Clair responded that this was not the case, but that "the president should decide as a political matter what should be made available to the House—that the court ought not be drawn into that decision. It is essentially a political dispute." The president's counsel went on to claim a broad and absolute privilege for the president to bar disclosure of documents or presidential conversations even if a criminal conspiracy was involved.

Justice Lewis F. Powell, Jr., asked St. Clair if it was that important that there be a flow of candid advice to the president, and what "public interest" would be served by refusing to reveal evidence of crime.

St. Clair fumbled with the answer because obviously there could be no public interest served by a president being permitted to cover up crimes, whether his own or those of his political associates. When St. Clair could only restate the claim of absolute privilege, I was certain of what the Court's decision would be.

Although Chief Justice Burger made comments and asked questions that seemed sympathetic to President Nixon's position, it was apparent that he too was distressed by the arguments that a president had a privilege which placed him above the law, above the courts, and even above the Constitution.

Those arguments before the Supreme Court focused attention on the dangers of executive privilege in a manner that I could not have anticipated when I warned of the evils of the doctrine ten and fifteen years earlier. I was pleased that the Supreme Court was going to speak on the issue that I believed central to the question of whether the United States could survive as a democracy or would evolve into a presidential dictatorship.

The day before a decision was handed down in the case of *United States v. Richard M. Nixon,* St. Clair said that he did not know whether the president would obey a Supreme Court order to turn over the tapes. He said that President Nixon was keeping open the option of defying the court in "the public interest" of saving the office of the president.

On July 11, the House Judiciary Committee made public the first volumes of evidence it had received on the impeachment inquiry, and the inevitability of President Nixon's ouster became apparent even to those who were following the case only casually.

But a little band of hard-core Nixon loyalists held tight, as they would until the very end. One of them, Vice President Ford, said that "new evidence as well as the old evidence" exonerated Nixon of any impeachable offenses. If Ford believed Nixon's story at this stage, he was either a damned poor judge of evidence, thoroughly negligent in his research, or blindly partisan in his judgment. I suspected that it was a little of each, and I was thoroughly disgusted with his speeches, for if Richard Nixon were impeached or resigned it was important that Gerald Ford retain a high degree of credibility. Certainly, I expected Ford to be appreciative for his appointment to the second highest office in the land. I did not expect him to lead the charge against his long-time friend, and would have understood a refusal to comment. But I did expect him to exercise a certain degree of good sense by not blindly defending Nixon to the end.

I called Ford on the telephone. In a brief, friendly conversation I expressed my views and listed the reasons for my opinion that the evidence established a serious criminal case of obstruction of justice against Richard Nixon. Ford offered no rebuttal to the facts I cited or to my legal conclusions.

It was not my desire to urge him to criticize President Nixon, but I did suggest that it was in neither his best interest nor that of the country for him to engage in a public defense which was without merit. He said that he appreciated my advice, had received similar advice from others, and did believe it essential for public officials—particularly the president—to have a high degree of credibility.

However, within a few days Ford was again peddling the White House line, knifing John Dean, accusing the Democrats of partisanship, and criticizing the Judiciary Committee. He called the House impeachment debate "a travesty" for not having produced more specific charges against President Nixon, even though he knew Nixon was withholding specific evidence in defiance of the constitutional right of the Judiciary Committee to have all of the evidence in an impeachment inquiry.

On July 23, Representative Lawrence Hogan of Maryland, became the first Republican to announce that he would vote to recommend the impeachment of Nixon for obstruction of justice. Hogan, a former FBI agent, declared, "After having read and re-read, sifted and tested the mass of information which came before us, I have come to the conclusion that Richard M. Nixon has, beyond a reasonable doubt, committed impeachable offenses which, in my judgment, are of sufficient magnitude that he should be removed from office."

The conservative congressman, a candidate for governor of Maryland, cut his ties with the White House and infuriated many Maryland Republicans by saying:

The evidence convinces me that my president has lied repeatedly, deceiving public officials and the American people. He has withheld information necessary for our system of justice to work. Instead of cooperating with prosecutors and investigators, as he said publicly, he concealed and covered up evidence, and coached witnesses so that their testimony would show things that really were not true. He tried to use the CIA to impede the investigation of Watergate by the FBI. He approved the payment of what he knew to be blackmail to buy the silence of an important Watergate witness. He praised and rewarded those whom he knew had committed perjury. He personally helped to orchestrate a scenario of events, facts, and testimony to cover up wrongdoing in the Watergate scandal and throw investigators and prosecutors off the track. He actively participated in an extended and extensive conspiracy to obstruct justice.

On the following day the Supreme Court dealt another telling blow by ruling 8 to 0 that Nixon would be required to produce the White House tapes and other White House documents for review by the trial courts to determine their relevance in the Watergate cover-up trial and in the trial of Ehrlichman and others for the burglary of the office of Dr. Ellsberg's psychiatrist. Chief Justice Burger, Mr. Nixon's appointee, wrote the opinion, declaring that Nixon could not be permitted to withhold evidence relevant to a criminal trial. Although he took inordinate care to give President Nixon credit for good faith in his claims of executive privilege, Burger was compelled to criticize harshly the use of presidential confidentiality to cover up serious crimes. He wrote that if President Nixon were permitted to do so it "would cut deeply into the guarantee of due process of law and gravely impair the functioning of the courts. . . . Without access to specific facts, a criminal prosecution may be totally frustrated."

In brief, the Supreme Court ruled that no man— not even the president— is above the law. It took eight hours for a stunned White House to reply. Then Presidential Counsel St. Clair, who had said that Mr. Nixon was keeping open the option to defy the court, announced that the president would accept the ruling and comply fully. The official statement issued from San Clemente repeated the drivel about President Nixon's challenge to the subpoena being based "on my strong desire to protect the principles of presidential confidentiality in a system of separation of powers." Faced with a definitive decision, Richard Nixon said he had no alternative but to "accept the court's decision, and I have instructed Mr. St. Clair to take whatever measures are necessary to comply with that decision in all respects." St. Clair said, "As we all know, the president has always been a firm believer in the rule of law, and he intends his decision to comply fully with the court's ruling as an action in furtherance of that belief." Then he added a last sentence which to my skeptical mind seemed a possible vehicle for further stalling on delivery of the tapes. St. Clair noted that "in accordance with his [Nixon's] instruction, the time-consuming process of reviewing the tapes subject to the subpoena, and the preparation of the index and analysis required by Judge Sirica's order, will begin forthwith." This seemed an assurance that all sixty-four tapes would be made available, but was "preparation of the index," etc., to be the technique used by Nixon to retain the evidence and cling to the power of the presidency?

The Supreme Court decision had strengthened the Democratic majority of the House Judiciary Committee, supported Representative Hogan, and provided the kind of atmosphere in which five other Republicans were able to vote in support of the first article of impeachment, charging President Nixon with obstruction of justice. On July 27, Republican Representatives Thomas Railsback of Illinois, Hamilton Fish, Jr., of New York, Caldwell Butler of Virginia, William Cohen of Maine, and Harold Froelich of Wisconsin joined with Hogan and twenty-one Democrats to provide a 27-to-11 margin. Two days later, the second article of impeachment charging abuse of power by President Nixon carried by an even margin, 28 to 10. On this vote, Representative Robert McClory of Illinois joined with those favoring impeachment.

The same day, the Nixon administration received another shock when former Treasury Secretary John B. Connally was indicted by the Watergate grand jury on charges of perjury, conspiracy to obstruct justice, and accepting bribes. The former Texas governor had switched from the Democratic to the Republican Party in the spring of 1973 and was believed to have President Nixon's support as a Republican presidential candidate in 1976. He was charged with five counts, including allegations that on two occasions in 1971 he had accepted $5,000 in cash for recommending an increase in federal milk price supports. It was charged that he made the recommendations for an increase as secretary of the treasury and conspired with Jake Jacobsen, a Texas lawyer who represented the Associated Milk Producers, Inc., to tell a false story to the grand jury and to the Senate Watergate Committee to conceal the bribery. It was alleged that Jacobsen paid the $10,000 in cash that he later testified falsely that he had kept the cash in a safe deposit box for several months but had not delivered it to Connally. Jacobsen was reported to be a government witness against Connally, who became the fourth Nixon cabinet member to be indicted on criminal charges.* Connally, who had headed Democrats for Nixon in 1972, denied that he had received payments from Jacobsen.**

There was no doubt in my mind that the indictment of Connally was a particularly heavy blow to President Nixon, not only because they were political cronies but because Connally had been symbolic of those strong, in-

* Former Attorney General Richard Kleindienst had entered a plea of guilty to a charge of giving incorrect testimony to a Senate committee. Former Commerce Secretary Maurice Stans and former Attorney General John N. Mitchell were indicted May 10, 1973, on criminal charges of conspiracy, obstruction of justice, and perjury in connection with a secret cash campaign contribution of $200,000 from financier Robert Vesco. It was charged that they interfered with a Securities and Exchange Commission investigation of Vesco. Mitchell and Stans were acquitted of the charges by a federal district court jury in New York City on April 28, 1974. Defense lawyers had challenged the credibility of key government witnesses, including John Dean. Mitchell was later convicted in the Watergate cover-up, and Stans entered a plea of guilty on a federal misdemeanor charge involving illegal handling of campaign contributions.
** Connally was aquitted of the bribery charges. The perjury charges were subsequently dropped on a motion by the special prosecutor's office.

vincible men of wealth whom the insecure Nixon admired. Only eighteen months earlier he was being discussed as a potential presidential candidate on either the Democratic or Republican ticket. His indictment must have forced Nixon to the chilling realization that a new era in American politics was beginning.

The next day, July 30, the House approved a third article of impeachment against Nixon for displaying contempt of Congress by his willful disobedience of the committee's subpoenas for White House tapes and documents. The 21-to-17 vote reflected the precise number of Democrats and Republicans, but it was achieved by two Democrats—Representative James R. Mann of South Carolina, and Representative Walter Flowers of Alabama—voting against the article and two Republicans—Representatives McClory and Hogan—voting in favor of it. It was hard to understand the reasons for the switches, but it was not important, because the House Judiciary Committee in open, televised hearings had discussed the issues at length and a bipartisan coalition had on three occasions voted to recommend impeachment.

Two articles, on the secret bombing of Cambodia and the fraudulent evasion of federal income taxes from 1969 through 1972, were rejected by lopsided 12-to-26 votes which had little to do with the merits of the charges. The article on Cambodia was rejected because the bombing was regarded not as a probable abuse of power but as a matter of judgement. The Judiciary Committee members obviously believed three articles were sufficient, despite the very persuasive case made by Representative Edward Mezvinsky, an Iowa Democrat, that President Nixon had to have known of the massive frauds in connection with the backdating of the deed to his vice presidential papers.

The impact of the televised discussions of the impeachment articles was overwhelming. This was particularly true among many well-meaning Nixon champions who had not understood the depth of evidence and had so much wanted to believe their president. The eleven Republican Judiciary Committee members who had stayed with President Nixon all the way took a tremendous political risk out of loyalty to the man and the party, and several were in serious political trouble in their home states because of their votes against the impeachment resolutions.

This was particularly true of Representative Wiley Mayne, from the far northwest district of Iowa. Mayne, an able lawyer and former president of the Iowa State Bar Association, had remained steadfastly with the Republicans on his votes against impeachment even though he was sharply critical of the president on each vote. By trying to please everyone, Representative Mayne pleased only a few in a district he had won by a bare 2 percent margin in the Nixon landslide of 1972.

President Nixon, on July 30, turned over to Judge Sirica eleven White House tape reels containing twenty of the forty conversations the Supreme Court had ruled should be made available.

On July 31, Representative Hogan urged Republicans to join in a demand that Vice President Ford be made President.

Not until the House leadership was taking the necessary steps for an impeachment hearing, to begin in the third week in August, did White House lawyer St. Clair learn that the contents of one of the tapes established clearly that within five days of the break-in President Nixon had known of the involvement of the re-election committee and had directed some phases of the initial obstruction of justice at the FBI. Special Counsel Buzhardt first came across the damaging evidence in a review of the tapes in the last week of July. He told Haig, St. Clair, and two other White House lawyers. St. Clair voiced his deep concern to White House Chief of Staff Haig and explained to him that the June 23, 1972 tape was to be turned over to Judge Sirica on August 5. Shortly after noon on August 1, Haig requested a meeting with Vice President Ford. He said that the tape would be "devastating, even catastrophic" for President Nixon and asked whether Ford was prepared to assume the presidency "within a very short time." Ford recalled later that he was "shocked and stunned."

Haig requested Ford's recommendations on the timing of the resignation and the handling of the transition. Together they discussed eight options being advanced by various people on the White House staff: fighting impeachment to the end; resignation "sooner" or "later"; Nixon stepping aside under the Twenty-fifth Amendment; delaying a resignation until later in the impeachment proceedings; trying to promote a censure vote in the Senate as a substitute for impeachment; Nixon pardoning himself; Nixon pardoning the Watergate defendants himself and then resigning; and Ford pardoning Nixon after Nixon resigned. Ford inquired about a president's pardoning power and Haig said that he understood that a White House lawyer, not further identified, was of the opinion that a president had authority to grant a pardon "even before any criminal action had been taken." Ford later said that he made no commitment but told Haig he wanted "time to think" and to talk with his wife and St. Clair.

At 8:00 A.M. the next day, St. Clair went to the vice president's office and reiterated the seriousness of the new evidence, but Ford told him that on further thought he did not wish to make any recommendations. Ford called Haig that afternoon of Friday, August 2, to repeat that "nothing we had talked about the previous afternoon should be given any consideration in whatever decision the president might make." On Saturday and Sunday, August 3 and 4, Ford kept scheduled speaking engagements in Mississippi and Louisiana, continuing to state that he believed President Nixon had committed no crime and should not be impeached.

Although the information on the damaging contents of the June 23 tape was confined to a handful of Republican leaders, the press was aware that something important was in the wind. On Monday morning, August 5, Assistant Senate Minority Leader Robert P. Griffin (R., Mich.) urged that the president resign. "We've arrived at the point where both the national interest and his own interest would be served by resigning," Griffin said. "It is not just his enemies but many of his best friends—and I number myself among them—who believe resignation would be the most appropriate course." For months, Griffin had been telling me privately of his great concern over the evidence that was piling up and his fear that Nixon's reason for withholding the tapes was they they contained even worse revelations. Although Griffin avoided sharp public criticism of the president, he had indicated agreement with Senator James Buckley's earlier suggestion that Mr. Nixon resign. As a Republican leader, he did not feel he should attack the president, but in the light of the record he could not justify defending him.

Griffin's call for Nixon's resignation was regarded as an indication of a developing move among Republican senators to make a joint demand for his resignation, even though the White House seemed to be preparing for still another televised attempt to rally public opinion. One more indication of a major development was House Republican Leader John Rhodes' cancellation, on Sunday night, August 4, of a press conference scheduled for Monday morning. He had planned to announce his position on impeachment. The postponement seemed to mean that some highly significant development was in the offing.

Late in the afternoon of Monday, August 5, President Nixon released the transcripts of three conversations with Haldeman on June 23, 1972, at the same time as St. Clair was making arrangements for them to be delivered to Judge Sirica. In releasing the tapes, President Nixon claimed that he had been unaware of the contents of the June 23 tape on April 29, 1974, when he told the nation on television that the release of the original set of White House tapes "will tell it all" as far as what he personally knew and did with regard to the Watergate cover-up. He claimed that he became aware of the seriousness of the evidence in the June 23 tape only later in May, when he made a preliminary review of the sixty-four taped conversations subpoenaed by the special prosecutor. Putting it in the best light possible, President Nixon said that he had realized that these tapes "presented potential problems" but "did not inform my staff or my counsel of it" nor "amend any submission to the Judiciary Committee in order to include and reflect it." Nixon admitted that he had permitted his lawyer and White House staff members to argue his case when he was aware that it was a material misrepresentation, but he rationalized: "At the time, I did not realize the extent of the implication which these conversations might now appear to have." He declared, "This was a serious act of omission for which I take full responsibility and which I deeply regret." This was the only time during his massive two-year obstruction of justice and deception of the American people that he ever admitted deviating from the truth.

After indulging in a series of falsehoods, half-truths, and self-serving declarations about his efforts to stop the FBI investigation, he concluded with the most blatant lie of all: "Whatever mistakes I made in the handling of Watergate, the basic truth remains that when all the facts were brought to my attention I insisted on a full investigation and prosecution of those guilty. I am firmly convinced that the record, in its entirety, does not justify the extreme step of impeachment and removal of a president. I trust that as the constitutional process goes forward, this perspective will prevail."

President Nixon's rhetoric no longer persuaded even his most ardent supporters in the Judiciary Committee. The ten Republicans who had voted against impeachment immediately scrambled to change their votes, announcing that they would now be in favor of the article of impeachment charging Mr. Nixon with obstruction of justice. The parade of Republican defectors was led by Representative Charles F. Wiggins, a California conservative who had been Mr. Nixon's most eloquent defender. St. Clair had advised Wiggins of the contents of the June 23 tape several days earlier, and Wiggins felt that it destroyed any possibility of continuing to oppose impeachment. House Republican Leader Rhodes joined the pro-impeachment forces on August 6 and, on the next day, accompanied Senators Goldwater and Scott to take to President Nixon the message that in a showdown on impeachment he couldn't count on more than a handful of votes in either the House or Senate. "The majority sentiment among Republican senators is that he should retire," said Senator Tower, who also reported a lack of support for a proposal that President Nixon be offered immunity from prosecution if he would resign.

Assistant Majority Leader Robert Byrd expressed his opposition to immunity from criminal prosecution in forceful terms: "I personally would be opposed to presidential amnesty. How can we tell our young people that they ought to respect the law if a man who commits a most heinous crime is granted immunity? Even if he resigns and admits guilt, I'd be opposed to any grant of immunity."

If Nixon went forward with his fight against impeachment he was doomed to lose, in addition to that fight, the right to a $60,000-a-year presidential pension, $96,000 a year for his staff, and other fringe benefits that the law provides for former presidents unless they are impeached, according to a GAO report made to Senator Philip Hart, Democrat of Michigan.

Richard Nixon had no real constitutional alternative when he announced on the evening of August 8 that he would resign. But, utterly lacking in sensitivity, he arrogantly compared his forced resignation to a personal tragedy in the early life of President Theodore Roosevelt:

Sometimes I have succeeded and sometimes I have failed, but always I have taken heart from what Theodore Roosevelt once said about the man in the arena, "whose face is marred by dust and sweat and blood, who strives valiantly, who errs and comes short again and again because there is not effort without error and shortcoming, but who does actually strive to do the deed, who knows the great enthusiasms, the great devotions, who spends himself in a worthy cause, who at the best knows in the end the triumphs of high achievements and who at the worst, if he fails, at least fails while daring greatly."

It was difficult to perceive how Nixon, exposed as a liar, a participant in a criminal obstruction of justice, and the instigator of a malicious, intentional effort to destroy a young man who had only told the truth, could dare compare himself to Teddy Roosevelt. Yet in his farewell statements to his staff on

August 9, Mr. Nixon enlarged upon that comparison, admitting that "some of my judgments were wrong" and adding: "He [Teddy Roosevelt] thought the light had gone from his life forever—but he went on. And he not only became president, but as an ex-president, he served his country always in the arena, tempestuous, strong, sometimes wrong, sometimes right, but he was a man." I did not understand how a man who had misled his family, his friends, and his political supporters; who had destroyed the lives of so many of his younger political supporters; who had disgraced the office of the presidency; who had brought a great nation to the brink of economic and political chaos could conceive of suggesting that he had "dared greatly."

I felt that Gerald Ford, in taking office as the thirty-eighth president of the United States, had properly characterized the last years of Nixon's administration as "our long national nightmare," and I applauded his promise of "a little straight talk" that would make "openness and candor" the hallmark of his administration. "Our Constitution works," President Ford said. "Our great republic is a government of laws and not of men." Ford displayed a commendable lack of bitterness about the personal embarrassment Nixon's deceptions had caused him. "May our former president, who brought peace to millions, find it for himself," he said of the man who appeared likely to be indicted for serious, willful, criminal acts committed through the misuse of his presidential powers.

At the time it seemed a decent thing to say.

*Chapter Forty-two*

# THE ULTIMATE EXECUTIVE PRIVILEGE

"IN ALL my public and private acts as your president, I expect to follow my instincts of openness and candor with full confidence that honesty is always the best policy in the end," President Ford told the nation when he took office on August 9, 1974. It was a refreshing thought, accepted by Democrats and Republicans alike as a welcome reaction to the Watergate scandals. I believed, as did many others, that Gerald Ford, former House Republican leader and consistent critic of executive secrecy, would understand the corruptive influence of secret decisions and abused discretion.

Ford declared that he was "acutely aware that you have not elected me as your president" and acknowledged "this enormous responsibility" to the Congress and the American people. "I believe that truth is the glue that holds government together, not only our government, but civilization itself," the new president said. "That bond, though strained, is unbroken at home and abroad." Drawing from a phrase in Nixon's resignation speech about the need for "healing the wounds of this nation," Ford asked that "we bind up the internal wounds of Watergate, more painful and more poisonous than those of foreign wars." And he requested "your prayers for Richard Nixon and for his family," in a spirit of "brotherly love." Ford's words seemed a proper expression of sympathy for members of Nixon's family, who, like himself, had been victims of the deceptions of the former president.

I shared the euphoria of the Democratic and Republican members of both houses of Congress who poured out praise for the Ford speech as the balm necessary to neutralize the bitterness of the last days of the Nixon administration. President Ford was reaching out with good will for the support he would need to face the tremendous problems of the nation at home and abroad. Democrats, including House Speaker Carl Albert, knew and liked Ford. Although they recognized him as a highly partisan Republican, they believed that because of his twenty-five years' experience in the House he understood and respected the importance of the legislative branch as a check on executive power. Republicans were particularly pleased, for Jerry Ford was a friend who would understand their election-year political needs. A popular and respected president could remove the weight of the Watergate scandals, a burden on every Republican as long as Nixon remained in the White House. Ford's simple, straight talk could perform political miracles in diverting the nation from the risk of a "veto-proof" Congress.

I was particularly pleased because of personal conversations with Ford on the evils of executive privilege. Although I had been deceived by personal assurances from Richard Nixon on the same issue, I was hopeful as I drew a distinction between the dissembling of Nixon and the frankness of Ford, who had never hesitated to scald Presidents Kennedy or Johnson on the corruptive influence of government secrecy. On April 3, 1963, Ford had declared: "To maintain that the executive has the right to keep to itself information specifically sought by the very people the executive is supposed to serve is to espouse some power akin to the divine right of kings. . . . Congress cannot help but conclude that the executive privilege is most often used in opposition to the public interest."

A careful analysis of Nixon's speeches revealed few comments on the importance of honesty in government, but Ford's record was filled with apparent outrage at the abuses of executive power and excessive secrecy of the Johnson administration. In October 1966, Ford had said: "We have strayed from the rule of law. Our government leaders, by dealing in half-truths and misinformation, led us to believe that honor and justice are just words. The measure is that the end justifies the means." And, on March 2, 1967, House Republican Leader Ford declared: "Any analysis of today's political picture in America of necessity revolves about a single phrase—four words—'a crisis of confidence.' . . . The American people are constantly engaged in a search for truth—for political truth, for moral truth, truth in government, for verities in our international relations . . . the credibility gap continues; the crisis of confidence grows."

Ford's deep interest in truth and candor apparently appealed to the nation, for within two weeks after he became the thirty-eighth president of the United States the Gallup poll showed 71 percent "approval" of the way he was handling the job and the Harris survey a short time later gave him a 67 percent "positive" rating. Affirmative public reaction to an issue I had long believed vital to the survival of American democracy was heartening.

A political dialogue started almost immediately on the question of prosecuting Nixon for the Watergate crimes, but President Ford indicated that such a decision was the responsibility of Special Prosecutor Jaworski. Unpublished reports circulated that Haldeman and Ehrlichman had pressured Nixon to grant them full and unconditional pardons before resigning and also to pardon himself. If there were substance to such suggestions, it was now obvious that they had been rejected as too outrageous even for the desperate Nixon. General Haig had had a conversation with Jaworski on the morning of Nixon's resignation, but the special prosecutor's office quickly issued a statement that "there has been no agreement or understanding between the president or his representative and the special prosecutor relating in any way to the president's resignation."

A long, unexplained conference of more than an hour had taken place between President Nixon and then Vice President Ford on August 8—just prior to Nixon's announcement of his resignation—but it was assumed that Ford would make no pardon deal with Nixon or his associates. During House and Senate hearings on Ford's nomination as Vice President, House Rules Committee Chairman Howard Cannon had asked: "If a president resigned . . . before his term expired, would his successor have the power to prevent or to terminate any investigation or criminal prosecution against the former president?"

Ford had replied: "I do not think the public would stand for it . . . and whether he has the technical authority or not, I cannot give you a categorical answer."

There was little doubt that the Watergate grand jury would take action against Nixon, whom they had named as an unindicted co-conspirator in March 1974. The June 23, 1972, White House tape revealed evidence against him so overwhelming that his most ardent supporters on the Judiciary Committee had to renounce him.

On August 19, just ten days after assuming office, President Ford made a speech opening up the controversial subject of amnesty for Vietnam deserters and draft evaders. That speech, before the Veterans of Foreign Wars (VFW) in Chicago, suggesting "earned re-entry" for Vietnam war evaders, not complete amnesty, was but a gratuitous broaching of a controversial subject that the president could have postponed until he implemented constructive measures against inflation which he had characterized as "public enemy Number One." Some commentators assessed this speech as the forerunner of a Nixon pardon, but I discounted that possibility because of Ford's testimony in his confirmation hearings. His comments to the VFW that he was "throwing the weight of my presidency into the scales of justice on the side of leniency" could have been just political rhetoric. "I will act promptly, fairly, and firmly in the same spirit that guided Abraham Lincoln and Harry Truman," Ford said. "As I reject amnesty, so I reject revenge."

On August 22 the House Judiciary Committee issued its final report—a 528-page document—giving details of the "clear and convincing evidence" from which its members had concluded that Nixon had obstructed justice, abused his presidential power, and defied congressional subpoenas. The universal appeal of the ideal of "equal justice under law" made it difficult for Nixon's friends to argue logically against prosecution of the ringleader of the Watergate gang. Even Representative Wiggins, who had been one of Nixon's stoutest defenders, concluded that, distasteful as it might be to send a former president to jail, it might be necessary "if we are truly to have 'equal justice under the law.'" Other Republicans were similarly cautious about requesting favored treatment for a president whose lies and deceptions had embarrassed them personally, damaged the image of the Republican Party, and destroyed the chances of election gains in either the House or Senate.

But by the third week in August, Senator Scott, still undismayed that the Nixon White House had made him appear foolish in his unjustified attacks on John Dean, argued that if Nixon were indicted he could not get a fair trial because of the publicity surrounding the Watergate scandals and his resignation. "The man has been punished," Scott said with some emotion. "For God's sake, enough is enough."

Scott was not dissuaded by American Bar Association president Chesterfield Smith's declaration that "no man is above the law." Said Smith, "Judgments should be made on the merits of Mr. Nixon's case just like anyone else."

But Scott continued to insist that the prosecution of Nixon would be a persecution. "He's been hung, and it doesn't seem to me [that] in addition he should be drawn and quartered."

A few days later Nelson Rockefeller, newly designated by President Ford as vice presidential nominee, offered his opinion that Nixon should not be prosecuted. A Rockefeller spokesman explained the statement to me as an effort by Rockefeller to appear compassionate in his bid for conservative support for his nomination, rather than to persuade the special prosecutor not to prosecute Nixon. "It is simply political posturing," the spokesman assured me. In fact, the statement had no impact on the special prosecutor, for he requested that Nixon be subpoenaed to appear as a witness at the Watergate cover-up trial scheduled for late September.

On August 27, it was revealed Nixon that had hired Herbert J. (Jack) Miller, Jr., to represent him. Miller, an assistant attorney general in the Kennedy administration, had many old friends and associates in the special prosecutor's office and had represented former Attorney General Kleindienst in negotiating a plea of guilty to a one-count misdemeanor for misrepresentations to the Senate Judiciary Committee in the ITT affair. Miller had been a friend of mine since 1957, when he had represented court-appointed monitors in the fight to keep James Hoffa out of the Teamsters presidency. An able advocate, he had good connections on the bench and in the Justice Department's Criminal Division, which he had headed for more than five years in the Kennedy and Johnson administrations. Although I was certain that Nixon was hiring the connections as much as he was hiring the talent, I recalled a discussion with Miller on the problems of earlier Nixon lawyers who had been deceived by their client. At the time, Miller had said that he would have insisted on the full truth and absolute control of the case. I wondered now what assurances he had received before taking on Richard Nixon. It seemed likely that Miller would have to defend the former president in at least one criminal trial and much related litigation. I did not envy him.

The presidential press conference of August 28, 1974, did not seem to change the outlook for a presidential pardon, even though President Ford endorsed Rockefeller's opposition to criminal prosecution of Nixon. Helen Thomas of United Press International had asked whether he agreed "with the Bar Association that the laws apply equally to all men, or do you agree with Governor Rockefeller that former President Nixon should have immunity from prosecution? Specifically, would you use your pardon authority if necessary?"

Ford, obviously prepared for some form of this question, recalled that at his swearing-in ceremony he had expressed a hope that our former president would find peace for himself. "Now, the expression made by Governor Rockefeller, I think, coincides with the general view and the point of view of the American people. I subscribe to that point of view, but let me add that in the last ten days or two weeks I have asked for prayers for guidance on this very important point."

"In this situation, I am the final authority," President Ford said with a boldness derived from his recognition of his new power, but he concluded, "There have been no charges made, there has been no action by the court, there has been no action by any jury, and until any legal process has been undertaken, I think it unwise and untimely for me to make any commitment."

Later a questioner noted, "Mr. President, you have emphasized your options of granting a pardon to the former president."

"I intend to," Mr. Ford said firmly.

"You intend to have that option," the questioner went on. "If an indictment is brought, would you grant a pardon before any trial took place?"

"I said at the outset that until the matter reaches me, I am not going to make any comment during the process of whatever charges are made," Ford said, appearing to leave the next move to Jaworski.

Later he was asked, "Do you feel the special prosecutor can in good conscience pursue cases against former top Nixon aides as long as there is a possibility that the former president may not also be pursued by the courts?"

He responded: "I think the special prosecutor, Mr. Jaworski, has an obligation to take whatever action he sees fit in conformity with his oath of office, and that should include any and all individuals." Had Richard Nixon been responding, we would have examined the fine print, but this was President Ford, who, at the same press conference, had promised to "be as candid and forthright as I possibly can" and to run "an open administration" as a safeguard against future Watergates.

Ford's answer on the question of a code of ethics for the executive branch was also bold and forthright, as he said, "The code of ethics that will be followed will be the example I set."

The press conference had been a series of warm and cordial exchanges, in sharp contrast to the carefully honed deceptions of President Nixon. However, the following day President Ford requested Congress to appropriate $850,000 for presidential transition expenses and Nixon's $60,000-a-year pension, $96,000-a-year staff allowance, and other incidentals through June 30, 1975. Most members of Congress considered these amounts excessive, but, in a spirit of cooperation with President Ford, they promised to give his request careful scrutiny and fair consideration. On the same day that President Ford requested nearly a million dollars for Nixon, however, Roy Ash, director of the Office of Management and Budget, revealed that the president would ask Congress to approve the deferral or recision of nearly $20 billion in funds appropriated in the federal budget for fiscal 1975.

With Nixon's request for custody of the still-secret White House tapes was pending in the Justice Department, the special prosecutor's office served him with subpoenas at his San Clemente estate.

Without notice, on Sunday morning, September 8, President Ford announced a full and unconditional pardon for Nixon which covered all possible crimes he might have committed between January 21, 1969, and his resignation on August 9, 1974. I couldn't believe it when Ernest Fitzgerald telephoned to ask if the radio bulletin he'd heard was true. In a short time the shattering news was confirmed on television. In that instant Gerald Ford destroyed his credibility with me and with millions of others who had wanted so much to put their faith in him. Fitzgerald's automatic reaction was that "a political deal" had been made to pardon Nixon within one month, and to a public disillusioned by the Watergate scandals no number of denials could allay those suspicions.

I reviewed what Ford had said and concluded that in his pledges to be "candid and forthright" he had actually been as duplicitous as Richard Nixon. I had difficulty accepting his explanation that he had been motivated by simple compassion and a desire to end the national turmoil caused by Watergate. As a lawyer, he should have foreseen the serious complications a pardon would create in connection with the Watergate cover-up case before Judge Sirica. As a politician, he should have known that greater turmoil would erupt because of his action. He had now irrevocably tied himself to the festering decay of Watergate. We were not freed from it; rather, he had compounded it.

Even a political novice could have foreseen the damage Ford's action would cause to his relationship with Congress and to Republican hopes in the fall election. In all likelihood, it would seriously jeopardize his chance for the presidential nomination in 1976, which he had expressed interest in. Ford might not be astute, but twenty-five years in Congress hardly made him a novice. Why had he done it?

Less than a year earlier Ford had said he would not seek the presidency in 1976 and would retire on his government pension of approximately $35,000 a year, as his wife wished. After becoming president, Ford said he had changed his mind and would probably seek the Republican nomination with Nelson Rockefeller as his running mate. If he had been serious about seeking the presidency in 1976, why would he risk dynamiting his chances without consulting political friends? Perhaps Ford's interest in the 1976 nomination was a pretense. Perhaps he intended to retire on his government pension plus the $60,000 pension for ex-presidents. That would explain the public-opinion-be-damned attitude that allowed him to grant Nixon a pardon without consultation.

President Ford said that he had consulted only his conscience in making the decision. He had conferred with White House Counsel Philip Buchen, a former Grand Rapids, Michigan, lawyer, only for verification of his authority to grant such a sweeping pardon before a crime had been charged. Buchen, in turn, discussed the possibility of a pardon only with Nixon's lawyer, Herbert J. Miller. It would take little imagination to project what course Miller had advised. I was troubled by the fact that President Ford had not consulted the attorney general or the special prosecutor before making such a momentous and unconventional decision. I wondered why he had not solicited opinions from such old friends as Robert Griffin, Melvin Laird, John Rhodes, or Hugh Scott. I wondered why he had kept the secret pardon from his own press secretary until the afternoon before the announcement. Since the White House taping system had been shut off in July 1973, the public would never know the substance of the conversation between Nixon and Ford in their hour-long meeting on August 8, 1974, unless it served Nixon or Ford to discuss it.

Though Ford deplored the fact that Nixon as a former president would not enjoy "equal treatment" under the law because of the widespread publicity the Watergate crimes and cover-up had generated, he averred that "it is not the ultimate fate of Richard Nixon that most concerns me." His major concern, he insisted, was "the immediate future of this great country . . . my conscience says it is my duty, not merely to proclaim domestic tranquility, but to use every means I have to insure it."

No admission of guilt was required of the former president, and in accepting the pardon he conceded only "mistakes and misjudgments" and said, "I was wrong in not acting more decisively and more forthrightly in dealing with Watergate, particularly when it reached the stage of judicial proceedings and grew from a political scandal into a national tragedy."

Significantly, simultaneously with the announcement of Nixon's pardon, an agreement was announced which gave Nixon title to and custody of White House tapes and documents. The arrangement provided for transfer of them to California and joint control of access by Nixon and Ford for five years, after which they could be destroyed.

Public and official outrage at the sweeping pardon brought an avalanche of telephone calls, telegrams, and letters to the White House charging "a crooked deal" and "a continuation of the cover-up." In the crescendo of fury over the pardon, most people overlooked the agreement on the tapes and documents. The next day, however, Senator Ervin accused Ford of aiding and abetting in "the cover-up operations" by granting the pardon and entering into the agreement on the tapes. Ervin did not question President Ford's authority to grant the pardon, but declared it "incompatible with good government." He said: "In granting to former President Nixon an absolute pardon exempting him from all the legal consequences of all crimes which he may have committed against the Constitution, the laws, and the people of the United States while serving in the highest office in the land, President Ford did infinite injury to the indispensable principles of good government embodied in the phrase 'equal justice under the law.' "

Senator John McClellan, an Arkansas Democrat who had been sympathetic to Nixon until a few weeks before he resigned, joined Ervin in expressing "regret" at President Ford's action. McClellan said that the pardon was "ill-conceived" and "premature" and would have "an adverse impact" on the criminal justice system.

Assistant Democratic Leader Robert Byrd said that the pardon was "an outrage" and that instead of putting Watergate behind us it "has put Watergate on the front page again." The West Virginia Democrat said that the pardon would be an issue in the 1974 senatorial and congressional campaigns and in the 1976 presidential race.

Senator Byrd said that it had destroyed Mr. Ford's credibility, "which was his greatest asset" in working with the Congress and the public in trying to solve the great economic problems which faced the nation.

Senator Ervin said that President Ford's belief that the pardon would put Watergate behind was "a false hope" and that the pardon "aids and abets the efforts of those who sought to hide the truth in respect to Mr. Nixon's involvement."

White House switchboards were jammed with thousands of calls. On the first day forty-nine thousand telegrams were received, 5 to 1 against Ford's action.

White House Press Secretary Gerald F. terHorst, who had followed Watergate for two years as a reporter, resigned in protest, saying that it was unfair to pardon a former president while his subordinates remained in jail or went on trial for serious crimes.

The next day, September 10, Deputy Press Secretary John W. Hushen declared that President Ford was studying a plan to pardon all of the Watergate criminals. This announcement touched off an even more furious protest from Republicans and Democrats alike. "I hope this will get no further than a study," Senator Byrd commented.

All the members of the Iowa delegation whom I polled that day were outraged at the suggestion that Ford would compound what Representative William Scherle called "his stupid mistake" by "letting all of the Watergate crooks off the hook." Representative H. R. Gross, a conservative Iowa Republican, had precisely the same response as Senator Dick Clark, a liberal Iowa Democrat: "Two wrongs do not make a right." Gross declared that "pardoning Nixon at this juncture did not make sense and obviously had not been thought through from a standpoint of its impact on other Watergate cases and on our whole system of criminal justice. It would be a further outrage if all of the Watergate defendants are pardoned and will destroy any respect that is left for our laws."

Disconcerted by the escalating furor, the White House retreated, saying that President Ford was not considering pardons for other Watergate defendants. Nevertheless, the Senate and House moved forward with legislation to express "disapproval" of any presidential action to pardon Watergate defendants "until the judicial process has run its full course with respect to such matters." The "sense of the Senate resolution" passed by a lopsided 55-to-24 margin, with the Republican leader and assistant leader siding with the Democratic assistant majority leader. Angry over President Ford's pardon of Nixon, but unable to rescind it, frustrated Congress took steps to block Ford's agreement to give Nixon the White House tapes, and cut deeply into Ford's request for a whopping $850,000 appropriation for Nixon's transition expenses. That fund was slashed to $200,000, and many believed even that amount was too generous.

At his press conference on September 16, President Ford faced blunt questions about "any deals."

"There was no understanding, no deal between me and the former president, no deal between my staff and the staff of the president," Ford told a skeptical press. It was called to Mr. Ford's attention that during his confirmation hearings "you said that you did not think that the country would stand for a president to pardon his predecessor. Has your mind been changed about such public opinion?"

Ford quibbled over his misleading answer under oath by replying: "I was asked a hypothetical question. In answer to the hypothetical question I responded by saying that I did not think the American people would stand for such an action." He further rationalized: "I think if you will re-read what I said in answer to that hypothetical question, I did not say I wouldn't. I simply said that under the way the question was phrased, the American people would object."

Another reporter asked, "In view of the public reaction, do you think the Nixon pardon really served to bind up the nation's wounds?"

Ford replied: "I must say that the decision has created more antagonism than I anticipated. But as I look over the long haul with a trial or several trials of a former president, criminal trials, the possibility of a former president being in the dock, so to speak, and the divisions that would have existed . . . I am still convinced, despite the pubilc reaction so far, that the decision I made was the right one."

After several attempts on my part, President Ford finally recognized me.

"Mr. President, at the last press conference you said, 'the code of ethics that will be followed will be the example that I set.' Do you find any conflict of interest in the decision to grant a sweeping pardon to your life-long friend and your financial benefactor with no consultation for advice and judgment on the legal fallout?"

Mr. Ford answered: "The decision to grant a pardon to Mr. Nixon was made primarily, as I have expressed, for the purpose of trying to heal the wounds throughout the country between Americans on one side of the issue or the other. Mr. Nixon nominated me for the office of vice president. I was confirmed overwhelmingly in the House as well as in the Senate. Every action I have taken, Mr. Mollenhoff, is predicated on my conscience without any concern or consideration as to favor as far as I am concerned."

Closely scrutinized, the answer was as craftily evasive as any Nixon reply. If this represented the ethical standards of the Ford administration, we were back in business at the same old stand, for such favoritism had precipitated hundreds of investigations during my twenty years in Washington.

In my column for October 5 publication, I wrote:

The American people can hope that cabinet officers and agency heads do not take too literally President Ford's statement that the code of ethics of his administration will be the example he sets.

It is doubtful if President Ford in his most compassionate moment would tolerate some of the conflicts of interest, favoritism, cronyism and outright illegalities he has permitted and encouraged in his first two months of office.

He gave us a lift with his talk of openness and candor and the clean breast of his finances before the Senate and House committees, and when asked about a code of ethics he said it would be his example.

We applauded for the moment, but there is much reason to wish that he will establish a code of ethics that is a more certain guideline than his example. His heart may be filled with pure compassion, but it looks like favoritism to some critics.

A number of House members, including Representative Bella Abzug, a New York Democrat, and Representative John Conyers, a Michigan Democrat, introduced resolutions of inquiry into the circumstances surrounding the pardon. The Judiciary Subcommittee on Criminal Justice, headed by Representative William Hungate, a Missouri Democrat, was given jurisdiction over the inquiry. After several unsuccessful efforts to obtain responsive White House replies, committee members charged stonewalling. President Ford then surprised the subcommittee and the Congress by stating that he would break precedent to appear in person to answer questions. A mutually agreeable time was found for his historic appearance on October 17, 1974.

Under rules limiting each of the committee members to five minutes, and with no advance questioning of other witnesses permitted, President Ford made the hearing his forum by reiterating the reasons for the pardon, expanding only slightly upon his conversations with General Alexander Haig on August 1 and August 2, but admitting that after being told of the incriminating June 23, 1972, tape he had continued to dwell on Nixon's innocence in speeches in Mississippi and Louisiana on August 3 and 4, 1974. Although several congressmen tried to raise the question of "equal justice under the law," President Ford avoided giving direct answers. Only Congresswoman Elizabeth Holtzman, a New York Democrat, in a staccato series of unanswered questions assailed him with the "very dark suspicions that have been created in the public's mind." She declared, "We must all confront the reality of these suspicions and the suspicions that were created by the circumstances of the pardon which you issued, the secrecy with which it was issued, and the reason for which it was issued which made people question whether or not, in fact, it was a deal."

"May I comment there?" President Ford interrupted. "I want to assure you, the members of this subcommittee, the members of Congress, and the American people, there was no deal, period, under no circumstances."

Rolling off a series of questions which she said should be answered if there was time, Ms. Holtzman charged that "suspicions have been raised that the reason for the pardon and the simultaneous tapes agreement was to insure that the tape recordings between yourself and Richard Nixon never came out in public." She asked, "To alleviate this suspicion once and for all, would you be willing to turn over to this subcommittee all tape recordings of conversations between yourself and Richard Nixon?"

"Those tapes, under an opinion of the attorney general . . . belong to President Nixon," President Ford said, rambling around the issue. "Those tapes will not be delivered to anybody until a satisfactory agreement is reached with the special prosecutor's office. We have held them because his office did request that, and as long as we have them held in our possession for the special prosecutor's benefit, I see no way whatever that they can be destroyed." Time ran out and no one pressed President Ford for a direct answer as to whether he would make the recordings of all Nixon-Ford talks available to the subcommittee. But the question would not fade, any more than Watergate burglary questions had faded over the past two years.

Only Richard Nixon and Gerald Ford knew what had been preserved on tape in the fall of 1972, when the Nixon White House enlisted the services of House Republican Leader Ford to block the hearings by Wright Patman's Banking and Currency Committee. Blocking that hearing was a vital part of the effort to keep the full Watergate story under wraps until the 1972 election. Only Ford and Nixon knew what the extent of Ford's knowledge of Watergate was when he carried out that mission. The full story could probably have been determined from those White House tapes, but President Ford now claimed that both he and Nixon had the executive privilege of keeping the tapes confidential unless the special prosecutor could first make a reasonable case that they contained evidence of crime.

For three weeks in August, I had exulted that the corrupting secrecy of executive privilege was behind us as President Ford talked of candor and truth and pledged cooperation with Congress. But on the issue of access to the tapes it was difficult to distinguish between Ford's rhetoric and the early pledges of Nixon never to use executive privilege to hide evidence of crime. When President Ford gave his views on executive privilege to the House Judiciary Committee in October 1974 he seemed to have forgotten his wise warning of 1963: "Congress cannot help but conclude that the executive privilege is most often used in opposition to the public interest." And a nation and press anxious to avoid another critical struggle over presidential power made little complaint, for everyone wanted to get on with the fight against inflation and "put Watergate behind us." In the process, there was a good chance that the nation would forget the expensive lessons of Watergate and that Gerald Ford would forget that unwise use of power had destroyed his immediate predecessor—Richard Nixon.

*Chapter Forty-three*

# CONTROLLING PRESIDENTIAL POWER

ON JANUARY 1, 1975, in Washington, D.C., a jury in United States District Court Judge John J. Sirica's court returned a verdict that brought to a conclusion the most important of the Watergate-related prosecutions. Verdicts of guilty on the charge of conspiracy to obstruct justice were returned against four of President Nixon's most important political aides—John N. Mitchell, H. R. Haldeman, John D. Ehrlichman, and Robert Mardian. All but Mardian were also found guilty of specific acts of obstruction of justice, false statements, and perjury in what had to be conceded was a Nixon-directed Watergate cover-up. The jury acquitted one defendant—Kenneth Wells Parkinson, a prominent Washington attorney who had represented the Nixon re-election committee—apparently accepting his lawyer's argument that he had been unaware of the manner in which some of his actions had aided the criminal obstruction of justice. The other major co-conspirators—John Dean, Charles Colson, Jeb Magruder, Fred LaRue, and Herbert Kalmbach—had entered pleas of guilty earlier and were serving prison terms at the time they testified for the prosecution in the Watergate cover-up case.

In the thirteen-week trial, evidence from more than eighty witnesses and more than thirty White House tapes of former President Nixon's conversations made it apparent that Nixon was deeply and actively involved in the cover-up beginning a few days after the June 17, 1972, Watergate burglary. Although there was no evidence that Nixon knew of or approved the Liddy plan in advance, all of the evidence indicated that he became aware of White House involvement within twenty-four or forty-eight hours after the arrests. From that time on, Nixon suggested or approved efforts to use all of the power of the White House, the Justice Department, the FBI, the CIA, and other federal agencies to limit the investigation to seven or less defendants.

Chief Prosecutor James Neal spelled out clearly the manner in which Nixon, Haldeman, and Ehrlichman used White House Counsel John Dean "to carry out their dirty work," and praising him privately and publicly but trying to destroy Dean when he decided to tell the truth. The tapes and other evidence corroborated Dean all the way and demonstrated why Special Prosecutor Leon Jaworski had concluded only a few weeks after he took office that President Nixon was deeply involved in the obstruction of justice even prior to the time the conclusive June 23, 1972, tape was produced. Jaworski, Neal, and others in the special prosecutor's office concluded, as Senator Sam Ervin had earlier, that Nixon and his White House gang would probably have succeeded with a vicious frame-up of Dean or any other defector if it had not been for the White House tapes.*

Nixon's mistake in establishing a system that recorded all conversations is now so indelibly inscribed in our history that it is unlikely that any future president will keep recordings that prove his involvement in crimes. The Watergate investigations and trials have made perfectly clear the scope of the problem of unbridled presidential power and arrogance. But the Congress has not reduced that power to any significant extent, nor has it taken any steps to insure greater accountability in the future. The Supreme Court decision that felled Nixon is not a barrier to future misuse of executive privilege if the magic words "national security" are uttered. Unless that decision is clarified, it will be an invitation for some future power-mad president.

The fatal defect in the present system is the president's supposed authority over all documents and witnesses in the executive branch of government, plus the political control he can assert over all legal opinions from the Justice Department. The use of a special prosecutor was effective in the Watergate case only because of the special circumstances surrounding the staffing of the office and the misjudgments by Nixon in naming Elliot Richardson to be attorney general and Archibald Cox and Leon Jaworski as successive special prosecutors.

The most important initial step for the Congress is to establish a truly independent ombudsman with full fact-finding power throughout the entire government, but without political responsibility or authority to prosecute or

---

* Shortly after taking office in 1969, Nixon had removed a taping system installed by former President Johnson, but he had a new taping system installed in 1971 on the advice of Johnson. Johnson told a committee researching a presidential library for President Nixon that the tapes he made of conversations in the Oval Office were the "most valuable things" in his whole library, and that if there was "one thing" he would advise Nixon to do it would be to reinstitute the taping of presidential conversations. But Johnson, who selected the conversations he wanted to tape by pushing a button on his desk, did not call attention to this in his discussions with the Nixon library committee. The efficient Haldeman, in carrying out Nixon's instructions to "go ahead with it," did not consider the legal ramifications of having a voice-actuated system that recorded *all* conversations.

to initiate legal actions. This fact-finding function would give a properly motivated president access to information now often denied him by the heads of departments and agencies who have a stake in covering up the facts. The ombudsman's periodic reports to the president should be made available at the same time to both the House and Senate to preclude any inclination by a president to engage in a political cover-up. These ombudsman reports, available to the executive branch, the House and the Senate in the same manner as General Accounting Office reports are now distributed, could be the basis for proper corrective action by the Justice Department if the president was motivated to take the initiative. To assure a proper vehicle for action against improprieties and illegalities in the event that the president or attorney general did not choose to act, I would suggest that Congress establish:

1. A permanent special prosecutor's office, in line with the suggestion of Senator Ervin, to be independent of, and insulated from, political pressure from the White House. Specific criminal and civil jurisdiction would be necessary in cases of alleged conflicts of interest and other cases where a political double standard is most likely to occur.

2. An office of legal counsel for the Congress, to provide legal opinions in cases involving conflicts between the authority of the Congress and the executive branch, having the authority to initiate court actions to settle such disputes. Over a period of years Senator Ervin, Representative John Moss, and many other congressmen and senators have suggested such congressional counsel as a way of preventing congressional investigations from being blocked by the arbitrary and capricious legal opinions of political attorneys general. Although a strong, independent, and honest attorney general could, and should, fill the functions of independent ombudsman, permanent special prosecutor, and congressional legal counsel, it is clear that our politically appointed attorneys general have had a conflict of loyalties. Even if President Ford and his immediate successors adopt a policy of appointing nonpartisan lawyers of stature to head the Justice Department, there is no assurance that this policy would continue to be followed. It should be helpful to any attorney general to receive the constructive prodding he may need in order to be reasonably aggressive in investigating the friends or political associates of an incumbent president.

Unless we establish a statutory independent ombudsman, a permanent special prosecutor, and an office of congressional legal counsel, this nation could be easy prey for a president set on dictatorship. With the federal government becoming bigger and more complex each year, such institutions are the only way to assure presidential accountability.

———

On June 27, 1975, it was revealed that Richard Nixon had appeared before two members of the Watergate federal grand jury for questioning under oath by several attorneys from Special Prosecutor Henry S. Ruth's staff. A total of eleven hours were consumed in questioning Nixon on June 23 and 24 at the Coast Guard compound adjoining Nixon's estate at San Clemente. The questioning covered Nixon's knowledge of the distorted editing of the White House transcripts, the 18½-minute gap in the tape of Nixon's conversations with H. R. Haldeman on the third day after the Watergate burglary, the fraudulent back-dating of papers filed with Nixon's federal tax returns in 1969 and 1970, and Charles G. (Bebe) Rebozo's handling of a $100,000 campaign contribution from billionaire Howard Hughes. Chief United States District Judge George L. Hart, Jr., made the special arrangements for two Watergate grand jurors and attorneys for the special prosecutor to travel to San Clemente to take the testimony they had been seeking for more than a year. President Ford's sweeping pardon of Nixon on September 8, 1974, meant that he could not be prosecuted for any crimes he might have committed while president, but he could be subject to perjury prosecution if he testified falsely.

# Index